A BRITISH RAILWAYS ILLUSTRATED SPECIAL

THE BOOK OF THE
BR STANDARDS

By Richard Derry

The Great Exhibition, Willesden 1954.

With contributions by
Richard Hardy
Bert Hooker
Terry Essery and
Harry Friend

Copyright Irwell Press
ISBN 1-871608-80-5

DEDICATION

To my late father, Prof. Leslie Watson Derry and my late mother, Ida Joan Derry, who greatly encouraged my reading, writing and interest in railways.

ACKNOWLEDGEMENTS

I must thank the following for help and encouragement in the preparation of this book: Peter Herring, K.P. Lawrence, P.B. Hands, creator of the *What Happened to Steam* series, Bob Miller, Chris Hawkins of Irwell Press, Mark Arscott, Phil Atkins of the NRM, and Nick Pigott of *Railway Magazine* for allowing me to quote from that periodical.

A Note on Photographs

It is not easy to illustrate 999 locomotives! The old riddle of the quart and the pint pot will be apparent to all readers. Pictures of the Standards under construction, such as they are, have mostly already been published and the BR 'officials' (again, such as they are - they are by no means super-abundant) are familiar from many published sources by now. Likewise the various detail differences - it would take page after page simply to illustrate those of the Britannias alone, and I shall be attempting this sort of thing in *British Railways Illustrated* (Editor willing) in the future. What I have aimed for here is a selection of photographs to show the Standards in everyday use, through most of their lives, across a fair range of duties. I've tried to bear in mind their geographical spread, and to give an impression of the way they changed and aged through those all-too brief years between 1951 and 1968. This, it has to be appreciated, includes a lot of muck and grime.... Having ridden the footplate of CAMELOT only weeks ago, the 'look and feel' of the Standards is very much in my mind. I hope this selection will convey that 'look and feel' to you, as it does to me.

Richard Derry, July 1997

First Published in the United Kingdom by
IRWELL PRESS 1997
59A, High Street, Clophill, Bedfordshire MK45 4BE
Printed in Huddersfield by The Amadeus Press

Contents

Bibliography

Steam Classic, Railway Magazine, British Railways Illustrated, Trains Illustrated, Railway ObserverRailway World, Steam Railway. BR Steam Motive Power Depots series by Paul Bolger, Ian Allan 1983 onwards; *The British Railways Standard 9F 2-10-0* by P. Atkins, Irwell Press 1993; *BR Standard Class 9F* ed. by G. Weekes, D. Bradford Barton 1975; *BR Standard Steam in Close Up* Vols 1 and 2 ed. by Tony Fairclough and Alan Wills, D. Bradford Barton; *BR Standard Steam in Action* by Derek Cross, D. Bradford Barton, 1974; *BR Standard Britannia Pacifics*, D. Bradford Barton; *A Pictorial Record of BR Standard Steam Locomotives* by E. Talbot, OPC, 1982; *The Power of the BR Standard Pacifics* by J.S. Whiteley and G.W. Morrison, OPC, 1980; *The Riddles Standard Types in Traffic* by G. Freeman Allen, Unwin, 1982; *BR Motive Power Allocations 1959-1968 1: BR Standards and Austerities* by Paul Teal; *Britannia Birth of a Locomotive*, by P. Atkins, Irwell Press, 1991; *The 9Fs BR's Heavy Freight Locomotives* by John Scott Morgan and Marina Knife, Ian Allan 1994; *BR Standard Pacifics in Colour* by Peter Swinger, Ian Allan, 1994; *British Railways Standard Steam* compiled by Keith Montague, OPC, 1977; *Riddles and the 9Fs* by Col. H.C.B. Rogers OBE, Ian Allan, 1982; *The Somerset and Dorset in the Fifties and Sixties* series by Ivo Peters, OPC; *Loco Profile No.12 Britannias* by Brian Haresape, June 1973; *The Britannia Pacifics: An Appreciation*, Stockport (Bahamas) Locomotive Society, 1968; *British Railways Standard Steam Locomotives* by E.S. Cox, Ian Allan, 1966; *Ivatt and Riddles Locomotives* by Brian Haresnape, Ian Allan 1977; *BR Standard Steam Album* by Alan Williams, Ian Allan, 1980; *The Stanier 4-6-0s of the LMS* by J.W.P. Rowledge and Brian Reed, David and Charles, 1977.

New 9Fs at Crewe, 19 January 1954.

Foreword

The BR Standard steam locomotive range consisted of twelve classes amounting to 999 locomotives, built between January 1951 (BRITANNIA) and March 1960 (EVENING STAR). By any measure it was a remarkable decade for British steam; it began as a New Era, in more ways than one, springing as it did out of wholly changed social and economic conditions. A truly comprehensive locomotive range, enjoying an extensive interchange of parts and roles was ushered in - dreamed of for years but rarely accomplished even by individual private companies. The nine brief years of Standard building ended with all the sombre ceremonial attached to Britain's last main line steam locomotive, though we were comforted that steam had a long, active and varied old age before it. By about 1964 the awful truth was beginning to dawn and in August 1968 came the withdrawal of the very last Standard from BR service, a Class 5 4-6-0 No.73069, from Carnforth. This was less than twenty years after the first one had been built and many had

very short working lives indeed. Forty six Standards have survived by diverse means - and all of them have now spent more years preserved or 'waiting to be preserved' than they ever did in revenue-earning service!

I write of the time in which I grew up; trainspotting (very respectable it was then, too) was my main hobby and interest and at times, a glorious obsession - to underline as many numbers as possible in my Ian Allan ABCs. The BR steam locomotive numbers appeared in all editions so a new Standard meant underlining the same number in all four books...... A simple enough, if not simple minded, pleasure, but one to relish still. I am happy to say I still possess all of these ABCs and often look through them just for sheer nostalgia. I never did see all 999 of the BR engines but I did come across representatives of every class and became very fond of the whole range.

Sadly, I gave up train spotting for a while and missed the finale of BR steam. I failed to truly appreciate that it was properly happen-

ing, becoming deeply involved with the opposite sex, pop music and under age drinking. It was a chance visit to Parkend in the Forest of Dean in May 1971 that revived my interest in steam once more and a visit to Barry scrapyard in March 1972 really triggered the 'itch' again. Since then I have delved a good deal into the background of the BR Standards and Steam Railway, British Railways Illustrated and Steam Classic magazines have been good enough to publish some of my efforts. Having written, mainly for my own satisfaction, pieces on all of the classes and more than one on most, an ambition grew inside me to develop them much further, for book form. Now I know there have been a good number of volumes concerned with the BR Standards but I wanted to write one more, from the enthusiast point of view; not a great technical treatise but a book to show how much I enjoyed these engines, to indicate some of the work they did and, sadly, where they were all scrapped. And that's about it really!

The Old Order and the New. Cardiff Canton, with 9F 92210 and GW 2-6-0 7321. Photograph J. Davenport.

Above. Standard at work 1. 78028 on the highly restricted Leicester West Bridge branch, at Glenfield on 4 May 1964. Photograph R.C. Riley.

Below. Standard at work 2. Class 3 tank 82005 at Barmouth on the Welsh coast, 17 July 1962. Photograph Stephen Gradidge.

Introduction

The twelve BR Standard steam locomotive classes can trace their origins back to the Transport Act of 1947 (passed by the post-war Labour Government) that brought about the British Transport Commission and British Railways. The Act also created five public authorities known as Executives and the one with which we are concerned, the Railway Executive, had the unenviable task of bringing four very different railway companies together to act as one. This was no easy task, for three of the four companies had already been convulsed by extensive amalgamation from many constituent parts. Only the Great Western had largely escaped this sometimes damaging process; most of the organisations to be absorbed into the new BR were thus only 25 years old and all still laboured under some problems from the days of the Grouping. All, moreover, still suffered from arrears of maintenance and damage repair from the Second World War. The Railway Executive of 1948 inherited over 400 classes of steam locomotives, with many run down and well past their best.

R.A. Riddles (rising to prominence in a more corporatist, bureaucratic age, he would never, sadly, achieve the status of the other great CMEs - Churchward, Bulleid, Stanier, Gresley and the like) was the Railway Executive Member for Mechanical and Electrical Engineering (it would never have the ring of *Chief Mechanical Engineer*) and he it was who had the task of paving the way for new motive power. The logical beginning, both technically and 'politically' was through a comparison of the types working on all the Regions, their procedures and practice, and to standardise the best within the limitations imposed by post-war conditions. This included lower standards in quality of fuel and shortage of skilled staff in both maintenance and on the footplate.

Claims have been put forward that interim dieselisation followed by electrification of the system should have been planned at this time. I do not intend to enter into such an argument (which owes in any event a great deal to wisdom after the event) and am content to describe and comment upon 'the 999'. Riddles inherited great power, but he was constrained by the committee system and the jealous independence of the Regions, with their ancient company allegiances, to a degree unthinkable to a Gresley or a Churchward. He had a thoroughly LMS pedigree and in the Second World War oversaw the development of the 'WD classes', the 2-8-0, 2-10-0 and Hunslet 0-6-0ST. The top posts directly under him went to LMS men and two of these were R.C. Bond, Chief Officer, Locomotive Construction and Maintenance and E.S. Cox, Executive Officer, Design. Between them they decided on a new series of standard steam locomotives for the new British Railways. But how did they go about this? Well, three major areas spring to mind:-

1. The Locomotive Exchanges of 1948.
2. The setting up of a Locomotive Standards Committee.
3. Initiation of the work on the nature of the proposed new Standards.

The Locomotive Exchanges ran between April and September 1948 and are well documented in two books by the late C.J. Allen and both published by Ian Allan; *The Locomotive Exchanges* (1949) and *New Light on the Locomotive Exchanges* (1950). Although the Bulleid Pacifics and LMS Royal Scots achieved the best all round results and the GWR engines were restricted by the loading gauge it was the expertise of the footplate crews that in the end influenced the performance of the locomotives. Everyone had an opinion but Cox summed up the virtues of the comparisons - they were 'rough justice' and little better could be expected in the circumstances. They proved some otherwise obvious points - that a good loco would work anywhere, with the appropriate duties for its power and size, and the ability to boil water *'was as vital as ever it was'*.

Early on, a mixed traffic concept was established. The BR Standards would have a definite LMS parentage, which would be clear in their derivation, design and 'look'. Much of this had been set even before the 1948 Exchanges, which many misinterpreted as a search for 'the best' - as if somehow there could be 'a best' and if there was, that it could be plucked from each category, and then built in. Cox was in no doubt- *'The prime objective was to continue the work successfully developed by Ivatt and his team in the latter days of the LMS towards simple robust machines which, while incorporating the results of available technical development, were nevertheless primarily economical units to build and maintain in sheds and workshops'*.

In June 1948 the twelve Standard classes were first proposed. This list (the keen-eyed will notice there are only 11 classes, the author presumably omitting by an oversight the new Class 3 2-6-0) is taken from Cox's *British Railways Standard Steam Locomotives*, Ian Allan 1966. The presence of a Class 5 Pacific and the 2-8-2 freight loco illustrates how much the 'final range' had yet to evolve in the creators' minds.....

'Entirely New Designs
Class 6 (later BR designation 7) 4-6-2 Express Passenger
Class 6 (later BR designation 7) 4-6-2 Mixed Traffic
Class 5 4-6-2 Mixed Traffic
Class 8 (later BR designation 9) 2-8-2 Freight
New Designs, but Developments of Existing Types
Class 7 (later BR designation 8) 4-6-2 Express Passenger
Class 4 4-6-0 Mixed Traffic
Class 3 2-6-2T Mixed Traffic
Existing Designs Modified in Detail
Class 4 2-6-0 Mixed Traffic
Class 4 2-6-4T Mixed Traffic
Class 2 2-6-0 Mixed Traffic
Class 2 2-6-2T Mixed Traffic'

For the background to the final choice of engine types, no account, of course, is better than Cox's which I mention not for the last time, no doubt. It was intended that the Standards should enjoy the maximum in steam production determined by weight and gauge restrictions; the number of working parts were reduced to a sensible working minimum, roller bearings or plain bearings were to be used and all types were to allow the maximum possible range of mixed traffic working. Rocking grates, self cleaning smokeboxes and self emptying ashpans would lessen time spent at the end of a working day; it was intended that more efficient regulators and sanding gear would improve adhesion and larger firegrates would ensure maximum thermal efficiency and thus lower rates of combustion. So the idea was to make the job easier - more attractive, if you like, through ease of maintenance and simplicity of operation, mainly by cutting the effort required to prepare and dispose of the locomotives. The outlook for coal quality was gloomy, and the new engines, it was intended, would make the best of what might be available a decade and more hence.

All of this more or less dictated the use of only two, outside, cylinders on all the locomotives (71000 was not in the original designs, in its final form) and this was based on the maxim 'the least number of cylinders for the job'. Cox analysed inside cylinder failures and found them far and away a major cause of breakdown and expense. It was both politic and practical to distribute design work and construction around the 'Big Four' works and this was done, as below. With the technical results garnered in from the Locomotive Exchanges and the work carried out by the inter-Regional committees, locomotive design could 'officially' begin in 1949. This work had to be divided between the former headquarters drawing offices of the four main line companies - Brighton, Derby, Doncaster and Swindon. No one office was made responsible for the design of a complete locomotive so each of the four offices was charged with the production of standard drawings for certain components in respect of all the engine types, as follows:

Derby - wheels, bogies and trucks, tyres; axles and spring gear, tenders.
Doncaster - valve gear and cylinders, connecting and coupling rods.
Swindon - boilers and smokeboxes, steam fittings.
Brighton - brakes and sanding gear.

The locomotives were designed to run within the L1 or L2 loading gauges and whilst the L1 gauge covered most of the running lines in Britain the L2 restricted the larger locomotives to the principal main line routes. The Locomotive Standards Committee was established at a meeting of the Mechanical Engineers Committee on 8th January 1948 with a remit, Cox relates, that included
i) design of consumable details and
ii) recommendations for 1950s construction.
What the committee set out to do it more or less achieved, with the final 12 classes of steam locomotives designed and built to run on British Railways all bearing a 'family likeness'. The following chapters cover the short working lives, and ends, of the majority of the 999 locomotives (there were 46 survivors) which, though they were never given a hope of adequately repaying their costs, left such a mark on British steam lore.

Shock of the New. 70021 MORNING STAR (one of the 'Venus' engines - see Note Three) starting a northbound express at Crewe on 6 August 1951. This would be a running in turn, for the engine went officially to traffic only a few days before. After this MORNING STAR went to Laira. The backdrop of a string of rapt spotters is particularly resonant of the times - note their cheerful (and tolerated) disrespect for the 'Not Beyond the Platform End' injunctions. A fitting audience for a Britannia's first days. Photograph E.R. Morten.

1. The Britannia Pacifics 1951-1968

Now that steam locomotive boiler design is a defunct science, it is interesting to reflect how remarkably compact (of necessity) a locomotive boiler was compared to its bulky counterparts in marine practice and stationary power generation. The BR 4-6-2 boiler barrel for example, had a mean internal diameter of 6ft and extended 17ft between tubeplates; within this was accommodated almost exactly *one mile* of firetubes, flues and superheater elements. Working hard it could generate about half its own empty weight (25 tons!) of steam in an hour.... *Britannia, Birth of a Locomotive*, by Philip Atkins.

70000 BRITANNIA, the flagship of the BR Standards, appeared in January 1951, the first of 55 engines, all built at Crewe between January 1951 and September 1954 when the last, 70054 DORNOCH FIRTH emerged from the one-time LNWR works. One of the first - maybe *the* first - published pictures of 70000 appeared in the March 1951 *Railway Magazine* and shows this first BR Pacific still in unlined black, leaving on a test run from Crewe on 12 January 1951. The engine was named on 30 January at Marylebone station by the Rt. Hon. Alfred Barnes MP, Minister of Transport and on 1st February, based at Stratford on the Eastern Region, 70000 entered service on trains out of Liverpool Street. No less than two pages of *The Railway Magazine* were devoted to the details of the new engine, for it was indeed a momentous development - the long-awaited outcome, if you like, of the 1948 Exchanges. The first brand new design since Nationalisation, a great future was expected for this and all subsequent BR Standard classes but who, then, would have dreamed, let alone forecast, that the whole of the class would have been withdrawn seventeen years on?

Riddles and his team had in mind a mixed traffic concept and though the Britannias were not the most powerful of steam engines, their wide route availability and high power put them easily on a par with the second string of Regional steam types. They were not intended to be as powerful as the LMS Coronations or the LNER A4s, but to be the equals of the Royal Scots, A3s, Bulleid light Pacifics and so on, though I could never really envisage them on the Southern's Withered Arm, west of Exeter. The

appearance of 70000 caused some ripples; BR was then only three years old, and the Big Four still had their adherents - very much so - among observers as well as on 'the inside'. Officers had barely yet begun to move around the giant new system. With the advent of the Britannias it seemed that the LMS had won the day in the design stakes.

First and foremost the Britannias were fitted with only two cylinders where British practice had been to fit Pacifics with three or four. Cylinders were of 20inch stroke by 28inch diameter, a departure from normal practice and about as large as the L2 loading gauge would permit. A third cylinder would have added up to £1,000 per engine and nearly 3.5 tons in weight, increase the preparation time each day and raise the repair costs. The driving wheels were down to 6ft 2in diameter, smaller than expected for a British Pacific - the engines had been designed for mixed traffic and it was slightly odd then that in practice, until their latter days, they spent most of their time on front rank passenger runs. Such wheels did not detract from running at speed, and 70021, 70031 and 70032 were recorded at different times at 80 mph. Another surprise was the fitting of a single chimney, strange considering the plethora of double blastpipes and double chimneys that front line engines were carrying. But the single chimney did not affect the performance of the class.

Everything about the class was aimed at accessibility, comfort for the footplate crew and reducing preparation, servicing and maintenance time. Shed staff benefited from the easy access to injectors, pipes and pipework with a

good provision of washout plugs and doors. Staff were also consulted, through the device of a wooden cab mock-up, with selected crews invited to examine and comment upon the arrangements. Whatever the subtleties and cunning craft of the layout, it was doomed really in the eyes of many Western men, who would never wholly take to driving controls on the left - including the pull-out regulator, reversing gear, blower valve, large ejector steam valve and so on, and the fireman's controls to the right. Further features, often duplicated on other Standard classes, included a deep fall plate between the smokebox and the buffer beam - some observers gave thanks for the smoke deflectors, which ameliorated what could have been an overly severe front view. The high running plate was not new, for the Ivatt class 4 2-6-0s, 43000-43161, had appeared thus in 1947, spreading (in anticipation of their quasi-Standard role, as precursors of the 76000 Moguls) far beyond the strict confines of the LMR. If one looks at the Britannias sideways-on, this high stepping feature, such an aesthetic failure in the 43000s, can be seen to add to a handsome design in the case of the Pacifics. Whatever, handsome is as handsome does; the pursuit of accessibility meant, for instance, that the cab sheet levels (to allow access to the fittings below the footplate) did not match the lower limits of the tender sides. Such aesthetic deficiencies, whilst any particular one might have been mortifying to a more traditional design, seemed only to bolster BRITANNIA's bold claim its part in the post-War 'New Dawn'.

Equipment that could be seen on either side and below the cab included the live steam

70004 WILLIAM SHAKESPEARE was justly famous for its 'exhibition finish' applied for the Festival of Britain in London in 1951. The last few wipes were applied once the engine was under a shelter of scaffolding, draped in canvas. In terms of display technique it was rather less than 'state of the art'. Still, it must be understood that 1951 was not a time for 'frippery' - it was a period of political change and economic crisis; rationing still refused to go away and Britain was at war again, in Korea. Photograph B.P. Hoper Collection.

The best work, and the best reception, for the Britannias was in East Anglia, on the GE Section. With this dizzy increase in power available the operating people were able to tear the old timetable up by the roots, much as the authorities were to do with the Deltics a generation later. This is a typical stirring scene - 70007 COEUR-de -LION of Norwich shed, leaving Ipswich on 28 May 1953 with The Broadsman. Note the Coronation headboard on the bufferbeam. Photograph H.N. James.

injector on the left hand side, in front of the pony truck and on the right (also in front of the pony truck) the Davies and Metcalfe class K exhaust steam injector with its associated pipework. Above the running plate, on the right hand side, were two steam valves, the lower for the live steam injector and the upper for the exhaust steam injector. To 'balance' this on the left hand side, also above the running plate, was the vacuum ejector, actually mounted on the firebox in front of the cab, a slightly shocking display for eyes used to A4s or Bulleid's efforts. At the front of the Britannias, not visible to the naked eye, the self cleaning screens inside the smokebox served their everyday purpose, deflecting ash through the chimney and hopefully keeping the smokebox clear for upwards of two weeks - thus cutting down disposal at the end of the day. What the incandescent ash

did to the passing countryside on hot days or to the washing hanging out in built-up areas is unrecorded. The blastpipe and chimney that much of this ash passed through was the result of much work and research by the legendary S.O. Ell at Swindon, a combination that proved a success on the Britannias.

These ideas, coupling a large boiler with medium size driving wheels, using just two cylinders with everything accessible, were new(ish) to the UK, though they had long been familiar in North America. Much of the performance in service however depended on the footplate crew and in this respect the class had a mixed reception. BRITANNIA and its ilk revolutionised the Norwich service out of Liverpool Street though, crucially, they were demonstrably streets ahead of what had gone before, and they had the benefit of an enthusiastic management,

which had actively lobbied for the new engines. These services had never seen their like. On the Western Region, except for the Cardiff Canton crews, no one seemed to get anything out of the class, and Cox relates a very telling instance of a senior WR manager barring the new engines from any train on which he was travelling..... The driving position would, in any event (see earlier) have condemned any stranger on the Western - moreover the new engines were relatively thinly spread and generations of men brought up on 4-6-0s, with their (comparative) surefootedness, would always take some convincing with something as radically new as a Pacific. Crucially, on the lines in the west, the Britannias (or any 'foreign' engine) could never be *so* superior that they could overcome the natural distrust of the new. Much has been said of the receptions given the Britannias, on the GE and, by contrast, the GW, but there is little recorded of their reception elsewhere, which might have been expected to throw up similar problems. How did the Holyhead or Longsight crews fare for instance, or the Midland men later in the 1950s - on a line where Pacifics had been unknown? All seemed to take to them like ducks to water...

As the flagships of the Standards, the Britannias had a high profile and, as Britain emerged from the years of post-War austerity, promised a Brave New World. The choice of names looked back to inspiring historical figures from literature and history; they were meant to embody the post-War revival in national pride, confidence and expectations (mind you, it was a while before I discovered who JOHN OF GAUNT was, who the IRON DUKE might be and that HOTSPUR was not a boy's comic). Included were some famous GWR names and also some Scottish Firths, the two groups going to the Western Region and Scotland respectively. For some reason 70047 was never named. The nameplates themselves, attached to the smoke deflectors, were cast in brass with raised four inch lettering with either a red or black background. Some of the shortest names were

Two Britannias, 70043 and 70044, appeared in mid-1953 with Westinghouse pumps, for experimental work on high speed air braked freights. What must have been an awesome highlight was a series of double headed 1,500 ton trials between Toton and Brent. This is 70043 at Euston with a Glasgow express in August 1953 - both engines were intended for the Eastern Region but the LM kept them, sending 70030 and 70034 in their stead. Photograph George Heiron.

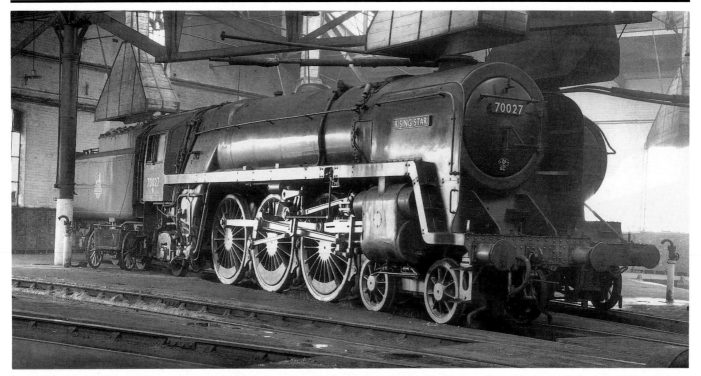

Photographs of Britannias inside roundhouses are, oddly, rather few and far between, which must be a reflection of their allocation. The only sphere of working where roundhouses predominated over straight sheds was on the Western Region, though both Laira and Canton were older, cramped examples. This would be the much more modern roundhouse, high and vaulted, at Old Oak, where Canton's 70027 RISING STAR resides in a pose much more familiar from Kings, Castes and the like. 12 August 1953. Photograph J. Robertson, B.P. Hoper Collection.

ARIEL, ARROW, VENUS, BYRON and ANZAC, and the longest must have been 70048 THE TERRITORIAL ARMY 1908-1958.

As with any new class there were teething problems and within two weeks of entering normal service 70000 shattered first one, then the other, cast iron piston heads, and the covers. The source of the problem was in the dome and with the carrying over of water into the cylinders - cast steel piston heads were fitted and alterations made which raised the point of steam entry further above water level. This meant new, higher dome covers. In July 1951 70014 IRON DUKE was whisked out of traffic to some alarm, as all the coupled wheels had shifted on the axles and 70004 WILLIAM SHAKESPEARE broke a rod on one side when

working the up Golden Arrow near Headcorn. At least five more of the class experienced shifting of the coupled wheels on their axles, resulting in bent coupling or connecting rods. By now twenty five Britannias were in service and all of them had to be withdrawn until the problem had been resolved. The cause was traced to the hollow axles - these were a weight saving device, compensating for the Timken Cannon roller bearing axleboxes. These required special fitting equipment which precluded traditional quartering, and some engines were turned out with cranks not set precisely at 90 degrees. A quarter of a degree could make .050in. difference. The rods had been machined to plus or minus .003in. between crank pin centres. This, with tiny distortion in the hollow axles, encouraged

wheel movement on the axles. The whole class was temporarily withdrawn in late 1951 for the axles to be plugged to the depth of the wheel seats. The 'plugging' appeared to solve the problem though there were sixteen cases of wheel movement on the Eastern Region between 1957 and 1960. In October 1965, near New Biggin, 70037 suffered a fractured wheel centre, breaking a coupling rod which pierced the boiler - fortunately without any injury to the crew. A further outcome of the 1951 modifications was the replacement of the original fluted coupling rods (fitted to 70000-70024 from new) by more robust tapered, plain section rods, weightier and stronger than the originals.

Even though the Pacifics were designed over forty years ago, to my mind they are still a

Another Western Britannia, 70018 FLYING DUTCHMAN, at Bristol Temple Meads on 8 August 1954. Photograph J. Robertson, B.P. Hoper Collection.

A remarkable view of double heading Britannias, 70017 ARROW and 70021 MORNING STAR at Aller Junction on 2 August 1955, with the 4.05pm Paddington - Penzance. Photograph J. Robertson, B.P. Hoper Collection.

'young' class and like all BR Standards I felt them to be a strong influence, at a tender age - they were 'my generation's' engines if you like. But then I never dreamed they would go so soon, lasting as a complete class only from September 1954 (when 70054 was completed) to June 1965 when 70007 was withdrawn, less than *eleven* years. If it was a short life it was a varied one, however, and in those few years the engines were at times allocated to all six of the BR Regions, including 70004 and 70014 to Stewarts Lane in September 1951, until they were transferred away in June 1958 to the Midland at Kentish Town and on to Trafford Park the following month. 70004 was exhibited at the Festival of Britain on London's South Bank in 1951 and was maintained in the exhibition

finish, receiving the 'treatment' from the cleaners at Stewarts Lane during 1951. For a good number of months it was the regular engine on the Golden Arrow Pullman but was replaced on Sundays by either 70014 or a Merchant Navy Pacific. 70004 was entrusted on 8th August 1954 with a heavy boat train on the South Western section from Waterloo to Southampton Docks. All went well until it crossed Canute Road into the Old Docks and on the sharply curved track that formed the entrance to No 1 shed it ended up caught by the platform edge, leaning up against it, so no more did a Britannia appear in the Old Docks. For a while, June - October 1951, 70009 ALFRED THE GREAT was to be found at Nine Elms, working trains between Waterloo and Bournemouth in part of

the country, Wessex, where Alfred indeed once ruled. 70009 had SR lamp irons fitted inside the smoke deflectors. Meanwhile the Laira based Britannias, 70016, 70019, 70021, 70022 and 70024 became the largest engines ever to work into Cornwall - though the 20¼ ton axle loading must have been close to the weight limit of engines allowed over the Royal Albert Bridge. Along with the other Western Britannias they were fitted with the GWR type of automatic train control, a feature which could be divined from the contact shoe, visible between the front bogie wheels.

There was a range of detail differences between the fifty five members of the class, and each loco was made up of over six hundred and fifty separate parts - various batches, moreo-

New Street, always a dramatic setting, serves as perfect stage for 70038 ROBIN HOOD on 2 October 1954. All but the last ten Britannias had the narrow bunker type of tender, a style which remained in production on the Standards until the last. It was a style, however, that was admitted to be less than perfect - the first shortcomings showed up with the LM Britannias sent to Holyhead. Their 7 tons compared badly with the 9 tons of a rebuilt Scot and they were removed to Longsight. Photograph A.G. Ellis, B.P. Hoper Collection.

70053 MORAY FIRTH with the bigger capacity BR1D tender, a very American looking design which many consider to have set the Britannias off at their best - certainly the overall look was altogether different. A splendidly volcanic view at Scarborough, 10 December 1958. Photograph B.P. Hoper Collection.

ver, were fitted with different types of tenders. The first thirty five were fitted with Timken roller bearings on all axles; 70035-70039 had roller bearings on the driving wheels only and 70040-70049 had plain axleboxes on all coupled wheels. There were problems of draughts caused by the cab design - dealt with in the chapter on tenders - and 70045-70054 were built with modified cabs. The BR1D tenders with which they were fitted had short footplates.

Another problem in the early days was a fore and aft movement between engine and train, something that occurred with other Standard types as well. It was soon solved, the cause being the degree of initial compression in the tender drawbar spring. This was modified so

that after coupling up, the drawhook would be pulled from its stock (even when the engine and rolling stock were stationary) against the compression of the buffers. Fitted as Standard were self cleaning smokebox, rocking firegrate, self emptying ashpan and manganese steel axlebox liners.

70000 and its sisters heralded the dawn of a new era, coming as they did in still-austere times of 1951; on the Regions they ran the peril of pleasing no-one and it was a burden I am sure, for R.A. Riddles and his team. The Britannias underwent a series of investigations including a number at the Rugby locomotive testing station. 70000 was tested between Crewe and Carlisle during January 1951, haul-

ing loads of 442 and 443 tons on January 12th and 13th respectively. 70006 ROBERT BURNS carried out test runs on the Great Eastern main line hauling the East Anglian express on both up and down runs on 4th and 5th June 1951. It hauled eight bogies with a dynamometer car and on the 6th and 7th eleven bogies, again with the dynamometer car. To help with the studies similar runs were made behind Thompson B1 No.61270. Elsewhere 70005 JOHN MILTON was at Rugby testing plant between April 25th and May of 1951, where it carried out performance and efficiency tests fitted with an exhaust steam injector.

Prominently described in the railway press of the time was the fitting of Westinghouse air brake equipment to 70043 and 70044, when outshopped from Crewe in 1953 - without smoke deflectors. Protracted trials were made, including the working of lengthy mineral trains between Toton and Brent on the Midland main line, for the purpose of comparing air brake and vacuum brake equipment, part of a process to decide which equipment would come into standard use in the future. 70043 and 70044 had a strange appearance, with the air brake equipment on both sides of the smokebox in place of the deflectors but unlike some experimentally fitted engines they did not look *disfigured* as such - merely 'foreign'. Once the trials were over the equipment was removed and they both received smoke deflectors and nameplates - LORD KITCHENER for 70043 and EARL HAIG for 70044. Both were allocated to Longsight until 70043 was transferred to Aston in August 1961 and 70044 to Holbeck in January 1959.

September 1954 saw the last of the class delivered, 70054 DORNOCH FIRTH and here we can speculate - would more have been ordered if the Modernisation Plan had not been introduced in 1955? This spelt the end of the steam on BR and the eventual sad waste of Standard locos built up to 1960, five years after the plan. By January 1968 only 70013 was left on the operational list, a sad end for a class of locomotives that should have been in service for another decade at least. A dismal epitaph which could be applied to all the Standard classes.

70024 VULCAN was the last of the 1951-built engines, coming out of Crewe Works in October of that year and of these 25, fifteen

Britannia on the Great Northern. 70036 BOADICEA leaves Peterborough North for the south in the early 1960s. Dieselisation had thrown them out of use on the GE and after a period languishing at March the celebrated GE line Pacifics, a lot dirtier than they had been but still in good nick mechanically, were distributed elsewhere. The last place anyone guessed they would end up was Immingham and the first three, 70039, 70040 and 70041 arrived at the end of December 1960. This, in a very small way, was a repeat of the experiences of 1951-52, for the Class 7 Pacifics were replacing 4-6-0s of much lower power ratings. Two of the three were out of action by the early summer of 1961 so they were not making the impact they should, but in the autumn four more arrived, 70035, 70036, 70037 and 70038. With this the Britannias were regular sights into Kings Cross. A brief Swansong, it was over by 1963. Photograph Barry Richardson, B.P. Hoper Collection.

The concentration of the Britannias on the LMR was the prelude to a protracted and painful decline. They moved to all sorts of sheds in the 1960s, as steam was extinguished in one area after another. One consolation was that they could be seen in hitherto very unusual places - such as 70020 (without its MERCURY plates) at West Hartlepool shed on 13 March 1965. It had brought in a train from Coventry, for a Rugby Union County Championship Final. Photograph Ian S. Carr.

were intended for the Eastern Region and the other ten for the Western. 70000-70014 should have gone to the ER to work on the Great Eastern lines but as we know 70004 and 70014 were diverted to Stewarts Lane in September 1951, 70004 having come from Stratford whilst 70014, having gone new to Norwich, went to Nine Elms in June before its move across London. 70015 APOLLO went new to Camden in June 1951 and to Stratford in January of the following year before arriving on the Western Region at Old Oak Common in September 1953. 70016 ARIEL was new to Leeds Holbeck in June 1951, moving to Stratford in March 1952 and onto the Western Region at Plymouth Laira in August 1953. 70017-70024 all went new to the Western Region and were later joined by 70025-70029 which were allocated new to Cardiff Canton, between September and November 1952.

Within railway circles and to some of the travelling public who saw the improvements in service, fame and popularity was assured. No better example of this was the improvement in service between Liverpool Street and Norwich where the Britannias enabled both a better frequency and punctuality. Indeed on the Great Eastern lines some of the first rosters involving the class included double return trips that could amount to 2,800 miles a week. For a number of years the GE section engines were 70000-70003, 70005, 70034, 70036-42 at Stratford and ten, 70006-70013, 70030 and 70035 at Norwich. The Britannias brought unprecedented Class 7 power to a line which had made do with nothing more than Class 4 in the shape of the B12 and B17 4-6-0s or Class 5 B1s. The Britannias appeared on the Harwich boat trains and the Kings Lynn and Cromer expresses but it was the Nor-

wich trains which really allowed them to show what they could do. A good example was the tightly timed Norfolkman, 10.00am from Liverpool Street, and on this the Britannias remained a favourite until replaced by the English Electric Type 4s.

Nothing was so alarming as the Britannias' ability to lose their tenders - on the GE in August 1957 70012, working an evening express, suffered a fracture of the pin of the coupling between the engine and tender with the result that the locomotive ran away and the train and tender stopped. Meanwhile the driver had to halt the engine by means of the reverser and the crew were most likely saved by the extended footplate. Nor was this a one-off; it occurred on a few occasions (though without the extreme consequences experienced on 70012) on the Norwich line, with one crew not realising the pin had fractured until arrival at Liverpool Street, when the broken pieces of the coupling dropped to the track. 70014 parted company with its tender whilst working the down 'Palatine' on 19 June 1958 and a photograph of the loco being unceremoniously hauled away appeared in *Trains Illustrated*. The fitting of safety links prevented any more such partings of engine and tender.

70052 FIRTH OF TAY also fell prey to a mishap, in January 1960 hauling the 9.05pm Glasgow (St Enoch) to St Pancras over the Settle - Carlisle main line, when the engine lost both right hand bottom slide bars. The crew became aware something was wrong but, unable to discover anything amiss, carried on at a slow speed on the south side of Ais Gill. The piston rod and union link nevertheless broke with the now loose coupling rod playing havoc with the

ballast. 70052 was not derailed but the free coupling rod had wreaked enough damage on the down road to cause the derailment of the engine on the 10.40pm Leeds to Carlisle freight. This had not been the first case of the slide bars being shed and although a solution had been arrived at, not all of the class had been dealt with by January 1960. 70052 was one of these not fitted with the newly designed front end fastening, and the accident hastened the fitting of this modification.

Sadly it is always the most notorious accidents that get the full publicity - on 20th November 1955, 70026 POLAR STAR, of Cardiff Canton, was involved in a tragic accident at Milton between Steventon and Didcot. Both engine and train of an up excursion from South Wales were derailed and eleven people killed. At the inquiry it was suggested that the driver's forward vision had been impaired and as a result of this the handrails on the smoke deflectors of most Western Region Britannias were removed to improve vision. Brass edged hand holds were cut to replace them. Oddly, 70021 MORNING STAR retained its handrails until withdrawn. As is well known (see earlier in this text for instance) the class had not proved popular on the WR, which did not enjoy any tradition of Pacific working. The fireman, who might not necessarily come across a Britannia with any great frequency, had to work out a different firing position, different to the one he had known for years and doubtless highly annoying. To complicate matters the regulator was deemed insensitive when compared with the Swindon type and Western drivers maintained that the BR equipment prevented them from getting away 'clean'. London and West Country crews famously did not take to the Britannias but once the men at Canton got hold of them, 70016-70020, 70022, 70023 and 70024 in late 1956/early 1957 (70025-70029 had gone there new in October/November 1952) there was a marked improvement in performances, on the South Wales expresses from Paddington and on the North and West route via Newport, Shrewsbury and Chester. In June 1960 70016 became the only Pacific to visit Caerphilly Works.

I count myself lucky in having seen many of the class, though I did not come across 70000 until August 1972 at Bridgnorth, in preservation. My most vivid memories of the Britannias are of them on shed, especially on Sundays, during glorious *Red Rover* visits, when it was possible to get round *six* London sheds using a five-bob ticket. I caught the Camden pair, 70048 and 70049 during their brief spell there but it was at Willesden that I saw the majority of my Britannias, including 70025-70027 when based at Aston. If not visiting sheds on a Sunday then it was London termini on a Saturday and there was no contest between the prospect of a Britannia at St Pancras and one of the new Deltics at Kings Cross. I came across 70053 MORAY FIRTH on an up train there, a rare instance and the only time I saw that engine. Later the same year I ventured back to the 'Cross having had my usual happy Saturday afternoon ration at Paddington but now intent on more A4s, so imagine my surprise on being confronted with 70041 SIR JOHN MOORE at the head of a down train. It was only in later years I discovered it to be part of a batch, 70039-70041, transferred to Immingham in December 1960 to work Grimsby and Hull expresses to London. They were later joined by 70035-70038 in the autumn of 1961. My last sighting of a Britannia in steam days was in August 1966 - oddly enough whilst waiting in the late afternoon on Surbiton station. A couple of days before, on 14th August, 70004 had worked the return leg of the LCGB 'A2 Commemorative Tour' from Westbury via Salisbury to Waterloo and on 16th August worked the 17.23 Waterloo to Southampton Docks boat train. I met it at Surbiton station whilst waiting for the 17.45 to Weybridge. 70004 (then based at Stockport Edgeley) eventually returned to the LMR on 17th August, on the 17.43 Southampton Docks to Crewe banana train, of all things.

70030-70033 were based from new at Holyhead at the end of 1952 and worked on the North Wales coast line to Chester, Crewe and beyond. Though liked well enough by their crews the BR1 tenders let them down, the 7 ton coal capacity at times proving insufficient. Within a couple of months these four were transferred to Longsight where 70034 had gone new in December 1952. In July 1953 70034 went south to Stratford, spending a number of years working out of Liverpool Street. It was one of the members of the class I was to see during its sojourn at Willesden. Eventually 70045-70049 went new to Holyhead, in June/July 1954 and with BR1D type tenders were well suited to the work, for they carried 9 tons of coal (with steam pusher) and had a better water capacity, 4,725 gallons compared with 4,250 gallons of the BR1. Often on the Irish Mail they worked turn and turn about with the Royal Scots. 70050-70054 (these final six were named after Scottish Firths) all had the BR1D tenders and for brief periods 70050, 70051 and 70053 were also at Holyhead. As the Modernisation Plan took effect the Britannias were transferred away from

The place to find Britannias as steam came to an end was of course Kingmoor, though the sights were increasingly unhappy ones. Nameless 70035 is at least a good illustration of the sort of handhold modifications (others were rectangular, and there were more of them) ordered in the wake of the Milton derailment of 1955. The edict regarding the handrails was not strictly interpreted and, famously, some 'Brits' retained the offending smoke deflector rail to the end. Photograph Ian S. Carr.

their first haunts; the Southern lost its two in June 1958, the Western its complement in September 1961, the North Eastern Region by August 1962, the Scottish by January 1963 and the Eastern Region by the end of 1963 - at one time Norwich had had twenty-two Britannias. Crewe North and Crewe South later had substantial allocations but they never seemed to stay long and it was often the case of the engine moving from North to South before going to another shed on the LMR. Spiritual home for the class in its final years was, indisputably, Carlisle, especially Kingmoor which, though it never had 70000, 70026, 70030, 70043 or 70044 on the books would certainly have received visits from them. All 55 spent their final years working out of LMR sheds and all were withdrawn from Carlisle Kingmoor save for the five above, and 70013 - as follows: 70000 Newton Heath 5/66; 70013 Carnforth 8/68; 70026 Stockport Edgeley 1/67; 70030 Carlisle Upperby 6/66; 70043 Crewe South 8/65 and 70044 Stockport Edgeley 10/66.

In January 1967 42 Britannia Pacifics were left in service but by December of the same year that number had been reduced to 14, all at Kingmoor. With this shed closing on 1 January 1968 there was only 70013 left in service, 13 more having been withdrawn. Of the 41 withdrawn in 1967, 40 of them were from Kingmoor.

DEMISE
June 1965 70007
August 1965 70043
March 1966 70019
May 1966 70000
June 1966 70030
August 1966 70050
September 1966 70001, 70017
October 1966 70036, 70044
November 1966 70037, 70054
December 1966 70018

January 1967 70002, 70008, 70009, 70020, 70026
March 1967 70003, 70052
April 1967 70040, 70041, 70053
May 1967 70006, 70034, 70042, 70048
June 1967 70027
July 1967 70005, 70033, 70046, 70047
August 1967 70015, 70016, 70038
September 1967 70010, 70028, 70032, 70039
October 1967 70029
November 70031
December 1967 70004, 70011, 70012, 70014, 70021, 70022, 70023, 70024, 70025, 70035, 70045, 70049, 70051
August 1968 70013

The Standards, Some Thoughts
By Richard Hardy

Many of the LNER locomotives had had drop grates for years, which saved both time and effort when the fire was being cleaned or thrown out. But when I came from Ipswich to the Southern at Stewarts Lane in 1952 there were few engines with such labour saving devices, other than the Ivatt tanks, the visiting 80000 Class 4MT tanks from the Brighton District and our two Britannias, 70004 and 70014, which had self cleaning smokeboxes, rocking grates and hopper ashpans. We also had sixteen Bulleid 'BoBs' with drop grates of a sort, but they were never used; once dropped, anything could happen! After I left, in January 1955, the Standard 5s arrived to replace some of the 'Arthurs' and they were manna from heaven for, not only were they splendid and economical engines but were easy to prepare and dispose. And what a boon this was to a hard-pressed foreman required to achieve the impossible in times of crisis in high summer.

A long way from the Festival of Britain, when the Empire's newest express loco stood under a large tarpaulin. 70004 at Holbeck on Sunday 20 August 1967 (D42 - just as grimy - stands in front), bereft of nameplates and shedplate, and carrying a lashed up tin smokebox plate. Photograph Gavin Morrison.

There used to be a national agreement with ASLEF and NUR which covered the time for preparation: thirty minutes for an engine with less than 1,500 sq. ft. of heating surface and forty five for more. This was in addition to the standard times for signing on and reading notices, so that the crew, say, for No.4 Duty signed on at 11.35, departed from the shed at 12.35 and left Victoria with the 'Golden Arrow' at 13.00. For the driver, the preparation of 70004 was relatively simple, all oiling points were readily accessible for an elderly driver as there was no shaft to attend to and, as the tools and oil bottles of all our engines were locked up in the tool boxes, there was no time wasted going to the stores or robbing other engines to make good the complement. The fireman had a wide firebox to cope with, which meant that he would spend maybe 15-20 minutes making up his fire in the back corners, after checking the water level and testing the injectors if he had enough steam to do so. In other words, it was a comfortable job for both men within the allotted time if they worked to a routine which also allowed them time to pull coal forward, trim the lamps, wash down the footplate, wipe over the firebox front and fittings, make the tea and get to the shed signal.

With locomotives with both inside and outside valve gear, such as the U1 or the 'Schools' classes, the driver had more to do and the fireman less, although he often did the underneath for a driver getting on in years. With the Bulleid Pacifics, it was plain sailing for the driver but harder work for the fireman, who needed plenty in the firebox against the climb out of London up to Knockholt, but with disposal things were different. There was no universal disposal time for any locomotive but the normal arrangement was one hour from arrival on the coal road to booking off, a snip with some, hard work for others. On the Southern, however, shorter disposal times for the few Standard and Ivatt engines were agreed. For example, 70004 would come on the coal road after working the up 'Arrow', the stoker locking the boxes and leaving the disposal for a shed crew. The fire would be cleaned, the clinker dropped through the hopper into the pit whilst alongside there might be an 'Arthur' which had been round Kent with a foot of clinker on the grate, the smokebox full of ash up to the cross bar and the ashpan solid, all to come out the hard way. The lucky men doing 70004 could be back in the messroom in half an hour, having taken coal, turned and berthed the engine in the shed. A piece of cake. So, in most ways, the Standard engines were popular with shed, artisan and footplate staff alike. The 80000s were preferred by Stewarts Lane men on the heavy Oxted line services, if only because the injectors were far more reliable than those on the ex-LM 4MTs. Both classes were strong but the LM engines were heavier on water and needed the full boiler pressure to keep time. If they had less than 160psi the ejector wouldn't have it and the brake would begin to drag.

And what of the Stratford Britannias on the Great Eastern, to which section I returned in 1955? Here the 7MTs were in regular hands, three sets of men to an engine and the diagrams were arranged so that the mileage was maximised and the visits to Stratford shed were kept to a minimum each working day. When at the shed, the engines were generally disposed and prepared by men in another link. But two of the three sets of men booked to the engine would do the trainwork whilst the third set acted as the relief at Liverpool Street between the early and late turn. For example, the 09.30 men would book on at the shed at 08.40, travel to London, relieve at 09.15 and work to Norwich and back. They were relieved on arrival by their opposite mates who would turn the engine and make it ready for the third set to go 18.30 Norwich and 22.45 return. With their own engine, the cab and footplate would be cleaned and the brass, copper and steelwork scoured, not only by the early turn men but by their relief at Liverpool St. These men would clean the fire and attend to all work within their ability, and if anything serious was amiss, Sam Chapman or 'Hoot' Gibson, the London fitters, would do the necessary. As at Stewarts Lane, the modern aids to disposal were of the greatest benefit if an engine were needed in a hurry. Relying on my memory, Stratford allowed an hour for the disposal of all engines, whether they had modern equipment or not. A good outside foreman kept a close watch on disposals. If a driver had got him out of a tight corner, one day he would have more than his share of Standard or drop grate engines by way of compensation, but a good foreman would also have some rough ones up his sleeve for anybody who had played him up!

Of the standard engines, I had most experience with the 7MTs. They were liked by everybody for they were powerful, fast, economical and responded to regular manning. The footplate was easily cleaned as there was little hot pipe work to obstruct the polishing and scouring that went on, often during a journey. Compared with a GE B12 or a Bulleid Pacific, the riding was harsh and the cabs draughty but, ever resourceful, in cold weather the Stratford drivers went in for surplus Army leather jerkins and jammed a disc board between the back of the seat and its frame to divert the air stream. Maintenance was straightforward although I seem to remember that the front end lubrication was not all it might have been, as piston and valve rings had a limited life. Unlike the Norwich District, life was far too hectic in our madhouse to keep details of serious mechanical derangements but I can recall few, if any, whereas Norwich had more than their share. Our troubles were largely with steaming and that was usually due to neglect in tube cleaning for which we were responsible. A Britannia, down to 160psi was a very poor tool and the blower would neither rally the fire nor clear the chimney of smoke. Yet a Bulleid light Pacific would time a heavy boat train up from Dover with 160psi - although it was slavery to do so. I made many journeys on our Britannias and of

course on 70004. Very rarely were we in difficulties but I remember going to Norwich with 70042 a good spare engine, Driver Albert Page and his mate, Charlie Gunner. We were below 200 psi most of the way. We could do little to improve matters, except to scheme and think ahead but back at Stratford I saw to it that the tubes were properly cleaned and many other small jobs attended to before 70042 went back to work. We kept time despite all the agony! One evening late in 1955 Dick Brock and Billy Hart lost 45 minutes getting to Shenfield with 70001: in June 1959 Norwich men with 70010 lost 80 minutes to Ipswich with tubes leaking but these were isolated instances in years of first class work. In 1958, when it was impossible to keep abreast of 7MT maintenance at Stratford, and before our thirteen engines were transferred to Norwich, we had Wally Mason, acting inspector, with a genius for getting the best from men, riding with the 7MT or B1 on the 09.30 and the 13.45 return six days a week with the remit 'Right time, Norwich or London, never mind the engine or the fireman's back, get there!' The Brits rarely if ever let us down.

In September 1959 I arranged for two SNCF enginemen with whom I had travelled in France to go to Norwich on 70041. Wally Mason saw to it that they got the feel of the 7MT even though it lacked the silky puissance of their own Chapelon Pacifics. On the return journey, they sampled D200 and an EMU to Thorpe-le-Soken where we waited for the 14.00 from Clacton, which soon arrived with 70007 and Driver Stan Pittuck in charge. As the engine

passed us, it was clear that the axlebox lubricator drive had come adrift and was flailing about. My French friends at once became fascinated spectators of what might be termed good old British make do and mend. Whereas the French crew's 231 E9 carried small spanners, pin punches, indeed every conceivable tool, 70007 made do with a few large spanners and a coal hammer. So Stan and his mate tied things up with signal wire and I got on the 'phone to Colchester for a fitter to meet us to strip the gear down, for we knew that the old Brit would manage with what oil she had for the next 42 miles.

Our Colchester fitter had the job done in a few minutes, threw the parts on board and Stan told me to get on with the driver. We had eleven minutes to regain and I know we went very fast between stops for we were going to show these Frenchmen how it should be done. In fact, they were thrilled by the speed, the noise from the stack, the vibration and our stop at Shenfield. I did not tell them that I forgot we were booked to stop until Stan whispered in my ear! We were 11 minutes late from Colchester and almost on time once more, only to be stopped by the Romford pilot crossing over: we had been too quick for the signalman. Never mind, we had a good run up to London and we were not far out when we stopped in Liverpool St. 70007 was none the worse, Sam Chapman fixed her up again, our Frenchmen had enjoyed every minute and Stan, his mate and I were pleased with a job well done and a delay avoided. All in a day's work to a Brit and what marvellous engines they were.

Striking view of 70049 (minus its SOLWAY FIRTH plates) running light to Citadel, near Kingmoor, on 10 July 1965. It shows the BR1D to good effect, with its steam coal pusher at the rear. Though by this time it mattered not at all, coal consumption had been an important factor when the Britannias were being designed. It had been an era of fuel crises after all, and tests with 70000 in 1951 revealed a very gratifying reduction over anything seen in the 1948 Interchange Trials. Philip Atkins in *Britannia, Birth of a Locomotive* (Irwell Press) records the rather amusing calculations that were made at the time. It was announced, somewhat breathlessly, that if BR Class 7s replaced all 533 pre-war equivalents, Castles, V2s, Scots and the rest, an annual saving of over 46,000 tons would result. The boast disappeared when it was pointed out that over 500 new Pacifics would cost £10 million, for an annual saving of £120,000. Thus, 80 years (or twice the engines' economic life) would be necessary to 'break even'.... Photograph James Stevenson.

DUKE OF GLOUCESTER spent much of its first year on exhibition or on test. It went to Willesden for the 16th International Railway Congress (it was towed there in company with 92014) May - June 1954 and after a summer on the LNW main line it went to Swindon for test work, both stationary and out on the road, with dynamometer car and indicator shelter. Here it is on arrival at Swindon in October 1954. Behind is 9F No.92001, which had been new earlier in the year, coming from Crewe to cause such consternation at Ebbw Junction. *Photograph Brian Morrison.*

2. Duke of Gloucester 1954-1962

It is worth recording that equivalent main line tests with a BR main line diesel and the Class '8' 4-6-2 No.71000 *Duke of Gloucester* have shown the latter's fuel costs on individual runs, in terms of pence per ton-mile, to be within 20 per cent of those attainable by the diesel. *British Railways Today and Tomorrow*, G. Freeman Allen.

In between trains, and perched on our local railway bridge, we would pore endlessly over the Ian Allan *ABC*s, whiling away the time before yet another Bulleid Pacific. We pondered numbers, seen and unseen, and in the section devoted to the BR Standards all agreed that the most desirable (this was a southern English viewpoint) were 70000, 71000 and 92220. In my case I did not see any of them until they were preserved - or, in the case of The Duke, in the scrapyard. So, imagine our collective astonishment on reading in the February 1963 *Modern Railways* that 71000 *had been withdrawn the previous November.....*

The disaster at Harrow and Wealdstone in October 1952 saw the writing off of Stanier Pacific 46202 PRINCESS ANNE, which was deemed to be beyond economic repair. When the range of new Standard engines had been under discussion a few years before, provision was made for the upper range of express passenger locomotives and E.S. Cox recounts that this putative Class 8P would 'be closely based upon the LM Duchess 4-6-2'. At the time, however, it had been determined that there was no need for further engines in this power class, as the Regions were well supplied with them - A4s and the rest on the East Coast, Duchesses on the LM and Merchant Navys on the Southern. The demise of PRINCESS ANNE gave Riddles the opportunity to seek a replacement.... In the words of E.S. Cox, in *British Railways*

Standard Steam Locomotives (Ian Allan 1966), experience would 'be gained against possible future needs for more of this kind of locomotive'. There was no foreknowledge then, as Cox duly points out, of the sheer pace of dieselisation; it was by no means certain that further Class 8s would not be required.

The first detailed published account of 71000 can be found in *The Railway Magazine* and *Trains Illustrated* July 1954, and the heading 'British Railways *Prototype* [my emphasis] Class 8 Express Passenger Locomotive' certainly did not suggest a one-off - which the word 'replacement' did. 'The Duke' seems in the end to have been several things - a prototype, a testbed and a demonstration of what could be done, of what might be possible. The publicity held that 71000 was '...the first locomotive to be built by British Railways specifically for working heavy passenger services...' but few realised then that it would be the last Pacific built for regular use on BR. The intention of Riddles and his team was to design and construct a prototype, put it through a tough testing programme to find any fault and then, if it was found necessary, production could begin. But by the time 71000 became part of the allocation at Crewe North, in May 1954, the writing was on the wall for steam on BR. There were enough front line Pacifics on the Regions, it was felt, to see out steam. If a need had arisen however (and this demonstrates the foresight in Riddle's ac-

tions) then the design, properly finely tuned and adjusted (which it never was, until preservation) would have been there. It was not as unlikely an outcome as might be thought. Despite the earlier decision against building any 8Ps, and the later decision not to replicate The Duke, from the operating standpoint of the early 1950s the 8P situation could hardly have seemed something to be sanguine about. Just fifty served for the entire length of the LMR from London to Scotland and most had been built before or during the War. The Western Region had King 4-6-0s already more than thirty years old and the New Order grouped around Riddles looked askance at the Merchant Navys. Only from the LNER tradition were any new, conventional big Pacifics emerging. If there were to be steam hauled expresses much past the 1960s (and who then could say this would not be the case?) then it would have been negligent not to have something in the kitty.

71000 was unique amongst the 999 BR Standards in that it had three cylinders. Each one had separate inlet and exhaust valves at each, with the inside cylinder driving onto the leading axle. All the other Standards had two cylinders; 71000 was thus the only one of the 999 to be fitted with a crank axle and the first to have a double chimney and blastpipe. It was easily differentiated from the Britannias, at a glance, by its oval buffers and flat bottomed smokebox. It was also the first of the Standards to be fitted

A famous picture at Crewe, 19 August 1955, when powering a Birmingham to Manchester express. Crewe was its home, but it was not liked overmuch. It was the old story of not being better, by an obvious margin, than the locomotives it was supposed to work with. Photograph Brian Morrison.

with British Caprotti valve gear. The prime advantage of this rotary cam poppet valve system was that it allowed excellent steam distribution - two inlet valves on the cylinders were driven by cams worked by circular rotating shafts and these in turn were connected to the return crank gearbox, linked to the driving wheel crankpins. The inside cambox, on the middle cylinder, was driven from an extension of the left hand wormshaft by way of a right angle bevel gearbox in front of the left hand cylinder. Apart from these features, it was intended that 71000 should have as much in common with the Britannias as possible, including the boiler, but 71000 had a 48.6 sq ft grate whilst the Britannias had 42 sq ft; the firebox heating surface area comparisons were 226 sq ft to 210 sq ft and 71000's firebox was a foot longer. True to standard though, the driving wheels were 6ft 2in in diameter with 3in tyres shrunk onto the wheels, Bulleid style. All driving axles were fitted with roller bearings. Problems with the trailing axle on the Britannias saw 71000 being fitted with coil springs instead of laminated springs but it still experienced vibrations in service, sufficient at times to break up the fire. Boiler pressure was 250lb/psi with tractive effort, at 85%, 39,080lb; tube heating surface was 2,264 sq ft and superheater heating surface 677 sq ft.

Built at Crewe under order number E486, 71000 emerged in May 1954 and on the 18th of that month and along with brand new 9F 92014, was towed to Willesden shed for the 16th International Railway Congress. The Duke of Gloucester was the president of the Congress and 71000 was named in his honour. A tender was taken from the 9F production line which became the unique BR1E, to carry 10 tons of coal (with pusher) and 4,725 gallons of water. After a while in service and with 71000 gaining a reputation for high coal consumption, still greater capacity was needed and another unique pattern emerged, a BR1J type constructed in November 1957. Though nominally it still had a 10 ton capacity in truth it carried more, though water was reduced to 4,325 gallons. It could be distinguished from the BR1E by the longer curved top sides of the coal space, which extended further to the rear.

71000 was based at Crewe North all its short working life, where it was not loved by crews accustomed to home bred Stanier Pacifics, two of the best designs, maybe, ever to work on a British railway. In the autumn of 1954 71000 was put on the same rosters as the other 8P Pacifics at Crewe North, including the 'West Coast Postal' and 'The Mid-Day Scot', tough assignments for any engine. This showed up 71000's appetite for coal and though some crews were able to get a good performance out of it, at times running at 90mph, the general preference remained for a Stanier Pacific.

In October 1954 71000 was in Swindon Works for a few months for efficiency test routines. Under the eagle eye of the experts at Swindon, the Pacific was tested on the stationary plant and in controlled road tests. On the main line 71000 was fitted with a front end indicator shelter and hauled a dynamometer car and 18 carriages or more, the load testing often taking place between Swindon and Westbury via the Reading West Curve. Boiler performance and efficiency were not up to par, though the cylinders produced excellent results and, as in service, vibrations at the rear end caused the firebed to be displaced and broken up. However the engine proved to be the most economical in

'The Duke' at Swindon 'Barn', minus smoke deflectors, 13 February 1955. The boiler efficiency was a disappointment compared to the Britannia ('an exceptionally well proportioned boiler') but the puzzle remains as to why no attempt was made to remedy the problem - though by now it was clear it would be the only one of its class. In any event matters greatly improved under road conditions and as Cox declares, 'as built', 71000 was 'a near miss'. He ruminates upon what might have been wrong in *British Railways Standard Steam Locomotives* but it would never occurred in his wildest dreams that, following half-scrapping, abandonment for seven years and slow loving rebuilding, the problems would at last be spotted and corrected... A collection of GWR chimneys look reproachfully on. Photograph Brian Morrison.

steam consumption per indicated horsepower of any on record in Britain.

71000 returned (a 'near miss' in Cox's words) to Crewe North in May 1955, symbolically close to publication of the *Modernization Plan*; the die was thus cast, and the engine, a year old and a one-off, had a bleak future. It worked both north and south of Crewe and its most regular task, as already mentioned, was 'The Mid-Day Scot', one of the heaviest and tightly timed trains on the LMR, Euston - Rugby, 82 miles in 80 minutes and often with loads of 500 tons. The engine maintained its reputation for being heavy on coal and water and of the men from No.3 link at Crewe North who drove and fired it, some hated 71000, others enjoyed the work. Like the 'Clans' it no doubt depended on how 71000 was fired and through research it appears that there was no way 71000 could be fired like a four cylinder Stanier Pacific - perhaps a better method would

have been to adapt the techniques used on three cylinder engines such as the Royal Scots. Whatever, 71000 was withdrawn on 24th November 1962, having covered nearly 300,000 miles in traffic. It was listed for preservation but after being stored at Crewe for some years, in 1967 the left hand cylinder and valve gear were removed, sectioned and put on display at the Science Museum, Kensington. The hulk that was now 71000 ended up at Woodhams scrapyard in Barry and in March 1972 I had my first sighting when walking round this atmospheric graveyard. Since then 71000, through its marvellous rebirth, has certainly turned into a true Phoenix. Minor rectifications have cured the problems which so perplexed Cox. He was denied a solution only through the curtailment of investigative work, and since this remedial treatment 'The Duke' has proved to be a very good performer on the main line, long after it first went to the breakers at Barry.

Above. The Duke at Shrewsbury shed, 11 June 1961. Since its renascence, it has recorded some of the highest power outputs seen in Britain in steam engines. Photograph W. Potter.

Below. Leaving Carlisle with the down Mid-Day Scot, 4 August 1954. This was its first summer of operation, between the Railway Congress at Willesden and the testing at Swindon. The engine was particularly associated with this train but men compared it badly with the existing Duchess Pacifics. One Camden fireman remembers it as 'a Monday-Tuesday loco'. What this meant was that by Wednesday it would be getting difficult to work and by Thursday/Friday nigh impossible. It was 'coal happy' and difficult to steam by the end of the week. The afterlife of this wondrous phoenix, with the discovery of misdrawn/misinterpreted drawings and the subsequent modifications to blastpipe and ashpan primary airways, has shown it to be an easy and efficient steamer and the equal of any Stanier Pacific. Photograph Peter Groom.

Above. 72000 CLAN BUCHANAN at Polmadie on 26 April 1952. The Clans shared many components with their larger brethren, the Britannias; even to the same chassis and wheel spacings. The smaller boiler was the only major difference. Photograph J. Robertson, B.P. Hoper Collection.

Below. 72001 CLAN CAMERON at Polmadie, 8 May 1954. The first Clans came to this great Glasgow shed (ex-LMS/Caledonian) from the end of 1951, and all of the first five were there by February 1952. Cox admitted the Clans to be a 'border line case'; the many Class 5 duties were, after all, being carried out by a highly efficient and numerous existing fleet of pre-Nationalisation 4-6-0s, all weighing less than the proposed BR Class 6 Pacific. Coal savings would make up for the increased capital cost of a 4-6-2, but there would be a further debit from increased maintenance. It was a fine balance, and the Class 6 seems to have gone ahead (the 1948 Exchange experiences with the Bulleid Pacifics were still very much in mind) on the basis that there would be circumstances where some increase in power over the Class 5 4-6-0s was desirable. Photograph J. Robertson, B.P. Hoper Collection.

3. Clan Pacifics 1951-1966

In spirit, the Clans were essentially Cox's original 1948 light 4-6-2 proposal, slightly enlarged at R.C. Bond's suggestion. The only *major* difference from the Class 7 4-6-2 was the smaller boiler. *BRITANNIA, Birth of a Locomotive*, by Philip Atkins.

Bulleid Pacific No.34004 YEOVIL, along with an LMS tender, proved a success on the Highland main line from Inverness to Perth during the 1948 exchange trials, albeit with a good footplate crew and a heavy coal consumption. Herein, maybe, was the genesis of the BR Class 6 Pacifics, a type that proved to be the Cinderellas of the BR Standards, though they carried stirring names. If the Clan names were rousing, then the further fifteen that were cancelled (there were to be even more, for the North Eastern but this hardly even got to the stage where cancellation was formally necessary) would have been even more so. Five for the Southern would have commemorated Saxon warlords and the rest further clans.

Was there, however, any need to build these machines? Hindsight suggests that the class should never have been constructed and though cancellation of the fifteen fuels this argument several other Standard classes were so cut short. In any case, the argument that says the Clans should not have been built could apply to the whole 'range'. The 'business history' of BR for instance, commissioned by the British Railways Board and published in 1986 (*British Railways 1948-1973*, T.R. Gourvish, Cambridge University Press) only just stops short of declaring the production of *any* steam locomotives in the 1950s perverse. 'It is quite clear' it states, 'that Riddles carried his enthusiasm for steam much too far'. The Standard were

'illogical' when Regional types were available and a full scale trial of diesels should have been embarked upon. Riddles won the argument, whatever a 'business history' may say and we can only be glad he did so.

At the time these engines were being planned Riddles and his team had arrived at a plan, whatever the wider merits, to restock the run down railways of Britain with a breed of modern, economic and efficient steam engines reflecting the conditions that existed in postwar Britain. These had to be capable of working under the severest of conditions and over the majority of lines that the six new Regions operated. All these years on, it might well be possible to demonstrate that far fewer individual Standard types were needed - the gradation between types did not need to be so fine, maybe. Thus the 'intermediate' engines *were* cut short - the 3MTs (tank and tender) and the 6MT Clans. Take the five 'Saxon warlords' cancelled for the Southern. How would these have looked amidst more than a hundred Bulleid light Pacifics roaming around the Southern Region?

The Clans have been described as 'scaled down Britannias' for they had an identical chassis, the same size driving wheels (6ft. 2in.) and identical wheel spacing, but a smaller boiler, type BR2 which produced 225lb boiler pressure with a 35 element superheater. Britannias were 250lb with 40 element superheater. The grate area on the Clans was 36 sq ft

compared with the Britannias' 42 sq ft. The Clan boiler had a smaller diameter of 5ft. 4in. compared to the 5ft. 8in. of a Britannia boiler and the cylinder diameter was half an inch less, 19°in. instead of 20in. for the Britannia, although the stroke was identical at 28in.. BR type 1 tenders were attached to all the Clans and these carried seven tons of coal and 4,250 gallons of water. Parent office for the design was Derby but as with all the Standards many other parts were sub-contracted to other British Railways workshops, with assembly taking place at Crewe under order number E480 to Lot 221 between December 1951 (72000 and 72001) and March 1952 (72007-72009). Details were given as below (Crewe incidentally provided flanged boiler plates to all other works, except Swindon which made its own for the Class 3 2-6-0s and 2-6-2Ts. Horwich and Derby did not build any boilers at all, but Doncaster, Darlington, Swindon and Brighton did).

Design
Derby: Parent office; wheels & axles; frames; bogie; pony truck; boiler; tender.
Doncaster: Motion.
Brighton: Brake gear.
Swindon: Standard boiler fittings.

Manufacturing Works
Crewe: Steel castings; drop stampings; large forgings; small forgings; cast steel cylinder cast-

Appropriate power at Crianlarich for the gathering of the Clan Cameron, on 16 June 1956 - 72001 CLAN CAMERON with a special from Queen Street to Spean Bridge. Apparently the Clan had friends at Court (in the person of a part time member of the BTC) and even the crew (including the guard) was made up of pure bred Camerons. To cap it all, the K4 2-6-0 61995 CAMERON OF LOCHIEL was also at Crianlarich in case of a failure. Whether this represented ordinary prudence or a special fear for 72001 is not clear. Photograph J. Robertson, B.P. Hoper Collection.

Majestic pose at Holbeck on 21 August 1961. 72006 was the engine which (quite incorrectly) was to have the ugly cabside yellow stripe applied, in August 1964. Photograph Gavin Morrison.

ing; general iron castings; brass castings; boiler flanged plates; smokebox front and door pressings; new boiler construction; flanged plates.
Derby: Small forgings; cylinder casting; general iron castings; brass castings; hot brass pressings; smokebox front and door pressings; flanged plates.
Horwich: Small forgings; cast iron cylinder casting; brake blocks; firebars; general iron castings; brass castings; flanged plates.

The light Pacifics emerged with a route availability similar to that of the Standard Class 5 (73000 came out from Derby in April 1951) and were fitted with taller chimneys than the Britannias which, I felt, suited them. Like the Britannias the Clans carried chime whistles when introduced but these were later exchanged for the standard BR whistle. Unlike the Britannias they retained their original handrails on the smoke deflectors until the end.

With the record of YEOVIL on the Highland the Clans, it was thought, would be suited to the Highland main line between Inverness and Perth. Research seems to indicate that the route never saw a Clan Pacific in operation, though it is reported that 72007 was at Inverness in August 1952. Adhesion factors (we all know how Pacifics love to slip) presumably scuppered any putative move to the Highlands, and whatever the success of the Southern Pacific, Stanier Black Fives reigned supreme on this line until the coming of the diesels. It has been said that Riddles came to the conclusion that a 4-8-0, with its increased adhesion, would have been the answer to the demands of the Highland, but sadly, we never saw if that could have been the solution.

When new, 72000-72004 went to Polmadie shed and 72005-72009 to Carlisle Kingmoor. Both sheds were then under the control of the Scottish Region with the London Midland Region responsible for maintenance. Crewe Works carried out the majority of overhauls and necessary repairs. With such a small body of locos it is easy enough to list here and comment on the few transfers and allocations for the entire class. (Carlisle Kingmoor came under the control of the London Midland Region from February 1958).

72000. New to Polmadie 12/51. Transferred to Haymarket in 10/57. Back at Polmadie in 4/58. Transferred to St Margarets in 11/59. Back at Polmadie in 3/60. Withdrawn in 12/62.
72001. New to Polmadie in 12/51. Transferred to Haymarket in 11/59. Back at Polmadie in 3/60. Withdrawn in 12/62.
72002. New to Polmadie in 1/52. Transferred to Haymarket in 10/57. Returned to Polmadie in 4/58. Back to Haymarket in 11/59. Final transfer to Polmadie in 3/60. Withdrawn in 12/62.
72003. New to Polmadie in 1/52. Transferred to St Margarets in 11/59. Back to Polmadie in 3/60. Withdrawn in 12/62.
72004. New to Polmadie in 2/52. Transferred to St Margarets in 11/59. Back to Polmadie in 3/60. Withdrawn in 12/62.

The first five were essentially Polmadie engines; even so, the transfers to Haymarket meant these members of the class could be used over the Waverley route, Edinburgh - Carlisle (though they didn't last too long). The withdrawal of all five in December 1962 was part of the Scottish

Region's drive to rid itself of express steam engines.

72005. New to Kingmoor 2/52. Transferred to Haymarket 10/57. Back to Kingmoor 4/58. Withdrawn from Kingmoor 5/65.
72006. New to Kingmoor 2/52. Transferred to Haymarket 10/57. Back to Kingmoor 4/58. Withdrawn from Kingmoor 5/66.
72007. New to Kingmoor 3/52. Withdrawn from Kingmoor 12/65.
72008. New to Kingmoor 3/52. Withdrawn from Kingmoor 4/66.
72009. New to Kingmoor 3/52. Transferred to Stratford (Eastern Region) 9/58. Back to Kingmoor 10/58. Withdrawn from Kingmoor 8/65.

The month that 72009 spent at Stratford in 1958 was for the engine to carry out trials on the GER where it worked the 'Essex Coast Express'. It was even seen at Norwich on 26th September 1958, but does not seem to have made much of an impression, which is hardly surprising given the success of the Britannias on this line and the arrival of the first main line diesels. The Eastern people would merely have seen an offer of a Class 6 for Class 7 jobs, and engines whose state of health was an unknown quantity. The trial didn't stand a chance.

72000-72004, after their withdrawal *en bloc* in December 1962, were first stored at their home shed, until May 1963 when they were moved to Parkhead for further storage until September 1963. In October they made their final move to Darlington Works. Here 72001 was the first one of the class to be scrapped, in February 1964; 72000, 72003 and 72004 followed in March and 72002 in April.

72005-72009 fared better at Carlisle Kingmoor and the footplate crews here found that, if pushed hard enough, the Clans could tackle the banks on the West Coast main line including Shap, with up to fourteen on. Of the Carlisle engines, 72007 was reputed to be the best of an average bunch.

Opinions varied widely on the attributes and/or deficiencies of the class, both among railway writers and, more importantly, the footplatemen that rode them. They seem to have been a tricky engine to handle, performance was seldom better than average but if they did steam well it was the coal consumption that suffered. They were, maybe, the 'least needed' of all the Standards. They were too few for a good part of the crews to become thoroughly used to them; if on a Jubilee job they probably seemed less sure-footed (lack of practice would contribute to this) and if on a Pacific job they would be noticeably underpowered. In June 1956 (after a trial run in May) 72001 CLAN CAMERON was used on the West Highland line for a week, the main working being to Spean Bridge where the Clan Cameron gathering took place at Achnasherry Castle. Verdicts differed as to the engine's capabilities - 72001 was said to have ridden roughly, grinding into the sharp curves of the West Highland line, whilst the driver commended the engine for treating the severest curves 'with disdain'. You takes your pick.

I have read that the class was well liked by enginemen *and* that Polmadie men did not like them at all. 'They were happy' when the engines were loaned (as well as sometimes transferred to) Haymarket at times to help with the annual seed potato traffic. Haymarket men, to whom the Clans would seem even more 'foreign' apparently considered them sluggish performers with an inadequate water supply compared with their LNER charges.

Steaming improved with the narrowing of the blastpipes, and Carlisle men seemed to get better performances out of the Clans - so it was all due to the firing technique? Polmadie men preferred to fill the firebox up, shut the firebox doors and let the blast do the rest and no doubt the Clans did not like it. Many Carlisle men used the Midland firing technique of little and often which seemed to suit the light Pacifics better. Derek Cross summed up matters with patent practicality - *'if you really hammered them, they would climb'*. The Carlisle men liked them on the 'Port Road', Dumfries to Stranraer, but on the heavier Euston - Stranraer boat trains preferred their Jubilees.

The geographical limits of the Clans were closely defined, but they did on occasion get to Bristol, Severn Tunnel and of course to Stratford. Few alterations were carried out but a footblock was added on the back of the tenders to aid the fireman when taking water. Other 'mods' included the fitting of AWS, powered from a battery box on the right hand side running plate ahead of the firebox and a speedometer, driven off the rear driving wheel on the left hand side. Finally, an LMS mounting appeared on the rear crank, one with four studs instead of a square pin. The nameplates were made of cast brass and had raised four inch letters, similar to the other Standard Pacifics.

Normal workings, which included fish trains and freights from Glasgow to Stirling, took the Clans as far north as Perth. The higher numbered ones, based at Carlisle, saw work on the Settle to Carlisle line and were regular engines on the Carlisle - Bradford stopping trains. For a period in the early 1960s, they could be found regularly on 'The Waverley' between Leeds and Carlisle and into Scotland, the express itself originating at London St Pancras. Lesser duties included freights to Wigan in the North West but

their most common workings were the Glasgow - Liverpool, Glasgow - Manchester and Glasgow - Birmingham expresses, the regular turns including the 09.25 Crewe - Perth; 1.15pm Manchester - Glasgow and 1.45pm Glasgow - Liverpool.

Frequent jobs included Carlisle to Perth parcel trains and taking over fish trains at Perth that ran from Aberdeen to the Midlands. Fast fitted van trains were rostered to them as were football specials; regular appearances on the GSWR route from Glasgow to Dumfries via Kilmarnock were balanced by workings on the Port Line through Dumfries to Stranraer. The Clans were recorded on boat trains from Stranraer to Newcastle via Ayr. By 1962 the Kingmoor based engines were being used on fitted freights and excursion trains, including Dundee - Blackpool and Glasgow - Blackpool via the West Coast main line.

I have few personal recollections of the class as I only got to the North West once in steam days and that on the way to Scotland. Dad drove and on the return journey south we once again ran parallel with the West Coast main line - here, by great good fortune I saw CLAN STEWART on a southbound express. A very exciting moment for a young trainspotter. My records also show 72000 CLAN BUCHANAN firmly underlined but inexplicably - and this seems impossible - I cannot recall where that was spotted.

Should the class have been built? From my wanderings through the literature the answer is no, for there were more than enough available types to cover their duties. They were not popular with many crews, moreover, and gained a reputation as poor steamers. When they were designed by Riddles and his team they were expected to have had a much longer life, working into the 1970s at least, but the with-

The Clans all went to the Scottish Region, the first five at Polmadie, the rest at Kingmoor. They were 'separated' when Kingmoor passed to the London Midland Region and this is just as well, for the whole class would probably have gone at the end of 1962. At that time the Scottish Region withdrew all its Clans (72000-72004) as part of a drive to reduce the number of classes in use (presumably some accounting device). As it was the LM five, 72005-72009, soldiered on into 1965 and even 1966. 72007 without its CLAN MACKINTOSH plates is turning, appropriately, at Kingmoor, on 10 August 1965. It was withdrawn a few months later. Photograph Peter Groom.

drawal of Polmadie's allocation in December 1962, whatever their shortcomings, was a great waste. Surely Kingmoor on the LMR could have found use for them and at least given them a longer working life? - ten after all, would be more economically worked than five survivors. In fact, the Scottish moves were probably an accountancy device to reduce the number of classes passing to 1 January 1963. Several classes thus became extinct in Scotland at the end of 1962, among them the Region's allocation of LMS 4-6-2s.

The last five, all Kingmoor engines, were in pretty lousy external state at the end, the BR Brunswick green livery often invisible under a coat of dirt, grime and grease and they were all withdrawn when they fell due for repairs or overhaul. 72005 was withdrawn in May 1965 and after a month in storage was sold and scrapped at the West of Scotland Shipbreaking Co Troon. Two more were withdrawn in 1965, 72009 in September and 72007 in December with 72009 stored for two months and then cut up at the Motherwell Machinery and Scrap Co Wishaw whilst 72007 survived until early 1966 before being scrapped at Campbells, Airdrie. 1966 saw the class extinct with 72008 withdrawn in April and 72006 the next month. Both were scrapped at McWilliams, Shettleston with 72006 lasting four months longer being cut up in October 1966. Thus 72004 was the shortest lived of the class (February 1952 - December 1962) with 72006 the longest, from February 1952 to May 1966. 72008 was only one month behind, February 1952 - April 1966. A sad end to a handsome class.

DEMISE
See text...

72000 CLAN BUCHANAN
72001 CLAN CAMERON
72002 CLAN CAMPBELL
72003 CLAN FRASER
72004 CLAN MACDONALD
72005 CLAN MACGREGOR
72006 CLAN MACKENZIE
72007 CLAN MACKINTOSH
72008 CLAN MACLEOD
72009 CLAN STEWART

Top. **CLAN CAMERON in glorious condition, at Polmadie on 16 February 1952. There were failures that year, the 'shifting axles' as experienced with the Britannias. Modifications were done at Crewe but there seems to be no record of the class being withdrawn 'en masse'. The reason seems to have been the same, for photographs show Clans in this period with hollow axles. Later photographs show the solid modification, though there are some puzzling inconsistencies. The sad fact is that the Clans are poorly recorded, compared to the 'Brits'. Photograph J. Robertson, B.P. Hoper Collection.**

Middle. **72009 CLAN STEWART at New Cumnock, Ayrshire, in August 1959. This was the engine non-too subtly rejected by the Eastern Region the previous year. Photograph George Heiron.**

Right. **Polmadie, where else? 72002 CLAN CAMPBELL 'at home' with fellow inhabitants, 14 May 1955. Photograph J. Robertson, B.P. Hoper Collection.**

Top. CLAN MACLEOD (minus nameplates) approaches Ais Gill summit with the morning Carlisle - Hellifield stopping train of six coaches, on 17 July 1965. Built February 1952 at Crewe to order No E480, its life typified the rather stay at home nature of the Class 6 Pacifics. 72000-72006 all enjoyed spells at Haymarket or St Margarets but that was really the limit of their peregrinations. Their normal haunts remained the north of England through to the middle of Scotland. 72009's first shed was Carlisle Kingmoor and that was where it stayed. Withdrawn from there in April 1966, it was stored at Kingmoor for a few weeks until May 1966, and was scrapped at McWilliams, Shettleston. Photograph Maurice Burns.

Below. Last days of the Clans. 72007 at Carlisle on 31 July 1965. Only three remained by now - 72009 would go in a few days and 72007 at the end of the year. The last, 72008, would last until April 1966. Photograph Ian S. Carr.

Top. New 73006 in Scotland. The BR Class 5s were the final manifestation of the '4-6-0 machine of all purpose utility' which had been outlined by Hughes as far back as the early 1920s.

Below. 73005, then only a year or so old, working an up freight through Dunblane station, on 28 July 1952. The only one of Hughes ideas to see fruition were the Crab 2-6-0s and the LMS did not have 'all purpose utility' 4-6-0s until Stanier's Black 5s in 1934. The quest for such a machine came down through varied paths, on the LNER and on the GW but the BR Class 5 was in essence the LMS version, and achieved a similar ubiquity, the length and breadth of the land. 73005 was however, not a far travelled example; built at Derby in June 1951 to order No 5122, its first shed was Perth and its second (and final) home Corkerhill, from where it was withdrawn in 1966. Photograph E.R. Morten.

4. 73000 4-6-0s 1951-1968

They are intended for mixed traffic duties, comparable with those now performed by LMR Class "5", ER "B1", and WR "Hall" class 4-6-0 locomotives. *The Railway Magazine, June 1951.*

The *Railway Magazine* was never fulsome or even mildly excited when greeting new locomotives, and traditionally confined itself to little more than the bare technical specifications. The words (above) in the issue for June 1951 were the nearest to a welcome a new engine would get and they rightly placed the new 5MTs formally in the British tradition of 'the Class 5' 4-6-0. The life of the first, 73000, ranged across more or less the entire 'Standard period', emerging as it did from Derby Works in April 1951 and ending its days at Patricroft, seventeen years on, in April 1968. It was scrapped later that year at Cashmores, Great Bridge. The last, 73171, was completed in May 1957 at Doncaster Works. Now, these two engines have left me with an abiding memory; it was my luck in steam days to visit a number of London sheds on a Sunday armed with a five bob Red Rover, all the trappings of a train spotter carried in the trusty duffel bag, conspicuous lack of permits and a fair amount of nerve. Kentish Town was always the first port of call, a lovely sight after tedious journeys along the 219 and 65 bus routes. A summer Sunday and always a good atmosphere in the roundhouses and on this particular day in No.2 shed, on adjacent lines I found 73000 and 73171. 73000 was at the time based at Canklow in the Sheffield district, once part of the LMR (it was an ex-Midland Railway shed) but was by this time under the Eastern Region. 73171 hailed from

Leeds Holbeck. This was really exciting for an impressionable urchin and they were the first two numbers carefully entered in the evening *ABC* ritual.

This memory, recalled with fondness over the years, helped endear the class to me though the ones I had first come across were the twenty, 73080-73089 and 73110-73119, that the Southern Region took to naming, after the withdrawn Urie 'King Arthurs'. From my favourite observation point overlooking Oatlands cutting, complete with signalbox, signal gantries and semaphores, those twenty Class 5s became so familiar that their passing often provoked ill-informed shouts to the effect that BR should 'scrap them' - and BR (save for 73082, now on the Bluebell) did just that a few short years on. A faint flush of embarrassment and guilt still accompany these memories... In those days I never looked at a timetable, save for when I was actually travelling and the only trains we really knew the times for were the up and down 'Bournemouth Belle' and the returning, late afternoon, milk empties, heading back to the West Country. However, these named engines, which for a good while were based at Nine Elms (not 73080, it went from Stewarts Lane to Weymouth in November 1959 and stayed there until withdrawn in January 1967 - it was scrapped at Cashmores, Great Bridge in 1968) worked mainly on the Waterloo - Basingstoke semi-fasts and returns.

Weighing in at 76 tons 4 cwt these were not small engines; 73080-73089 were fitted with BR1B tenders (51 tons 5 cwt) and 73110-73119 with BR1Fs, at 55 tons 5 cwt apiece. Both of these tender types suited the class well; the BR1B was flush sided with a capacity of 4,725 gallons and 7 tons of coal and the BR1F, fitted only to these ten engines, were high sided with capacities of 5,625 gallons and 7 tons, perfectly necessary on the Southern Region which was devoid of water troughs. When I saw them in action in those 'early' days the difference in the tender type meant nothing, especially when one of them emerged under the roadbridge in the distance near Walton-on-Thames station, on the down fast with yet another Basingstoke semi-fast. A hulking black shape, very little exhaust and some rolling (for crews appeared to push these engines given half a chance), with a crisp sound from the single chimney. A glimpse as engine and train disappeared under our road bridge, the nameplate announcing it was no stranger to this working and it was gone. But where was 73080 MERLIN? It never seemed to come up to London - it was 'rare'. A glorious summer's evening and on my own for a change, and resigned to going home after the next up Bournemouth - at last 73080 appeared and I had the twenty named members of the class. It remained my only sighting of MERLIN.

Parent office for the class 5s was Doncaster, but like the majority of the Stand-

73005, a few weeks old and with its very first coat of grime, on one of the Glasgow turntables, 21 July 1951. In detail, most of the BR Standards were anything but and the Class 5s were no exception. As more emerged many details changed - fluted coupling rods gave way to plain section for example. One of the earliest alterations was to cut away the running plate to make the lubricator accessible, as here. Photograph B.P. Hoper Collection.

73005 again, a well photographed engine if not a widely travelled one. Kept in beautiful condition, the first Scottish batch (the second five, 73005-73009) seemed to enjoy a slightly higher profile than the others of that time, lost on the LM amid so many existing Black 5s. Smartly turned out 73005 (note the bulled-up buffers, handrails, smokebox front etc.) is at Aberdeen, on 12 April 1954. Photograph J. Robertson, B.P. Hoper Collection.

ards they bore all the hallmarks of LMS origin. This was particularly true of the 5MTs and the point has frequently been made that they were simply a continuation of the successful Stanier class 5 4-6-0, with a few refinements. Perhaps then, it was fitting that the majority were built at Derby, one hundred and thirty in all, the remaining forty two coming out from Doncaster. Crewe did not build one of the Standard 5MTs. The boiler, designated BR type 3, was a near copy of the Stanier design, with an outside diameter of 5ft 8½in, tapering to 4ft 11in. There was the customary high running plate and a deep fall plate beneath the smokebox which led (I have heard it said) to the early nickname of 'Town Halls' - presumably a reference to the Town Hall steps. Dimension differences were minor - coupled driving wheels at 6ft 2in were two inches larger than the Stanier type and the Standards had 19in diameter cylinders, half an inch more than the Stanier engines. BR fittings were used on the Standards and the Stanier top feed was replaced by clack valves derived from the Southern Railway type. When new, members of the class had the tri-tone whistle as fitted to the Pacifics and this was mounted directly behind the chimney. Later it was replaced by a traditional whistle carried on the manifold in front of the cab.

None carried double chimneys though in later years it was found, from scientific testing at Swindon, that a decrease in the blastpipe diameter from 5in to 4in could mean an increase of *up to 26%* in steam production. The narrow stovepipe chimney of the class was not pleasing to British eyes so this was fitted with an outer casing that was larger than the bore of the internal lining. The result was a handsome chimney that suited the class.

Early examples - 73000 and 73001 - had hollow axles on the coupled wheels and 'I' section coupling rods though later engines emerged

with solid core axles on the driving wheels and plain section coupling rods, which were found to be stronger in everyday use. From April 1951 to May 1957 was the time it took to complete the building of the class and during that period the cost of construction, not surprisingly, went up. While 73000 and its tender had cost £17,603, 73171 ran out at no less than £27,000. Original livery for the class was LNWR black, fully lined out but examples did emerge from Swindon from 1956 in lined green, including 73029, 73031, 73035 and 73054. Personally, I felt the class looked much better in the original livery.

When introduced the cab was fixed to the boiler with the footplate extended by cantilever to the tender. Along with this came problems of draughts - later members of the class had a fallplate fitted between the tender and the rear of the cab.

When new, 73000 went on display at Marylebone, on 26th April 1951, for inspection by the Railway Executive and the press; it was followed into service that year by a further twenty-eight, 73001-73028 but 1952 saw only one finished, 73029, completing works order No.5122 at Derby in the January. 73030 was not built until June 1953, again at Derby, the first of works order No.6230. Crewe supplied 142 boilers, including 10 spares, whilst Doncaster built only ten boilers - the remaining 32 being supplied by Darlington.

The Railway Magazine of February 1957 describes the one great development within the class, the fitting of British Caprotti valve gear to thirty, 73125-73154. The gear was fairly new in British practice, with 71000 already fitted and various Black 5s before that. The *Modernization Plan* for British Railways, unveiled in 1955, meant a limited future (however far off the end seemed then) for steam. Nevertheless experimentation and development was still be-

ing carried out. 'The Caprottis', something of a throw back to 1953 or thereabouts, appeared from Derby between July 1956 and June 1957 to works order No.9247; ten of each were allocated to the London Midland, Scottish and Western Regions - the last ten equipped with automatic train control gear. It was a textbook example of how not to allocate a new and different species of locomotive, for to get the best from such developments, it was vital, really, to concentrate them so that both fitting, footplate and management staff could properly familiarise themselves with the things, in order to get the best from them.

The prime advantage of the Caprotti rotary cam poppet valve system was that it allowed excellent steam distribution. The two inlet valves on each of the cylinders were driven by cams worked by rotating shafts and these were connected to the return crank axlebox, linked in turn to the driving wheel crank pins. Another change from the basic Standard 5 design concerned the mechanical lubricators, activated from the rear coupled wheelset. On the rest of the class the mechanical lubricators were activated from the motion above the leading wheelset - however, on all the engines the mechanical lubricators were fitted under the running plate.

Caprotti 73125-73134 were the only Class 5s to be allocated to the Western Region from new, all going to Shrewsbury between July and October 1956. In September 1958 they were transferred *en masse* to Patricroft and stayed there until withdrawn, most of them in 1968. 73135-73139 went new to Holyhead in October - November 1956 and 73140-73144 to Leicester Midland, in December 1956. After a few transfers, mainly to Rowsley, they joined their earlier sisters at Patricroft, nine in June 1964 and 73135 later, in September. The final ten Caprottis, 73145-73154, had gone new to St Rollox in Glasgow, between March and June

1957 and spent their time operating from Scottish sheds.

One of the Caprottis, 73129, has survived and has been resident at the Midland Railway Centre since 1973. Once it has been steamed perhaps the claims that the Caprottis were stronger than their sister engines can be put to the test. It is on record that some of the 73125-73154 batch operated trains at 80mph plus but I have been told the conventional engines were stronger on the banks.

The Western Region's ten Caprottis had moved away *en bloc* in 1958 (as described above) but conventional examples were transferred in from other Regions. As with the 9Fs, the Somerset & Dorset has the benefit of records and writings far beyond that merited purely by the line's importance in the global scale of things and the transfer to Bath Green Park of brand new Derby built 73050-73052 in June 1954 was a celebrated move. 73050 was the first to arrive, having on the way taken part in the display at the International Railway Congress at Willesden. 73051 is known to have undertaken its first run over the Somerset & Dorset on 29th May 1954 on the 3.35pm Bournemouth to Bath, working down from its birthplace, Derby, light engine via Brent, Willesden, Feltham, Basingstoke and on to Bournemouth. On this most famous of cross country lines these three 5MTs worked singly or double headed with the 'native' engines, both as pilots and train engines. It was not unknown for combinations of Standard 5s to double head over the Mendips. Some S&D crews were said to prefer the Standard 5s to the Stanier Black 5s which had worked over the line for a number of years. Of the original trio, 73051 and 73052 remained whilst 73050 moved on to Llanelly in March 1964; it went to Shrewsbury in April 1964, to Agecroft in April 1966 and finally to Patricroft in October 1966. It is now one of the five preserved members of the class.

Although the SR had its wealth of Bulleid light Pacifics, 110 in all, a good number

of the Standard 5MTs at one time saw service on the Region, especially on the Kent lines and the South Western section. These included 73002, 73016-73018, 73020, 73022, 73029, 73037, 73041-73043, 73046, 73065, 73074, 73080-73089, 73092, 73093, 73110-73119, 73155 and 73167-73171.

Those coming to the Southern new, 73080-73089 and 73110-73119, had additional lamp brackets fitted to meet the demands of the Region's headcode system. 73080-73089 began their careers at Stewarts Lane between June and September 1955, though most moved on to Nine Elms in May 1959. 73110-73119 had been at Nine Elms, new, from late 1955 with others following later. As well as becoming regular performers on the Basingstoke semi-fasts the Class 5s were frequently found on Waterloo - Bournemouth trains, often proving adequate substitutes for Pacifics.

Elsewhere on the SR, there were allocations at Eastleigh and Weymouth; in May 1965 Eastleigh had 73022, 73029, 73037, 73041, 73043, 73087, 73089, 73092, 73093, 73110, 73111, 73113-73115, 73117-73119, 73155, 73168-73171, and Weymouth 73002, 73018, 73020, 73042, 73080 and 73083. Workings included local services in Hampshire and Dorset.

Just twelve years after their introduction on the SR the Class 5s shared the last rites of steam on the Region, in 1967. Amongst these final workings on July 7th (the last weekday) was 73029 on e.c.s. from Fratton to Clapham Junction via Guildford and Woking and 73092 on a Waterloo - Bournemouth. 73093 was noted on a goods train and 73018 undertook a Weymouth - Bournemouth local. The survivors were a cosmopolitan lot. At the end, of the final Nine Elms complement, 73029 had once been based at Shrewsbury and Swindon, 73037 at Shrewsbury and Oxford; 73043 had counted Patricroft, Grimesthorpe and Canklow amongst its former sheds and 73065 was late of Millhouses and Canklow. Guildford's list included 73018, once

of Nottingham and Swindon, 73020 late of Chester and Swindon, 73092 and 73093 both earlier based at Patricroft, Shrewsbury and Gloucester Barnwood, and 73155, whose former homes included Neasden, Millhouses and Canklow. The tale of the last few at Nine Elms and Guildford demonstrates just how far and wide some had moved about the Regions during their short careers.

On the London Midland, especially on the Midland lines, the 5MTs saw extensive use, including the semi-fasts out of St Pancras. Patricroft, as we have seen, became a stronghold with 73030, 73044, 73125-73134 on the books by 1959; by April 1965 the Patricroft band numbered 73006, 73010, 73011, 73125-73144, 73157, 73158, 73160, 73163 and 73165. Although this shed was the last redoubt of the class, closing on 1st July 1968, the last active member was 73069. It had been amongst the last transfers away from Patricroft, having arrived from Bolton in April 1968; it moved in July to Carnforth but was reduced, in its final days, to collecting scrap. Better memories of 73069 are of it working railtours during the last week of steam in August 1968. After that it was withdrawn and stored at Lostock Hall for six months before being towed to South Wales to meet its fate at Cashmores, Newport. A poignant photograph exists of the engine complete, save for its right hand side connecting rod and smokebox number plate, awaiting its fate in the yard at Newport, the very last BR steam engine to be cut up in there.

When fairly new 73000 and 73001 double headed a vacuum fitted coal train over the southern end of the Midland main line, in October 1952. Also when new, in June - July 1953, 73030 and 73031 were fitted with Westinghouse air brakes for a similar series of fitted freight trains trials, in which Britannias 70043 and 70044 also took part. One compressor was fitted to each of the Class 5s, attached to the right hand side of the smokebox with the air reservoir fixed

Leaving 73005 behind at last, but still in Scotland, for a contrast in tenders, rods and other detail on 73106, at Haymarket on 10 June 1956. In August and September 1955 a batch had gone new to Corkerhill, 73100-73105, and from 73100 onward Doncaster did away with the rather fetching whistle behind the chimney, mounting it on the firebox instead. 73106 broke a run of five new engines going to Corkerhill and went to Eastfield, in December 1955. Photograph J. Robertson, B.P. Hoper Collection.

Perhaps the most familiar 'location' of Standard engines is Nine Elms, the roads of the 'Old Shed' left open by wartime bombing. The blizzard of photographs date from 1966 and 1967 as the end drew near but this is a rather earlier time, with a surprisingly scruffy 73089 MAID OF ASTOLAT. It had been the first of the Class 5s to be named, in May 1959; the fair maid in question turns out to be Elaine and 'Astolat' was, bathetically, Guildford. Photograph J. Robertson, B.P. Hoper Collection.

under the running plate just in front of the cab. In this condition 73030 also hauled an empty coaching stock train, (it was noted thus near Radlett on the Midland main line), whilst 73031 also spent a while at the Rugby Testing Station. Once these experiments were finished the equipment was removed from the 5MTs and both were transferred away from Derby in the summer of 1957.

The Eastern Region saw few of the class allocated thoughfive, 73155-73159, did go new to one shed, Neasden. All were used on the GCR line out of Marylebone to Leicester, Nottingham and Sheffield; 73155 stayed until 1959 when it moved to Millhouses; 73156 moved on in December 1958, to Grimesthorpe and back to Neasden in September 1960, and 73157-73159 went to Kings Cross, in September 1957. During a short stay there they worked mainly on Cambridge and Peterborough semi-fasts and on race specials to Newmarket.

A good number of the 5MTs went new to the Scottish Region, starting with 73005-73009 to Perth, already a renowned centre for Stanier Class 5s. This was in June-July 1951 and next to go north, in July - September 1953, were 73032, 73034 and 73036 to Carlisle Kingmoor, then part of the Scottish Region as 68A. 73033 and 73035 went to Polmadie in the same period, and 73055-73064 arrived at this great Caledonian shed during June - October 1954. Subsequent Scottish arrivals were: 73075 and 73076 to Polmadie, April 1955; 73077-73079 to Eastfield, May 1955; 73100-73104 to Corkerhill August - September 1955; 73105-73109 to Eastfield late 1955 - early 1956; 73120 to Perth and 73121-73124 to Corkerhill January - February 1956; 73145-73154 to St Rollox between January and June 1957. Several ended up in sheds in England: 73006 withdrawn March 1967; 73033 withdrawn January 1968, 73034 withdrawn March 1968 and 73035 withdrawn January 1968 all from Patricroft; 73036 withdrawn from Shrewsbury September 1965.

One of the first duties of the 5MTs in Scotland was the working of the Royal Train,

undertaken by 73005 and 73006 from Perth to Aberdeen. Other early duties for the Perth engines were on the Highland line north to Inverness, as well as to Glasgow and Aberdeen on named expresses such as the 'Saint Mungo' and 'The Granite City' from Glasgow to Aberdeen. These Perth-based engines also reached as far west as Oban. At St Rollox the Caprottis, 73145-73154, eventually found themselves with A4 Pacifics on the Aberdeen - Glasgow express passenger trains. The 4-6-0s proved themselves good hill climbers and at times just as good on the flat, reaching the high 'eighties at times.

Some of the Scottish engines led a nomadic existence whilst others stayed at one shed, such as 73059-73064 at Polmadie and 73100, 73100-73104, 73121-73124 at Corkerhill. One or two were fitted with miniature snowploughs and others with a cabside tablet exchanger for the stretches of single line abundant in Scotland. One such was the Highland and the Class 5s sometimes worked to Inverness via Forres over the original Highland line (now closed) that ran via Grantown-on-Spey. They were even noted working tender first with a single carriage on the Crieff branch from Gleneagles.

My abiding memory of the class remains the Sunday afternoon visits to Neasden, for we were on our way home, our heads full of the images of Willesden and Old Oak Common. Gritty and begrimed, we would fall out of the

Close up of the Caprotti gear, on 73144. There is little doubt that, had the wind not gone from steam's sails (an awkward phrase in the circumstances) by the mid-1950s, then the Caprotti gear would have seen far wider adoption. All those wonderful gears, bevels and joints required specialised care to ensure the best and by allocating the Caprottis as it did, ten each to the Western, LM and Scottish Regions, BR more or less ensured that this was not done. Photograph Eric Sawford.

'bus on the North Circular Road and after crossing that great girder bridge over the lines from Marylebone (if you looked to the north you could see the towers of Wembley Stadium) we crunched our way along the inevitable cinder path to the shed and its six roads. Nobody seemed to mind as we walked around and I always appreciated the high-numbered Class 5s based here, 73156-73159 (73155 had already gone) even though I had seen them during my earlier visits.

The working life of the 5MTs spanned 17 years but they only remained a complete class for just seven, from the completion of 73171 in May 1957 at Doncaster to the first withdrawal of 73027 in February 1964, from Swindon. The withdrawals continued each year:-

Sadly down at heel 73000, covered in priming deposits, at Leicester shed on 8 March 1961. This was a long way from its flagship days, running at 76mph with an Ipswich - Liverpool Street train in 1952 (timed by Allen and recounted by Cox). Photograph Alec Swain.

DEMISE
1964. Feb: 73027; July: 73076; September: 73046, 73074; October: 73017, 73109; November: 73012, 73024, 73058, 73116; December: 73047, 73052, 73061, 73161, 73164.
1965. January: 73077; March: 73044, 73049; May: 73091, 73123, 73162; June: 73041, 73056, 73062, 73106, 73112; August: 73015, 73021, 73023, 73030, 73032, 73042, 73051, 73054, 73147, 73167; September: 73008, 73031, 73036, 73038, 73122, 73148, 73165; October: 73090, 73103, 73104, 73111; November: 73163; December: 73001, 73003, 73068, 73075, 73084, 73124, 73152, 73166, 73168.
1966. January: 73121; March: 73007, 73057, 73098; May: 73013, 73055; June: 73005, 73063, 73082, 73114, 73170; July: 73009, 73078, 73081; August: 73095, 73101, 73151; September: 73083, 73089, 73105, 73107, 73145; October: 73072, 73086, 73087, 73088,

73089, 73169, 73171; December: 73016, 73028, 73080, 73102, 73108, 73120, 73149, 73150, 73153, 73154.
1967. January: 73019, 73100, 73110, 73113, 73130; March: 73002, 73006, 73115, 73117, 73119; April: 73022, 73026, 73066, 73070; May: 73059, 73060, 73064, 73079, 73094, 73097, 73139, 73146; June: 73137; July: 73014, 73018, 73020, 73029, 73037, 73043, 73065, 73085, 73092, 73093, 73118, 73141, 73155; August: 73045, 73144; September: 73039, 73071; October: 73004, 73025, 73048, 73140, 73158, 73159; November: 73011, 73073, 73096, 73127, 73156, 73160; December: 73129.

1968. January: 73033 73035, 73131; March: 73000, 73034, 73053, 73067, 73132, 73135, 73136; April: 73126, 73138, 73142; May: 73040, 73128, 73157; June: 73010, 73050, 73125, 73133, 73134, 73143; August: 73069.

Below. Re-routed because of engineering work on the main line, 73082 CAMELOT heads a Southampton Docks - Waterloo train near Alton on Sunday 2 October 1960. Photograph Bryan H. Kimber.

AN APPRAISAL OF THE BR 5MT 4-6-0 AND 9F 2-10-0
By Terry Essery

From the earliest days of steam traction on railways the opinions of working enginemen have been sought as to how particular locomotives measured up to their contemporaries. This is especially so when a number of engines designed to perform similar duties originate from entirely different backgrounds. We all like, indeed need to make comparisons, for only by so doing are we able to judge what suits us best, but as with most things, personal opinions are just that. They are highly individual and although a certain machine could be ideal for one person it may not appear so admirable to another.

Steam locomotives are no exception so it must be emphasised that the following remarks, based on personal experience, derive from *my* view of them. Others, quite possibly and properly, hold entirely different opinions. It must also be borne in mind that these comments are coloured by the needs of a working footplateman and therefore biased towards the practical rather than the aesthetic - which after all, is in the eye of the beholder.

Perhaps the first lesson I learned was that it is not possible to assess the merits of a locomotive by studying its diagram, table of dimensions and general specification. Far more is involved and in any case individual locomotives of the same class can vary considerably, as indeed can a particular engine during its progression between periodic shoppings. I was extremely fortunate that my footplate career encompassed the buoyant and innovative 'fifties when new BR Standard locomotives began to mingle not only with designs from the Big Four but also with those hosts of old faithfuls from the pre-grouping era.

Birmingham's Saltley MPD was principally a freight shed at which passenger work took second place to the super long-distance Water Orton - Carlisle express fitted freights run over the arduous Settle to Carlisle route. Unfortunately this background only enabled me to become acquainted with two BR types, Class 5MT 4-6-0s and 9Fs, although in the case of the latter it did include the Crosti and mechanical stoker variants.

It is now generally accepted that in terms of overall performance there was not much to choose between the latest products of the grouped companies. However, when it came to longevity of components, visibility and accessibility, with consequent ease of maintenance and servicing, the LMS had, under the guidance of H.G. Ivatt, progressed further than most. Certainly at Saltley his excellent 2MT and 4MT Moguls enjoyed great popularity, if for no other reason than being equipped with self-cleaning smokeboxes, hopper ashpans and rocking grates, all of which reduced disposal from an hour's onerous and dirty labour to but a few minutes

light work. We enginemen were therefore delighted to see that not only were these designs perpetuated by BR - albeit in improved form - but also their 'user friendly' innovations were adopted for the whole range of Standard locomotives.

With both BR5s and Black 5s sharing the same 3B boiler, direct comparisons between the two types were inevitably made, particularly at Saltley where there was great pride in the Stanier engines, which were reckoned to be the best maintained on the Region. General appearance apart, the cab is to many the centre of interest and it is possibly this feature which showed the most obvious improvement over the Black 5. On viewing the footplate for the first time, probably the most notable innovation was its extension rearwards and the absence, in the case of BR1 tenders, of a movable fall plate. This provided a very stable, tank engine-like platform to fire from and was much appreciated by firemen, particularly when travelling at high speeds. The boiler face was impressively uncluttered and the few exposed pipes were clipped in neat runs, giving the appearance of well thought out tidiness. A further encouragement to this conclusion was the placing of the main steam manifold outside, at the front of the cab.

Ergonomically, the general layout was a vast improvement over the Black 5s, since all the driver's controls were sighted around him within easy reach from a very comfortable padded seat complete with back rest. To add to this unaccustomed luxury, a partition behind the seat rose to the roof and incorporated a window which gave further protection from the elements when running tender first. The regulator, with

73078 (note the big ScR cabside numerals) takes the 3.45pm Queen Street - Fort William train onto the West Highland line at Craigendoran, heading fellow Eastfield Class 5, 44956, on Thursday 11 August 1960. The BR Class 5s represented, in a sense, simply further production of the LM Black 5s. The charge has been levelled since, that they were one of several 'unnecessary' classes but this is simplistic, ignoring important considerations and drawing heavily on hindsight. The Black 5s themselves had 'evolved' and the BR version should perhaps be more properly regarded as the latest development, refined and honed in the light of experience, of a successful type. Tests with 73008 at Rugby and afterwards between Carlisle and Skipton led to some modifications and showed the LM and BR types to be close. As, really, we should expect. Cox's 'biggest regret' was that no tests were done with the Caprotti engines - like the work on 71000, it wasn't worth the candle...

its fore and aft movement, was relatively unobtrusive and likewise the end-on positioning of reversing screw occupied less lateral space. Operation of these controls proved, as the designers had envisaged, more natural to the human form than the traditional arrangement. Bracketed to the cab side at the left of the driver was the very effective steam-operated cylinder drain cocks valve, while directly to his front above the reversing screw were the large and the small ejector valves. The operating handle for the combined vacuum and steam brake system was mounted horizontally on a pedestal convenient to the driver's right hand and above this was located a separate, independent steam brake. This pedestal formed an anti-glare shield and also housed the blower and sanding valves.

On the other side, the fireman also enjoyed a padded seat, albeit without a back rest, and a rather lower partition minus a window - an omission necessary for the unobstructed withdrawal of fire irons from the tender tunnel. As with the driver, all relevant controls were positioned within easy reach around him and he could enjoy the benefit of operating both injectors and the damper controls without leaving his seat. Even the whistle could be reached from either side without having to get up and grope under the roof, which was a considerable improvement on previous locomotives.

The Western type water gauges were easier to read in poor light whilst the accompanying gauge lamp was more sophisticated and reliable than the former LMS pattern. Instrumentation too, was not only clearer and more logically laid out but also more comprehensive. A steam chest pressure gauge was provided for drivers who were interested in such matters while a matching speedometer registered the results and did much to banish guesswork at permanent way slacks and other speed restrictions. The cab weather boards were angled, not only presenting a pleasing effect but also largely eliminating unwanted reflections at night.

In many respects the BR tenders were a considerable improvement over their Stanier forebears with the front plate extending to the cab roof, to give a neat flush appearance. Only the hand brake and water scoop handles, together with the shovelling plate, projected into the cab, the latter possessing a tapered lip at its leading edge. This lip tended to restrain small coal from shaking on to the footplate while at the same time was less hostile to the crew's shins.

Much appreciated was the extra locker space provided and an excellent highly visible tank gauge mounted flush with the front plate adjacent to the water scoop handle. It must be said though that the original BR inset tenders were not as well liked as the later BRC curved sided versions. The intended improved rearward vision of inset tenders was negligible and in any case was of little use when setting back on to stock when the driver would be concentrating on buffers or a shunter at ground level. Also the fireman preferred an extra couple of tons of coal at the front of the tender where it would fall on the shovelling plate. It was undoubtedly this immensely improved cab and layout providing a much higher level of comfort and convenient which in turn reduced fatigue, that was so endearing to crews. With all things being equal, this alone would have determined the choice, but there was more to come.

Most new engines feel taut, are relatively quiet and generally ride well but BR5s

with cabs attached to the boilers and having a continuous floor, provided a stability of ride approaching that only hitherto experienced on passenger tank locomotives. Nor did this seem to deteriorate when higher mileages were attained, which was certainly not the case with Black 5s. Perhaps I was lucky but I cannot recall ever having a rough BR locomotive in the true sense of the word, even though many had been in service long enough for a Regional type to become distinctly uncomfortable. One can but speculate that this was due to improved design, materials and lubrication and so the Riddles team should be applauded for achieving exactly what they set out to do.

Driving the BR5 was in many respects a new experience because apart from the driver being able to operate all relevant controls while seated, the regulator remained where it was set and did not tend to shake shut as was often the case (unless fully opened) with Stanier 5s. When moving light engine or working unfitted trains they were quieter and more economical, since there was no need to keep the small ejector open as with locomotives equipped with the LMS vacuum controlled steam brake. Keener types were for the first time able to relate regulator openings to steam chest pressure and then experiment with precise alternative settings of shut off, whereas before it had been mainly a matter of guesswork. For those who wished to take the trouble, with this instrument alone it was possible to engender a far higher consistency of driving over any given section. However, as with Black 5s, they were extremely tolerant as to the driving methods adopted and gave a good showing whether worked with a partially open regulator and longish cut off or fully open with the shortest practical cut off. It was noticeable, though, as drivers became more familiar with them, that the latter method was used more frequently than with Black 5s.

Despite altered cylinder design, the two inch increase in coupled wheel diameter and the slight tractive effort advantage, there was in all honesty little detectable difference in performance on the road. Both Class 5 4-6-0s possessed reliable adhesion, accelerated well and with ten bogies would quickly settle into the mid-seventies on level track using around 160psi in the steam chest and 20/25% cut off. If conditions were favourable a fully opened regulator would ensure a further 10/15mph or they could be hammered for long periods up inclines using perhaps 35 to 50% cut off without showing too much distress. Economy regarding fuel and water was equally good but the BR5 completely outclassed the Stanier engine in terms of comfort, convenience and quality of ride, which made the job so much more pleasant.

Firemen likewise benefited from the superior disposition of controls which were in any case a considerable improvement over previous equipment. For example, the dampers were screw operated and they could not only be adjusted within a very fine limits but they would remain exactly as set. Damper controls on Black 5s frequently had to be propped open with a spanner, particularly on higher mileage locomotives. Both the live steam and exhaust steam injectors functioned more efficiently and reliably and they too could be operated while still seated. Perhaps most appreciated though, was having a continuous platform to fire from and not being obliged to perform perpetual balancing acts while straddling a mobile fall plate. This, coupled with the absence of violent knocking in

motion bearings and axleboxes, provided a quieter, more stable environment which did much to reduce fatigue on long runs.

As may be expected, the same 3B boiler required the same firing methods used with Black 5s and provided one adhered to normal techniques it steamed very freely for long periods. Regular use of the rocking grate in its limited stroke mode of course tended to keep the fire very much cleaner than with the fixed grates of earlier Black 5s.

Drivers found preparation of BR5s somewhat easier, since apart from better accessibility, even greater use was made of grease lubrication, for the multitude of pin joints to be found in the motion, suspension and brake system. For firemen it was a case of swings and roundabouts, a higher climb when filling sandboxes but generally a tidier footplate; however, it was during disposal that he benefited most, since all BR locomotives were provided with rocking grates whereas only the later Black 5s possessed them.

With overall performance virtually the same, choice was therefore dependent on comfort and convenience of operation and in both aspects BR5s completely outclassed the Stanier engines, to such a degree that there was, as far as I am concerned, never any doubt which to select.

****

The 9F was a complete surprise to everyone, for although designed as a heavy mineral locomotive it soon proved to be just about the finest general purpose, do-anything, mixed traffic engine ever produced in this country. Nearly all the features, including tender variations already described for the BR5, apply to 9Fs and even in the cab the main differences lay in the size and shape of the boiler back plate. Being higher and wider and devoid of carriage warming apparatus and speedometer, it was even less cluttered, presenting a remarkably tidy appearance.

Opening the sliding firedoors revealed a large oval firehole through which could be seen its 40-42 sq. ft rocking grate, of almost square dimensions. Being level over the rear half and sloping gently towards the front it was rather more shallow than usual since it was placed over the rear coupled wheels. In keeping with other BR types, the firehole was at a convenient height for men of average stature and lined up nicely with the tender shovelling plate.

Despite its size, drivers found preparation of 9Fs just as clean and straightforward as other BR Standards which likewise were designed with visibility and accessibility in mind. With only the normal six sandboxes to fill, firemen also found no extra hardship, except that a little extra care was needed when climbing up to and walking along its foot framing, due to the wide boiler and smoke deflectors.

Driving 9Fs was a delightful experience, difficult to describe, for they seemed to possess every attribute ever desired in a locomotive and even then managed to produce some pleasant surprises. At Saltley, many of our northbound freight workings departed from Water Orton Sidings, some seven miles distant from the loco shed. Travelling main line to this starting point gave crews an insight as to what they might expect from their engine.

Easing open the light and sensitive regulator brought immediate response so that its one hundred and forty ton bulk flowed into motion without apparent effort. Once on the main line with a clear road, 40psi steam chest pressure and with the reverser notched fairly quickly back to 15% cut off, speed built up rapidly to the fifties. At this pace the ride was as rock steady as any 2-6-4 tank engine, the only noticeable noise being the click of wheels on rail joints and a faint intermittent drumming from the cab roof ventilator. This may sound like a description of a brand new locomotive, but although there are always exceptional examples in every class, the above is pretty typical of these engines as a whole.

My acquaintance with 9Fs did not really begin in earnest until 1957, by which time some of the earlier engines had covered sufficient mileage to be showing the effects of wear, but even so I cannot recall any of them being much different and certainly there was never an incidence of knocking in motion bearings or axleboxes.

Every class has its star performers and within the scope of my own personal experience, No.92137 shone brighter than the rest. I had the pleasure of driving this wonderful locomotive on just about its first trip after running in and was completely deceived by its incredibly smooth, turbine-like progression. With only a very light fully fitted train in tow this Water Orton to Toton duty required little more steam than when running light engine and with a clear road over the section from Stenson Junction to Trent I was able to experiment with regulator and cut off settings. On the 1:220 falling gradient to Castle Donington with 80psi showing in the steam chest pressure gauge and notched back to rather less than 10%, we fairly hurtled along with such uncanny smoothness and silence we may well have been in a Pullman Coach. In darkness so complete that even the trackside was invisible, the only indication of speed was the click of wheels on passing rail joints. Without the normal buffets of footplate travel I found it difficult to judge our true pace and was consequently obliged to make some pretty hefty brake applications when the distant at Sheet Stores Junction was seen to be on. I later found that we had covered the twelve and a half miles from Stenson Junction to Trent Station in rather less than fifteen minutes. This gave an average speed of 51mph which indicated, taking acceleration and braking periods into account, that we probably touched around 70mph over the fastest section; somewhat quicker than a fully fitted was then permitted to travel.

The following July, when booked in the Carlisle Link with a competent but conservative driver (the last person I would have expected to go breaking records), I travelled at the highest speed ever on a 9F or indeed any other class over the Carlisle runs. Strangely enough, although the venue and situation was different, similar conditions of total darkness prevailed and that same incomparable engine, 92137, deceived him just as it had deceived me nine months earlier. We had started using 9Fs on that arduous two hundred and twenty six mile journey which up to then had been the domain of Black 5s, and many drivers were still a little doubtful how well a small wheeled heavy mineral locomotive would cope with this prestigious, fast, fully fitted duty.

Hauling just about the heaviest train I can recall to Carlisle, 48=52 wagons, and suffering temperatures in the high eighties, we encountered violent thunderstorms at Hellifield which lasted until Appleby, causing a block failure at Garsdale en route. Having over 56% more

tractive effort than Black 5s, 9Fs were able to demonstrate their vast superiority with this weight of train so that despite the delays we were only ten minutes late at New Biggin. However, it was from here, with improved weather conditions and a clear road, that my mate set about regaining lost time. Approaching Lazonby the power was really turned on and with the steam chest pressure showing 180psi and at around 20% cut off, speed rapidly increased.

In pitch black conditions on that beautifully riding 9F I am quite sure my driver had no idea just how quickly we were travelling, but the fact remains that the last fourteen and a half miles from Lazonby to a dead stand at Carlisle Petteril Bridge took just eleven minutes, an average speed of 78mph. So incredible did this seem that I double checked the timings, but they were quite definite and I could only come to the somewhat sobering conclusion that we must have achieved a maximum speed of around 90mph.

It was sobering in as much that fitted freights were then limited to 55 mph and one could not help wondering how near to derailment the wagons may have been and how many other drivers on 9Fs could have been similarly deceived. There was absolutely no concern whatsoever regarding the engine, for at no time did it seem any different from when travelling at half that rate, just a soft purr from the chimney, the rapid click of rail joints and the same silky, rock steady, effortless progression.

9Fs steamed superbly and under normal running conditions were not too sensitive regarding shape or profile of the firebed. It did not seem to matter whether it was conventional, haycock or saucer shape, provided normal firing rules were adhered to and the area under its brickarch not choked. In fact it would stand terrible mismanagement even to the extent of having dead patches on the grate and still make steam, and I know of no other locomotive that would behave quite that way.

Of course if really serious work was to be performed, over a considerable period then, as with all other engines, the fire had to be as near-perfect as possible. With so much power available, 9Fs could often be worked quite lightly over long stretches and for these conditions a thin firebed sufficed, although it was necessary to keep the back corners of the grate well filled. While a large oval firehole was provided to facilitate this, the shovel blade needed to be placed well inside, which then brought the fireman's hands very close to that searing white heat generated under normal working conditions. For those of us not familiar with wide shallow fireboxes it was initially puzzling why we suffered so much from heat radiation, but the reasons soon became obvious. The flat shallow grate brought the incandescent firebed much higher in relationship to the firehole than with deep narrow fireboxes, and being of larger area and nearly square in plan meant that a far greater proportion was nearer the fireman. Finally a larger firehole allowed more radiation to pass through it. Because 9Fs steamed so well and the reduced free area over their grate required rather more secondary air to consume smoke, doors were generally set more open than for other types. However, it did not take too long to discover a way of greatly reducing the emission of unwelcome heat - before commencing a round of firing, it was policy to drop two or three shovelfuls just inside the firehole so that a small hump of dead coal was formed. This not only blan-

keted off much of the radiation, but also acted as a deflector, since by bouncing the shovel blade against this hump at the correct angle, coal could be shot into the back corners with the minimum of effort and without need to get too near. As with the 5MTs, one live steam and one exhaust steam injector was provided; both of these had excellent flow rates, proved extremely reliable and could be operated along with the dampers while still seated.

The bulk of my experience with 9Fs, at least from a mileage point of view, was obtained working the Birmingham to Carlisle fitted freights and this marathon run encompassed just about every working condition imaginable. It was therefore interesting to compare fuel consumption with Black 5s, which at one time were rostered with them on these same duties. On lighter trains in good weather Black 5s were somewhat more economical because they too were running well within their capacity. With medium loads they broke about even, but with heavy trains, particularly in wild conditions, 9Fs won handsomely. However, if the run became unduly protracted by delays then with every passing hour, the advantage began to swing back to Black 5s.

This is not altogether surprising when one considers the grate areas involved - 28.65 sq. ft. as to 40.2 sq. ft. for 9Fs, because even when standing the fire still has to be kept alight and the water boiling. Although there was therefore a tendency to use more coal with the 2-10-0s, being able to stand on a continuous stable platform rather than perform perpetual balancing acts across a mobile fall plate saved a lot of effort. Furthermore, 9Fs possessed such a reserve of energy in their large boilers that they could run for miles when working lightly, without need of firing or the use of injectors. This ability, plus the high level of comfort, enabled firemen who knew the road well to even snatch a quick sandwich at selected places, which more then compensated for an extra ton of coal fired on the grate.

In the autumn of 1958 No.92165 the first of three 9Fs fitted with Berkley Mechanical Stokers, arrived at Saltley to be tested on the Birmingham to Carlisle duties, since these were the longest and most demanding freight runs in the country. In order to familiarise the crews with their intricacies and also to run in the brand new engines, it was arranged that they would initially work local trip jobs up the Camp Hill Bank into Bordesley Sidings.

By chance, I was rostered on the afternoon turn to Carlisle the following week when it was planned to make a trial run and so I was selected to take the first day's training session. I must confess to being intrigued by the prospect of sitting down twiddling valves as an alternative to seven or eight hours of almost continual effort, since apart from the obvious reduction in labour, it would allow more time for road learning. Unfortunately it did not work out quite as expected, not because of any deficiency in the design by mainly because of unsuitable fuel.

The firebed had to be first built up by hand but this in itself proved to be a very slow and difficult process. The principle obstacle was the raiser conduit which angled upwards from the centre of the footplate to just below the firedoors. These firedoors were of the butterfly type and of necessity were placed above waist height on the boiler face. In order to remind firemen of a potentially lethal conveyer screw laying at the bottom of the tender coal space, a low safety barrier ran transversely across the shovelling plate. This barrier effectively blocked coal from falling on to the plate and therefore lumps had to be extracted from the tender piece by piece until there was sufficient for a decent shovelful. It then had to be carried across the footplate and while straddling the raiser conduit, lifted up and thrust through the firehole as best one could. Just covering the grate involved far more effort and physical pain than firing a ton of coal on a normal engine.

The Firing Inspector in charge of training explained that, pending arrival of special fuel, tenders would be coaled from the hopper and any large lumps should be broken up by a gang of cleaners acquired for the purpose. Knowing of the problems this could create, tenders on training trips were only partially filled and just in case any blockages should occur, a substantial inching bar had been provided to assist in clearing them.

Once the knack had been duly acquired, the stoker units worked adequately although never as efficiently in terms of steam production and fuel consumption as with hand firing. This was mainly due to the stoker jets having to deal with both dust and pieces of coal one and a half inches in diameter, with the result that a percentage of fines passed through the combustion passages unburned. For the same reasons it was not possible to maintain an ideal firebed shape and there was a tendency for small particles to build up under the brickarch, thereby considerably reducing the active grate area. This problem was particularly noticeable after periods of heavy working and the fiery slurry thus formed had to be levelled by means of a rake at the first opportunity.

Because manually building up fires was so slow and tedious I soon found that a quantity of coal could be dumped under the firehole by running the feed screw with the distributor jets turned off. The resultant mound could then be quickly spread over the rear part of the grate, including back corners with the firing shovel. However, despite a partially filled tender, blockages to the conveyor screw were far too frequent and much time and energy was wasted clearing them. I was assured though, that for our Carlisle run greater attention would be given to breaking up all lumps. Surprisingly, the latest arrival, 92166, was selected for the maiden run to Carlisle which, in the event, proved an unwise choice since it had acquired only delivery mileage. Indeed one axlebox overheated to a point when failure at Leeds seemed inevitable but after some judicial nursing it eased sufficiently for us to continue.

Setting off with a mountain of seemingly well-broken coal on its tender the stoker performed reliably until Tamworth when the first of a series of blockages spoilt what should have been a relatively effortless journey. With an overfilled tender it was almost impossible to clear jams with the heavy inching bar so that the only alternative was laborious hand firing. Fortunately the Firing Inspector accompanied us as far

as Leeds and he shared some of the misery, but after that I was on my own.

The return from Carlisle followed much the same pattern with blockages seemingly occurring when they were least welcome, i.e. approaching long inclines. Our reports along with those of other crews who experienced exactly the same difficulties on subsequent trips, emphasised the need for small coal for reliability to be assured and were it not for the 9Fs all-round excellence we would have been forced to a halt on a number of occasions.

Regrettably, all the while I was involved, Saltley still persisted with the same coaling methods and this culminated in one run best-forgotten, when I was obliged to hand fire 92167 virtually all the way from Water Orton to Blea Moor. Some special inch-and-a-half fuel suitable for mechanical stokers was eventually provided at Carlisle. This should have been ideal but unfortunately BR's timing went awry and instead of consuming it in the stoker trio we used it on standard engines instead, where the tiny chips caused problems of an entirely different nature. Had correct fuel been supplied then I am sure mechanical stokers would have been very popular - with the Carlisle Link firemen at least. Although they did not steam quite so well as standard engines, used more fuel and were not so friendly to the environment, when working properly they allowed the fireman more time for road learning and reduced his labours. In the event, with lumps of coal sometimes as large as coffins blocking the screw trough, firemen often expended far more effort than would be required for normal firing - precisely the opposite to what had been the objective. Nevertheless, it was an interesting exercise which probably came a few years too late, since by then extra power was being sought from other methods of traction.

9Fs fitted with Franco-Crosti preheater drums were another variation which did not prove too popular with fireman, although they were devised to give them a slightly easier time. Generally speaking, they steamed well enough and rode as impeccably as other 9Fs but having the chimney placed a few feet from the fireman's face proved more than a little troublesome. Apart from the physical obstruction this created, the cab seemed to be perpetually engulfed in exhaust steam and fumes which made life very miserable and often reduced visibility on that side to zero. No one was particularly sorry when their preheater drums were removed and they reverted to normal draughting, albeit with the original, smaller boilers.

From the foregoing it may be deduced that the 9F was my favourite locomotive; well I would not deny that, for I honestly believe that no other British steam engine possessed such versatility. As a heavy mineral it was in a class of its own, offering immense brute power, inexhaustible steaming capacity, superb adhesion, remarkable economy and the very highest level of comfort and convenience. For long distance express freights, it was equally unbeatable since in addition to the above attributes, it provided probably the most stable ride of any tender locomotive on a footplate so free from vibration and noise that it was positively uncanny. On stopping passenger trains it would out-accelerate all competition whatever the load, whilst even expresses were handled in its stride, running smoothly at 90mph and showing Britannias a clean pair of heels on banks.

What other locomotive could do all these things in such comfort and with equal competence? Indeed if asked to operate a railway with just a single class of steam engine then there is only one possible answer - the 9F.

Waiting to go. 73040 at Patricroft shed, Manchester in April 1968. Built at Derby in October 1953 to order No 6230, its first shed had been Chester. Withdrawn in May 1968 it was stored at Patricroft until June, 'ready for the off' to Cashmores, Great Bridge, with connecting rods hoisted up on the handrail. Photograph Tom Heavyside.

Above. Some sheds might have looked askance at the light 4-6-0s but, in country districts especially, they were a marked success. Sheds like Rhyl of course (note the 6K plate) had never seen the like - powerful, versatile, easy to service and - *new*. 75033 threads the hills with that little known tourist train, the Radio Cruise.

Below. Crewe North on 29 June 1952. The 75000 light 4-6-0s were a tender version of the LMS 2-6-4T, a type which, as Cox says, had 'a high reputation for speed, reliability and general effectiveness'. There were areas, however, which needed a longer operating range than a tank could manage, rural places for which a Class 5 axle loading was too high. The classic area was Central Wales, for which the GW Manors were ideal; they were too wide for general use, however, and the BR 75000s ended up, in a sense, as 'universal Manors'. It is in this sort of role that 75000, new the previous year, has run into Crewe. Photograph E.R. Morten

5. 75000 4-6-0s 1951-1968

The design is similar in many respects to the new Class "5" 4-6-0, but it is a lighter engine, having almost universal availability over main and secondary lines throughout Britain.
The Railway Magazine, August 1951.

The smaller BR 4-6-0 was introduced in 1951, a time when *The Railway Magazine* (of August of that year) could devote a mere two pages to the new development. 'Twenty of these engines are to be built during 1951' it announced; the first ten, Nos.75000-75009, would go to the Western Region and the second batch of ten, Nos.75010-75019, to the London Midland. 75016-75019 were not actually completed until 1952, between January and March. All the 75000s were built at Swindon, the final engine emerging from there in June 1957.

The 4MT 4-6-0s were always favourites of mine and they spent their working lives operating out of sheds in England and Wales. Unlike their sister tank engines (the 2-6-4Ts, Nos.80000-80154) they were never shedded in Scotland - though in later years some appeared north of the border and were overhauled at Cowlairs, running in on passenger turns around Glasgow. Some were eventually scrapped in Scotland having been stored at Carnforth, Tebay or Kingmoor before their final journey. They included familiar faces from the last days of banking on Shap and four of the last five to be withdrawn from Carnforth in August 1968 - 75009, 75019, 75020 and 75048, were all scrapped at Campbells of Airdrie. The fifth engine was 75027, now preserved on the Bluebell Railway in Sussex.

Design work was carried out at Brighton but as *The Railway Magazine* of August 1951 reminds us, certain sections were designed at Swindon, Derby and Doncaster. The 75000s were derived from a tank design, the Fairburn LMS 2-6-4T (the last of which, No.42095, was built at Brighton, in 1951); the BR boiler was nine inches longer than the Fairburn version with the firebox dimensions the same. The 75000 boiler tapered from 4ft 9in to 5ft 3in; the two outside cylinders were 18in diameter by 28in stroke, driving wheels were 5ft 8in diameter with an axle loading of 17 tons 5 cwt on the leading and rear coupled wheels and 17 tons 1 cwt on the middle set. Principally through width across the cylinders, the 4MT 4-6-0s (and this determined much of their future work) could be used on routes barred even to GWR Manors. The majority when new had the BR black livery with red, cream and grey lining. When built the class was fitted with three different types of tender, as follows:-
75000-75049, type BR2. 75050-75064, type BR2A. 75065-75079, type BR1B. With their extra water capacity (4,725 gallons) this final fifteen went to the Southern Region, where there were no water troughs. Later in its working life 75075 was fitted with a BR1F tender, which held 5,625 gallons. In June 1957 the first alteration in design came when, after draughting tests,

75029 was adapted and fitted with a double blastpipe and chimney at Swindon from where it emerged, moreover, in fully lined passenger green. The Swindon double chimney did not sit well on the engine; the result was ugly, and spoilt the appearance of a handsome engine. Technically, however, the experiment proved a success. It was planned to convert the whole class but diesels were the order of the day by now and the scheme was not carried through. Eastleigh nonetheless produced its own double chimney design, a much neater and more handsome form, and between October 1960 (75069) and November 1961 (75079) all fifteen, 75065-75079 of the SR 75000s got the home-grown double blastpipes and chimneys, improving the performance and proving popular with the footplate crews, especially when they could have these engines on lines barred to the heavier Class 5s. Other Class 4s fitted with double chimneys were 75003 (12/59), 75005 (1/62), 75006 (12/60), 75008 (9/62), 75020 (1962) and 75026 (7/62).

As built the 4MT 4-6-0s was allocated thus:-
Western Region. 75000-75009, 75020-75029.
London Midland Region. 75010-75019, 75030-75064.
Southern Region. 75065-75079.
When withdrawn the allocations were:-
Western Region 75000, 75001, 75003, 75005,

One of the last regular jobs for the light 4-6-0s was the Grassington branch quarry workings: 75020, its smokebox plate pinched, is en route to Grassington, about half way along the branch, on Tuesday 13 June 1967. Photograph Gavin Morrison.

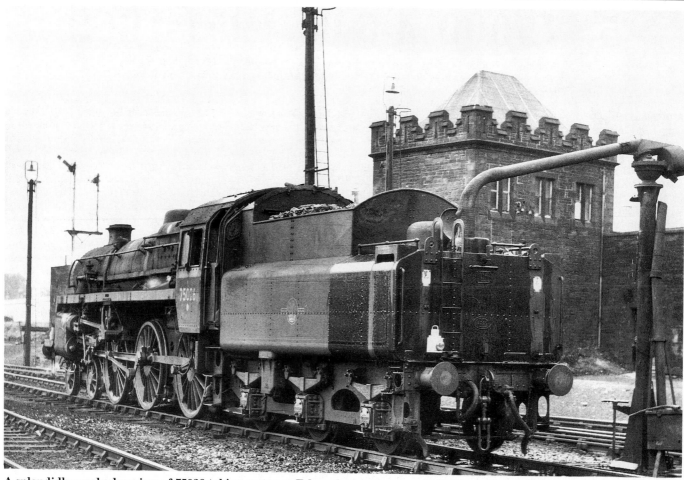

A splendidly workaday view of 75026 taking water at Tebay shed in October 1967. They went to Tebay for the last year or so of steam banking on Shap but were not popular. Half of any shift on the bank, by definition involved tender first running, and the old complaints of draughtiness soon resurfaced. Photograph Tom Heavyside.

75007, 75008, 75022, 75025, 75072 and 75073. London Midland Region 75002, 75004, 75006, 75009-75021, 75023, 75024, 75026-75064 and 75071.
Southern Region 75065-75070, 75074-75079.

There were to have been ten more of the light 4-6-0s, for the Eastern Region, but with the Modernisation Plan of 1955 and ever encroaching dieselisation they were cancelled. The numbers would have been 75080-75089.

Being a wholly new class, one was selected for extensive investigation soon after construction, and 75006 ran on the WR complete with indicator shelter and a mixed rake of carriages on a controlled road test.

During their short but varied working lives the engines had a couple of problems, not uncommon amongst the BR tender Standards. The cab layout, designed with the footplate crews so much in mind, made for draughts and dust, and the familiar complaints were voiced. In some cases canvas draught screens were fitted to try and combat the swirling blasts but these were not a resounding success and in most cases had been removed before the engines were withdrawn. If one studies photographs of the 75000 4-6-0s when new, close up, it will be noted that they were fitted with coupling rods of a fluted design. After a time in service these were found to suffer from excessive stresses and they were replaced by rods of a rectangular section. These are heavy indeed, as I discovered when an active member of the group that owns 73082 CAMELOT; it was a struggle for *six* of us just to lift and carry one!

The Class 4 4-6-0s enjoyed only the short working life, 1951-1968, that was given

to the Standards, though they were 'whole' as a class for a mere seven years, just like the 5MTs. Last built was 75064 in June 1957, entering service at Nottingham and the first withdrawn was 75067 from Eastleigh, in October 1964. There was little variation in the livery, though 75003, 75016, 75019, 75023, 75024, 75027 and 75029 were known to carry fully lined green.

I am not ashamed to say I spent some enjoyable years trainspotting in my younger days and wish I had been able to visit more parts of the UK in the quest for numbers, especially the North East of England. I saw less than half of the light 4-6-0s but all of the Southern Region ones were familiar to me - though 75071-75073 on the Somerset and Dorset were a bit harder to root out. One I saw at Eastleigh and the other two at Bournemouth. The remainder were seen on the Waterloo - Basingstoke semifasts, where they worked turn and turn about with the Class 5s. Of the others I was pleased, long ago, to note 75008 and 75022 on my only visit to Oxford, a trip organised by the London Railfans Club. I saw 75020 and 75024 during my summer holidays in Shropshire when they were based at Tyseley and during my frequent Sunday visits to some London sheds 75013, 75028 and 75038, then of Bletchley, turned up at Willesden - which also had some of its own at home, including 75030, 75031 and 75052.

By far the majority of the class were based in England and by 1955 (when most had been built) could mainly be found working on the LMR and WR. The allocation is a good illustration of the jobs the designers had in mind, the new 4-6-0s replacing any number of obsolescent types - 0-6-0s, 4-4-0s and others, tank and tender, and it had probably been a long time

indeed since such 'second rank' sheds had received brand new engines. On the LMR they were operating in the North West of England out of Patricroft (75010-75014); Southport (75015-75019) and Accrington (75045-75049), and in the south from Bletchley (75030-75039) and Bedford (75040-75044). The few examples on the Southern, though they were the last numerically, were not the last actually built; these were 75050-75064 put to traffic from Swindon between November 1956 and January 1957. When new these last fifteen engines were allocated to the LMR as follows:- Llandudno Junction, 75050; Chester, 75051, 75053 and 75054; Bletchley, 75052; Bedford, 75055; Nottingham, 75056, 75062-75064; Leicester, 75057-75061.

On the WR, some had worked on the Cambrian with 75020, 75023 and 75024 at Oswestry and 75001-75003, 75005 and 75007-75009 at Shrewsbury. The 4MT 4-6-0s were the last steam engines to work over the Cambrian lines. Elsewhere on the Western, Cardiff Canton had a couple - 75020 and 75021 - whilst Plymouth Laira had five, 75025-75029.

Of the SR batch, 75065-75069 went new to Dover and 75070-75079 new to Exmouth Junction, though by June 1956 75070-75072 had been transferred to Bath Green Park for the S & D. 75072 and 75073 spent the rest of their working lives here before both were withdrawn from Templecombe in December 1965, to be scrapped at Wards of Ringwood, Hampshire. 75071 was moved to Croes Newydd in August 1964 and was withdrawn from Stoke in August 1967. Though emphatically mixed traffic engines, I only ever saw them on passenger work on the SR, or on parcel trains at Christmas. Of course they worked freight trains, for there are enough photographs and films showing them on such work.

Even amongst the BR Standards, the Class 4 4-6-0s enjoyed a wandering life, with constant movements between sheds. This owed a good deal to the upsets of closure and retrenchment as the 1960s wore on, and the newer engines were pushed around the system in order to find them further work, but it might also be taken as an indication of a great Standard principle - a wide-ranging suitability for any task on offer. Amongst the most Gypsy-like was 75033; new to Bletchley, spells followed at Chester, Llandudno Junction, Chester again, Rhyl, Chester Northgate, Workington, Mold Junction, Rhyl and Llandudno Junction, Nuneaton, Southport, Bank Hall, Heaton Mersey, Chester again, Croes Newydd, Shrewsbury, Croes Newydd again and finally Carnforth, from where it was withdrawn in December 1967. It was scrapped at Wards, Killamarsh in 1968. One of its claims to fame was the working of the last up Cambrian Coast Express on 4th March 1967.

When new to the SR at Dover, 75065-75069 were used on such trains as the 9.20am to Victoria, non-stop Canterbury East to Chatham and the 8.59am to Charing Cross. 75070-75079 at Exmouth Junction worked west of Exeter, especially to Plymouth via Okehampton though by 1957 all ten had been transferred east to other parts of the South Western section. Even a brief look at their peregrinations, just on the Southern, gives an impression of the activities of the class - exactly the sort of un-noticed secondary *milieu* in which the light 4-6-0s saw out their lives, quietly and competently - precisely in the way the designers intended.

Southern steam finished in July 1967 and 75068, 75074, 75075, 75076 and 75077

survived to the end, all withdrawn from Eastleigh. 75078, withdrawn July 1966 and 75079 withdrawn November 1966, both from Eastleigh, still survive, 75078 having worked longer on the Worth Valley Railway than it did for BR. These double chimneyed members of the class had proved a great success on the SR and elsewhere where they could often be called on to perform duties normally timetabled for a 5MT.

When new to the LMR the Bletchley engines could be seen working between Euston and Rugby and in September 1957 75037 turned up at Cambridge off the Bletchley line. They also acted as station pilots at Bletchley. Bedford was the first shed for 75040-75044 and 75055 and they remained there until January 1960, when they moved to Leicester. At Bedford they were common user engines on St Pancras to Bedford semi-fasts, superseding (in a classic instance of the Standards' declared purpose in life) Midland Compound 4-4-0s and loading up to eight carriages. The class will be associated with the end of steam, for a number went to Tebay, replacing older engines and serving out the last two years of banking over Shap. Here again the old complaints of draughts in the cab resurfaced, especially with tender first working when returning light from a banking duty.

Other workings in the North West saw, surprisingly late on 2nd April 1966, 75012 and 75015 coupled tender to tender on snow plough duty working from Skipton, clearing the Settle and Carlisle as far as Kirkby Stephen. Carnforth shed became the final home for the working members of the class and although the great boast is that Stanier designs saw out the end of BR steam, no less than five Class 4 4-6-0s were there until the bitter end - 75009, 75019, 75020, 75027 and 75048. One of the regular duties for the five survivors was working the Grassington

branch, hauling ballast from Rylstone Quarry, working first out of Skipton and then Carnforth sheds. August 1968 saw the final withdrawals with 75009, 75019, 75020 and 75048, cut up later at Campbells of Airdrie.

DEMISE

1964. October 75067. December 75001.
1965. March 75007. October 75003. November 75005. December 75000, 75008, 75022, 75025, 75028, 75038, 75072, 75073.
1966. January 75023. February 75031, 75057, 75066. March 75044. April 75045. May 75063. June 75036, 75056. July 75078. August 75054. September 75053, 75065, 75069, 75070, October 75049, 75051. November 75011, 75050, 75079. December 75014.
1967. January 75012, 75017. February 75061. March 75004, April 75060. May 75055, 75064. June 75018. July 75016, 75035, 75059, 75068, 75074-75077. August 75002, 75006, 75013, 75029, 75046, 75047, 75052, 75071. September 75039. October 75010, 75040. November 75024, 75042. December 75015, 75026, 75030, 75033, 75037, 75043, 75058.
1968. January 75041. February 75021, 75032, 75034, 75062. August 75009, 75019, 75020, 75027, 75048.

Below. **The Nine Elms 'Old Shed' roads again, 17 July 1964. The double chimney (fitted for an extra power margin on jobs where Class 5s were prohibited through their weight) was not a success aesthetically though it certainly marks out 75078 from its fellow Standards. Q 0-6-0 30530 is the only native among four Standards - the one chalked HOT is 73087 LINETTE. Photograph Peter Groom.**

Above. 76000 at Polmadie when new. The first five had gone to Motherwell when new and had all been received at the shed in December 1952. They were used on local and through freight and an occasional passenger turn depending on 'the power position' as a contemporary Scottish Region report put it. Mileages were thus low and by the end of May 1953 ranged from 12,717 (76003) to 14,709 (76001). 76002 was much lower, at 7,903; it had suffered a collision which required it to be in shops from 12 February to 6 March 1952 and this, together with the inevitable waiting period, would account for the loss of miles. The first five weren't very lucky at all in fact, for 76000 was also in the wars. It collided with something and went into shops for nearly a fortnight in December 1952, in between leaving Horwich and its arrival at Motherwell! Photograph W. Hermiston, B.P. Hoper Collection.

Below. The other end of the country, and 76016 at Eastleigh, on 2 August 1955. Photograph W. Hermiston, B.P. Hoper Collection.

6. 76000 2-6-0s 1952-1967

.....an engine whose 5ft. 3in. coupled wheels destined it primarily for freight work, but which like its 2-10-0 big brother sometimes showed a clean pair of heels on occasional passenger jobs. In this latter role its principal appearances were at the opposite ends of the country, on the Southern Region and in Scotland. *British Railways Standard Steam Locomotives*, by E.S. Cox.

*T*he Railway Magazine of February 1953 introduced "the seventh of British Railways standard designs" in a brief two page piece with the usual outline information, line drawing and photograph of the first of the class, 76000. "They have been designed for mixed traffic operating with maximum route availability..." which certainly summed up much of the thinking that went into the BR Standards. The engines were drawn relatively seamlessly from late LMS practice, as developed by Ivatt. The point has been made that the BR locomotives were largely an extension of matters LMS, with as many 'foreign' detail extras as possible, where such equipment had been thoroughly proven on other lines. Some suspected that even this bore a hint of the cosmetic..... No better demonstration of this (unless it may be the case of the little 2MT Moguls) is provided in the case of the Class 4 2-6-0 niche. Here the existing Ivatt 'doodlebug' was dressed up - tidied up indeed - to match the various BR features, the running plate, cab and so on. The engines were fundamentally identical to the LMS-designed single chimney Nos.43000-43161, though only the first three (3000-3002) had been constructed by the LMS. The two classes were distributed as if both constituted Standard classes, and most of the 'LMS' examples went to Regions other than the LM. The 43000s became familiar engines for instance in Norfolk, of all places.

Employing the psychological dexterity that passed off the 1948 Exchanges as the theoretical proving ground of the Standards, the BTC saw that Doncaster was given 'parent design' responsibility, though it would have had little to do that was fundamental. The cab and footplate were tidied up with the boiler mountings and footplate controls provided to match other Standards. Fitted with a single blastpipe and chimney the 4MTs also enjoyed improved draughting arrangements. Designed with a bias towards freight operation (driving wheels were 5ft 3in, as on the Ivatt 'parent') the Moguls also had self cleaning smokebox, drop grate and hopper ashpan - standard ingredients for easy servicing. Grease nipples on mechanical parts and the mechanical lubricators under the running plates eased matters further. In any event the work done by Doncaster certainly gave the new Class 4s a vastly improved appearance.

The majority of the class had plain bearings on all axles but 76053-76066, fitted with type BR1B tenders, had Timken roller bearings on the tender axles. All of them, 76000-76114, were fitted with the BR7 boiler which had a maximum diameter of 5ft 3in, tapering to 4ft 9$\frac{1}{2}$in and a barrel length of 10ft 10$\frac{1}{2}$in with a narrow firebox, grate area 23 sq ft. The boiler was sometimes shown up as too small when called upon to work heavy trains on stiff gradients for a length of time, but a high adhesion factor made them amongst the most sure-footed of steam engines. Other features were the external rodding to the regulator on the left hand side; the attachment of speedometers, also on

the left hand side with a cable connected to the rear coupled wheel and the fitting of AWS (Automatic Warning System) to some of the class. Those allocated to the Southern Region had additional lamp irons fitted to the front and as already mentioned, 76053-76069 (new to the SR) had BR1B tenders, capacities 7 tons of coal and 4,725 gallons of water. Otherwise there were two further tender types, though there was little difference between them. The first 45, 76000-76044, were fitted with the type 2 and 76045-76052 and 76070-76114 with the 2A. Both carried 6 tons of coal and had a water capacity of 3,500 gallons with water pick up apparatus fitted only 'if required'. The main difference was the fallplate and gangway doors fitted to the type 2A.

Construction was divided between Doncaster and Horwich and when new the engines went to the following Regions:-
Scottish: 76000-76004, 76070-76074 and 76090-76114.
Southern: 76005-76019, 76025-76029 and 76053-76069.
North Eastern: 76020-76024 and 76045-76052.
Eastern: 76030-76044.
London Midland: 76075-76089.

76000 was built in December 1952 and 76114 (the last new steam engine to come out of Doncaster) in October 1957. The class, like the rest, had only a short working life, the first withdrawal coming in May 1964 with 76028 from

76045 heading a pick up goods for Bishop Auckland, at Hunwick on 30 April 1962. The Class 4 2-6-0s were the Ivatt 43000 engines modified with Standard features. They were identical in operation and performance, to the extent that the Swindon tests for the class were done with Ivatt 43094. Photograph Ian S. Carr.

The Book of the BR Standards

Eastleigh, followed by six more in the same year. Thus the 76000s were complete for less than seven years. Regional withdrawals were as follows:-

Scottish: 76000-76004, 76021, 76024, 76045, 76046, 76049, 76050, 76070-76074, 76090-76094, 76096-76098, 76100-76105, 76107-76114.

Southern: 76005-76019, 76025-76034, 76053-76069.

London Midland: 76020, 76022, 76023, 76035-76044, 76047, 76048, 76051, 76052, 76075-76089, 76095, 76099, 76106.

From the foregoing it can be seen that the Eastern and North Eastern Regions lost their allocations before the engines were taken out of service. The Eastern's 76030-76034 went to the Southern and its 76035-76044 to the LMR whilst the NER lost 76020, 76022, 76023, 76047, 76048, 76051 and 76052 to the LMR and 76021, 76024, 76045, 76046, 76049 and 76050 to Scotland. The ScR transferred a few to the LMR, 76095 in September 1964 to Saltley (after withdrawal in July from Corkerhill); 76099 in September 1964 to Saltley (after withdrawal in July from Ardrossan) and although 76106 moved in August 1965 from Bathgate to Willesden, this was probably a paper transfer as the engine was withdrawn the next month, stored at Crewe Works and scrapped at Cashmores, Great Bridge at the end of the year.

Although none of the class went new to the Western Region a number were withdrawn from one-time WR sheds: 76022, August 1966 from Oxley; 76037, June 1967 from Croes Newydd; 76038, September 1966 from Machynlleth; 76039, June 1967 from Croes Newydd; 76040, April 1967 from Croes Newydd; 76042, June 1966 from Oxley; 76043, September 1966 from Machynlleth; 76048, February 1967 from Croes Newydd; 76086, September 1966 from Croes Newydd; 76087, January 1967 from Oxley.

When the class was complete the ScR had 35, SR 37, NER 13, ER 15 and LMR 15. On the Scottish Region 76000-76004 were first based at Motherwell along with 76070 and 76071; 76072 and 76073 went to Dumfries and 76074 to Eastfield. Of the final 25, 76090-76114, 76090-76099 were built at Horwich and delivered between June and November 1957 and 76100-76114 came from Doncaster, delivered between May and October 1957. Thus, 76099 was the last of the class to enter service. These all went new to the Scottish Region with Corkerhill getting 76090-76099, Dawsholm 76100 and 76101, Parkhead 76102 and 76103, Kittybrewster 76104-76108, Thornton 76109-76111, Dumfries 76112 and St Rollox 76113 and 76114.

For a while 76001 served as the Blair Atholl banker but the Highland was not really to be a haunt of the new Moguls. They tended to concentrate in the Glasgow area and on the lines of the old Glasgow and Southern Western - Ayr and Kilmarnock - but were later seen more widely in the Region. 76001 returned to Motherwell and in June 1960 moved to Fort William where it stayed until August 1962, although some records show it on loan, for over two years. It was often used on the Fort William to Mallaig stretch, frequently the 3.15pm to Mallaig and the 5.40pm return. In August 1962 76001 moved to Corkerhill, on to Ardrossan in April 1964 and finally to Ayr in February 1965, from where it was withdrawn in August 1966, to be scrapped at Arnott Young, West of Scotland

An unlikely redoubt of the class formed in the area around Sutton Oak where, as latter-day successors to the 4F 0-6-0s, they saw out some of the last local freights on BR. This is 76084, at Sutton Oak shed on 30 June 1967. Photograph Tom Heavyside.

Shipbreaking Co., Troon. Of the first five, 76000, 76002 and 76003 remained at Motherwell whilst 76004 moved to Greenock Ladyburn in January 1963 and in December 1964 to Polmadie. Elsewhere on the ScR, which used them very much as a mixed traffic engines, the 4s saw a variety of workings and these included Littermill to Ayr Harbour, Motherwell to Bathgate coal trains, and regular workings on the Dumfries to Stranraer line, Dumfries shed at times having 76072-76074, 76102 and 76103 on the books, with 76101 and 76112 at Stranraer. 76104-76108 were regulars on the Elgin to Aberdeen route whilst based at Kittybrewster in Aberdeen where they had gone when new in July and August 1957, and all later moved on to Ferryhill. 76109-76111 of Thornton could be seen working trains to Dunfermline and Rosyth including a variety of local freights. All three moved on to Dunfermline early in 1960. A modest degree of fame came when they were used as banking engines on Beattock: 76070 was there from April to December 1964, 76090 from July 1962 to December 1966, 76094 from November 1966 to May 1967, 76098 December 1965 to May 1967, 76100 December 1965 to June 1966, 76103 April to June 1966 and 76114 which arrived in November 1966 but was withdrawn the next month. During my one family holiday in Scotland during steam days (I've been back a few times since) amongst the mass of Stanier Black Fives I was lucky enough to see 76071 and 76114. This last one was destined for a rather lonely existence, forlornly underlined in my ABC. According to the photographer Derek Cross, the Ayr men thought highly of their Class 4s, with 76096 being the last of 'Ayr's Pets' - engines that were kept in good order for working the special passenger trains. These included holiday trains from the Butlin's holiday camp at Heads of Ayr to Edinburgh or special trains to and from Prestwick Airport (Ayr) especially when other airports were fog -bound. A good part of my trainspotting days was spent close

to home, especially on summer Saturdays. Warm weekday evenings after hurried homework meant a quick walk to the railway bridge and two hours looking down on Oatlands Cutting, near Weybridge station. A good selection of steam was guaranteed and with luck one of the Eastleigh Class 4s might work up from the South Coast. I saw all that were based on the Southern, including 76030-76034 when they were transferred from the ER. All ended up at Guildford - though 76030 was withdrawn from Eastleigh. A summer camp at Lulworth Cove took me past Eastleigh and Bournemouth and an Ian Allan special to Southampton Docks revealed the last of the SR Class 4s. They came to the fore at summer Saturdays, when all sorts of extra trains required (often unusual) motive power, including some of the Class 4s. When new to Eastleigh the 2-6-0s worked to Reading and over the one-time Didcot, Newbury and Southampton line, on Brighton to Bournemouth through trains, to and from Salisbury on the Cardiff to Portsmouth through trains and other services between South Wales and the South Coast. At times they were noted at over 70mph (a clean pair of heels, as Cox rightly records). When Salisbury shed got hold of them they were sometimes used on express or stopping trains to Exeter.

76053-76062 went new to Redhill between April and July 1955 and were often seen on heavy cross country trains, though rarely east of Tonbridge. All transferred to the South Western section by the end of the decade, 76053-76055, 76059 and 76060 to Salisbury and 76056-76058, 76061 and 76062 to Eastleigh. It was then that I was able to see them in action on summer Saturdays, when their BR1B tenders were put to good use and they worked summer extras to and from London - a great bonus to us local lads.

Other workings on the Southern included rare appearances at Tunbridge Wells, Tonbridge and Hastings, but they were common in the

Southampton and Bournemouth areas working on both freight and passenger trains. The 4s worked to and from Basingstoke and Portsmouth, on parcel trains, Weymouth to Eastleigh stopping trains, Littlehampton to Totton via Southampton, Salisbury to Yeovil Junction stoppers and on the SECR line between Reading and Redhill. My favourite memory was the Saturday Waterloo to Lymington boat train, the Class 4s gaining this prestige working by dint of the turntable at Brockenhurst, which could not take larger engines. Further down, the Swanage branch saw 76000s (mainly Bournemouth based) right up to the end of steam.

The NER had thirteen of the class from new. Nos.76020-76024 when delivered in December 1952 (76024 in January 1953) went to different sheds: 76020 Darlington; 76021 York; 76022 Hull Dairycoates; 76023 Sunderland and 76024 Gateshead. Others went more logically - 76045-76049, new in March/April 1955 to Gateshead; 76050, new in August 1956 to Darlington and 76051, 76052 new in August/September 1956 to York. Better known than the far more remunerative work these engines did in the industrial areas of North East England was that over the Stainmore route, crossing the Pennines to Tebay and Penrith via Kirkby Stephen. Because of the weight restriction on a couple of viaducts only engines of a low axle loading, such as the Class 4s, were allowed and eventually 76020, 76022, 76023, 76047, 76048, 76051 and 76052 were based at Kirkby Stephen, and 76021, 76024, 76045, 76046, 76049 and 76050 at West Auckland. They found work over the route during its last days, the main duties being coal and return empties to and from the Durham coalfield as well as local passenger trains and excursions from Newcastle to Blackpool. January 20th 1962 was a sad day, class 3 2-6-0 77003 and 76049 hauling the last passenger train over the line, an RCTS special.

On the Eastern Region 76030-76034 had gone new to Stratford in November/December 1953 moving south of the Thames to Brighton (after a time at March) in December 1962, as dieselisation took hold on the GE Section. They were distinguished by a recess in the cabside for a token exchanger but it is uncertain whether any were actually fitted or used.

76035-76044 were new to Neasden between May and August 1954 and Neasden became part of the LMR on 20th April 1958. During my Red Rover 'six shed tours' around London the last visit was always Neasden and at this time on a Sunday, late afternoon, the six road shed was always packed. Several 'raids' off the nearby North Circular Road meant to I was able to see all ten of these engines before they were scattered to other parts of the LMR, most of them seeing out their days in the Chester area or on the former Cambrian lines.

The London Midland Region had one batch of the class from new, 76075-76089, the first five going new to Sutton Oak between December 1956 and February 1957. The next five went to Lower Darwen between February and April 1957 with 76085 and 76086 arriving at Leicester Midland in April and May 1957 respectively. The final three, 76087-76089, were new to Trafford Park between May and June 1957. Those at Sutton Oak later included 76080-76084, all transferred there in March 1965. Their duties were mainly on freights, especially in the Liverpool area and one diagram included a St Helens - Warrington - Chester passenger train, returning the next morning on the Hooton - Heaton Mersey freight empties. Another working was hauling sand trains to the Pilkington glass factory at St Helens. Later in their working lives they could be found on coal trains on the Chester to Holyhead route. 76087-76089 when based at Trafford Park were involved in trans-Pennine work, one duty being passenger trains between Manchester Central and Sheffield Midland. 76085 and 76086 of Leicester were recorded working passenger trains between Nottingham Midland and Chesterfield and by the end of 1963 and along with 76087 all three were based at Saltley. Those at Lower Darwen were also involved in freight work, in the Liverpool, Manchester and Preston areas. A few of them, 76075, 76077, 76079, 76080, 76081 and 76084, spent their last few months at Wigan Springs Branch, working mainly on coal trains before being withdrawn as follows:- 76075 October 1967; 76077 December 1967; 76079 December 1967, 76080 December 1967; 76081 July 1967 and 76084 December 1967. 76077 achieved a small measure of fame in August 1967 when it hauled an LCGB brake van special on a tour of lines in the Warrington and Widnes area, whilst 76084 was the last of the class in service, in December 1967.

DEMISE

1964

May 76028. July 76097. August 76032. September 76034. October 76029, 76054, 76072.

1965

April 76030. July 76017. September 76050, 76106. October 76015, 76023, 76025, 76027,76055, 76056, 76062, 76065, 76068, 76107, 76112. December 76060.

1966

January 76045, 76049,76071, 76105, 76111. February 76019. March 76003. April 76020. May 76035. June 76042, 76073, 76085. July 76103, 76108. August 76001, 76022, 76070, 76092, 76099, 76100. September 76010, 76012, 76013, 76014, 76038, 76043, 76059, 76086, 76089, 76109. October 76004, 76016, 76018, 76021, 76044, 76057, 76074, 76082, 76083. November 76076. December 76002, 76024, 76047, 76052, 76078, 76090, 76091, 76096, 76101, 76102, 76110, 76113, 76114.

1967

January 76033, 76036, 76053, 76061, 76087. February 76048, 76093. March 76058, 76095. April 76040, 76041, 76051, 76063. May 76000, 76008, 76046, 76094, 76098, 76104. June 76037, 76039, 76069, 76088. July 76005, 76006, 76007, 76009, 76011, 76026, 76031, 76064, 76066, 76067, 76081. October 76075. December 76077, 76079, 76080, 76084.

76034 stored out of use at March (its home shed) on 9 September 1962 - in the December it was transferred to Brighton. Note the recess in the cab for tablet exchanging mechanism. Built at Doncaster in December 1953 to Engine Order No 396 its first shed was Stratford, and its final home Guildford, where it was withdrawn in September 1964. It was scrapped at Woods (Shipbreaking) of Queenborough, Kent.

Above. The two smallest classes (apart from the Duke of course) were the Clans and the 77000 3MT Moguls, and both were remote, to anyone south of a line from Birmingham to the Wash. To us poor benighted southerners they had an exotic air, something which goes some way to explaining the warm reception of 77014 in 'Maid of Astolat' country in latter years - see anon. Here is 77009 under a dramatic sky at Blair Atholl on 4 September 1954. On its return from London (where it represented the class at the Railway Congress in Willesden roundhouse earlier in the year), it was put on banking duties. Such 'low activity' applications were rooted out when BR investigated some disappointing mileages on the smaller classes. It turns out that sheds around the country were putting some smaller Standards (the original Ivatt versions - Class 2 2-6-0s in particular - were favourites too) on duties for the comfort they afforded crews, rather than grander reasons of maximum utilisation. Whatever the shortcomings of the Standard cabs (and the 77000 were not liked, at least in Scotland), they were fine places in which to spend a cold night in February compared to say, a pre-Group 0-6-0, especially if much of the shift involved standing around. Photograph J. Robertson, B.P. Hoper Collection.

Below. More mundane setting. 77004 at Darlington shed, 7 July 1956. Photograph Eric Sawford.

7. 77000 2-6-0s 1954-1967

The two Class 3 designs, 2-6-0 and corresponding 2-6-2 tank, arose from the existence at the time of nationalisation of a number of routes having a 16-ton axle load restriction which Class 4 engines could not satisfy. *British Railways Standard Steam Locomotives*, E.S. Cox. **The high running plate, concealing so much pipe work, might have seemed unsightly by more traditional measures but in world design terms, the new BR locos were still astonishingly 'clean' in their externals.** *The Invisible Standards, British Railways Illustrated*, August 1996. **.....a very ugly engine.** *The Observer's Book of Railway Locomotives of Britain*, H.C. Casserley.

The late Derek Cross did not have too a high an opinion of this class, considering them well, unnecessary. They were not popular with the crews either, and more than once he had asked footplatemen what they thought of the 77000 Moguls. The common complaint was that the footplates were dirty and draughty and worse, steaming was suspect. On summer Saturday trains the class worked over the Stainmore route from Newcastle to Blackpool, and Cross records that crews felt the boiler lacked the capacity for the adverse gradients on this route, though they were free running on the flatter stretches.

Perhaps the most telling elements in the poor reception of the 3MTs were the two simple, straightforward, stock ones - they were not demonstrably, *absolutely* superior to existing types in power and in any given area they were present in no more than handfuls, so men got them only occasionally and haphazardly. The example of the GE Britannias was not taken to heart. On the Norwich jobs the Pacifics allowed of an undreamed-of increase in power, and they were in sufficient numbers to become 'the norm' in the relevant links, quickly. The 3MT situation - lack of *marked and significant* power over that of the types to be replaced and lack of numbers - was repeated across BR in different places, at different times and with different

classes. Since at least the 1930s the cry of the sheds (distrusting all new developments) had been 'more of the same'. If more of the same meant more generic '4F' 0-6-0s and what turned up on a particular job was a smattering of strangers, sometimes in power class 3 and the next week class 4, then trouble was in store, Whatever the new engine's advantages of versatility and ease of maintenance, this so-called modern engine, if it failed to quite live up to the indigenous examples on some obscure colliery shunt, stood condemned forever.

The entry in *The Railway Magazine* for the 3MTs comes in the June 1954 issue, with the usual photograph and line drawing; the new engine was the tender version of the 3MT tank, enjoying almost universal availability over main and secondary lines throughout Britain. It was designed to replace 'various tender engines of similar classification now becoming obsolete' but with only twenty built (further orders were cancelled) they certainly did not replace many ageing 0-6-0s. Loss of traffic did far more in that particular direction.

Parent office for design was Swindon, where all twenty were built but none saw service on the Western Region, other than running in - in this, they could turn up at Exeter. By a turn of fate the boiler was based on the GWR No.4, used on GWR types such as the 51XX, 56XX

and 81XX tanks. It served for the 82000 Standard tanks too, and became the BR type 6. There were minor dimensional modifications from the GW base design and the plates were made of high tensile instead of mild steel. In the case of the 3MT 2-6-0s the principles of maximum accessibility, laid down from the first, evolved perhaps to their highest level of development. Many observers, as a result, found the 3MT Moguls aesthetically the worst by far of the Standards. All moving parts were almost alarmingly on show but there was exceptional forward vision when running tender first. The tenders were the BR2A type, 6 tons of coal and 3,500 gallons, which gave the class, in my heretical opinion, a handsome appearance. The engines were fitted with a tall and shapely chimney which helped balance the front end and it was quite surprising to see 77005 fitted with the wider and squatter class 4 chimney - a queasy effect altogether - when the engine was based at Motherwell.

The Class 3s were amongst the nearest to a wholly new design in the Standard range, for no pre-Nationalisation company had a Mogul in such a power class. So the idea behind the new 2-6-0 was to provide a modern machine of medium power to handle the traffic on certain lines limited to a 16 ton axle loading - though loading in fact just exceeded the 16 ton require-

Two of the 'wee Standards' at Polmadie (note the customary glistening smokebox front) on 14 April 1956. Side views accentuated the engines' eccentric lines, which observers found either repulsively ugly or oddly attractive. The design was wholly new and the 'house style' combined with such small drivers made it inevitable that a startling gap should be opened up between the wheels and the running plate. Photograph J. Robertson, B.P. Hoper Collection.

The 3MT 2-6-0s ploughed a lonely furrow, seeming to positively shun human habitation, which all added to their mysterious quality. This is 77011 of Blaydon shed, arriving at a desolate Kielder Forest (passenger services ended a few months later) with the 11.10 Newcastle - Hawick, on 28 July 1956. Photograph Ian S. Carr.

ment. It was nevertheless hard to justify the existence of the class; only a few were built and many lines for which they were suited closed relatively early, or traffic declined precipitately. There was not much of the work that could not be carried out by a Class 2 locomotive in any event, especially the 78000 introduced at the end of 1952. Civil engineering progress in some instances, moreover, made for upgraded lines, so that they could take engines of Class 4. In any event the all-conquering diesel sets were soon on the scene. A gallant little experiment, the 3MTs maybe owed more to a feeling that all the available power niches should be filled.

Being the penultimate class of Standards (the last were the mighty 9Fs) the Class 3s had the advantage of design development and improvements gleaned from the others whilst in service. This included rectangular shaped coupled rods instead of fluted ones, a speedometer attached to the rear coupled wheel on the left hand side and footsteps to the rear of the tender. From new the class had the redesigned cab and tender arrangement which meant gangway doors to the tender but no canvas draught screens. Grab rails were also fitted and large footblocks were added to the rear of the tender tank top. The other main addition was a fall plate on the front of the tender, resting on a rearward extension of the cab floor - hence no need for the draught screens. AWS apparatus was later fitted to some of the class, at the front, where it was protected from the screw coupling (which hung down when not in use) by a steel guard. As built the engines were allocated as follows:-

77000-77004; February - March 1954 to NER Darlington.
77005-77009; March - June 1954 to ScR. 77005-77007 to Hamilton and 77008, 77009 to Perth.

77010-77014; June - July 1954 to NER Darlington.
77015-77019; July - September 1954 to ScR Hurlford.

77009 was exhibited at the International Railway Congress in May 1954 held in the roundhouse at Willesden, complete with polished rods, tyres and cylinder covers, a star indeed. Twelve years to the month the engine was withdrawn from Motherwell, to where it had moved in October 1965. It was scrapped by the end of 1966 at Motherwell Machinery & Scrap Co, Wishaw.

Evenly split between the Scottish and North Eastern Regions, the ER and NER shared works maintenance of the 3MTs. The engines spent a good deal of their time working away from the main line - it was part of the design concept after all - and were thus not too well photographed. 77005-77009 spent the majority of their time at Polmadie, Motherwell and Hamilton on Glasgow suburban services, on which they were replaced by stock supplied under the Modernisation Plan of 1955. They went to Motherwell and 77005 ran for a while with MOTHERWELL on the front buffer beam - applied, in Scottish tradition, during an overhaul at Cowlairs. 77015-77019 spent all their working lives at Hurlford, apart from a brief move to Polmadie for 77019 in 1963. It came back to Hurlford after a few months, in the October. This group of engines worked local freights and passenger trains to and from Ayr, over the hilly and twisting line from Muirkirk to Lanark and Carstairs; they worked south to Stranraer and occasionally took heavy coal trains over mineral branches with restricted weight limitations that Class 2s could not handle. Freight trains over the border to Carlisle gave a chance of catching one of them, on shed at Kingmoor.

All five were withdrawn between March and November 1966 and scrapped in yards in south west Scotland.

When new, the North Eastern complement all started work at Darlington, and although they moved around the NER, none of them really found a permanent home like 77015-77019 on the ScR. However, 77014 did go further afield at the last. First (extraordinary enough in itself) it moved to Northwich, in November 1964, but it then went south *to Guildford,* in March 1966, from where it was withdrawn in July 1967. 77014 was thus rendered very much the odd one out; it came to work a special and stayed with Guildford as its base. It was here, on a rare visit for me, in 1966, that I caught my only glimpse of a 77000, awaiting a turn of duty in the shed yard. An 'exotic', more used to far off climes such as the Alston branch, it became a regular and a favourite on the Mid-Hants line where it worked freights and even piloted the diverted 'Bournemouth Belle'. It got as far west as Weymouth and was used on several special trains. By early 1967 it was rostered to work the daily Woking - Farnham waste ballast train and was noted on this on 10th January. On the final weekday of Southern steam, 7th July 1967, it was seen on the 7.20pm Salisbury - Northam Yard parcels. It was a stranger in which we all delighted; withdrawn and stored at Weymouth shed, unhappily 77014 did not go to Woodhams and was instead cut up at Birds, Risca in 1968.

DEMISE
1965. November 77010.
1966. January 77001. February 77011. March 77006, 77013, 77016. May 77009. June 77008. July 77015. November 77005, 77007, 77017, 77018, 77019. December 77000, 77003, 77004.
1967. June 77002, 77012. July 77014.

Above. Ugly ducklings side by side at Hull Dairycoates, in one of the demolished roundhouses, 9 June 1962. Partly through their low numbers and partly because they were used on local and branch line jobs, the 77000s strayed beyond their own haunts very rarely. In this they were unlike most of the Standards, which were truly ubiquitous. Photograph Ian S. Carr.

Below. We are back in the land of Astolat with the celebrated wanderer, 77014, looking perfectly at home behind the Guildford shed pilot, USA Tank No 30072 (now resident on the Worth Valley Railway), in the final days of Southern steam. Though traditionally (pressing home a point) they rarely emerged from their moorland and coalfield homes, there was a time when it was not all that unusual to see 77000s *at Exeter...* The hard pressed Swindon shed foreman would grab anything on running in work and these included brand new 77000s. A favourite turn was the overnight fish from the north east, and Major J.M. Jarvis of the Engine Shed Society, writing in *British Railways Illustrated* in April 1997, recalled (instead of the usual Swindon Dukedog or St Philips Marsh Dean Goods), a shiny new 77006 pulling in at the London end of Exeter St Davids, with its malodorous cargo. Photograph K.P. Lawrence.

Above. 78048, at an unknown location (St Margarets? - the date is given as 19 May 1956) and *left*, 78022 fussing about at Preston, on 30 May 1964. At Class 2, the 78000 Moguls were in the smallest Standard power class. They were among the group of four designs that were purely LMS, altered to incorporate Standard details. The others were the Class 4 2-6-0s, Class 2 2-6-2Ts and the Fairburn-derived 2-6-4Ts. Photographs J. Robertson, B.P. Hoper Collection and Peter J. Fitton.

8. 78000 2-6-0s, 1952-1967

The smallest of the BR Standard types and, amongst the tender classes, alone possesses a running plate of moderate height, resulting in the best proportioned engine of all the new designs. *The Observer's Book of Railway Locomotives of Britain,* H.C. Casserley.

The Ivatt Class 2 2-6-0, introduced by the LMS in 1946, was simply adapted, in a few small details, to make it of wider use in the matter of loading gauge. Derby, the design office, did not trouble to apply the 'family look'. In effect, the 65 engines were only built insofar as further Ivatt Class 2MT Moguls were deemed necessary. Construction effectively overlapped with No.46527, the last of the Ivatts which emerged from Swindon Works in March 1953 - 78000-78009 came from Darlington (where the entire class was built) between December 1952 and April 1953.

The differences between the 78000 Mogul and its Ivatt 46400 progenitor were minor ones, of appearance only. The BR engines had fall plates between the running plate and front buffer beam, the chimneys were taller and wider and the top feed was uncovered. The most marked visual difference concerned the cabs; the 78000 upper side sheets sloped inwards so that the BR engines could be used where the narrowest of loading gauges existed. Technically, there were no differences; both Class 2 Moguls had 5ft driving wheels and a boiler pressure of 200lb, the Ivatts weighing in at 47 tons 2 cwt and the Standards at 49 tons 5 cwt. The Ivatts numbered 46400-46464, had two cylinders 16in x 24in producing a tractive effort of 17,410lb. The remainder, 46465-46527, had a half inch increase

in the bore - the size adopted for the Standards - which produced a tractive effort in the Ivatts of 18,510lb and in the Standards, 18,515lb.

The 78000s, like the Ivatts from which they derived, had a traditionally mounted cab, attached to the frames instead of being cantilevered back from the frames and the class lacked the deep side valences beneath the running plates so characteristic of the other Standards. The boiler was similar to that of the Ivatts and was classified BR type 8. The reversing gear was of LMS pattern, on the left hand, driver's side. The LMS top feed of the Ivatts was replaced by the BR clack valve arrangement and the BR regulator in the dome was a vertical grid type, operated by an external rod at the side of the firebox. Mechanical lubricators on both sides of the engine were situated on top of the running plate, directly over the valve gear and leading coupled wheel. Mechanical lubricators have been mentioned elsewhere in this book but how do they work? Well study photographs of this class (or go and see 78022 on the Worth Valley Railway) and you can see they are driven off the motion, the mechanical lubricators delivering oil through atomisers, in front of the main steam pipe in the case of the 78000s. In these, the steam disperses the oil into particles, tiny ones, before they are delivered into the steam chest and thence the cylinder. When the cylinder

drain cocks are shut the atomiser steam valve opens, so a constant supply of oil is available when the engine is in motion.

Two live steam injectors were situated on the right hand side beneath the cab, the fireman's side where the controls were grouped. The class was fitted with AWS equipment in the 1960s and on the right hand side of the smokebox was a small steam cock to which a steam lance could be fitted for cleaning out the boiler tubes. On the lower part of the smokebox door could be seen the letters SC, familiar from the rest of the Standards. It indicated of course that the smokebox was 'self cleaning', and that wire mesh screens had been set up inside the smokebox at a predetermined angle, ensuring that particles of unburnt fuel were suspended above the blastpipe and cooled before exiting through the chimney. This *should* have meant that the smokebox would only need emptying say, once a fortnight, but this all depended on a number of factors. The quality of coal was important, as well as the method of firing, how good the driver was and how long the engine had been in traffic before it was available for routine maintenance. There was also a subversion factor. The screens could inhibit steaming, if the last refurbishment had been rather far in the past - a collapsed screen could fail a locomotive after all - and it is clear that sheds (*some* sheds?)

78012, doing what was intended, somewhere in the North East in 1959. Photograph B.P. Hoper Collection.

habitually removed the things and refitted them only for works visits.....

The 78000 tender was unique among the Standards; BR type 3, they took 4 tons of coal and 3,000 gallons of water, weighing 37 tons. They carried a tender cab which gave reasonable protection and good forward vision when running tender first. Fitted with Timken roller bearings on all six wheels, like all the Stand-ard tenders they were equipped with water sieves - developed on the earlier Ivatts - to filter out impurities and prevent the injectors getting blocked. Water pick up apparatus was fitted inside the tanks but water scoops were put on only when required.

The last 2MT Mogul emerged from Darlington in November 1956, No.78064 which, like 78063 completed the same month, went new to the old L&Y shed at Wigan, where they were later joined by 78040 and 78060-78062. Yet the 78000s, like other Standards, remained complete for just seven years, the first withdrawal taking place at Darlington shed: 78015, taken out of service in November 1963, was the only BR Standard, along with some of the Clans, to be cut up at Darlington Works. The final Class 2 to be condemned seems to have been

'The best proportioned engines of the new designs' as H.C. Casserley (who thoroughly disliked the look of the Class 3 Moguls) wrote in the 1950s. They certainly lacked the family look of the Standards, though it would have been interesting to see the results if the external details had been refashioned after the manner of the 43000/76000 Class 4 Moguls. This is 78003 at Shrewsbury shed, in August 1957. Photograph B.P. Hoper.

The 78000 Mogul was perhaps odd in that all the test work had been done before even a pair of frames was laid, for Ivatt's original design was more or less exactly similar. 46413 had been tested at Swindon from the summer of 1949, so the 'fine tuning' of the chimney proportions were well established before the first 78000 saw the light of day. The 2MT Moguls, both versions, were very well received by footplate crews and could anything they were given in their power class - and beyond. Cox notes that 46413 on road test lifted 15 coaches (455 tons) up five miles of 1 in 300 between Little Somerford and Badminton at a minimum speed of 40mph! This is one of the 78000s sent to work out their days at Willesden on empty stock - no sinecure but traditionally carried on out of Euston by locos in their twilight years. 78059, with chalk embellished number is under the (unenergised?) wires, about to return to shed, 22 September 1965. Photograph B.P. Hoper Collection.

78062 from Bolton in May 1967, though 78007, 78012, 78013, 78023 and 78044 were also withdrawn from Bolton that month, as well as 78020, 78021 78037 and 78041 from Lostock Hall.

The Railway Magazine of April 1953 gave details of the class, declaring that the first ten, 78000-78009 were going to the Western Region for the sort of duties carried out by 2251 and 2301 0-6-0 classes. The older 0-6-0s were the obvious 'targets' as the new engines became available. Like other Standards, the 78000s were fitted with the fluted type of coupling rods when new but after various faults manifested themselves in service they were replaced by rods of a rectangular cross-section. Some had a speedometer fitted, driven conventionally through a cable fitted to the left hand rear driving wheel. When built they were allocated as follows:-

Western: 78000-78009.
North Eastern: 78010-78019.
London Midland: 78020-78044 and 78055-78064.
Scottish: 78045-78054.

In each case the operating Region was responsible for maintenance. The 78000 Moguls were turned out in black livery, lined in red and white, though Swindon once again took an independent path, painting 78000 in BR Brunswick green during a heavy repair. After the delivery of 78000 in December 1952, through to 78009 in April 1953, there was a break until 78010 appeared in December of the same year. Deliveries continued to the end of 1954 with 78044, some appearing every month except August (perhaps due to the Works annual holiday - just a theory...). 78045 did not arrive until October 1955, the first of a batch which finished with 78054 in December. 78055, first of the final batch, appeared in August 1956 and the final engine, 78064, came in November 1956. The

late Kenneth Hoole in his book *North Road Locomotive Works, Darlington 1863-1966* (Roundhouse Books, 1967) gives the typical cost for a 2MT in 1953 as £14,377 - 'weight for weight the Class 2MT was the most expensive engine ever built at Darlington' - condemnation indeed from a Yorkshireman.

Route availability was wide due to the low axle loading of the engines; the leading axle carried 13 tons 15 cwt; the middle axle 13 tons 12 cwt and the rear axle 13 tons 3 cwt. Unlike the 3MTs the locos were spread far and wide across the operating Regions - though none was ever based on the Southern. The little Moguls were a powerful, light design, intended to work over light track on any type of duty - the late Derek Cross called them versatile and useful little locomotives - many of the secondary tasks and routes for which they were intended were, however, soon ended or closed - diesel sets took over the passenger work and freight declined.

G.C. Bird praises the 78000 Moguls in the summer 1976 edition *Severn Valley Railway News*. The author was a Junior Inspector at Darlington shed and for a time covered the vacancy of Shed Master at Kirkby Stephen. Here he came across 78016-78019 and found them to be 'marvellous little engines... which would stand up to the vagaries of Stainmore, within the expected capacity, of course, of a small engine'. During his short time at Kirkby Stephen he found 78018 to be the best of the four and this was the engine that got snowed up in Bleath Gill cutting during the bad winter of 1953/1954 - memorably preserved on celluloid by the British Transport Film Unit. He found from personal experience that these engines could shorten the time of the trips between Darlington and Penrith without breaking any speed limits, mainly through good steaming capacity up the hills. The 2-6-0s, he records, were never short of

steam or water. After his short and enjoyable stay at Kirkby Stephen Mr. Bird returned to Darlington and later had an extended relief spell at Northallerton; on his recommendation 78010-78014 were transferred there from West Auckland - to some chagrin at the latter place. The Moguls did good work again but Mr. Bird's dealings with them came to an end in April 1956 when he became Shed Master at Hull Botanic Gardens where, incidentally, he became acquainted with the Class 3MTs 77000, 77001 and 77010 which he felt were '... machines par excellence'.

Not one of the class stayed at a single shed, unlike other Standards - 73121-73124 at Corkerhill for instance, or 77015-77018 at Hurlford, but neither did they have the real gypsy in them, like some of the 4MT 4-6-0s, such as 75033 and 75055. They did tend to stick with the original Regions, though some of the WR allocation (78000-78009) after a spell at Oswestry were eventually distributed across the LMR, a consequence of Machynlleth and other sheds being taken into that Region.

The majority worked on the LMR, ScR, NER and WR with a little work on the Eastern, 78022-78025 moving to Doncaster for instance, in January 1962 and on to March in September 1962 where they were joined by 78027. All moved to the NER in the December. In their short time at March they were reported working to Cambridge and *Trains Illustrated* of October 1962 told of 78022-78025 and 78027 being transferred to Stratford - to replace J15 0-6-0s, the account (probably mistakenly) assumed. At the end of the year the 2-6-0s were reported back at March, so it was probably a 'paper move' at best.

78000-78009 going new to Oswestry from December 1952 to April 1953 arrived at the same time as brand new Ivatt 2-6-0s from

78023 at Nottingham Midland in June 1955. Even as construction of the 78000s was drawing to an end, DMUs were being introduced, particularly across the rural areas which provided most of the passenger work for this sort of engine. By the 1960s these sort of duties had declined steeply. Photograph B.P. Hoper Collection.

Swindon works, 46503-46524 delivered between November 1952 and March 1953. (46525-46527 went to Bristol St Phillips Marsh). These later Ivatts had the same size cylinders as the Standards and they worked side by side on the Cambrian lines, both passenger and freight trains - bread and butter stuff which attracted few headlines. Later, 78000, 78002, 78005 and 78007 moved to Machynlleth and one of their everyday duties was to work local trains between Machynlleth and Barmouth along the picturesque Cambrian coast. Up to four carriages, they were easy enough jobs for the Class 2s. Later, after overhaul at Swindon, some were seen in green livery - including 78000, 78001, 78004-78006 and 78009. They were subsequently based at Gloucester, from where they were all withdrawn.

For a time 78001, 78004, 78008 and 78009 found a home at Worcester and at the end of 1953 could be noted on Kingham to Chipping Norton turns and on the daily Moreton-in-Marsh to Shipston-on-Stour goods. Early in 1954 78001 had a regular duty on the 7.15am Honeybourne to Leamington Spa and then 9.15am Leamington Spa to Stratford on Avon.

The Scottish based 78000s were seen in all parts of the North Kingdom. 78045 went new to Kittybrewster; 78046 and 78047 to Hawick; 78048 and 78049 to St Margarets and 78050-78054 to Motherwell. 78016 was new to West Auckland and moved to Motherwell in August 1963 and was eventually withdrawn from Stranraer in August 1966. 78026 moved to Ayr in January 1962 and was withdrawn from Corkerhill in August 1966. Otherwise the original Scottish allocation remained north of the border and was withdrawn as follows:-

78045 January 1966, Bathgate; 78046 November 1966, St Margarets; 78047 September 1966, St Margarets; 78048 July 1964, Hawick; 78049 August 1966, St Margarets; 78050 January 1966, Bathgate; 78051 November 1966, Ayr; 78052 January 1966, Bathgate; 78053 July 1964, Stirling and 78054 December 1965, Bathgate. 78052 must have the one to venture farthest north, for at one time it could be found working out of Helmsdale, on the Dornoch branch which left the Inverness to Wick line at The Mound. Later it was based at Inverness, and at Aviemore too, from where it worked up to Forres over the old Highland main line and on to the former GNSR. It was withdrawn from Bathgate in January 1966, and scrapped at Motherwell Machinery & Scrap Co. Wishaw.

Much-photographed duties were the passenger workings between Berwick and St. Boswell via Kelso, a route of some 35 miles - just one carriage, often worked tender first. Coal trains for Ravenscraig Steelworks were a striking and surprising contrast. 2MTs based at Keith, between Inverness and Aberdeen, included 78045, 78053 and 78054, employed on the line from Craigellachie to Boat of Garten (GNSR), closed in October 1965. This line passed through a beautiful part of Scotland, now famous for its 'Whisky Trail' and the engines would have passed Knockando station, now the reception centre for the Tamdhu distillery, home of *The Famous Grouse*. This mention should at least enhance my chances of a substantial free sample next time I visit...

The LMR received the greater part of the class, 78020-78044 and 78055-78064, and they were widely distributed across the Region, from 78020 and 78021 at Kettering to 78032-

78036 at Rhyl. For a while they became quite common in the Midland Division of the LMR and around Liverpool and in North Wales, on both local passenger and freight trains. 78028 at Kettering might represent a typical mix of duties before dieselisation and closures took too much of a hold - in 1959 it worked trains to Cambridge as well as freights in the Leicester area. At one time the 78000s were put to work on the Leicester West Bridge to Desford line, which had closed to passengers on September 1928. The restricted Glenfield Tunnel meant that engines of modest outline were necessary - Midland 2Fs had long served but these were wearing out. Even the replacement Moguls required some reduction in the roof profile and 78028, based at Nottingham, was one so treated.

The 78000 duties were myriad, from 78025 on the Nottingham Midland to Chesterfield run to 78043 (once of Bank Hall and Aintree), working Rochdale to Wigan passenger trains. The work encompassed all that was secondary, really - as the Ivatts before them, though one or two sheds had to be firmly advised against putting them on the most obscure duties, particularly in winter. The cabs were palatial compared to some pre-grouping engines and it was the suspiciously low mileages of some brand new 2-6-0s which alerted 'authority' that these expensive new engines were ending up on some of the most obscure shunts and pilot turns - for reasons of crew comfort rather than efficiency of working.

Transfers within the LMR took the 2-6-0s to such places as Nuneaton, Bolton, Barrow, Toton and Derby, mainly for trip or pick up work but most unexpected was the batch transferred to Willesden, and a visit to this shed

Cross country links and pilot work at provincial stations was the very stuff of the Class 2 Moguls. 78063 at Rugby in the declining years of such jobs, 7 May 1963. Photograph B.P. Hoper Collection.

was the only time I saw any of the class in steam days. By June 1965 the following were based in London, 78003, 78018, 78019, 78029, 78032-78035, 78038, 78039, 78043, 78058-78060 and 78063 and they proved able performers on e.c.s. duties in and out of Euston, last in a long line of engines (traditionally elderly 0-6-0s - ex-MR and ex-LNW) for which nobler work could no longer be found.

DEMISE
1963. November, 78015.
1964. February, 78009. **July,** 78048, 78053. **September,** 78005.
1965. February, 78024, 78025. **June,** 78000. **September,** 78011, 78014, 78027, 78042. **October,** 78029, 78030, 78032, 78033, 78043. **November,** 78004. **December,** 78001, 78006, 78035, 78054.
1966. January, 78034, 78040, 78045, 78050,

78052. **May,** 78057. **June,** 78002. **July,** 78056. **August,** 78016, 78026, 78038, 78049. **September,** 78010, 78022, 78047. **October,** 78008, 78031, 78039, 78060. **November,** 78018, 78019, 78046, 78051, 78059, 78061. **December,** 78003, 78017, 78036, 78058, 78063, 78064.
1967. February, 78028, 78055. **May,** 78007, 78012, 78013, 78020, 78021, 78023, 78037, 78041, 78044, 78062.

More pottering. 78061 at Burscough Bridge with the 12.40pm 'Wigan Parcels', 6 March 1964. It was for just such duties, in between more demanding and lucrative roles, that the Class 2s were designed. Unfortunately, by this time the racier jobs had disappeared. Photograph B.P. Hoper Collection.

Above. The BR 80000 tank was the Fairburn engine modified to fit the L1 loading gauge. Though mixed traffic, they went almost exclusively to bolster areas where longer distance, heavier suburban/country traffic needed more up to date power. This meant the Southern, (which had already built over forty Fairburn tanks to cover a shortfall in such locomotives), Scotland (for Glasgow passenger work) and the hard-pressed LT&S section. Smaller groups went to the forefront of commuter working - what were often regarded as 'business trains' - out of Euston for instance. 80027 is at Polmadie on 21 June 1952; it was one of the first Scottish engines, built at Brighton and arriving at Glasgow in January that year. Photograph J. Robertson, B.P. Hoper Collection.

Below. 80007 of the Derby batch (Brighton got started earlier, with 80010) at Polmadie on 8 May 1954. Photograph J. Robertson, B.P. Hoper Collection.

9. 80000 2-6-4Ts 1951-1967

Less well known is the curious fact that at no time were *all* 999 Standard locomotives in operation simultaneously, quite apart from visits to works .... At the end of August 1962 the first BR Standard steam locomotive was condemned - Class 4 2-6-4T No.80103. ....it was a harbinger of things to come, for during the latter half of 1962 the slaughter of BR steam stock was particularly savage. From that time on, nothing was sacred. *The First One To Go*, by Philip Atkins, *British Railways Illustrated* August 1996.

The aim, in the case of the notional BR 4MT tank, had been to continue the building of the successful Fairburn design of the LMS, which could be traced back, through Stanier, to Fowler's design of 1927. But this foundered on the question of fitting the design within the L1 loading gauge. The BR 2-6-4T was therefore an outcome of Riddles/Cox thinking; it became a very successful one, outshone - it could be said - only by the final Standard design, the mighty 9F 2-10-0. Brighton was the design office responsible for producing a tank that would fit inside the universal L1 loading; the Fairburn was too large for this, though more were built at Brighton in the interim, for the Southern - 42066-42106 during 1950 and 1951.

For the new class to conform with the loading requirements the solid, square, LMS outline was reformed, imparting subtle and distinctive curves which were absent from the earlier LM classes. This was the reason for the marked inward curve of the cabsides, bunker and side tanks. Thus the Class 4 2-6-4T was born, eventually totalling 155 locos numbered 80000-80154. Brighton was responsible for the overall design though detail work came from Derby, Doncaster and Swindon. All but twenty five were constructed at Brighton, Derby turning out fifteen and Doncaster the other ten.

The L1 loading gauge dictated the use of smaller cylinders than those employed on the Fairburn design. To compensate for the reduced

size the boiler pressure was increased to 225lb/sq in, giving a tractive effort of 25,515lb compared to the 24,670lb of the Fairburn. The boiler itself was the same as the Class 4 4-6-0: this was the Ivatt c

Class 4 boiler but with modifications to make it the BR type 5. It proved to be free steaming and gave the 2-6-4Ts a good acceleration. Modifications included the replacement of the Stanier pattern top feed system (as used on the Fairburns) by the Southern-style clack valves and external rather than internal rodding linking the cab regulator handle with the regulator in the dome.

Another restriction to meet the BR L1 constraints was the inset bufferbeam, which meant that, while the maximum width of the engine was 8ft 9in, the width across the footsteps was 7ft 7$\frac{1}{2}$in. This was the only standard class to carry oval buffers, quite a visual contrast with the original LMS engines. In full working order with full tanks of 2,000 gallons (100 less than the Fairburns) and 3$\frac{1}{2}$ tons of coal, the engines weighed in at 86$\frac{1}{2}$ tons, with 53 tons available for adhesion on the coupled wheelbase, as follows:-

Leading coupled 17 tons 7 cwt
Middle coupled 17 tons 19 cwt
Rear coupled 17 tons 15 cwt

The trailing bogie was similar to the class 4 4-6-0 leading bogie and the wheel diameter, 3ft, was the same as the leading two wheels.

The 80000 tanks were close sisters to the 75000s, introduced the same year (1951); motion components were largely duplicated between the two classes though the coupled wheelbase of the tanks was 4in larger at 15ft 4in. For the convenience of the crews footsteps were incorporated on the back of the bunker and a level recess on the rear corners so footplatemen could climb into the coal space. Ventilation holes were cut in the cab weatherboards. The principal difference in 'the look' of the 2-6-4Ts derived from their fully welded and *curving* side tanks; designed to fit the engines within a tighter loading gauge, these were wholly unlike the Fairburns, which had a riveted, upright construction.

Advance publicity in 1951 declared that the first 54 of the 2-6-4Ts then ordered and under construction were to be divided between the Southern Region (10), Scotland (21), the London Midland (20) with a mere three to the North Eastern Region. Subsequently the Eastern Region received its quota as well and thus one presumes the Western Region was happy with its Churchward Prairies. The original allocations planned for the class were as follows:-

ScR 80000-80009, 80020-80030, 80054-80058, 80106-80115, 80121-80130.
SR 80010-80019, 80145-80154.
NER 80031-80033.
LMR 80034-80053, 80059-80068, 80081-80095.
ER 80069-80080, 80096-80105, 80116-80120, 80131-80144.

80146, powering its way through the Southern chalk in the 1950s. The 2-6-4T was ideal for much of the work in southern England; they could run important morning trains into Victoria or wherever, hoist out heavy trains of commuters in the evening to smart timings, and still ramble around during the day with a couple of coaches, alone with the skylarks. Photograph Ted's Dad.

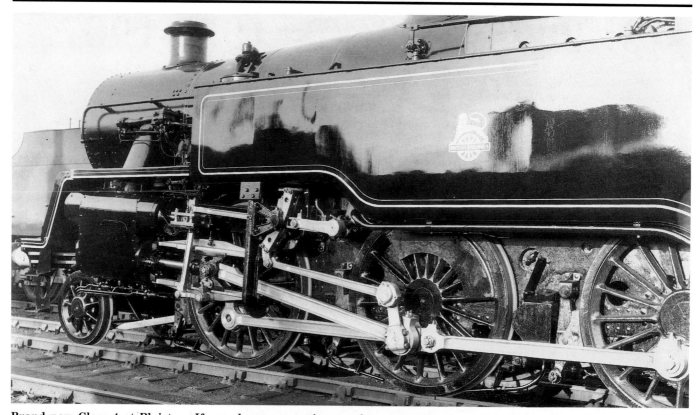

Brand new Class 4 at Plaistow. If anywhere was crying out for new power it was the LT&S, for it enjoyed even then something of its later 'misery line' reputation. The injection of brand new locomotives aided reliability but the men always preferred a good Stanier three cylinder engine and the line increasingly suffered from manpower shortages. Thameside boomed as the 1950s advanced and it was one of the first areas to reveal that, given well paid jobs in clean conditions without heavy, dirty, manual labour, workers, not surprisingly, deserted engine shed and steam locomotive work in droves. Oddly, the first BR Standard to be withdrawn, 80103, ended its time at Plaistow, in 1962. A shaken fitter called the foreman over to the pit to see a frame broken so badly that the fire was ordered out and the engine stopped immediately. When 80103 later went to Stratford, for safety's sake it travelled between two other engines.

80000 appeared in September 1952 from Derby Works, fourteen months after the first one, 80010, came out of Brighton - by which time Brighton had completed up to 80046 of the first order. 80010, unveiled in July 1951, went new to Tunbridge Wells West along with 80011-80019. 80000, when new, was based at Ayr so there was very little chance of seeing 80000 and 80010 alongside one another, especially as the Regions on which the class were based were

originally responsible for their maintenance. The exceptions were the NER (for which the ScR was responsible) and the Eastern. At the same time that 80000 went to Ayr, 80045 and 80046 from Brighton went new to Bedford. The remaining nine of the first Derby order, 80001-80009, were complete by the December, all going to Scottish sheds. Derby did not build more of the class until December 1954 when 80054-80058 appeared and again these engines went

new to Scotland, all to Polmadie, with 80058 arriving in January 1955. Doncaster completed its one order, 80106-80115, between October and December 1954, and again all went to Scottish sheds. Otherwise the rest of the class were completed at Brighton, the last one, 80154, emerging in March 1957. Like 80145-80153 it did not have far to travel for its first shed, going across the way to - Brighton. All this Brighton batch finished their working days at Southern

Unusual overview, at Holbeck on 27 April 1963. Photograph Ray Farrell.

sheds, mainly on the South Western section. 80154 was the last steam engine to be constructed at Brighton but sadly did not survive the cutter's torch, at Buttigiegs, Newport, 1967, after withdrawal from Nine Elms.

First of the Brighton engines to reach Scotland was 80020 which, like a lot of its sisters, had a daunting journey north from Brighton - its first shed was Kittybrewster, Aberdeen. This began a Scottish association with the class that lasted until the end of steam north of the border, seventeen years later. By then, but not from new, 80045-80047, 80049, 80051-80053, 80060-80063, 80071, 80073-80077, 80086, 80090-80093 and 80116-80120 had arrived in Scotland to finish off their days, a number of them exiled from the LT&S lines. Scotland made good use of this class, on various suburban services out of Glasgow and Edinburgh, their good acceleration put to good effect from Glasgow to the Lanarkshire towns and the Clyde coast resorts. The Kittybrewster allocation was employed on the one-time GNofSR lines out of Aberdeen including the branch to Ballater. Later they were used on the Dumfries to Stranraer line, as bankers on Beattock, on transfer freights around Glasgow, short haul goods traffic in Ayrshire and the border counties, and saw out the last rites on the Killin branch in Central Scotland.

Withdrawals of the class from the Scottish Region began in 1964 with 80030 and 80049 going from Corkerhill in June. At the same time the LMR was disposing of some of the tanks it had just acquired from the ScR, such as 80056, once of Eastfield, transferred to Lostock Hall in September 1964 only to be condemned the following month - one of the few cut up by BR, at Crewe Works, in November 1964. 80125 moved from Stirling to Lostock Hall in August 1964

and was withdrawn in the October and cut up by Maden & McKee, Stanley, Liverpool. 80129 suffered exactly the same fate as 80125 but was scrapped at Crewe Works whilst 80044 and 80050 both moved from Corkerhill to Bangor in July 1964. Both were withdrawn in the November. But while 80044 finished its days at Crewe Works in January 1965, 80050 survived until the middle of 1965 before being cut up at Central Wagon Co., Ince, Wigan.

May 1967 was the final month for the class in Scotland and the last ones in service were 80045 (Polmadie), 80046 (Corkerhill), 80086, 80116 and 80120 (Polmadie). 80045, 80046, 80116 and 80120 were cut up at Campbells, Airdrie and 80086 met its end at McWilliams, Shettleston.

The NER had just five of the class from new, 80116-80120, the first one going new to York and the others to Whitby, where they worked the coast line south to Scarborough. By 1957 80116 was also a Whitby engine and in May 1958 they were all reallocated to Leeds Neville Hill. They left the NER in the autumn of 1963, going to Scotland where they finished their days. Six others had a brief period on the NER when 80071 and 80073-80077 arrived at Ardsley in December 1962, all from March. They spent less than a year working from Ardsley before they were all moved north of the border in October 1963, mainly to Carstairs.

On the LMR the class first saw service out of Watford, Bletchley and Kentish Town sheds, on London commuter services. They carried out similar duties in the Manchester area when working out of Newton Heath and Bury, working in tandem with the existing Stanier and Fairburn tanks.

By the 1960s thirty five of the LMR allocation had either migrated to Scotland or been

exchanged for SR Fairburns. It is said that the SR came off worse in the deal, but certainly Watford, which saw its immaculate BR tanks swapped for scruffy run-down Fairburns, did not agree...

A route which benefited greatly from the introduction of the BR 2-6-4Ts was the London, Tilbury and Southend which had an intensive commuter timetable. Plaistow first received one, 80069, in September 1953; this was followed right through to 80080, delivered in March 1954. To complete the allocation 80096-80105 came between November 1954 and April 1955 and 80131-80136 from March to May 1956. These engines worked fast, 300 ton trains out of London's Fenchurch Street station. Once the LTS lines were electrified the class became redundant, more or less at a stroke. They were too modern to send straight to the scrapyard (except for 80103, which had suffered damage); some went to Stratford in June 1962 to work on the Liverpool Street suburban trains, but this only lasted for three months before the engines moved onto the WR.

When Plaistow closed a good number of engines were in store there and along with a group of friends, I paid a visit late on an autumn Sunday afternoon. At the end we were filthy and, in the gathering dark, walked back through the large graveyard to the District line station. I became re-acquainted with some of these engines in August 1962, during the school holidays when a friend and myself paid a mid-week visit to Old Oak Common - there we found a good number of the Class 4s in store, minus their smokebox numberplates. I still have one of my few surviving photographs from steam days and it shows a line of these engines with a member of staff cycling in between them. What it does not show is the (BR) man stopping by

The Standard principle at work. 80065 was one of the Watford BR 2-6-4Ts working important business trains in and out of Euston - but here is a 2-6-4T between times, hauling a hefty up Saturday pick up goods south of Tring yard, 3 October 1953. The Watford 2-6-4Ts were lavished with care and there was much grumbling when the Southern 'repatriated' its often scruffy and run-down Fairburns for Standard 4MTs off the LM - 'short changing' was easily the most printable description.. Photograph E.D. Bruton.

The end of the 'big tanks' in Scotland coincided with the end of steam itself, in April 1966, and on the last day 80116 and 80120 were in steam at Polmadie. The 2-6-4Ts had predominated for some time - this is the scene at Polmadie on 26 September 1965 with, left to right, 80118, 80086, 80120 and 80027. Photograph Ken Fairey.

each engine and checking the numbers in his Ian Allan *ABC!* In the main these were in transit either to WR sheds or to the ScR or SR. I cannot say whether every single one of the LTS allocation were stored at Old Oak but they eventually finished their days on the Regions thus:-

WR 80072, 80078-80080, 80097-80101, 80104, 80105, 80131, 80135 and 80136
SR 80069, 80070, 80096, 80102, 80132-80134
ScR 80071, 80073-80077

In September 1962 80103, only seven years old, was not only the first of the class to be withdrawn but also the first of the Standards to go. It was stored at Plaistow for a couple of months and was moved to Stratford in September 1962, the same month that a party from my school were given a guided tour. The great, rambling depot was deep in the process of changing to diesel and the only steam engines we saw were in the scrap lines. I was in the forefront of our guided party, frustrated at having seen only a couple of B1s, destined for scrap at Doncaster. I found 80103, climbed into the cab and stuck my head out of the bunker as tour, guide and teachers came round the corner, the latter not amused. 80103 was scrapped at Stratford Works the same month.

80000s allocated to the WR ended up mainly working on the Cambrian lines out of such sheds as Shrewsbury, Croes Newydd and Machynlleth. Others went to Swansea East Dock to work over the Central Wales line to Shrewsbury. This included 80069 which was recorded on a Swansea to Shrewsbury train in June 1964 - the engine was withdrawn from Nine Elms in January 1966.

The original SR allocations were 80010-80019 and 80145-80154, the first and last orders from Brighton Works, and they all stayed true to the Region. With one hundred and twenty constructed at Brighton many worked on Southern metals, even if only on running in turns or working through to their first sheds. The final tally of the class on the SR was over sixty, ending their days at Southern sheds or one-time SR sheds taken over by the WR. The final list was

80010-80019, 80031-80043, 80059, 80064-80066, 80068-80070, 80081-80085, 80087-80089, 80094-80096, 80102, 80132-80134 and 80137-80154. Which actually totals up to sixty three, for some only spent their last few months on the Southern. Duties embraced all of the SR, from the Kent Coast in the east to the 'withered arm' in deepest Cornwall in the west. See for instance *From Kent to Cornwall*, a three part article on Standard Tanks on the Southern in *British Railways Illustrated*, May - July 1996 (Irwell Press).

In May 1964 80040 from Laira was the second of the class to be withdrawn, and was scrapped at Crewe Works in the July. No less than thirty more followed that year including 80010, the first-built in June, from Brighton. The end was more than nigh.....

DEMISE
1962. September 80103.
1964. May 80040. June 80010, 80030, 80049, 80087 and 80148. July 80008, 80021, 80052, 80053, 80071, 80073, 80074, 80075, 80076 and 80127. September 80009, 80017, 80031, 80038, 80107. October 80056, 80062, 80077, 80106, 80115, 80125 and 80129. November 80036, 80044 and 80050.
1965. January 80042. February 80003. March 80035, 80090, 80149 and 80153. April 80018. May 80014, 80066, 80099, 80108, 80110 and 80131. June 80020, 80022, 80067, 80070, 80081, 80084, 80088, 80119 and 80147. July 80048, 80072, 80078, 80079, 80080, 80097, 80098, 80100, 80101, 80104, 80105, 80135 and 80136. September 80064. October 80023, 80137 and 80150. November 80059 and 80109. December 80029, 80096 and 80102.
1966. January 80034 and 80132. February 80039, 80060, 80069 and 80141. March 80037, 80041, 80043, 80117 and 80142. May 80144. June 80013, 80054 and 80121. July 80001, 80007, 80058 and 80094. August 80005, 80024, 80025, 80047, 80051, 80063, 80083, 80112, 80123 and 80130. September 80006, 80026, 80028, 80055, 80065, 80082, 80092, 80093 and 80113. October 80033, 80068,

80089, 80095 and 80138. November 80027, 80091, 80111, 80118 and 80126. December 80000, 80057, 80061, 80114, 80122 and 80124. **1967. January 80032. March 80002, 80012 and 80019. April 80128 and 80154. May 80004, 80045, 80046, 80086, 80116, 80120 and 80151. June 80145. July 80011, 80015, 80016, 80085, 80133, 80134, 80139, 80140, 80143, 80146, 80152.**

On Standards
By Bert Hooker

The only BR Standards I had any regard for were the Class 3 Tankies and the Class 4 tender engines with double chimneys. The former were compact, cosy, willing little engines which were like a breath of fresh air after our ageing M7 0-4-4Ts, which were just about clapped out. The 3s were ideal locomotives for empty stock working and the van trains which always seemed to be on the move in the Waterloo area. They were fitted with a ratchet steam brake (as were all the Standards) and were a delight to us on the shunting jobs, the only drawback to that type of work being winding the 'bacon slicer' wheel reverser to and fro, although it was seldom necessary to go to full forward or reverse to get them to move. The little 3s were speedy, quite economical with coal and water and the driver had a good look out in either direction. It was easy to keep down the dust and keep the footplate clean and I appreciated that. For the class of work we had at Nine Elms I would prefer a 3 to a 4 Tankie; on our outer suburban work to Basingstoke the reverse would have to apply but a tender locomotive was usually provided for those jobs.

I considered the Standard Class 4 tender engines with the double chimneys much superior to the single blast ones as they steamed more freely and were not so noisy, in addition to being able to run without too much effort. I was just as happy on a double chimney 4 as on a class 5 except on heavy boat trains when the extra power was needed. The 5s gave one a harsh ride and, especially when run down, lateral play would develop in the trailing axleboxes. The driving wheels would gouge a furrow in the main frames and when that was spotted you'd know the locomotive would 'wag her tail', with consequently a rougher ride than usual - though at least it kept the fire on the move! The 5s were cold, draughty engines for the driver during wintertime, especially the early ones, so it was not uncommon to see a headboard stuck in behind the seat to ward off the draughts on the driver's back. They had one redeeming factor though - at least there was a clear view of the road ahead. But they were not an engineman's engine, needing to be driven fairly hard (by my standards) to keep up the boiler pressure. I discovered that on my first main line trip with one - a non stop to Salisbury. The fireman 'Bill Botten advised me to use ear plugs and 'open her up' which I did with the desired result.

The Standards were produced when shed maintenance was falling in some parts of the country; they were robust and easy to maintain with their self cleaning smokeboxes, rocking and drop grates and hoppers, but even so they were harder to fire than a Bulleid Pacific. When I had a turn on the shovel I could never get them in the palm of my hand - I would be watching them all the time. To my mind they were hard coal engines and did not take kindly to the 2nd grade Welsh coal supplied to Nine Elms. Some chaps would fill the fireboxes, then thrash them along to get the fire alight and though the locomotives thrived on this treatment, it went against my grain.

One Bank Holiday Sunday my mate Bob Payne and I worked down to Salisbury with the 16.00 ex Waterloo, having an excellent trip with a Merchant Navy. After relief we walked to the Depot to prepare a Standard 5 to work a special to Waterloo, picking up our empties in the sidings adjacent to the loco. The ten-

der was loaded up with ovoids but Bob was careful with the preparation of the fire, giving the bars a good shake to dislodge the inevitable dust, after which the hoppers were cleared. Bob built up a good fire with the wretched briquettes (while I oiled around) adding a few at a time as the previous lot burnt through. By starting time the needle was on the red line and the water bobbing in and out of the top nut on the gauge glasses, an excellent start. But we struggled up through Porton with 160 psi, an inch of water in the glass and the injector had not been started! Half a mile further on the boiler feed HAD to go on, the exhaust injector was set on minimum range and the pressure was still falling despite Bob's efforts. As we turned the top of the bank just before Grateley I shut the regulator, even though the water level was very low. The water range on the injector was opened up and I was thankful we did not have to make a sudden stop, as that would have possibly made the water flow off the crown sheet and uncover the fusible plugs, which is disaster. However we coasted down the bank into Andover, now with about half a glass of water. I ran the locomotive off the platform ramp, grabbed the rocker bar as we came to a stand and hit the ground, I opened the ashpan hoppers and immediately the roar of the fire altered and the glow in the ashpan brightened. I regained the footplate and the difference in the fire was already apparent. Bob asked, 'What have you done Bert?'. 'I've opened the hoppers, Bob, we'll see what happens now'. The boiler was gaining steam and water as we stood awaiting the 'right away' and upon receiving that we departed, determined to regain the time lost on the first leg. I hustled her along but the open hoppers left a trail of red hot cinder along the track and I hoped none would bounce into adjacent fields with possible claims against British Railways for crop damage! We regained the lost minutes as the boiler was steaming freely, proving to me that the primary air intake was insufficient to deal with the ovoids. I've seen Basingstoke men go along with their

new Standard 4s with the hoppers open when burning soft coal but the steaming was improved when double chimneys were fitted. With hard coal, primary air was needed of course but more secondary was needed to burn the coal satisfactorily and to kill the smoke.

I disliked the tenders with their inadequate shovelling plates which were made too short (by 6 or 8 inches) so that when the tender was full of coal the fireman was continually picking it up off the floorboards until 'it got back a bit', this was typically an LMS failing and I sighed for the ideal shovelling plates as on the Nelsons, King Arthurs and Bulleid Pacifics on which the coal would feed forward without dropping onto the floorboards.

I did not have any main line experience on the 'Brits' as a driver or fireman except for a couple of trips to Norwich from Liverpool Street. I found them fast, free running locomotives in the hands of their regular crews but the riding was not of West Country quality. On the Great Eastern, of course, they were very popular.

As regards the Standard Class 4 2-6-0s I had one on a Summer Saturday up from Southampton to Waterloo on one of the Lymington trains and it was a good 'un until the injector was started! But I must say the locomotive was very economical on water, coming up from Southampton on about a thousand gallons less than a WC though, I hasten to add, not with the same sectional timing competence. On the running ground east of Basingstoke and moving at 70 mph the engine was a good more stable than a Maunsell U or N 2-6-0. I looked over the side at the rods and they were just a blur as the small driving wheels revolved. The front end was excellent, admitting steam and releasing it without hesitation.

I did most of my driving of the Standards on the class 5s, 73110 was the best of the class that came my way, give me a good King Arthur, but then I'm a Southern man!

80146 again, this time with a run of vans Weymouth - Bournemouth, passing Upwey on 3 July 1967. Though by this time the engine would be relegated to such duties as this, it nevertheless illustrates that versatility once more. Photograph S.C. Nash.

82018 passing Exmouth Junction. It came there early on, in 1952, after a brief spell at Redhill and stayed for ten years. It ended its days on the Waterloo empty stock trains. Photograph J. Robertson, B.P. Hoper Collection.

10. 82000 2-6-2Ts 1952-1967

The Class 3 2-6-0 and 2-6-2T proved to be somewhat unnecessary, owing to the upgrading of routes, which meant that much of the work they had been designed for could be undertaken by Class 4 engines. *A detailed history of British Railways Standard Steam Locomotives, Volume One*, **Railway Correspondence and Travel Society.**

The Class 3 2-6-2Ts were originally included in the building programme of 1951 but the first, 82000, did not emerge from Swindon Works until April 1952. The engines were numbered 82000-82044, and all were constructed at Swindon. 82000-82019 appeared between April 1952 and September of that year; there was a gap of two years before 82020 was completed in September 1954, and then engines followed at regular intervals to the last, 82044, which entered service in August 1955. It was withdrawn ten years later in November 1965, from Bath Green Park.

The public 'unveiling' came in *The Railway Magazine*, in July 1952 - an advantage of the new engines, it was declared, was their 'almost universal availability over main and secondary routes in Great Britain.' 82000 had the usual standard features as the account tells us: *'The rocking grate, self emptying ashpan and controls are similar in design to those on other Classes of standard locomotives. The boiler mountings, regulator, clack valves are similar to those fitted to the Classes 4 and 5 standard locomotives, as is also the smokebox self-cleaning equipment.'*

When the type was first mooted it was felt that a tank of intermediate power was required to work within a 16½ ton axle weight; parent office for the design was Swindon though

certain sections were done at other offices including Brighton, Derby and Doncaster. 'There was no existing LMR boiler in this category, or at least none that was sufficiently satisfactory' Cox relates in *British Railways Standard Steam Locomotives*; it was decided eventually to use the flanging blocks of the Swindon 5100 2-6-2Ts, but 'in all other respects the locomotives were built as first diagrammed, conforming to the general standardisation in all their details.' However, this original design was domeless and to allow the fitting of standard components to the 82000 version, such as regulator and top feed, a dome was provided with the standard clack valves placed astride the front ring of the boiler. There was a water capacity of 1,500 gallons in the side tanks, three tons of coal (maximum) in the bunker and a boiler pressure of 200lb per sq. in., which resulted in a tractive effort of 21,490lb. The pony trucks were similar to those on the Class 4 tanks with a wheel diameter of 3ft. Driving wheels were 5ft 3in diameter.

In full working order the new engines weighed 74 tons 1 cwt. The straight sided tanks and bunker were of welded construction throughout; their high tops made for relatively poor forward visibility and this was not helped by the cab spectacles, which were on the small side. The overall width of the locos was 8ft 6in, which put them within the L1 loading gauge.

There was a considerable amount of pipework hidden under the running plate, with a pair of live steam injectors below the fireman's side of the cab. Whilst the mechanical lubricators were mounted on the very front of the running plate they were in front of the outside steam pipes and the front driving wheel and motion. Metal plates shielded the front of the mechanical lubricators though some of these went missing in the last days of steam. BR mixed traffic black was the first livery though both lined and unlined green was applied to engines allocated to WR sheds. Principle strongholds became the SR and WR, with a few based on the NER where they became familiar for working over the Stainmore route, and on the equally spectacular Yorkshire coast. When new the 82000s were allocated as follows:-
Western Region: 82000-82009, 82030-82044
Southern Region: 82010-82025
North Eastern Region: 82026-82029

I saw a few, 82006, 82010-82019 and 82022-82029, mainly during three visits to Swindon Works in steam days when some were in for overhaul, but all the other entries in my *ABCs* came about through engines ending up at Nine Elms for empty stock working between Waterloo and Clapham Junction. In the last days of steam I often travelled up to Waterloo from my

82016, with 76061 beyond, at Eastleigh on 22 August 1959. As there was no LMS boiler in the Class 3 range, an entirely new design was prepared; suitable flanging blocks were available, for the GW 5100 tanks, and so Swindon had the task of building the Class 3s, tank and tender. Photograph Stephen Gradidge.

82016 again, in company with 82014, at Fawley on 13 May 1960. Both had been at Eastleigh since 1952. Photograph J.H. Aston.

home in Weybridge by electric train and usually the Class 3s could be observed going about their business.

Of the first twenty, introduced between April and September of 1952, 82000-82009 went to Tyseley on the WR and 82010-82019 to the Southern, at Exmouth Junction (82010-82013, 82017); Eastleigh (82014-82016) and Redhill (82018, 82019).

Working on West Midlands suburban trains, the Tyseley contingent did not prove too popular with drivers, who preferred their GWR tanks. The main reason was, as ever, the driving position - left hand on the Class 3s and right hand on the GWR types. Drivers grumbled at having to lean out of the window to view the signals which were, of course, sited for GWR engines. Throughout May 1952 82000 was rostered to work the 8.45am Westbury to Swindon local and in the same month 82004 was reported working between Weston-super-Mare and Bristol, with 82002 noted at Banbury. The group that arrived at Exmouth Junction was reported to have taken the lion's share of the Exmouth branch work and also the Sidmouth branch. In July 1953 82000 went on loan to Barry and either it proved popular or Tyseley wanted rid of its engines, for in the September 82000 was moved to Treherbert and 82001-82009 to Barry. Right through the following year the 82000s were seen working in the Cardiff area and on holiday trains to Barry Island. The three engines at Eastleigh were noted working on the Fawley branch, which lost its passenger service in February 1966. 82017 later moved from Exmouth Junction to Eastleigh.

In the summer of 1954 Swindon began the final batch, 82020-82044 completed in August 1955. They were allocated as follows:- Exmouth Junction: 82020-82025; Kirkby Stephen: 82026, 82027; Darlington: 82028, 82029; Barry: 82030-82032, 82035, 82036, 82039-82044; Newton Abbot: 82033, 82034, 82038; Swansea Victoria: 82037.

Perhaps the most interesting of these allocations was to the NER, 82026-82029 in November/December 1954. Over the next few years these engines were recorded at work over the Pennines on the Stainmore route, a line well served by the lighter members of the Standard classes, the 2MT, 3MT and 4MT 2-6-0s. The Class 3 tanks were normally used on the lighter passenger trains, Penrith - Darlington, or the six coach Saltburn - Penrith. By 1960 82026-82029 had moved to the coast, at Scarborough, and at the end of 1962 82026 was at Low Moor and the others at Malton. The sort of services which suited the 82000s were succumbing either to the axe or to dmus and, as with many of the Standard classes, a process of grouping into strongholds, to ease maintenance in the last years, began. To this end the NER examples moved south in September 1963, 82026, 82027 and 82029 to Guildford and 82028 to Bournemouth - all four were 'down south' by December. During what was to be a short stay, 82027 was observed working a two coach train on the Swanage branch. Eventually all four were based at Nine Elms from where they could be seen on e.c.s. duties - see above - between Clapham Junction and Waterloo and on the suburban service between Clapham Junction and Kensington Olympia. 82029, along with 82019, which had always been an SR engine, survived until the end of steam on the Region in July 1967. On the last day of service 82019 was noted as a Waterloo station pilot and in the afternoon worked the Clapham Junction to Kensington Olympia service. Both engines were stored at Salisbury and cut up at Birds, Risca early in 1968.

The 3MT tanks were another of the Standards used on the Somerset & Dorset but not with the success experienced with the others. They were introduced by the WR in 1958 for local services and examples were based at Bath Green Park and Templecombe. These included 82001 and 82002 at Templecombe between April 1961 and September 1962; 82004

at Green Park from October 1959 until withdrawn in October 1965; 82039 at Templecombe from February 1959 to September 1960; 82041 at Green Park from March 1959 until withdrawn in December 1965. 82030 was withdrawn from Gloucester Horton Road in August 1965, reinstated to Green Park in the November and at last withdrawn in January 1966. 82044 was also withdrawn from Gloucester in August 1965, duly reinstated to Green Park in the September and withdrawn in November. Green Park used its small complement for local trains over the Midland line to Bristol Temple Meads as well as on the S&D. The Class 3s were little used over the Mendips as the operating authorities felt they were underpowered for the steep starts from the S&D stations. They were not closely associated with the S&D but one regular working was the 6.05pm (SX) Bath to Binegar and the 7.20pm return - 82041 in fully lined green livery was noted working out of Bath on February 28th 1959 on a local to Bristol Temple Meads and from March of that year it stayed on the S&D, until withdrawal in December 1965. The last WR based Class 3 2-6-2T, 82001, was withdrawn in December 1965 from Bath Green Park.

In 1958 Bristol Bath Road shed started to receive some, starting with 82001 and 82003 in the March, and both stayed until the August. Over the next two years the following spent different periods of time at the shed, 82002, 82005-82007, 82009, 82030 and 82032-82044. In 1959 they were still working out of Bristol - in November 82030, now at Barrow Road, was noted on a train working from Andover to Swindon Town.

The first year of the 'sixties still saw some of the 82000s at Bristol Bath Road. By now the class was spreading around the WR and although 82004, 82006 and 82009 left Newton Abbot in the middle of 1959, the West Country still saw them, Taunton gaining an allocation in November 1961 - 82008, 82030,

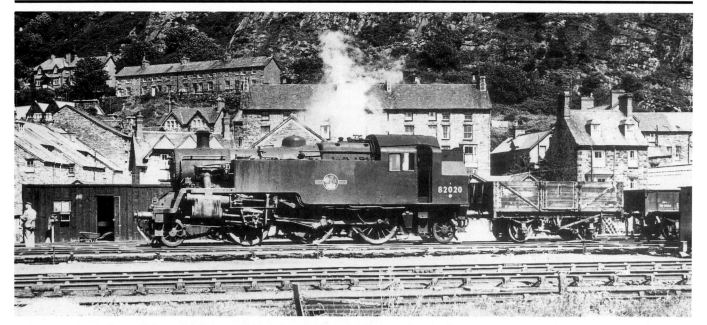

82020 at Barmouth, 19 July 1962. This would be the plain green livery, which emphasised the high flat sides of the tanks and subtly altered the whole look of the locomotive. There were a number of subtle variations in this class in fact - the WR lamp irons on the front seemed far more prominent than usual and there were livery differences, the Western applying two sorts of green, lined and unlined. The number could appear on the tank side rather than the bunker side and there were of course the 'mods' familiar from many of the other Standards - rectangular section rods and the addition of a speedometer. Photograph Stephen Gradidge.

82042 and 82044, with 82001 and 82043 arriving in December 1963 and January 1962 respectively. Elsewhere, Machynlleth, at the heart of the Cambrian, received several early in 1960: 82031 in January, 82020 in February and 82021 in March. These were later followed by 82003, 82005, 82006, 82008, 82009, 82032-82034 and 82036. In September 1961 82031 and a 2251 Class 0-6-0 double headed the Pwllheli portion of the Cambrian Coast Express. A regular working was to act as pilot to a Manor 4-6-0, often with twelve carriages on, either from Machynlleth or Aberystwyth over Talerddig Summit, the Class 3 staying on until arrival at Shrewsbury to save a light engine path on the single line.

There were transfers from Bath Road to St Phillip's Marsh by 1962 and transfers from Machynlleth in April 1965 saw 82000, 82003, 82005, 82006, 82009, 82020, 82021 and 82034 leaving Wales. Some went to Nine Elms but 82000, 82003, 82009 and 82034 made a surprise move north to Patricroft; for the first time the LMR had an allocation. 82031 joined them at Patricroft in June 1964 from Bangor, where it had moved in June 1964 from Machynlleth. (82033 also moved to Bangor in June 1964 but then proceeded to Nine Elms in April 1965). For a short period the Class 3s worked in the Manchester area and 82003 even appeared on the LCGB 'Cotton Spinner' rail tour at Manchester Central on April 16th 1966. 82009 was withdrawn in November 1966 and the following month 82000, 82003, 82031 and 82034 went the same way.

In 1954 BR had planned to build further examples, all at Swindon, 82045-82054 for the WR and 82055-82062 for the NER. This order was cancelled. With a left hand drive and poor forward vision the Class 3s were regarded as something of a nuisance on the Western. The engines had good acceleration but it has been written (a bit uncharitably) that they '...did not sparkle and on the road were little in advance of similarly sized machines of earlier vintage'. Their building was unnecessary as there was '...little or no real work for them to do.' They suffered,

like many of the Standard engines, especially on the Western, simply through not being what they replaced, and were frequently present only in very limited numbers. Crews therefore seldom had them for prolonged periods and they were easy victims of innate conservatism and suspicion of the new.

Simultaneously, civil engineering improvements meant that many of the routes over which the Class 3s were designed to run were passed to take the Class 4 tanks; this, together with loss of traffic and the fall of many services to the diesel multiple unit fleet sealed their fate on many lines. The late Derek Cross wrote that when withdrawn their passing was 'unwept by their drivers and unsung by the operating authorities' which seems now a little harsh. I'd wager a few preserved railways would like to

own one or two now. Their epitaph might be that they never had the chance, in sufficient numbers, to prove themselves.

DEMISE
1964. February 82002, 82008, 82043. May 82012, 82014. June 82007, 82013. August 82011, 82025. December 82015.
1965. April 82010, 82016, 82017. May 82032. July 82035, 82036, 82038-82040. August 82042. September 82005, 82020, 82033, 82037. October 82004, 82021, 82022. November 82044. December 82001, 82041.
1966. January 82027, 82030. February 82024. June 82018, 82026. September 82006, 82028. November 82009, 82023. December 82000, 82003, 82031, 82034.
1967. July 82019, 82029.

82026 makes a spirited passage through the trees, approaching Bournemouth Central on 9 June 1964. Photograph John Scrace.

That wonderful Willesden Exhibition of 1954, when an averagely filthy steam shed was closed off, cleaned to a level never seen anywhere before or since and repainted to Exhibition Hall standards. After getting all the locos in, the turntable was then covered so completely that the floor appeared continuous. The real miracle was in cleaning the complex roof structure, ridding it of years of accumulated soot, so that no rogue flake should fall on the shining exhibits below. 84019 had been new to Bury in the autumn of the previous year, and went to Fleetwood after the show. It is fairly safe to say that, like the Willesden roundhouse, 84019 is unlikely to have been cleaner than this, ever again.

11. 84000 2-6-2Ts 1953-1965

Though the smallest tank locomotives to be built in the British Railways standard range, they incorporate as far as practicable all the modern developments in design which have proved themselves on the larger types. A rocking grate with self-emptying ash-pan has been fitted, and the smokebox is self-cleaning. *The Railway Magazine*, **November 1953.**

The 84000s, appearing in 1953, merely represented a continuation of the Ivatt 2-6-2Ts introduced in 1946 by the LMS, 130 of which were in service when the BR version appeared. The new 2MT Standards had minor detail differences from the Ivatts and only 30 were built. The Ivatt forerunners weighed, in working order, 63 tons 5 cwt and the BR version 66 tons 5 cwt. So there were some differences but nothing of import - both had driving wheels of 5ft diameter for instance. The Ivatts were divided into two cylinder sizes, 41200-41289 having 16in x by 24in stroke while 41290-41329 had half an inch extra on the stroke; this meant the first group had a tractive effort of 17,410lb and the second 18,510lb. The 84000s, with cylinders of 16½ x 24in had a tractive effort of 18,515lb. A minor difference was apparent on the rear of the bunkers, the Ivatts having a ladder for access whilst the BR engines had steps and grab rails.

Like the other Standards, the Class 2 tanks were equipped with rocking grates, hopper ashpans and self cleaning smokeboxes which eased servicing. There was more welding in the construction of the 84000s compared to the Ivatts and they had different boiler feed clack valves in place of the LMS type. The Standards also carried external regulator rodding on the BR type 8 boiler. The water tanks held 1,350

gallons and the bunker had a maximum capacity of 3 tons. One major difference, compared with the other tank classes in the standard range, was the fitting of push-pull gear. This meant having regulator valves in the steam pipes and these were operated by a system of levers from the diaphragm vacuum cylinder, situated by the front of the smoke box.

Main design work was carried out at Derby though parts were designed at Brighton, Doncaster and Swindon. The boiler was the same as that used on the Class 2 2-6-0 (as with the existing Ivatt 2-6-0 and 2-6-2T) having a diameter tapering from 4ft 8in to 4ft 3in at the front. 'Features somewhat similar to the standard Class '3' tank engine' ran *The Railway Magazine* account, included crossheads, coupling and connecting rods. Skefko self-aligning roller bearings were also fitted to the return cranks.

With hindsight it is possible to wonder why this class was introduced at all; the Ivatt Class 2s had proved good performers on the road, easy to maintain and with a maximum axle loading of 13 tons 5 cwt on the middle driving wheels (the other two sets were 13 tons each) had a wide route availability. As mentioned above, in essence the 84000s (like the Class 2 2-6-0) were nothing but the further promulgation of the original LM type, so close were they in form and design. The 84000s were, in effect,

another batch of Ivatt's tanks, and this was the reasoning behind their production. This process can be recognised in four types among the Standards - the three Ivatt designs (Class 2 2-6-0 and 2-6-2T, and Class 4 2-6-0) and the 2-6-4T. Only the latter had to be substantially altered to fit the universal L1 loading gauge. As Cox says, the existing London Midland designs 'already included all of the design features for easier maintenance which it was desired to introduce, they were first-class performers in their different power categories and their low axle loads gave them the required route availability. They were already accepted for wide use outside their parent system on the Eastern, North Eastern and Southern Regions'.

The first twenty, 84000-84019 built at Crewe, appeared between July and October 1953 and all went to LMR sheds. The next ten did not appear for another four years, 84020-84029 delivered between March and June 1957 from Darlington works. This batch went to Southern sheds. The LMR remained responsible for the works maintenance of the whole class.

84000-84019 were fitted with push pull gear, though this was removed from most of them before withdrawal. In the early 1950s examples thus fitted were used on a number of traditional duties. They were the natural expression, if you like, of the BR Standard principle,

84010 on a typical duty (the 84000s were of course a continuation of the Ivatt 2-6-2Ts), the motor-worked 'Delph Donkey' - an Oldham Clegg Street to Delph train passing Measurements Halt. Photograph J. Davenport.

84028 in more familiar guise, encrusted with dirt and grease, at Tonbridge on 28 March 1959. Photograph Stephen Gradidge.

applied to branch line push pull duties that then existed in such profusion, unchanged since before the War. The 84000 tanks could perform all day on a branch formerly worked by some pre-Grouping 0-4-4T yet afforded their home sheds all the flexibility on freight and passenger work a modern powerful locomotive could offer. Servicing was easier, and they were more comfortable; so comfortable that some sheds had to be strong-armed into putting them to greater effect. As mentioned elsewhere, some sheds found that such engines were of more value on winter pilot 'waiting around' jobs - it made a foreman's job easier, to stop a crew moithering, but it subverted the aims and policies of the Standards as expounded by Riddles and Cox. It was rather as if LNW 0-8-0s had stayed on jobs whilst a new 9F had been kept back as 'spare' pottering about in place of an engine seeing out its days before works, just because the cab was more agreeable on a January night.

Many duties can be listed for the 84000s; a classic so far as the LMR was concerned could well be the Oldham to Delph shuttle, the 'Donkey'. The Delph to Greenfield line lost its passenger service as early as May 1955. 84000 and 84001 had gone new to Crewe North for the Northwich push pull, and there were many other examples. At the end of their working lives 84021-84024 were allocated to Crewe works, in July 1962 and here we had a case of a 'Midland'-designed, Darlington-built engine employed in the LNWR works. Crewe had the last word, withdrawing all four in September 1964 and after a short period of storage cut them up in the autumn of the same year.

Many of the duties for which the 84000 tanks were to have been such saviours soon disappeared, either with the closure of branch lines (as in the case of the Delph Donkey) or replacement by diesel multiple units. The first twenty were widely dispersed on the LMR and worked from London, up through the Midlands

and into the North West. The sheds ranged from Kentish Town, Neasden and Bedford, to Wellingborough via Crewe North, Llandudno Junction and Skipton, Bolton and Fleetwood. The duties covered the branches from Irchester Junction to Higham Ferrers; Llandudno Junction to Llandudno; Bradford to Penistone, Northampton to Wellingborough and Leicester to Burton-on-Trent. At one time Skipton had two on its books, 84015 from August 1958 until withdrawn in December 1965 and 84028 from September 1961, until it too was withdrawn, in December 1965. Both were scrapped at the Central Wagon Co., Ince, Wigan.

By their nature the 84000 2MTs spent most of their time on passenger trains, whatever the 'mixed traffic' notation, though they were frequently to be found on freights on the LNW - 84002 for instance (then of Rhyl) on the Gaerwen to Amlwch branch goods in 1962. 84005 of Bedford was noted in 1961 shunting at Chinnor on the truncated Watlington branch (closed between Watlington and Chinnor for freight in January 1961) and 84028 was recorded on the Barnoldswick freight to Skipton yard.

Several of the class finished their working days in North Wales, 84001, 84003, 84009 and 84020 bowing out at Llandudno Junction. They worked to Llandudno and on the branch to Amlwch - elsewhere in Wales 84000 and 84004 were withdrawn from Croes Newydd, in November 1965.

In the south it proved possible to see a number of the BR 2MT tanks, mainly on shed or from a passing train. I travelled quite widely in Kent and recorded all the SR examples, 84020-84029, when I spent time on Ashford station. Furtively consulting my ancient *ABC* I find 84002 and 84004, then of Bletchley, seen on visits to London sheds whilst 84005, 84006 and 84008 were noted during their short periods at Neasden. Both 84004 and 84005 could be found at Kentish Town a few months later.

84029 was at one time based at Neasden, the last of six sheds visited on our normal 'Sunday tour'; here 84005, 84008 and 84029 joined the list.

84009 was an odd one out as it spent a while in the north east; in 1957 it had been based at Royston and in June 1959 moved to Hull Dairycoates before returning to the LMR in December 1962. It went to Llandudno Junction, from where it was withdrawn in November 1965.

The Darlington engines, 84020-84029, made their way south to the Southern, 84020-84024 going new to Ashford and 84025-84029 new to Ramsgate. May 1959 saw Ramsgate lose its allocation to Ashford and for a couple of years this shed had a third of the class on its books. The 84000s were highly suited to the lightly loaded trains on the easily graded lines in the Ashford area and duties included Ashford to Maidstone locals, Maidstone to Dover workings, Ramsgate to Hastings and Minister to Shorncliffe trains. Although they replaced, in typical fashion, the old H 0-4-4Ts on passenger trains; they themselves were soon replaced by diesel or electric units. They stayed on the SR, mainly in the South East Section with some transfers to the Central and South Western Sections. These included 84020-84023 to Exmouth Junction in May 1961, 84028 and 84029 to Eastleigh in June 1961 and 84024-84027 to Brighton in May 1961. In September 1961 all ten were transferred to the LMR to various sheds mainly in the North West and thus, like the Britannia Pacifics, all the engines saw out their days on the LMR.

Oddly, the earlier Ivatt locos outlasted their Standard brethren, with the last of the BR engines (84010, 84013-84017, 84019, 84025, 84026 and 84028) withdrawn in December 1965. The Ivatt survivors worked until the last days of Southern steam in 1967. 84012 had been the first of the 84000s to go, in October 1963 from Southport. It was cut up at Crewe Works. Nine more went in 1964 - 84001, 84007, 84020, 84021-84024, 84027 and 84029, with the remainder withdrawn in 1965. In the autumn of 1965 the idea emerged of using the class on the Isle of Wight and ten were transferred 'on paper' to Eastleigh. Those involved were 84010 and 84016 of Fleetwood, 84013, 84014, 84017, 84026 of Stockport; 84015, 84028 of Skipton and 84019 and 84025 of Bolton. It is doubtful if any worked their way south though 84014 is reported to have reached Eastleigh. Eventually they were 'transferred' back to the LMR and withdrawn. A couple of reasons given for the failure of the venture was the cost of ferrying them over to the Island and the cost of adapting Ryde workshop for them. In any event steam finished on the Isle of Wight at the end of the following year.

84028 might have been preserved but like the others it is now just a memory - by way of footnote, the summer 1965 edition of *Push & Pull* (the journal of the Keighley & Worth Valley Railway) refers to 84028, 'thought to be ideal for the branch ... the locomotive is still in service at Skipton.' The spring 1967 edition reported the purchase of the Ivatt 2MT No.41241 for the line instead, and pondered the speculation regarding 84028. Soon after the 1965 report, a picture figured large in the June *Railway Magazine*, of 84028 being cut up! This was at the Central Wagon Co. of Ince, Wigan where 84010, 84015 and 84016 were also scrapped. It is a pity that none survived for they would have been at home on some of today's preserved railways. History continues to be re-wrought however, and 78059, of the comparable tender class and now based on the Bluebell Railway in Sussex, is - wonder - being converted into an 84000 tank. It should appear as 84030...

Above. 84025, with at least eight coaches, dwarfed by the Shakespeare Cliff on 5 August 1957. Photograph J. Robertson, B.P. Hoper Collection.

DEMISE
1963: October 84012
1964: January 84007: **May** 84027: **June** 84029: **September** 84021-84024: **October** 84001, 84020.

1965: April 84002, 84011, 84018: **October** 84000, 84003-84006, 84008: **November** 84009: **December** 84010, 84013-84017, 84019, 84025, 84026, 84028.

84005 (with forebear 41271 behind) at Bedford shed, 25 February 1956. The BR 2-6-2Ts were direct descendants of that great host of 0-4-4Ts and 2-4-2Ts and others, representatives of which could be found at many sheds well into the 1950s. Even before the full effect of passenger tanks such as the 84000s could be felt, diesel sets were robbing them of many duties. The closures of the 1960s rendered the decline in work precipitous. Many of us must now ponder the great 'might have been', of the 84000s and the Isle of Wight. Very soon it would have been the only conventional railway (not a specially preserved line) fully steam worked in western Europe; years before the fashion for chasing steam in ever more exotic locations, visitors would have flocked from the world over. And the locos would have been BR Standards - ironically of a type that was never preserved. Photograph Eric Sawford.

Above. One of those 'little and large' photographs beloved of the railways and used since before the turn of the century to demonstrate progress. The comparison is striking enough between the old LNW 2F 'Cauliflower' which someone had thought to drag out (a Widnes engine, and in for scrap?) and the mighty 9F alongside. What is also surprising is that 58413, of a class introduced in the 1880s was still around (the last Cauliflower went in 1955) at all, at the same time as this vast 2-10-0. The 9Fs lasted barely fourteen years, the Cauliflowers seventy or more...

Below. 92003 at Crewe on 19 January 1954, where it was displayed along with 92000 and 58413 (see above) as well as 92001 and 92002 - see *Fourum* in *British Railways Illustrated* Vol.1 No.6 for the extraordinary scene.

12. The 9F 2-10-0s 1954-1968

The 9F, if only through its extraordinary power classification, broke new ground in British practice and it is a strange revelation now to learn that it was *not* officially regarded in the beginning as a *standard* class as such. The rest of the Standards, despite their bold new looks, were in many ways straightforward replacements of existing designs - the 2-10-0 was something different..... *The British Railways Standard 9F 2-10-0*, by Philip Atkins.

The 9Fs arrived (in force) late on the steam scene, only to mark (as it turned out) the waste of a great deal of money. There were 251 in service by 1960, only a few of them more than five years old, yet the whole class had been withdrawn by June 1968 - only eighteen of them, indeed, made it to BR service at the start of that year. The costs in 'lost work' are unimaginable, but the 'booked' construction figures are: 92000, the first, completed January 1954 - £23,975 and the last, 92220, £33,497, 1960. So, over six years, the cost of construction of a 9F had gone up by just under £10,000 - not far off 50%; the cost of the whole fleet ran into millions of pounds. The cost of their unnaturally foreshortened working lives (and you would have to find a steam age accountant for this) is, probably, incalculable. Time, in the end, was agin 'em.

While they were in service the 9Fs proved the most popular and reliable of the BR Standards; they are certainly the most numerous and the most interesting for me to scribble about. The time spent compiling this chapter was one of the most enjoyable aspects of this book - an inspiration was travelling on an eighteen wagon freight train hauled by 92240 the complete length of the Bluebell Railway in April 1995.

The concept of the 9Fs was nothing if not straightforward - "a heavy freight locomotive intended principally for working mineral traffic". Parent office for the 9Fs was Brighton, though none of the class was built there. Other sections were designed at Derby, Doncaster and Swindon though only the last mentioned of these works actually built any of them. *The Railway Magazine* concentrated heavily on the working parts of the class but gave no hint as to where "the initial order, comprising 20 locomotives, Nos.92000-92019" would work or be allocated.

What a class they turned out to be; the late Derek Cross felt the 9Fs were far and away the most efficient of the Standard classes and certainly they were the most widely used and appreciated of the Standards on the WR. Originally the class was conceived as a 2-8-2 but the eventual result, with a ten coupled wheelbase was just as alien to British practice - though of the WD 2-10-0s designed by Riddles in 1943 twenty-five, 90750-90774, were working in the Scottish Region.

The 9Fs were European in concept and many felt the class matched the best ten coupled locomotives then working on the continent. Although they appeared larger than the Britannia Pacifics the boilers on the 9Fs were slightly smaller, tapering from 6ft. 1in. to 5ft. 9in., to incorporate the fitting of a wide Belpaire firebox and grate above the rear coupled wheels. The grate area was 40.2 sq ft. and the length between tubeplates 15ft. 3in., shorter than the Britannias by 1ft. 9in. Boiler pressures remained the same at 250lb per sq in.

At the front of the motion the three bar type of slide bar was used to support the underhung crosshead. On other Standard classes with a pony truck that had to meet the L1 loading gauge, this had proved unsatisfactory, but the arrangement was fine for the 9Fs as they were designed for the larger L2 loading gauge. The driving wheels, at 5ft. diameter, were larger than the average British freight size, and (a revelation) proved excellently suited to running passenger trains at some speed. 9Fs at times were recorded at 90mph but this was frowned upon by higher authority. The middle set of flangeless driving wheels - an unusual sight - allowed the 9Fs to negotiate a six chain curve. The pony truck wheels were 3ft. in diameter and had load bearing vertical springs and a horizontal coil which controlled lateral movement.

In 1957 92178 was fitted with a double chimney and blastpipe and noted on road trials between Reading and Stoke Gifford, minus smoke deflectors. It was also tried and tested in the stationary plant at Swindon. The experiment was deemed a success and from 92183 locos (except the Giesl 92250) were turned out with double chimneys from new. However, it was felt that in general freight service there was little to choose in the performance of single and double chimney varieties and only a few of the earlier members were converted - these were 92000, 92001, 92002, 92005, 92006, 92079 and 92165-92167.

Crosti 92026 at Wellingborough, 22 July 1956. When the test results actually favoured the conventional locomotive over the Crostis (!) to great Italian consternation, the great man himself was called in to adjudicate. André Chapelon visited Cricklewood (Wellingborough was too far out in the country, maybe) but it took two years for his report to be presented. Atkins in *Britannia Birth of a Locomotive* makes the point that the Crosti boiler had only showed dramatic effects when applied to older, inherently inefficient designs - the 9F boiler was very good indeed to begin with. The sort of improvements in coal consumption found in Italy were impossible on the 9F unless the firing rate could be increased far beyond that of the time.

fundamental redesign work - most notably the Crosti boiler episode. The minor alterations included the fitting of rectangular section coupling rods, footsteps on the top of the rear of the tender and the securing of the return crank to the big end, where the LMS method of using four studs replaced the original Gresley style.

The decision to construct ten of the class with Franco-Crosti boilers (an Italian invention which both the Italians and Germans had experimented with) came in 1952, once the design of the 9Fs had got under way. The engines were 92020-92029 and, working from their first shed, Wellingborough, constituted a strange sight, with the exhaust emanating from halfway along the right hand side of the boiler. The ten were built at Crewe Works under order No.E488, and appeared between May and July 1955. Because of the British loading gauge the preheating drums, so important to the design, could not be fitted on the side of the engines and in the 9Fs a single pre-heater drum was slung below the main boiler barrel. Based on a design by Piero Crosti, they appeared at a time of coal shortage, with the inventor claiming a saving of up to 19% in service. This, in the straitened, still-rationed times of the early 1950s, was the spur for the Crostis. Atkins, in *The British Railways Standard 9F 2-10-0* (Irwell Press 1993) puts it into context: *"Within five years this major project would be regarded as something of a fiasco, but it is important to view this decision sympathetically in a contemporary context. Only a few months earlier, in late 1950, the Government had directed British Railways to reduce its weekly coal consumption by 10,000 tons, which was achieved by curtailing passenger services. It was pointed out that if a large main line locomotive reduced its coal consumption by 1lb a mile, it would achieve a saving of 25 tons per annum..."*

How did this all work? The boiler was necessarily of a smaller size, and although a chimney at the front gave the engines a 'standard' appearance, this was only used when lighting up and was blanked off when steam was raised. The principle of 92020-92029 was for the boiler to extract further heat from the hot gases by passing them through the pre-heater situated beneath the boiler, which raised the temperature of the incoming water to boiling point before entering the boiler. Flue gases were then passed into a third 'final' smokebox and then exhausted through the side chimney. The draughting required the exhaust steam to be fed into a blank chamber below the side chimney.

One of the 9Fs at Crewe, 19 January 1954. These were the very engines which made such an inauspicious start for the class on the Western. Maybe, with hindsight, Crewe might have sent them somewhere closer to home - Crewe South would presumably have been perfect, but there was a feeling abroad that 'foreign' works should provide for the Regions without fear or favour. The first six or seven 9Fs were at Ebbw Junction by February 1954 where the unfortunate incident of the sticking regulators occurred, and 92004 collided with 92005.

On the right hand, fireman's side, there was a lot of pipework below the cab where two injectors were fitted, the lower one being the exhaust steam injector. As freight locomotives, the 9Fs did not have any steam heating connections so the only visible item on the buffer beam beside the coupling hook and screw coupling was the hose for the vacuum brake. In their short working lives the class saw the usual run of the mill minor modifications as well as some

Crostis were hated at Wellingborough, for the unpleasant working conditions, and a report of 1958 recommended that the Crostis be transferred elsewhere. Wellingborough, it was said, was an unenterprising shed and more might be got from the Crostis at say Annesley or Woodford. Doubtless Wellingborough could have happily lived with the slur if the Crostis could be got rid of but it was not to be. BR, noticeably, did not attempt to lumber anyone else with them and they stood around the shed yard for months waiting conversion. Wellingborough was much happier with the conventional 9Fs - here is 92009 working out of the shed, a few months after delivery, on 22 June 1954.

Prominent Westinghouse pumps on 92064, at Tyne Dock on 7 July 1956. Photograph Eric Sawford.

Meanwhile the live steam was moved from the superheater header to the lower part of the first smokebox and then via elbow pipes to the cylinders. Exhaust steam was ejected by large pipes under the boiler to the blast chamber and rear chimney. All this equipment meant the sandboxes had to be resited, with those for the leading wheels situated behind the front fall plate. The proximity of the exhaust chimney to the cab was a key problem. The footplate became dirty and periods of light steaming led to the production of sulphuric acid which caused corrosion in the system. Complaints from footplate crews about the exhaust chimney led to smoke deflector plates being fitted but the hoped-for economies did not come and the ten Crostis were converted to normal Stephenson arrangements, with the pre-heater drum removed and the main smokebox retained. 92026 was the first to be dealt with, by September 1959, and the last one was converted by July 1962. These engines were never fitted with the proper smoke deflectors and because of the smaller boiler were never as powerful as their sisters. They were downgraded to 8F in the power classification when returned to traffic.

In 9F terms, then, the Crostis were a failure and though the class saw many variations none were as fundamental as the Crosti experiment. Air pumps for operating hopper doors were fitted to 92060-92066 and 92097-92099 with considerable success; the first seven were completed in November and December 1955 and the other three in June and July of the following year. They were destined for Tyne Dock where they spent most of their short working time and though 92097-92099 went straight to the north east the earlier series spent time at Wellingborough covering for the Crosti 92020-92029, then receiving modifications in works. The air pumps that distinguished the 9Fs at Tyne Dock were fitted on the right hand side in a gap in the running plate, above the middle driving wheel. The engines worked the heavy iron ore trains between Tyne Dock and Consett steel works, the trains made up of 56 ton bogie tippler wagons. The pumps were independent and served to operate the side doors of the wagons - whilst one held the discharge doors closed the second one opened the doors when required. These trains were very successful, often operating with a second of the class

acting as a banker. These ten engines lasted nearly to the end of steam in the north east; all but one (the exception was 92065, withdrawn from Wakefield in April 1967) ended active life at Tyne Dock. Of these, 92066 went in May 1965 and the rest   92079 carved a small place in railway history for itself, for it was selected to replace the Midland 0-10-0, 58100, better known as 'Big Bertha', as banker on the Lickey Incline, south of Birmingham at Bromsgrove. It had a BR1G tender, to facilitate tender first running when returning from banking duties and the electric headlight that had been fitted to 58100 was transferred to 92079. This was apparently a good aid when buffering up to the rear of an ascending train during the hours of darkness but was removed about 1960. 92079 had gone new to Toton in March 1956 and reached Bromsgrove in the May, to carry out its banking duties uninterrupted, except for works visits, boiler washouts and so on until October 1963. After that it moved to Birkenhead, from where it was withdrawn in November 1967 when the shed closed.

92165-92167 were also distinguished from the common run of 9Fs - though so numerous were the detail differences that it is hard to talk of the 'common run'. The trio were fitted with the American Berkley design of mechanical stoker, another last-ditch effort at prolonging the life of BR steam. Completed at Crewe in April and May 1958 the three engines (originally five had been earmarked for the stokers but this was reduced) went new to Saltley. The idea of fitting the stokers was to increase the firing rate beyond the capacity of one fireman, so that a fully fitted freight could be hauled at improved speeds and schedules, in trains of fifty or more 16-ton wagons. Specially crushed coal had to be supplied and the engines worked north to Carlisle via the Settle and Carlisle, often with crews from Saltley working throughout. After a few years the experiment was quietly abandoned and the three engines passed through Crewe Works late in 1962 for the removal of the mechanical stokers and conversion to normal hand firing. All three had several transfers during their working lives. 92166 even going to the WR, in August 1959, first to Canton and in September to Ebbw Junction, for use on the Ebbw Vale iron ore trains. By February 1960 it was back at Saltley. All three then remained LMR engines, though 92167 was at Tyne Dock between May and October 1962. The tree engines ended up as follows:
92165 withdrawn from Speke Junction in March 1968, scrapped at Cashmores, Newport.
92166 withdrawn from Birkenhead in November 1967, scrapped at Campbell's, Airdrie.
92167 withdrawn in June 1968 from Carnforth, scrapped at Campbell's, Airdrie.

A final experiment, reported to have been 'imposed' on the running authorities, was carried out on the highest numbered BR steam locomotive and one of the last to be built, 92250. Completed in December 1958, this engine was fitted with a Giesl Oblong Ejector, the invention of Dr Adolf Giesl-Gieslingen of Austria. This consisted of an oblong chimney through which seven nozzles exhausted the steam from the cylinders, an arrangement providing reduced back pressure, and leading to a lower coal consumption with normal grades of coal. It was also hoped that lower quality, cheaper grades of coal could be burnt. Savings were found when comparisons were made with a double chimney (which

With that wide overhanging firebox prominent, 92056 comes through Harrow with a train of coal, 11 March 1957. Photograph C.R.L. Coles.

The principal purpose of the 9Fs was to work long heavy coal trains over long distances - Toton to Brent was a classic case, and this was mirrored on the east coast, where Doncaster and New England had substantial fleets for the London coal workings. This is one of them, 92146, at New England shed on 16 May 1963. Photograph Ken Fairey.

in turn used less coal than the single chimney variety) but this was not enough, given the extra costs. In any case it was all really too late, with the rundown of steam underway. 92250 went new to Banbury shed and stayed a WR engine all its short life until withdrawn in December 1965 from Gloucester Horton Road - still fitted with Dr Giesl's invention. The engine was scrapped at Cashmores, Newport in the summer of 1966.

From the introduction of 92220 EVENING STAR in March 1960, the class was 251 strong until the first withdrawals in May 1964, all from the ER: 92034, 92169-92171 and 92175-92177.

When new the 9Fs were allocated to Regions as follows:-

WR: 92000-92007, 92203-92250.
LMR:92008, 92009, 92015-92029, 92045-92059, 92077-92086, 92100-92139, 92150-92167.
ER: 92010-92014, 92030-92044, 92067-92076, 92087-92096, 92140-92149, 92168-92202.
NER: 92060-92066, 92097-92099.

The first eight went new to the Western Region between January and February 1954, all to Ebbw Junction, where alarming problems manifested themselves - the steam brake was slow to act after a time standing, and at slow speed the regulator tended to stick open. Lagging went a good way to resolving the delay in brake action, though Riddles was worried throughout the construction of the Standards. The new horizontal opening grid of the regulator was being held open

by the sheer volume of steam pressure, pressing the regulator hard down on the seat. A cure was effected by using a smaller valve, off the Class 4 4-6-0. The poor reputation of the 4-6-2s was already passing into WR legend, which did not augur well for the 9Fs; this, the very *strangeness* of the 2-10-0s, and the foreign left hand drive, cast a shadow over the 9Fs for all their Western Region lives. Question marks over the braking were never wholly resolved, and other Regions also found the 9Fs (and Standards in general) lacking in this respect in comparison with home types. The regulator business was cured by investigation and modification to the regulator valve. Not until 92221, going new to Banbury in May 1958, did the WR receive further more brand new 9Fs; the sequence ran to 92250 in December 1958 but 92203 did not go new (to Bristol St Philip's Marsh) until April 1959, and the last was 92220 in March 1960 - new to Canton. Indeed only three were new that year, 92218-92220, all constructed at Swindon, the last three steam engines built for BR.

The ER received 85 9Fs from new but under regional boundary changes the Annesley fleet, 92010-92014, 92030-92033, 92043, 92067-92076 and 92087-92096 went to the LMR from February 1958. The shed lay north of Nottingham and the 9Fs, of course, became famous for the Annesley - Woodford Halse coal trains, the 'Windcutters'. Elsewhere on the ER two sheds - New England and Doncaster - had substantial complements from new. New England first received 92030 in November 1954, followed by 92034-92042, 92140-92149 and 92178-92188, the last one in February 1958. New England closed in January 1965 and of its original 9Fs, 92036 (December 1964) and 92142, 92143 and 92181 in February 1965 were withdrawn from the shed. Doncaster received 92067-92076, 92087-92094, 92168-92177 and 92192-92202, the last one delivered in December 1958 but by May 1965 the allocation had been reduced to 92168, 92172-92174, 92183, 92186, 92190, 92200 and 92201. The Eastern Region 9Fs were used side by side with the V2 2-6-2s on such work as the fish trains originating from

It is an impossible job to illustrate the variations even within this one class, let alone among 'the 999' but this one has to have a place - EVENING STAR (the third 'Venus' - see page 76) at Cardiff Canton shed, Sunday 3 June 1962. EVENING STAR had gone new to Canton in 1960 and by the summer it was on Paddington trains with The Red Dragon. Photograph Gavin Morrison.

The naming ceremony of EVENING STAR in March 1960, one of the few steam locomotive namings in which both fur coat and turban could be found among the audience...

employed, a distance of 226 miles and a near seven hour journey.

The class was celebrated for a relatively insignificant facet of its very varied work - the Somerset & Dorset between Bath and Bournemouth in the 1960s. Peter Smith in his book *Mendips Engineman* (OPC 1972) declared the reason for this development to be the need to reduce the necessity for double-heading, and so alleviate the footplate staff shortage. It all began on Tuesday 29th March 1960 when 92204 of St Philips Marsh made a test run from Bath down to Bournemouth with a van and ten carriages in tow, in appalling weather. The weather was just as bad on the return run but with the engine less than a year old the test run was a complete success. As a result 92203-92206 were allocated to Bath Green Park for the summer service and though some records show the transfers taking place in July 1960 others just show the re-allocation at the end of the season, in October; 92203 to Old Oak; 92204 to Southall and 92205, 92206 to Westbury.

March 1960 saw completion of the class of 251 engines; no glorious long life awaited them, and the first withdrawals came in May 1964. The class was thus complete for just over four years.

In the 1950s a requirement for a small number of 9Fs on the Southern Region had been recognised but it was not until January 1961 that 92205, 92206 and 92231 were based there, at Eastleigh, with 92211 and 92239 joining in the August. All came from WR sheds. They worked 1,200 ton oil trains from the Fawley oil terminus along the Fawley branch to Toton, normally over the Didcot, Newbury and Southampton route. By mid-1963 the duties were finishing and in June all five were transferred to Feltham where they spent three months before moving north to York in September 1963, a complete contrast to their former GWR haunts.

Throughout the 1960s the Tyne Dock engines could be seen hard at work on the steep line to Consett and this lasted until the final steam hauled iron ore train to Consett on No-

South Humberside and on fitted freights but most notably on the endless London coal trains. They also appeared on summer Saturday extras, for once the operating department realised the potential of these engines they were put on relief expresses, some being timed at 90mph. 92069 was once noted on the 'South Yorkshireman' and 92179 worked a down relief from Kings Cross in August 1958. These passenger workings would normally have been restricted to the summer months because of the lack of steam heating equipment.

By far the largest numbers were sent new to the LMR, while the Scottish and Southern received none - though the class did work through to the ScR, especially with through goods trains - as far north as Perth.

The main shed on the LMR to receive 9Fs from new was Wellingborough, starting with 92008 and 92009 in March 1954 and followed by 92015-92029 (92020-92029 were the Crostis), 92045-92049, 92082-92086, 92105-

92108, 92121-92127, 92154 and, in November 1957, 92159 and 92160. Two other sheds, Toton and Saltley, received a fair number of new 9Fs. Toton first received 92050 in September 1955 followed by 92051-92059, 92077-92081, 92100-92104, 92109, 92110, 92128, 92153, ending with 92156-92158 in November 1957; Saltley got its first 2-10-0 in April 1957, 92129 followed by 92130-92139, 92151, 92152, 92155 and 92165-92167, the last in May 1958. These engines were at work in the 1950s on the Midland main line, on coal trains between Toton and Brent - a reflection of their use on the Eastern.

The Saltley engines certainly travelled, working Esso oil trains from the Fawley branch near Southampton to Carlisle. It has been said, and I think few would argue, that amongst the most difficult trains to work on in the later days of steam were the two return freights between Water Orton yard near Birmingham to Carlisle over the Settle to Carlisle, a job for which the mechanical stoker engines, 92165-92167 were

Amongst the everyday grit and grime. Wellingborough Finedon Road, 25 March 1964, and 92084 heads north past a 4F on a ballast - the crossing had just been re-laid by the look of it. Photograph Alec Swain.

Converted Crosti (now 8F) 92022 approaches Ais
Gill summit with a southbound freight on 17
July 1965. Photograph Maurice Burns.

vember 19th, 1966, 92063 carrying the head-board 'The Tyne Docker'. This engine and 92064 were the final two of the original Tyne Dock allocation to be withdrawn, in November 1966. 92065 had moved the same month to Wakefield and was withdrawn in April 1967. 92063 and 92064 were both broken up at Thompsons, Stockton-on-Tees whilst 92065 was cut up at Arnott Young, Parkgate and Rawmarsh in the late summer of 1967.

Though the ER had carried out the first withdrawals in May 1964, 92223 had in fact been the first to be 'withdrawn'. This had been from Bromsgrove, in February 1964, but the engine was reinstated in the March and trans-ferred to Tyseley, surviving to become one of the last of the class. Its second withdrawal took

place in April 1968 from Carnforth. It was scrapped at Arnott Young, Dinsdale in the autumn.

Steam working on the Western Region finished at the end of 1965 (officially, 1st January 1966) but not before the 9Fs (maybe because they were supplied in decent numbers) had became the most (grudgingly?) popular of the BR standard classes with WR crews. Besides working heavy coal trains out of South Wales and similar heavy coal trains and iron ore trains into Wales for the steelworks, they could be seen working between London and the Midlands, with batches based at Old Oak and Southall.

In its rush to be the first region to eliminate steam power, the WR withdrew a lot of

engines with plenty of working life left, including 9Fs completed at Swindon only a few years before. In December 1965 the last were condemned: 92007, 92230, 92244, 92246 and 92250 from Gloucester Horton Road (the shed closing the same month) and 92209 and 92243 from Bath Green Park. The ER was only four months behind, also condemning modern 9Fs and sending them to the scrapyard.

Steam lasted a little longer on the North Eastern Region and besides the original allocation to Tyne Dock other 9Fs finished their days at NER sheds. By April 1965, York had gained 92005, 92006, 92205, 92206, 92211, 92221, 92231 and 92239. As late as June 1966, 92077 of Newton Heath was noted on the York to Manchester parcels train.

The LMR, perhaps, got the best out of its 9Fs and by 1957 had 95, increasing to 129 by 1958 through the acquisition of Annesley, along with its thirty 9Fs. By 1963 there was a maximum of 147 on the books, reduced by scrapping to 105 in 1966 and a dismal 18 by 1967. Towards the end the 9Fs were of course reduced to the redoubt of the North West; of the former bastions, Wellingborough had closed to steam in 1966 and Toton in 1965. Birkenhead for a while became an extraordinary centre for the class as did Kingmoor, whilst Speke Junction and Carnforth were the final homes - as follows: Speke Junction 92027, 92054, 92055, 92069, 92091, 92094, 92153-92155, 92158, 92160, 92165, 92204, 92218, 92227, 92228, 92233 and 92249; Carnforth 92004, 92009, 92016, 92077, 92087, 92088, 92091, 92118, 92128, 92160, 92167, 92212 and 92223.

There is little record of the class at work in 1968; the Stanier survivors, after all, outnumbered the 9Fs - a curious outcome, given the original breadth of the Standard programme. 92077, 92160 and 92167 were the last three withdrawn, in June 1968; by a grotesque chance,

92061 in charge of a Consett ore train, at South Pelaw 20 August 1965. The line climbed to 900ft over 22 miles, some of it at 1 in 35. The train looks short but iron ore was far denser than coal and an ore train would only be half as long as a coal train of similar weight.

92167 finished up running without its rear trailing coupling rods as a 2-8-2, the original concept for BR's 'heavy freight locomotive'.

DEMISE
1964
May 92034, 92169, 92170, 92171, 92175-92177
August 92198, 92199
November 92210, 92229
December 92036, 92196, 92207, 92232, 92245

1965
February 92037, 92142, 92143, 92181, 92184, 92185, 92187, 92188, 92192
March 92003, 92220, 92222, 92236
April 92038, 92044, 92140, 92147, 92180
May 92066, 92195, 92221
June 92149, 92168, 92193, 92242, 92248
July 92000, 92225, 92241
August 92005, 92040, 92041, 92186
September 92033, 92197, 92214, 92219, 92226, 92237, 92238, 92240
October 92039, 92057, 92178, 92190, 92200, 92216
November 92179, 92235
December 92007, 92042, 92141, 92144, 92148, 92174, 92189, 92191, 92194, 92202, 92209, 92230, 92243, 92244, 92246, 92250

1966
January 92068, 92072
February 92035, 92053, 92081, 92115, 92145
March 92173, 92183, 92201
April 92010, 92146, 92172, 92182
May 92130
June 92062
July 92043, 92098, 92158, 92164, 92217
September 92059, 92061, 92075, 92099
October 92013, 92028, 92060, 92092, 92095, 92097, 92136, 92247
November 92063, 92064, 92067, 92116, 92155, 92213, 92231, 92239
December 92085, 92124, 92134, 92161

1967
January 92001, 92031, 92105, 92228
February 92030, 92076, 92083, 92087, 92089, 92096, 92104, 92107
April 92006, 92015, 92018, 92032, 92065, 92074, 92150, 92151
May 92078, 92080, 92090, 92100, 92103, 92206, 92211
June 92019, 92135, 92205, 92215
July 92106, 92114, 92120, 92121, 92129, 92133, 92138, 92154, 92156, 92159
August 92027, 92052, 92126, 92127, 92157

September 92045, 92048, 92050, 92093, 92119, 92131, 92137, 92139, 92224
October 92008, 92012, 92014, 92016, 92020, 92046, 92051, 92101, 92111, 92113, 92123, 92132, 92208
November 92002, 92011, 92021-92026, 92029, 92047, 92049, 92056, 92058, 92070, 92071, 92073, 92079, 92082, 92084, 92086, 92102, 92108, 92109, 92112, 92122, 92128, 92152, 92162, 92163, 92166, 92203, 92227, 92234

December 92017, 92055, 92110, 92117, 92125, 92204

1968
January 92153, 92212
February 92233
March 92004, 92009, 92165
April 92088, 92223
May 92054, 92069, 92091, 92094, 92118, 92218, 92249
June 92077, 92160 and 92167.

Dog days. Speke Junction, along with Carnforth, provided a final home for the 9Fs, including some of the Crosti conversions. 92025 and 92021 maintain some dignity in the face of obvious neglect, on 26 May 1966. Photograph I.G. Holt.

Happier times, and a 9F, 92210, at Canton on 20 September 1959. Appropriately at a shed noted for its enthusiastic reception of the Standards, 92210 is flanked by two Britannias. One is at the extreme left, recognisable by the new cut-out handholds whilst on the right is 70019 LIGHTNING. Photograph P. Hutchinson.

Swansong. 92118 assisted by, or pushing, a Type 2 (which hardly seems in that much better condition) and approaching Hest Bank from the Morecambe line, with the Heysham - Leeds oil tanks in August 1967. The perfect 9F task, but the addition of the diesel is sadly symbolic. 92118 had gone to traffic in December 1956 and went for scrap in May 1968. As such, it did rather better than most 9Fs. Assuming a working life of 45 years, the class achieved on average a mere 20% of the expected working life.... Photograph Tom Heavyside.

STANDARD EXPERIENCES
By Harry Friend

A brief note about myself first. I started on the railway in 1941 at a freight depot called Borough Gardens. It was in the heart of Gateshead and the other shed, which dealt with passenger trains, was the High Shed, known to most people simply as Gateshead.

For the first month at the Gardens I learnt how to fire on a goods pilot, the J72 designed by William Worsdell. I had been issued with a new copy of the LNER rule book and on the following Monday was made passed cleaner by Mr. Pagnall, the shedmaster. In 1941 the War was well and truly on; I did hardly any cleaning at all, for there was an acute shortage of labour and the foreman put whatever men he had to clearing smokeboxes.

At the Gardens I did 95% firing on old engines designed by Worsdell, Raven and Robinson, including class Q5, Q6, J27, N9, N10, J24, O4s and finally a Gresley 0-6-0, the J39, which had drop bars, unlike the others which had fixed fire bars. Fires in the main, dropped by the likes of me, required two shovels to throw them out, one short, one long, then clean out the ashpan and the smokebox. Bloody hard work...

In 1943 I was promoted to be a young fireman at Durham where I lived and here we had another class designed by Worsdell, the 0-4-4T G5. In October 1943 I volunteered for air crew and joined the RAF, and was demobbed in January 1947.

I now moved as a fireman to South Dock, Sunderland as there was no vacancy at Durham for about seven months. There I fired the G5 and the A8 which was a very large Pacific tank engine designed by Raven; again the fireman needed two shovels to dispose of the confounded things.

I returned to Durham at the end of 1947, remaining there until 1958 when the shed closed, upon which I moved to Gateshead as a passed fireman. I passed for driving in 1949 at the age of 25, very young indeed. In those 11 years I did over five hundred driving shifts, all on the main line, on G5s, A8s, J21s and J39s.

Then the Standards began to creep in, the tanks and the tender engines and in 1958 I worked as a driver on the BR4 2-6-0s stationed at West Auckland. I did two trips on these. In 1958 I was the senior passed fireman and at Durham shed there was a system whereby a passed fireman or passed cleaner or a regular driver would be with work for twelve weeks. The man concerned would be made a 'red ink' driver, that is, work as a driver or fireman full time and perform the shifts the absent man would have performed, including Sunday. So I was marked up - in red ink - as the cover for my regular driver, Billy Woodward, who was laid off for 13 weeks with a double hernia. By the time Bill returned to work I was a keen 'red ink' driver, substituting for other drivers at Durham who took a fortnight's holiday. In all I drove for five months, then I went back firing to Billy Woodward, with the occasional driving shift.

In 1958 at Durham we had lost our G5s and they were replaced by a large tank engine, the 'Teddy Bear', a Raven 4-6-2T - big awkward engines, slow off the mark, three cylinders, but at least they could pull a heavier load than a G5.

Saturday Miners Day 1958

On the Friday, I noted my working, a very nice job indeed and the fact that West Auckland would provide a tender engine. I expected an Ivatt Class 2 and found I was allotted a BR4 2-6-0 built at Doncaster in 1953; there it was, standing over the pit. The chargeman met me and with it being 'Miners Day' he was alone, for all the cleaners were rostered to fire that day. 'You've got a good 'un here Harry' he exclaimed. This was the first Standard engine I

had worked, either as driver or fireman. For a start there was no going underneath to oil the shaft and it was a two cylinder engine with outside Walschaerts valve gear - all I had to do was oil round the motion, big ends and both mechanical lubricators. Inside the cab was a revelation, rocker bars, a full tender, both injectors on the fireman's side, one pull up regulator, one vacuum brake, one steam brake and a speedometer which worked. No sign of the fireman (big, lazy Cyril, always late) so I did his work, made the fire up in the medium sized firebox, filled the tank and then with the shunter shunted the five coaches to work the first service train to South Shields. Still no fireman, only five minutes to go, then he arrived at the last minute. 'I slept in Harry' he said.

We kept the same set all day, on stopping trains to South Shields and back to Durham, fifty miles. Then empties to Waterhouses and a loaded train back to Durham, fourteen miles. Empties to Washington then a special to Bishop Auckland, twenty miles, loose off, to West Auckland shed to fill her with coal and clean the fire, six miles. Special to Durham, ten miles, get relieved by another set at Durham then go home, one hundred miles altogether.

With five on it was a light load for this marvellous engine but the only trouble was my mate, coal all over the floor, steam kept up to the mark. He turned sullen when he realised the work involved, but I used only half regulator throughout, never pulling the reverser beyond 25%, sometimes dropping it down to 40% just to run to time. I could drive a good engine being abused by its fireman. At West Auckland Cyril retired to the mess room for his bait so I had to get the coal on (an overhead crane shovel) filling the tender right up and deciding to try the rocker bar. I did the ashpan myself, then finally filled the tank. My fault, but Cyril did pass the buck and shortly afterwards, as he said, 'Too much work in this job'. He was aged about 23, while I was at the time 34.

On the Monday the engine was still there, rostered to me again and the fireman was Austin Caulfield, who was a passed cleaner and a bloody good Mate. Our first stopping train, engine first, was to Middleton, 35 miles, then a stopping train to Sunderland, 50 miles, down to South Dock to coal, turn and run back to Durham. We started at 07.30 and first shoved two express trains out at Durham, then worked the 09.00 to Middleton, stopping at every station. Austin drove to Middleton, all uphill, by the way, from West Auckland station and with three coaches on, a doddle. Austin revelled in the work, no more than half regulator except the pull up to Gibbs Neese when he fully opened the regulator and pulled it up to 20%. No problem at all with the steaming and we registered 55mph running down into Barnard Castle. The tank served us to Middleton, then no more water at all until we got to South Dock shed where Austin cleaned the fire.

I drove tender first all the way back as the turntable at Barnard Castle was too small to turn a BR4. Top speed 70mph down the bank from Cockfield to Evenwood, then another 60mph on Brassiare Viaduct near to Durham. I let Austin drive back to Durham but there a set of West Auckland men met us on the platform and took the 2-6-0 to its shed and that was it, no more Standard engines at Durham.

Gateshead
Now to Gateshead, no more the senior passed fireman, only a fireboy now. In January 1959 I was spare turn on the night shift on shed with a passed fireman called Gilbert, acting as driver. The foreman gave Gilbert a job: 'Turn out the Peterborough engine Gilbert, take it to Heaton Yard, load up with a full brake, down to Newcastle, get relieved by Peterborough men'. The engine was a 9F and it stood outside, made ready by the pits. Gilbert explained the job to me. The Peterborough men worked up early each morning to be relieved at Newcastle then lodged in a hotel at Newcastle. The load was a 45mph brakey and the Gateshead men worked the load to Heaton then took the 9F to the shed for stabling. That night another set took the 9F to Heaton and loaded up with a full brakey of 50 wagons, took it to the Central station at Newcastle, and got relieved by the Peterborough men who worked the train to Whitemoor near Peterborough - it took around six hours to do the journey.

Gilbert was a true Geordie, very kind, and helped me find the gear including two firing shovels. Then we entered the coal stage and while I made up the fire in the large box, Gilbert filled the tender right up. It was a rough job for any fireman, pretty slow speed and I reckon he would have shovelled at least four tons of coal - maybe five - to do it. That was it then, tender full, also the boiler; the men were thankful when they relieved us though sometimes the Gateshead men were not fussy about filling the tender right up, thus making the fireman enter the tender to trim the coal forward.

The 9F was just like the BR4, a bigger firebox, rather shallow but like all the Riddles engines, a good steamer.

3MT 2-6-0
Now - there were not too many of them around - to the BR 3MT 2-6-0. It was a Saturday, I was working my rest day at Gateshead shed and my mate again was a passed fireman, Reg. Now Reg was a Gateshead man through and through, a canny fellow but in my opinion he did not have a clue about driving steam engines, certainly not Standard ones. The job we had was tool vans to Haydon Bridge on the Carlisle line, up line from Hexham where a freight train had been derailed and both lines were blocked. We got on the 3, Reg made ready and we had a good fire burning and the tank was full. He tied onto the tool van train and we left, though for some reason we ran tender first to Haydon Bridge, perhaps not the best way going uphill from Hexham. We got the road right through of course, running as an express. Now, I could really fire but Reg simply hammered the engine along. He did not pull her up at all, the lever seemed to be in full gear all the way and did I work. We did not stick or anything like that but the steam was well back

and of course the boiler did the job. Working back the engine blew off all the way to Gateshead shed and I had an enormous fire on. Reg's fault I think - I heard later he was a corker on any job, braying fireman cold with a grin on his face!

Working with Good Mates
I worked with a regular mate, Maurice Rhodes 63, the senior driver and the best mate I ever had, on passenger and freight. We worked to Edinburgh, Leeds, Doncaster, Carlisle and to Middleton in Teesdale. One week we worked a night shift, Gateshead to Carlisle, the class 2 'Forth Yard Goods'. We turned our engine at Carlisle London Road and worked a heavy loose fitted freight back. Thirty two wagons for Prudhoe, ICI then light engine to shed. We had a V2, B1, B16, K1 and finally a BR4. We had no trouble at all with all the engines bar the BR4. It was the Wednesday when we got the 2-6-0 and had no trouble working to Carlisle with 35 wagons on, turning the engine at London Road where I cleaned the fire using the rocker bars. But running back *was* a problem. We were banked from London Road to Low Row up Carlisle Bank by a Standard Class 4 tank engine. During the rest of the week we had had engines in the Class 5 category - at least our class 4 was well loaded and the banking engine did not get stuck in at all.

That night it was bat for bat! Maurice had the regulator well open, reverser right over to about 50%. The engine steamed beautifully but the banker took a hammering indeed. I was obliged to put the second injector on at Branston Fell otherwise we would have dropped the plug. Once over the top however the engine flew, excellent driving from Maurice backed up by good firing by me.

Then Maurice and I got a 9F on the day shift, a full load turn, Gateshead to York, then leave the engine at York shed, home on the cushions. We had exactly 50 on and maximum speed on this job was 60mph. Maurice was on the little valve throughout, except for the pull up Durham bank but he never notched up and we stopped at Darlington for water. (There was no scoop fitted to the tender). We liked the engine and agreed it could do 70mph pulling passenger coaches.

Final Trip with a 9F as Fireman
I had George Lees, another good mate, again on a Saturday. We worked an express parcels to York that morning, the train going on to Kings Cross, with a Peppercorn A1. Then we walked to York shed and got our engine, a 9F; our job was to work the Scarborough train via the coast to Newcastle, stopping at Northallerton, Stockton, Hartlepool, Sunderland and Newcastle. The train came in from Scarborough with 10 on and we tied onto the other end and made off. Again it was a Heaton engine and George used full regulator pretty well all the way, but pulling the engine well up, probably about 20%. We attained about 80mph running down Picton Bank and 70mph going over the flat to Northallerton - a great engine.

Consett Days
By 1961 I was a driver at Consett and had learnt a few roads. The first week, working to South Pelaw with a Consett man, I got off and learnt the road with a Tyne Dock driver called Jack Laws, my age, driving a 9F assisted in the rear by another 9F.

I fired the 9F up the first day and drove it back to Pelaw. The rest of the week Jack let me drive it while he stood behind to give counsel. It was all full regulator work but about 25%. They were very heavy iron ore trains and I also rode the banker up one day, one fitted with a mechanical stoker (92167) and operated by an expert, but it was no good at all, not on those heavy banks. Because of this it was sent back whence it came.

Traction Inspector at Newcastle
When I was a Traction Inspector at Newcastle, Dick Taylor was the Area Manager. He loved steam locomotives and arranged for 92220 EVENING STAR to do four trips from Newcastle to Hexham, then work back to York Museum. Dick thought that 12 coaches would do but with my experience I thought of the bank at 1 in 60 from Bensham Curve to the High Level Bridge cabin which was protected by a signal so I said 10 coaches, no more. John Lovett, our driver, did get stopped at this signal to let a HST go by. 92220 then walked it when the signal came off, proving me wrong.

I drove 92220 on one trip and then on another, using full regulator to get them moving, pulling the lever up to no more than 25% to reach the speed we wanted. I partially closed the regulator to halt, still leaving it at 25% though a 9F was not a Gresley engine - so 25% was the maximum. We got up to 60mph, no bother, on a really beautiful engine. The 9F was the best that Riddles ever designed, that is for certain. That day the locomotive ran light engine from York and Dick Taylor arranged for the coal lorry to supply the essentials and I tipped 40 cwt of coal into the tender, filling it right up. The driver and fireman were being interviewed by the press. At the end of the day 92220 returned light engine to York with still plenty of coal in the tender. The 9F was one of my favourite classes.

Postscript
I nearly forgot the Standard tank engines - though my own personal favourite by a long way was the Gresley V3 designed in 1939, 200 psi, a real racehorse capable of 80mph on the main line to Carlisle, pulling 7 coaches. I worked on them quite a lot at Durham and again at Gateshead. Of the Standard tanks, my favourite one and one that could be seen recently on the North Yorkshire Moors Railway is the 4MT 2-6-4T No.80135, a lovely engine. I work on the NYMR as a traction inspector - there are three of us of whom the chief is the paid superintendent of the line and he passes fireman into drivers. I go about three or four times a year, the old cloth-capped person who boards every locomotive, a pass conspicuous in his hand. Otherwise they would not let me board at all. I also pass out drivers from steam onto the Type 2 diesels.

All the drivers I have seen are good though the firemen differ, but that is lack of experience. Occasionally I pick the shovel up and try to demonstrate how it was done, but I am now over 70, arthritic - though I can still try. I once drove 80135 hauling the maximum load allowed from Grosmont to Pickering and with the maximum speed being 25mph it is hard work on the 1 in 49 three miles from Grosmont to Goathland. All the drivers on the NYMR prefer 80135 because it has full protection and there is no tender first running. The best engine to have in the winter and it's a Standard!

Appendix

Note 1 - Tenders

When the Standard tender designs were first conceived just three variations were envisaged, called simply type 1, type 2 and type 3. The first two were built to suit the original standard cab layout. In this case the fireman was intended to benefit, as the traditional fall plate, in use on other British tender locomotives was done away with and in its place the cab floor was lengthened to come *under* the tender shovelling plate when engine and tender were coupled together. An inset coal bunker was included in the three types with the one aim of allowing the footplate crew to have improved vision when travelling tender first. It soon became apparent that footplatemen did not really appreciate all this, for it was no help when setting an engine back onto a train. In service the lengthened cab floor created excessive draughts and crews complained of swirling coal dust - as we have seen plenty of times through the text. Doors were fitted to the cab and a handrail extended from the corner of the roof down to the end of the cab floor. One of the solutions to the excess air rushing around was to fit flexible screens behind the rear of the cab and to the front of the tender. As we now know, this was not really effective so a re-design took place; the one-piece cab floor remained and the front of the tender received a short but full width fallplate, resting on the rear of the cab floor. Shorter grab rails were fitted to the tender, thus doing away with the aforementioned handrail and doors were now fitted to the tender, with anti-draught flaps attached.

How many tender types were there? BR found the standardisation principle unravelling a little, but of the *fourteen* types in all, two were unique - BR1E and BR1J, both fitted to 71000 DUKE OF GLOUCESTER. A further oddity was the BR1K, of which only three were built, to take mechanical stokers. They were attached to 9Fs Nos.92165-92167. Types BR1B to BR1F and the aforementioned types had the inset coal bunkers done away with and thus had no spectacle plates for tender first running. The coal bunkers were fitted out to the limits of the loading gauge and the now flush sides curved inwards to give a very neat look - they may well have been descended in direct lineage from Stanier efforts but I'd wager that somewhere along the line, someone had taken a good look at the American 141Rs built for the French.

BR1 (inset) Capacity, 7 tons of coal, 4250 gallons of water.
Weight. Leading axle: 16T 8cwt, Middle axle 16T 12 cwt. Rear axle 16T 3cwt.
Total weight: 49T 3cwt. Pick up apparatus fitted.
Attached to 70000-70024. 70030-70044. 72000-72009. 73000-73049.

BR1A (inset) Capacity, 7 tons of coal, 5000 gallons of water.
Weight. Leading axle 16T 10cwt. Middle axle 17T 10cwt. Rear axle 18T 10cwt.
Total weight: 52T 10cwt. Pick up apparatus fitted if required.
Attached to 70025-70029.

BR1B Capacity 7 tons of coal, 4725 gallons of water.
Weight. Leading axle 17T 2cwt. Middle axle 17T 1cwt. Rear axle 17T 2cwt.
Total weight: 51T 5cwt. Pick up apparatus fitted if required.
Attached to 73080-73089, 73100-73109, 73120-73134, 73145-73171. 75065-75079. 76053-76069. 92020-92029, 92060-92066, 92097-92099.

BR1C Capacity 9 tons of coal, 4725 gallons of water.
Weight. Leading axle 17T 18cwt. Middle axle 17T 15cwt. Rear axle 17T 12 cwt.
Total weight: 53T 5cwt. Pick up apparatus fitted if required.
Attached to 73065-73079, 73090-73099, 73135-73144. 92015-92019, 92045-92059, 92077-92086, 92100-92139, 92150-92164.

BR1D Capacity 9 tons of coal, 4725 gallons of water.
Weight. Leading axle 17T 10cwt. Middle axle 18T 10cwt. Rear axle 18T 10cwt.
Total weight: 54T 10cwt. Pick up apparatus fitted if required. Fitted with coal pusher.
Attached to 70045-70054.

BR1E Capacity 10 tons of coal, 4725 gallons of water.
Weight. Leading axle 18T 10cwt. Middle axle 18T 10cwt. Rear axle 18T 10cwt. Pick-up apparatus, coal pusher, fitted.
Total weight: 55T 10cwt.
Attached to 71000.

BR1F Capacity 7 tons of coal, 5625 gallons of water.
Weight. Leading axle 18T 5cwt. Middle axle 18T 10cwt. Rear axle 18T 10cwt.
Total weight: 55T 5cwt. Pick up apparatus fitted if required.
Attached to 73110-73119, 92010-92014, 92030-92044, 92067-92076, 92087-92096, 92140-92149, 92168-92202.

BR1G (inset) Capacity 7 tons of coal, 5000 gallons of water.
Weight. Leading axle 16T 10cwt. Middle axle 17T 10cwt. Rear axle 18T 10cwt.
Total weight: 52T 10cwt. Pick up apparatus fitted if required.
Fitted with fall plate and gangway doors and the only difference between BR1A and BR1G.
Attached to 73050-73052. 92000-92009, 92203-92250.

BR1H (inset) Capacity 7 tons of coal, 4250 gallons of water.
Weight. Leading axle 16T 8cwt. Middle axle 16T 12cwt. Rear axle 16T 3cwt.
Total weight: 49T 3cwt. Pick up apparatus fitted if required.
Fitted with fallplate and gangway doors and the only difference between BR1 and BR1H
Attached to 73053-73064.

BR1J Capacity 10 tons of coal, 4325 gallons of water.
Weight. Leading axle 17T 18cwt, Middle axle 17T 18cwt. Rear axle 17T 18cwt.
Pick up apparatus fitted. Fitted with coal pusher. Total weight: 53T 14cwt.
Attached to 71000 in 1958.

BR1K Capacity 9 tons of coal, 4325 gallons of water.
Weight. Leading axle 16T 6cwt. Middle axle 17T 19cwt. Rear axle 18T 2cwt.
Total weight: 52T 7cwt. Fitted with pick up apparatus and mechanical stoker.
Attached to 92165-92167.

BR2 (inset) Capacity 6 tons of coal, 3500 gallons of water.
Weight. Leading axle 15T 2cwt. Middle axle 13T 9cwt. Rear axle 13T 12cwt.
Total weight: 42T 3cwt. Pick up apparatus fitted if required.
Attached to 75000-75049. 76000-76044.

BR2A (inset) Capacity 6 tons of coal, 3500 gallons of water.
Weight. Leading axle 15T 2cwt. Middle axle 13T 9cwt. Rear axle 13T 12cwt.
Total weight: 42T 3cwt. Pick up apparatus fitted if required.
Fitted with fallplate and gangway doors - these constituted the only differences between BR2 and BR2A.
Attached to 75050-75064. 76045-76052, 76070-76114. 77000-77019.

BR3 (inset) Capacity 4 tons of coal, 3000 gallons of water.
Weight. Leading axle 13T 15cwt. Middle axle 11T 16cwt. Rear axle 11T 6cwt.
Total weight: 36T 17cwt. Pick up apparatus fitted if required.
Attached to 78000-78064.

As a wide-eyed youngster these differing types of tender (inasmuch as I noticed only the more obvious variations) meant little to me - I saw representatives of all of the classes (except 71000) at work or on shed and when visiting the latter (normally without permission) we were concerned with getting down as many numbers as possible before someone ejected us. The finer detail of tender construction eluded us. The BR tenders, all of a new design but to well established principles, did not prove at first to be what the footplatemen wanted. Let us

not forget that these men, many with years of service behind them, were faithful to the old company locomotives and looked upon the new Standard designs with suspicion. A good example is the GWR men's attitude to the Britannias; they did not like them, whereas the Pacifics proved a revelation on the GER lines out of Liverpool Street. Then there were the Southern men, used to electric lighting and steam powered reverser in the cabs of their Bulleid Pacifics. Suddenly they were back to darkened cabs and manually controlled reversers. A one-time Nine Elms man has declared to me in no uncertain terms that the BR Standards were a retrograde step, in far stronger language than I can reproduce here.

With 25 Britannias in service by the end of 1951 experience was soon gained with the BR1 tender. All was not well, as we have seen throughout the book. To mention it one last time, a considerable backdraught was created at speed in the gap between the rigid cantilevered floor and the tender shovel plate, making for a draughty and noisy ride. Swirling coal dust (again, already mentioned) hardly improved a crew's humour and one of the first solutions was the rubber bellows that were added between the cab edge and tender. Other problem solvers have already been listed but another early nuisance was a fore and aft surging between the tender and front coaches that often occurred around 60mph. The cure was an alteration to the tender drawbar spring.

Some Britannias were tried on the Euston - Holyhead trains, with 70030-70033 allocated from new to Holyhead at the end of 1952. They were fitted with BR1 tenders and it was found that capacity was inadequate for this route. 70045-70054 had the hulking BR1D tenders which carried two more tons of coal and 525 more gallons of water than the BR1; these were more suited to the job and to the general operational requirements of the London Midland Region, with its longer daily runs. 70045-70054 proved masters of the job and popular with crews. Amongst the features that made the BR1D tenders more popular were the curved, self trimming sides, doing away with the inset coal bunkers. There was also a steam operated coal pusher, designed to save the fireman time and work. 70014 and 70032 later acquired BR1D tenders from withdrawn sisters.

71000 had the BR1E tender, No.1271, from new until November 1957 when it was converted to a BR1C, involving a decrease of a ton of coal but the same water capacity, 4,725 gallons. From then until withdrawal 71000 was fitted with the unique BR1J which, given the engine's appetite for coal in BR service must have been put to good use. 71000 now runs with BR1C No.1344 purchased from Barry scrapyard (the BR1J was long ago disposed of) converted to BR1J and renumbered 1271.

The Clans, something of an enigma amongst the Standards, were all fitted with BR1s. It appears that if handled correctly the engines were good steamers with fair economy of coal and water and when the steaming was improved in 1953/54 some crews found them easier to operate then the Britannias.

With 172 Class 5s there were bound to be a variety of tender types. The first fifty, 73000-73049 had type BR1; 73050-73052 type BR1G; 73053-73064 BR1H; 73065-73079 BR1C; 73080-73089 BR1B; 73090-73099 BR1C; 73100-73109 BR1B; 73110-73119 BR1F; 73120-73134 BR1B; 73135-73144 BR1C and 73145-73171 BR1B.

73050-73052 went new to the Somerset and Dorset in June 1964 and were fitted with BR1G tenders with inset coal bunkers, 7 tons of coal and 5,000 gallons of water, the only members of the class thus fitted, though the only real difference between BR1A and BR1G tenders was the fitting of a fallplate and gangway doors to the latter. 73053-73064 were Derby built, like 73050-73052 and had the BR1H type which was identical to the BR1 except (again) for the fitting of fallplate and gangway doors. (BR1G carried 5,000 gallons compared to the 4,250 of BR1 and BR1H). Earlier problems in operation had now been solved and 73053 and 73054 went new to Holbeck and 73055-73064 to Polmadie. Twenty of the class allocated to the Southern were fitted with other types because that Region had no water troughs and tenders needed greater water capacity. 73080-73089 had type BR1B, 4,725 gallons and all went new to Stewarts Lane in the summer of 1955, whilst 73110-73119 received BR1F tenders with a capacity of 5,625 gallons. These all went new to Nine Elms where their increased water capacity was put to good use on the longer non-stop jobs out of Waterloo. These last two designs had flush sides which proved more popular than the original inset models. The BR1B had good locker space at the front above the shovelling plate, the axle boxes had Timken roller bearings and the steps leading to the cab were fitted to the tender, a practice introduced by Bulleid. On both sides of all the Standard tenders, between the leading and middle axle, were feed water sieves, acting as a filter to remove sediment or any object that might foul the injectors. Engine and tender had steam brakes and it was possible to work these separately or combine them with the vacuum brake system.

The 75000s, introduced in 1951, were the first in the BR range to work with the type 2 tender and the inset coal bunker gave a nice balance to the appearance of the whole ensemble. This applied to 75000-75049. 75050, new at the end of 1956, was the first of the class to have a BR2A tender and as with the BR2, pick-up apparatus could be fitted if required. The major difference between the two types was of course the addition of a fallplate and gangway doors. After 75064 the remainder were allocated to the Southern Region and fitted with BR1B tenders. Brackets on the inside on the bunker sides, for lifting purposes, were a feature of these tenders. Water capacity was 4,725 gallons, for the longer non-stop journeys of the Southern Region.

BR1Bs were also attached to 76053-76069 when they went new to the SR and this type of tender enhanced the appearance of both the 75000 and 76000 classes. 76000-76044 were fitted with BR2 tenders and the remainder, 76045-76052 and 76070-76114 with BR2A. As the twenty 77000s did not appear until 1954, they had BR2A tenders and the fallplate and gangway doors must have pleased the footplate crews that worked in the wilder areas of the North East and Scotland.

78000-64 were the only class to have the type BR3 tender and with its capacity of 4 tons of coal and 3,000 gallons of water (giving a weight in working order of 36 tons 17 cwt) it was the smallest in the BR range, ideal for branch line work. A tender cab was fitted which gave reasonable protection when running tender first, with upright bars fitted over the tender cab windows. Like the other designs it had footsteps at the sides, front and back and a ladder at the rear, giving access to the tender top and the lid of the water tank.

251 9Fs were constructed between January 1954 and March 1960 and enjoyed a complex mix of tenders - twenty had the BR1B, 92020-92029, 92060-92066, 92097-92099; eighty-five had the BR1C, 92015-92019, 92045-92059, 92077-92086, 92100-92139, 92150-92164; another eighty-five had the BR1F, 92010-92014, 92030-92044, 92067-92076, 92087-92096, 92140-92149, 92168-92202; fifty-eight had the BR1G, 92000-92009, 92203-92250; and three the BR1K, 92165-92167. Whilst the BR1B carried 7 tons of coal the BR1C carried 9, the basic difference being the length of the interior coal space. At times the back end of a BR1C would not be cleared of coal, leaving degraded slack and other undesirable material for months on end.

The real oddities among the 9Fs were the mechanical stoker BR1Ks, built new at Crewe in the summer of 1958 and numbered 1529-1531. The Berkley mechanical equipment meant there was a fallplate in three parts, to fit over the screen, and steam jets distributed the coal around the firebox. The engines spent the early part of their working lives at Saltley and from there worked long distance freights, especially over the Settle - Carlisle main line. For a compelling account of a nightmare journey on one of these engines, read the second half of Chapter V *The Summit* in Terry Essery's *More Firing Days at Saltley*, published by D. Bradford Barton.

Table of tenders first allocated.

Locomotives	Year	Built	Type	Tender Numbers
70000-70014	1951	Crewe	BR1	759-773
70015-70024	1951	Crewe	BR1	774-783
70025-70029	1952	Crewe	BR1A	844-848
70030-70034	1952	Crewe	BR1	849-853
70035-70044	1952/3	Crewe	BR1	854-863
70045-70049	1954	Crewe	BR1D	979-983
70050-70054	1954	Crewe	BR1D	984-988
71000	1954/8	Crewe	BR1E/BR1J	1271/1528
72000-72009	1951/2	Crewe	BR1	784-793
73000-73009	1951	Derby	BR1	794-803
73010-73029	1951/2	Derby	BR1	804-823
73030-73049	1953	Derby	BR1	864-883
73050-73052	1954	Derby	BR1G	989-991
73053-73064	1954	Derby	BR1H	992-1003
73065-73074	1954	Derby	BR1C	1004-1013
73075-73079	1955	Derby	BR1C	1014-1018
73080-73089	1955	Derby	BR1B	1206-1215
73090-73099	1955	Derby	BR1C	1272-1281
73100-73109	1955/6	Doncaster	BR1B	1282-1291
73110-73119	1955	Doncaster	BR1F	1292-1301
73120-73124	1956	Doncaster	BR1B	1302-1306
73125-73134	1956	Derby	BR1B	1413-1422
73135-73144	1956	Derby	BR1C	1423-1432
73145-73154	1957	Derby	BR1B	1433-1442
73155-73171	1956/7	Doncaster	BR1B	1443-1459
75000-75019	1951/2	Swindon	BR2	824-843
75020-75029	1953/4	Swindon	BR2	884-893
75030-75049	1953	Swindon	BR2	894-913
75050-75064	1956/7	Swindon	BR2A	1014-1028
75065-75079	1955/6	Swindon	BR1B	1029-1043
76000-76019	1952/3	Horwich	BR2	914-933
76020-76024	1952/3	Doncaster	BR2	934-938
76025-76044	1953/4	Doncaster	BR2	1044-1063
76045-76052	1955/6	Doncaster	BR2A	1226-1233
76053-76069	1955/6	Doncaster	BR1B	1234-1250
76070-76074	1956	Doncaster	BR2A	1251-1255
76075-76099	1956/7	Horwich	BR2A	1460-1484
76100-76114	1957	Doncaster	BR2A	1485-1499
77000-77019	1954	Swindon	BR2A	1064-1083
78000-78009	1952/3	Darlington	BR3	939-948
78010-78044	1953/4	Darlington	BR3	1084-1118
78045-78054	1955	Darlington	BR3	1261-1270
78055-78064	1956	Darlington	BR3	1500-1509
92000-92009	1954	Crewe	BR1G	949-958
92010-92014	1954	Crewe	BR1F	959-963
92015-92019	1954	Crewe	BR1C	964-968
92020-92029	1955	Crewe	BR1B	969-978
92030-92044	1954/5	Crewe	BR1F	1119-1133
92045-92059	1955	Crewe	BR1C	1134-1148
92060-92066	1955	Crewe	BR1B	1149-1155
92067-92076	1955/6	Crewe	BR1F	1156-1165
92077-92086	1956	Crewe	BR1C	1166-1175
92087-92096	1956/7	Crewe	BR1F	1176-1185
92097-92099	1956	Crewe	BR1B	1307-1309
92100-92139	1956/7	Crewe	BR1C	1310-1349
92140-92149	1957	Crewe	BR1F	1350-1359
92150-92164	1957/8	Crewe	BR1C	1271/1361-1373
92165-92167	1958	Crewe	BR1K	1529-1531
92168-92177	1957/8	Crewe	BR1F	1378-1387
92178-92202	1957/8	Swindon	BR1F	1388-1412
92203-92220	1959/60	Swindon	BR1G	1510-1527
92221-92250	1958	Crewe	BR1G	1532-1561

Note 2 - Building Details By Class

Jan 1951 to Oct 1951. 70000-70024. Order no E479. Crewe.
Sept 1952 to June 1953. 70025-70044. Order no E483. Crewe.
June 1954 to Sept 1954. 70045 - 70054. Order no E486. Crewe.

May 1954. 71000. Order no E486. Crewe.
Dec 1951 to Mar 1952. 72000-72009. Order no E480. Crewe.

Apr 1951 to Jan 1952. 73000-73029. Order no 5122. Derby.
June 1953 to Dec 1953. 73030-73049. Order no 6230. Derby.
June 1954 to Aug 1954. 73050-73059. Order no 6735. Derby.
Aug 1954 to Oct 1954. 73060-73064. Order no 8035. Derby.
Oct 1954 to Dec 1954. 73065-73074. Order no 8025. Derby.
Apr 1955 to July 1955. 73075-73089. Order no 8241. Derby.
Oct 1955 to Dec 1955. 73090-73099. Order no 8845. Derby.
Aug 1955 to Sept 1955. 73100-73104. Engine order no 402. Doncaster.

Dec 1955 to Jan 1956. 73105-73109. Engine order no 404. Doncaster.
Oct 1955 to Dec 1955. 73110-73119. Engine order no 403. Doncaster.
Jan 1956 to Feb 1956. 73120-73124. Engine order no 404. Doncaster.
July 1956 to June 1957. 73125-73154. Order no 9247. Derby.
Dec 1956 to Mar 1957. 73155-73164. Engine order no 406. Doncaster.
Mar 1957 to May 1957. 73165-73171. Engine order no 407. Doncaster.

May 1951 to Oct 1951. 75000-75009. Lot no 390. Swindon.
Nov 1951 to Mar 1952. 75010-75019. Lot no 391. Swindon.
Nov 1953 to May 1954. 75020-75029. Lot no 400. Swindon.
June 1953 to Oct 1953. 75030-75049. Lot no 401. Swindon.
Nov 1956 to June 1957. 75050-75064. Lot no 408. Swindon.
Aug 1955 to Jan 1956. 75065-75079. Lot no 409. Swindon.
Dec 1952 to July 1953. 76000-76019. Horwich.
Dec 1952 to Jan 1953. 76020-76024. Engine order no 395.

Oct 1953 to Dec 1953. 76025-76034. Engine order no 396. Doncaster.
May 1954 to Aug 1954. 76035-76044. Engine order no 397. Doncaster.
May 1955 to April 1955. 76045-76049. Engine order no 401. Doncaster.
Aug 1956 to Sept 1956. 76050-76052. Engine order no 399. Doncaster.
Apr 1955 to July 1955. 76053-76062. Engine order no 400. Doncaster.
July 1956 to Aug 1956. 76063-76069. Engine order no 399. Doncaster.
Sept 1956 to Nov 1956. 76070-76074. Engine order no 405. Doncaster.
Dec 1956 to Nov 1957. 76075-76099. Lot no 249. Horwich.
May 1957 to Aug 1957. 76100-76109. Engine order no 408. Doncaster.
Aug 1957 to Oct 1957. 76110-76114. Engine order no 409. Doncaster.

Feb 1954 to Mar 1954. 77000-77004. Lot no 406. Swindon.
Mar 1954 to June 1954. 77005-77009. Lot no 407. Swindon.
June 1954 to July 1954. 77010-77014. Lot no 406. Swindon.
July 1954 to Sept 1954. 77015-77019. Lot no 407. Swindon.

Dec 1952 to Apr 1953. 78000-78009. Darlington.
Dec 1953 to July 1954. 78010-78029. Darlington.
Sept 1954 to Dec 1954. 78030-78044. Darlington.
Oct 1955 to Dec 1955. 78045-78054. Darlington.
Aug 1956 to Nov 1956. 78055-78064. Darlington.

Sept 1952 to Dec 1952. 80000-80009. Order no 5124. Derby.
July 1951 to Dec 1952. 80010-80053. Order no 3621. Derby.
Dec 1954 to Jan 1955. 80054-80058. Order no 6231. Derby.
Mar 1953 to Aug 1953. 80059-80068. Order no BR 5271. Brighton.
Sept 1953 to Feb 1954. 80069-80078. Order no BR 5788. Brighton.
Mar 1954 to July 1954. 80079-80088. Order no BR 6166. Brighton.
July 1954 to Apr 1955. 80089-80105. Order no BR 6167. Brighton.
Oct 1954 to Dec 1954. 80106-80115. Engine order no 398. Doncaster.
May 1955 to Sept 1955. 80116-80124. Order no BR 6360. Brighton.
Oct 1955 to Apr 1956. 80125-80134. Order no BR 6941. Brighton.
Apr 1956 to Mar 1957. 80135-80154. Order no BR 7739. Brighton.

Apr 1952 to June 1952. 82000-82009. Lot no 392. Swindon.
June 1952 to Sept 1952. 82010-82019. Lot no 393. Swindon.
Sept 1954 to Dec 1954. 82020-82029. Lot no 398. Swindon.
Dec 1954 to Jan 1955. 82030-82034. Lot no 399. Swindon.
Mar 1955 to Aug 1955. 82035-82044. Lot no 410. Swindon.

July 1953 to Oct 1953. 84000-84019. Order no E484. Crewe.
Mar 1957 to June 1957. 84020-84029. Darlington.

Jan 1954 to May 1954. 92000-92014. Order no E487. Crewe.
Sept 1954 to Oct 1954. 92015-92019. Order no E491. Crewe.
May 1955 to July 1955. 92020-92029. Order no E488. Crewe.
Nov 1954 to Mar 1955. 92030-92049. Order no E489. Crewe.
Sept 1955 to June 1956. 92050-92086. Order no E490. Crewe.
Aug 1956 to Apr 1957. 92087-92096. Lot no 421. Swindon.
June 1956 to June 1957. 92097-92134. Order no E493. Crewe.
June 1957 to Mar 1958. 92135-92177. Order no E494. Crewe.
Sept 1957 to Dec 1958. 92178-92202. Lot No 422. Swindon.
Apr 1959 to Mar 1960. 92203-92220. Order no 429. Swindon.
May 1958 to Dec 1958. 92221-92250. Order no E497. Crewe.

Note Three - A Variety of Names

A few notes on the naming of the Standards ('an extraordinary variety') would not go amiss. 70000 was named BRITANNIA on 30 January 1951 at Marylebone by Alfred Barnes, the now long-forgotten Minister of Transport. 'The Britannias' they were, ever after. (It is only, perhaps, the brief tenure of most Ministers of State that has largely spared us the 'political' locomotive name - imagine some of the possibilities...) 70001 turns out to be a warning - LORD HURCOMB was no Hammer of the French or Pillar of Empire, but a civil servant, and first Chairman of the British Transport Commission. However worthy a man, he hardly ranked among the likes of Shakespeare, Oliver Cromwell and the other greats! We have to think ourselves lucky that a proposal to name 70000 after him was not acted upon. Would we have had the *Hurcomb Pacifics?*...... After this things got better, though JOHN BUNYAN, to someone forced to read *Pilgrim's Progress* at school, was suspect. Literature soon gave way to some decent warlike figures, COEUR-de-LION, BLACK PRINCE, ALFRED THE GREAT, HOTSPUR, OLIVER CROMWELL and IRON DUKE and the stirring broad gauge monickers APOLLO and suchlike. FLYING DUTCHMAN seemed odd to me but the various 'stars' were wonderful of course. Literature, war and Empire followed and apart from the stirring Firths, inspiration (ANZAC aside) largely dried up. In fairness, of course, all of the best names had already been taken - heroes, the aristocracy/royalty, the fruits of Empire, stately buildings/ancient monuments, even public schools and racehorses. There remained one Britannia of course, 70047, which inexplicably never received a name. I have never read of a particular explanation other than that of the process 'running out of steam', though *British Railways Illustrated* ran a competition some years ago. Readers came up with OVERLORD.

70000   BRITANNIA
70001   LORD HURCOMB
70002   GEOFFREY CHAUCER
70003   JOHN BUNYAN
70004   WILLIAM SHAKESPEARE
70005   JOHN MILTON
70006   ROBERT BURNS
70007   COEUR-de-LION
70008   BLACK PRINCE
70009   ALFRED THE GREAT
70010   OWEN GLENDOWER
70011   HOTSPUR

70012   JOHN OF GAUNT
70013   OLIVER CROMWELL
70014   IRON DUKE
70015   APOLLO
70016   ARIEL
70017   ARROW
70018   FLYING DUTCHMAN
70019   LIGHTNING
70020   MERCURY
70021   MORNING STAR
70022   TORNADO
70023   VENUS
70024   VULCAN
70025   WESTERN STAR
70026   POLAR STAR
70027   RISING STAR
70028   ROYAL STAR
70029   SHOOTING STAR
70030   WILLIAM WORDSWORTH
70031   BYRON
70032   TENNYSON
70033   CHARLES DICKENS
70034   THOMAS HARDY
70035   RUDYARD KIPLING
70036   BOADICEA
70037   HEREWARD THE WAKE
70038   ROBIN HOOD
70039   SIR CHRISTOPHER WREN
70040   CLIVE OF INDIA
70041   SIR JOHN MOORE
70042   LORD ROBERTS
70043   LORD KITCHENER
70044   EARL HAIG
70045   LORD ROWALLAN
70046   ANZAC
70047
70048   THE TERRITORIAL ARMY
         1908-1958
70049   SOLWAY FIRTH
70050   FORTH OF CLYDE
70051   FIRTH OF FORTH
70052   FIRTH OF TAY
70053   MORAY FIRTH
70054   DORNOCH FIRTH

The one-off 8P became DUKE OF GLOUCESTER; it was a name fully in keeping with the Britannia tradition already established but it related not to the role of the Duke in history but rather more prosaically to the then Duke's role as President of the 16th International Railway Congress. The Clans reflect a far more tangled history, with one lot murdering another at Glencoe in 1692; the cancelled locomotives would have represented further Scottish Clans and even more warlike names were planned for the Southern ones. The only other 'original' name was of course EVENING STAR and the tale of the ballot to choose it is well known. MORNING STAR (70021) can denote Jupiter, Mars, Saturn or especially Venus when rising shortly before the sun, and was therefore less specific than it might be. EVENING STAR was 'a bright star just after sunset' and, once again, applied in especial to Venus. So, with 70023, there were three Standards named after Venus!

The Southern names continued the Region's own private Arthurian tradition; certainly it made for wonderful names, though the plates themselves were poor things in comparison to the plates of the other Standards. The names were taken from the withdrawn Urie Arthurs Nos.30736-30755 but the sequence was not followed:

73080   MERLIN (30740)
73110   THE RED KNIGHT (30755)
73081   EXCALIBUR (30736)
73111   KING UTHER (30737)
73082   CAMELOT (30742)
73112   MORGAN le FAY (30750)
73083   PENDRAGON (30746)
73113   LYONESSE (30743)
73084   TINTAGEL (30745)
73114   ETARRE (30751)
73085   MELISANDE (30753)
73115   KING PELLINORE (30738)
73086   THE GREEN KNIGHT (30754)
73116   ISEULT (30749)
73087   LINETTE (30752)
73117   VIVIEN (30748)
73088   JOYOUS GARD (30741)
73118   KING LEODEGRANCE (30739)
73089   MAID OF ASTOLAT (30744)
73119   ELAINE (30747)

All these ran past my 'back door' and were a familiar sight for some years. Namings took place between May 1959 with 73089 and September 1962, with 73116 ISEULT the last to be dealt with. The plates were modest things, like their forerunners, but did not carry any explanatory legend, in the manner of the originals, with their KING ARTHUR CLASS. The names were fixed to the running plates and 'the centre of the nameplate coincided with the centre line of the dome on the boiler'.

ALLOCATIONS

70000 NEW 1/51; STRATFORD 1/51; NORWICH 1/59; MARCH 9/61; WILLESDEN 3/63; CREWE NORTH 5/63; CREWE SOUTH 5/65; NEWTON HEATH 3/66; WITHDRAWN 5/66. ENGINE PRESERVED.

70001 NEW 2/51; STRATFORD 2/51; NORWICH 1/59; MARCH 9/61; WILLESDEN 3/63; ASTON 12/63; KINGMOOR 10/64; WITHDRAWN 9/66.

70002 NEW 3/51; STRATFORD 3/51; YARMOUTH SOUTH TOWN 1/59; NORWICH 1/59; MARCH 6/61; KINGMOOR 12/63; WITHDRAWN 1/67.

70003 NEW 3/51; STRATFORD 3/51; NORWICH 1/59; MARCH 7/61; KINGMOOR 12/63; WITHDRAWN 3/67.

70004 NEW 3/51; STRATFORD 3/51; STEWARTS LANE 9/51; KENTISH TOWN 6/58; TRAFFORD PARK 7/58; WILLESDEN 12/60; ASTON 3/62; WILLESDEN 4/62; CARLISLE (CANAL) 5/63; KINGMOOR 6/63; WILLESDEN 7/63; CREWE NORTH 1/65; STOCKPORT (EDGELEY) 5/65; KINGMOOR 6/67; WITHDRAWN 12/67.

70005 NEW 4/51; STRATFORD 4/51; RUGBY TESTING STATION 12/51; STRATFORD 2/52; NORWICH 1/59; MARCH 9/61; WILLESDEN 3/63; ASTON 12/63; KINGMOOR 10/64; WITHDRAWN 7/67.

70006 NEW 4/51; STRATFORD 4/51; NORWICH 5/51; STRATFORD 10/51; NORWICH 11/51; MARCH 12/61; KINGMOOR 12/63; WITHDRAWN 5/67.

70007 NEW 4/51; STRATFORD 4/51; NORWICH 5/51; MARCH 11/61; KINGMOOR 12/63; WITHDRAWN 6/65.

70008 NEW 4/51; NORWICH 4/51; MARCH 9/61; KINGMOOR 12/63; WITHDRAWN 1/67.

70009 NEW 5/51; NORWICH 5/51; NINE ELMS 6/51; NORWICH 10/51; MARCH 9/61; KINGMOOR 12/63; WITHDRAWN 1/67.

70010 NEW 5/51; NORWICH 5/51; MARCH 12/61; WILLESDEN 3/63; CREWE NORTH 1/65; CREWE SOUTH 5/65; KINGMOOR 6/65; WITHDRAWN 9/67.

70011 NEW 5/51; NORWICH 5/51; MARCH 9/61; KINGMOOR 12/63; CARLISLE (UPPERBY) 2/65; KINGMOOR 12/66; WITHDRAWN 12/67.

70012 NEW 5/51; NORWICH 5/51; STRATFORD 10/58; YARMOUTH SOUTH TOWN 1/59; NORWICH 1/59; MARCH 9/61; WILLESDEN 3/63; CREWE NORTH 1/65; CREWE SOUTH 5/65; LLANDUDNO JUNCTION 2/66; CREWE SOUTH 4/66; KINGMOOR 8/66; WITHDRAWN 12/67.

70013 NEW 5/51; NORWICH 5/51; IPSWICH 9/58; NORWICH 1/59; MARCH 9/61; KINGMOOR 12/63; CARLISLE (UPPERBY) 2/65; KINGMOOR 12/66; CARNFORTH 1/68; WITHDRAWN 8/68; ENGINE PRESERVED.

70014 NEW 6/51; NORWICH 6/51; NINE ELMS 6/51; STEWARTS LANE 9/51; KENTISH TOWN 6/58; TRAFFORD PARK 7/58; NEWTON HEATH 12/60; WILLESDEN 9/61; NEASDEN 9/61; ANNESLEY 6/62; WILLESDEN 10/62; LLANDUDNO JUNCTION 12/62; WILLESDEN 5/63; CREWE NORTH 1/65; CREWE SOUTH 5/65; LLANDUDNO JUNCTION 2/66; CREWE SOUTH 4/66; KINGMOOR 8/66; WITHDRAWN 12/67.

70015 NEW 6/51; CAMDEN 6/51; STRATFORD 1/52; OLD OAK COMMON 9/52; CARDIFF (CANTON) 12/56; TRAFFORD PARK 7/58; NEWTON HEATH 12/60; WILLESDEN 9/61; NEASDEN 9/61; ANNESLEY 6/62; WILLESDEN 10/62; LLANDUDNO JUNCTION 12/62; CREWE NORTH 1/65; STOCKPORT (EDGELEY) 5/65; KINGMOOR 6/67; WITHDRAWN 8/67.

70016 NEW 6/51; LEEDS HOLBECK 6/51; STRATFORD 3/52; LAIRA 8/53; CARDIFF (CANTON) 12/56; CARLISLE (CANAL) 9/61; LONGSIGHT 5/62; CREWE NORTH 9/62; LLANDUDNO JUNCTION 12/62; HOLYHEAD 2/63; ASTON 5/63; KINGMOOR 10/64; WITHDRAWN 8/67.

70017 NEW 6/51; OLD OAK COMMON 6/51; SALISBURY 5/53; OLD OAK COMMON 6/53; CARDIFF (CANTON) 12/56; KENTISH TOWN 6/58; TRAFFORD PARK 7/58; WILLESDEN 12/60; ASTON 9/61; RUGBY 10/62; ASTON 2/63; LLANDUDNO JUNCTION 5/63; CREWE NORTH 9/63; CREWE SOUTH 5/65; NEWTON HEATH 7/65; KINGMOOR 5/66; WITHDRAWN 9/66.

70018 NEW 6/51; OLD OAK COMMON 6/51; CARDIFF (CANTON) 12/56; CARLISLE (CANAL) 9/61; LONGSIGHT 5/62; CREWE NORTH 9/62; CREWE SOUTH 5/65; CARLISLE (UPPERBY) 3/66; KINGMOOR 12/66; WITHDRAWN 12/66.

70019 NEW 6/51; NEWTON ABBOT 6/51; LAIRA 9/51; CARDIFF (CANTON) 12/56; KINGMOOR 9/61; LONGSIGHT 5/62; CREWE NORTH 9/62; ASTON 5/63; CREWE NORTH 9/63; CREWE SOUTH 5/65; CARLISLE (UPPERBY) 7/65; WITHDRAWN 3/66.

70020 NEW 7/51; OLD OAK COMMON 7/51; CARDIFF (CANTON) 12/56; KINGMOOR 9/61; LONGSIGHT 6/62; CREWE NORTH 9/62; CARLISLE (CANAL) 1/63; WILLESDEN 5/63; CREWE NORTH 1/65; CREWE SOUTH 5/65; CARLISLE (UPPERBY) 7/65; KINGMOOR 12/66; WITHDRAWN 1/67.

70021 NEW 8/51; LAIRA 8/51; CARDIFF (CANTON) 1/57; TRAFFORD PARK 7/58; WILLESDEN 2/61; ASTON 3/62; WILLESDEN 3/62; CREWE NORTH 1/65; CREWE SOUTH 5/65; NEWTON HEATH 7/65; STOCKPORT (EDGELEY) 5/66; KINGMOOR 6/67; WITHDRAWN 12/67.

70022 NEW 8/51; LAIRA 8/51; NEWTON ABBOT 4/52; CARDIFF (CANTON) 12/56; KINGMOOR 9/61; LONGSIGHT 6/62; ASTON 9/62; RUGBY 10/62; ASTON 2/63; KINGMOOR 10/64; CARLISLE (UPPERBY) 11/64; KINGMOOR 12/66; WITHDRAWN 12/67.

70023 NEW 8/51; OLD OAK COMMON 8/51; SALISBURY 5/53; OLD OAK COMMON 6/53; CARDIFF (CANTON) 2/57; KINGMOOR 9/61; LONGSIGHT 6/62; ASTON 9/62; RUGBY 10/62; ASTON 2/63; CREWE NORTH 9/63; HOLYHEAD 9/64; CREWE NORTH 2/65; CREWE SOUTH 5/65; LLANDUDNO JUNCTION 2/66; CREWE SOUTH 4/66; KINGMOOR 9/66; WITHDRAWN 12/67.

70024 NEW 10/51; LAIRA 10/51; EXMOUTH JUNCTION 5/53; LAIRA 6/53; CARDIFF (CANTON) 12/56; ASTON 9/61; RUGBY 10/62; ASTON 2/63; WILLESDEN 4/63; CREWE NORTH 11/63; HOLYHEAD 9/64; CREWE NORTH 2/65; CREWE SOUTH 5/65; LLANDUDNO JUNCTION 2/66; CREWE SOUTH 4/66; CARLISLE (UPPERBY) 8/66; KINGMOOR 12/66; WITHDRAWN 12/67.

70025 NEW 9/52; CARDIFF CANTON 9/52; RUGBY TESTING STATION 9/52; CARDIFF (CANTON) 5/53; ASTON 9/61; CREWE NORTH 5/63; CREWE SOUTH 5/65; LLANDUDNO JUNCTION 2/66; CREWE SOUTH 4/66; KINGMOOR 9/66; WITHDRAWN 12/67.

70026 NEW 10/52; CARDIFF (CANTON) 10/52; ASTON 9/61; HOLYHEAD 4/63; STOCKPORT (EDGELEY) 5/65; WITHDRAWN 1/67.

70027 NEW 10/52; CARDIFF (CANTON) 10/52; ASTON 9/61; HOLYHEAD 5/63; CREWE NORTH 2/65; CREWE SOUTH 5/65; LLANDUDNO JUNCTION 2/66; CREWE SOUTH 4/66; KINGMOOR 9/66; WITHDRAWN 6/67.

70028 NEW 10/52; CARDIFF (CANTON) 10/52; EXMOUTH JUNCTION 5/53; CARDIFF (CANTON) 6/53; ASTON 9/61; LONGSIGHT 3/62; ASTON 6/62; LONGSIGHT 7/62; ASTON 9/62; WILLESDEN 5/63; CREWE NORTH 9/63; CREWE SOUTH 5/65; LLANDUDNO JUNCTION 2/66; CREWE SOUTH 4/66; KINGMOOR 9/66; WITHDRAWN 9/67.

70029 NEW 11/52; CARDIFF (CANTON) 11/52; EXMOUTH JUNCTION 5/53; CARDIFF (CANTON) 6/53; ASTON 9/61; KINGMOOR 10/64; CARLISLE (UPPERBY) 11/64; KINGMOOR 12/66; WITHDRAWN 10/67.

70030 NEW 11/52; HOLYHEAD 11/52; LONGSIGHT 12/52; LEEDS (HOLBECK) 1/53; LONGSIGHT 2/53; DOVER 5/53; LONGSIGHT 6/53; NORWICH 7/53; YARMOUTH SOUTH TOWN 10/58; NORWICH 1/59; MARCH 6/61; CREWE NORTH 7/63; CREWE SOUTH 5/65; CARLISLE (UPPERBY) 7/65; WITHDRAWN 6/66.

70031 NEW 11/52; HOLYHEAD 11/52; LONGSIGHT 1/53; TRAFFORD PARK 4/60; LONGSIGHT 9/60; ASTON 9/61; WILLESDEN 4/63; CREWE NORTH 1/65; CREWE SOUTH 5/65; CARLISLE (UPPERBY) 7/65; KINGMOOR 12/66; WITHDRAWN 11/67.

70032 NEW 12/52; HOLYHEAD 12/52; LONGSIGHT 1/53; TRAFFORD PARK 2/60; WILLESDEN 1/61; KINGMOOR 10/64; CARLISLE (UPPERBY) 11/64; KINGMOOR 12/66; WITHDRAWN 9/67.

70033 NEW 12/52; HOLYHEAD 12/52; LONGSIGHT 1/53; TRAFFORD PARK 2/60; WILLESDEN 2/61; LLANDUDNO JUNCTION 12/62; HOLYHEAD 3/63; WILLESDEN 5/63; CREWE NORTH 9/63; CREWE SOUTH 5/65; KINGMOOR 6/65; WITHDRAWN 7/67.

70034 NEW 12/52; LONGSIGHT 12/52; STEWARTS LANE 5/53; LONGSIGHT 6/53; STRATFORD 7/53; NORWICH 1/59; MARCH 6/61; WILLESDEN 3/63; CREWE NORTH 6/64; CREWE SOUTH 5/65; NEWTON HEATH 7/65; KINGMOOR 5/66; WITHDRAWN 5/67.

70035 NEW 12/52; NORWICH 12/52; MARCH 6/58; NORWICH 1/59; IMMINGHAM 10/61; MARCH 6/63; KINGMOOR 12/63; WITHDRAWN 12/67.

70036 NEW 12/52; STRATFORD 12/52; NORWICH 1/59; MARCH 11/60; IMMINGHAM 10/61; CARLISLE (UPPERBY) 12/63; KINGMOOR 2/64; WITHDRAWN 10/66.

70037 NEW 12/52; STRATFORD 12/52; NORWICH 1/59; MARCH 11/60; IMMINGHAM 9/61; CARLISLE (UPPERBY) 12/63; KINGMOOR 1/64; WITHDRAWN 11/66.

70038 NEW 1/53; STRATFORD 1/53; NORWICH 1/59; MARCH 11/60; IMMINGHAM 10/61; CARLISLE (UPPERBY) 12/63; KINGMOOR 1/64; WITHDRAWN 8/67.

70039 NEW 2/53; NORWICH 2/53; STRATFORD 5/53; NORWICH 1/59; IMMINGHAM 12/60; CARLISLE (UPPERBY) 12/63; KINGMOOR 2/64; WITHDRAWN 9/67.

70040 NEW 3/53; NORWICH 3/53; STRATFORD 5/53; NORWICH 1/59; IMMINGHAM 12/60; CARLISLE (UPPERBY) 12/63; KINGMOOR 2/64; WITHDRAWN 4/67.

70041 NEW 3/53; STRATFORD 3/53; NORWICH 1/59; IMMINGHAM 12/60; CARLISLE (UPPERBY) 12/63; KINGMOOR 1/64; WITHDRAWN 4/67.

70042 NEW 4/53; STRATFORD 4/53; KENTISH TOWN 5/58; TRAFFORD PARK 6/58; WILLESDEN 12/60; CREWE NORTH 5/63; CREWE SOUTH 5/65; HOLYHEAD 6/65; KINGMOOR 12/65; WITHDRAWN 5/67.

70043 NEW 5/53; LONGSIGHT 5/53; TOTON 9/53; LONGSIGHT 10/53; TOTON 10/53; LONGSIGHT 12/53; M & EE DEPT DERBY 10/54; LONGSIGHT 12/54; ASTON 9/61; LONGSIGHT 3/62; ASTON 6/62; WILLESDEN 4/63; CREWE NORTH 6/64; CREWE SOUTH 5/65; WITHDRAWN 8/65.

70044 NEW 6/53; LONGSIGHT 6/53; M & EE DEPT DERBY 10/54; LONGSIGHT 12/54; LEEDS (HOLBECK) 12/58; CREWE NORTH 8/62; CREWE SOUTH 5/65; NEWTON HEATH 7/65; STOCKPORT (EDGELEY) 5/66; WITHDRAWN 10/66.

70045 NEW 6/54; HOLYHEAD 6/54; CHESTER (MIDLAND) 11/59; CREWE NORTH 11/59; CAMDEN 12/59; NEWTON HEATH 1/60; NEASDEN 9/61; ASTON 6/62; HOLYHEAD 12/62; OXLEY 6/65; BANBURY 9/65; KINGMOOR 1/66; WITHDRAWN 12/67.

70046 NEW 6/54; HOLYHEAD 6/54; CREWE NORTH 11/59; LONGSIGHT 2/60; WILLESDEN 9/61; KINGMOOR 9/61; WILLESDEN 10/61; ASTON 4/62; HOLYHEAD 12/62; CREWE NORTH 2/65; CREWE SOUTH 5/65; HOLYHEAD 6/65; BANBURY 9/65; KINGMOOR 1/66; WITHDRAWN 7/67.

70047 NEW 6/54; HOLYHEAD 6/54; CREWE NORTH 11/59; HOLYHEAD 8/60; WILLESDEN 6/61; KINGMOOR 9/61; WILLESDEN 10/61; ASTON 3/62; WILLESDEN 12/63; HOLYHEAD 1/64; OXLEY 6/65; BANBURY 9/65; KINGMOOR 1/66; WITHDRAWN 7/67.

70048 NEW 7/54; HOLYHEAD 7/54; CREWE NORTH 11/59; CAMDEN 12/59; NEWTON HEATH 1/60; NEASDEN 9/61; ANNESLEY 6/62; WILLESDEN 10/62; LLANDUDNO JUNCTION 12/62; HOLYHEAD 12/62; ASTON 4/63; WILLESDEN 12/63; KINGMOOR 10/64; CARLISLE (UPPERBY) 11/64; KINGMOOR 12/66; WITHDRAWN 5/67.

70049 NEW 7/54; HOLYHEAD 7/54; CHESTER (MIDLAND) 11/59; CREWE NORTH 11/59; CAMDEN 12/59; CREWE NORTH 1/60; NEWTON HEATH 2/60; NEASDEN 9/61; ANNESLEY 6/62; WILLESDEN 10/62; LLANDUDNO JUNCTION 12/62; HOLYHEAD 12/62; ASTON 5/63; CREWE NORTH 10/63; WILLESDEN 3/64; KINGMOOR 10/64; CARLISLE (UPPERBY) 11/64; KINGMOOR 12/66; WITHDRAWN 12/67.

70050 NEW 8/54; POLMADIE 8/54; CORKERHILL 4/62; CREWE NORTH 10/62; HOLYHEAD 12/62; CREWE NORTH 1/63; CREWE SOUTH 5/65; BANBURY 9/65; KINGMOOR 1/66; WITHDRAWN 8/66.

70051 NEW 8/54; POLMADIE 8/54; CORKERHILL 4/62; CREWE NORTH 10/62; HOLYHEAD 12/62; CREWE NORTH 1/63; CREWE SOUTH 5/65; BANBURY 9/65; KINGMOOR 1/66; WITHDRAWN 12/67.

70052 NEW 8/54; POLMADIE 8/54; CORKERHILL 4/62; CREWE NORTH 10/62; CREWE SOUTH 5/65; BANBURY 9/65; KINGMOOR 1/66; WITHDRAWN 4/67.

70053 NEW 9/54; POLMADIE 9/54; LEEDS (HOLBECK) 10/58; CREWE NORTH 8/62; HOLYHEAD 6/64; OXLEY 6/65; BANBURY 9/65; KINGMOOR 1/66; WITHDRAWN 4/67.

70054 NEW 9/54; POLMADIE 9/54; LEEDS (HOLBECK) 10/58; CREWE NORTH 8/62; WILLESDEN 3/64; CREWE NORTH 7/64; CREWE SOUTH 5/65; BANBURY 9/65; KINGMOOR 1/66; WITHDRAWN 11/66.

71000 NEW 5/54; CREWE NORTH 5/54; SWINDON 10/54; CREWE NORTH 5/55; WITHDRAWN 11/62. ENGINE PRESERVED.

72000 NEW 12/51; POLMADIE 12/51; HAYMARKET 10/57; POLMADIE 4/58; ST MARGARETS 11/59; POLMADIE 3/60; WITHDRAWN 12/62.

72001 NEW 12/51; POLMADIE 12/51; HAYMARKET 11/59; POLMADIE 3/60; WITHDRAWN 12/62.

72002 NEW 1/52; POLMADIE 1/52; HAYMARKET 10/57; POLMADIE 4/58; HAYMARKET 11/59; POLMADIE 3/60; WITHDRAWN 12/62..

72003 NEW 1/52; POLMADIE 1/52; ST MARGARETS 11/59; POLMADIE 3/60; WITHDRAWN 12/62.

72004 NEW 2/52; POLMADIE 2/52; ST MARGARETS 11/59; POLMADIE 3/60; WITHDRAWN 12/62.

72005 NEW 2/52; KINGMOOR 2/52; HAYMARKET 10/57; KINGMOOR 4/58; WITHDRAWN 5/65.

72006 NEW 2/52; KINGMOOR 2/52; HAYMARKET 10/57; KINGMOOR 4/58; WITHDRAWN 5/66.

72007 NEW 3/52; KINGMOOR 3/52; WITHDRAWN 12/65.

72008 NEW 3/52; KINGMOOR 3/52; WITHDRAWN 4/66.

72009 NEW 3/52; KINGMOOR 3/52; STRATFORD 9/58; KINGMOOR 10/58; WITHDRAWN 8/65.

73000 NEW 4/51; STRATFORD 11/51; DERBY 3/52; MILLHOUSES 1/53; DERBY 2/53; NOTTINGHAM 10/53; GRIMESTHORPE 5/58; CANKLOW 1/61; DERBY 1/62; WOODFORD HALSE 9/62; OXLEY 1/65; SHREWSBURY 4/65; AGECROFT 4/66; PATRICROFT 10/66; WITHDRAWN 3/68.

73001 NEW 5/51; DERBY 5/51; SHREWSBURY 3/56; SWINDON 11/56; BRISTOL (BARROW ROAD) 1/64; GLOUCESTER (HORTON ROAD) 1/65; BATH (GREEN PARK) 2/65; WITHDRAWN 12/65.

73002 NEW 5/51; DERBY 5/51; STRATFORD 11/51; DERBY 1/52; NOTTINGHAM 10/53; BRISTOL (BARROW ROAD) 1/58; CANKLOW 5/58; MILLHOUSES 1/60; CANKLOW 4/61; EASTLEIGH 11/62; WEYMOUTH 9/63; WITHDRAWN 3/67.

73003 NEW 6/51; LEICESTER (MIDLAND) 6/51; BRISTOL (BARROW ROAD) 1/58; SHREWSBURY 3/63; BRISTOL (BARROW ROAD) 9/63; OXFORD 6/65; WITHDRAWN 12/65.

73004 NEW 6/51; LEICESTER (MIDLAND) 6/51; DERBY 12/51; LEICESTER (MIDLAND) 1/52; HEATON MERSEY 1/57; LEICESTER (MIDLAND) 3/57; MILLHOUSES 5/58; CHESTER (MIDLAND) 2/60; WILLESDEN 5/60; BLETCHLEY 3/64; NUNEATON 1/65; CROES NEWYDD 6/65; BOLTON 4/66; WITHDRAWN 10/67.

73005 NEW 6/51; PERTH 6/51; CORKERHILL 1/63; WITHDRAWN 6/66.

73006 NEW 7/51; PERTH 7/51; CORKERHILL 1/63; PATRICROFT 7/64; WITHDRAWN 3/67.

73007 NEW 7/51; PERTH 7/51; GRANGEMOUTH 6/64; STIRLING 10/65; WITHDRAWN 3/66.

73008 NEW 7/51; RUGBY TESTING STATION 7/51; PERTH 4/52; ABERDEEN (FERRYHILL) 7/64; WITHDRAWN 9/65.

73009 NEW 7/51; PERTH 7/51; CORKERHILL 1/63; WITHDRAWN 7/66.

73010 NEW 8/51; LEEDS (HOLBECK) 8/51; LEICESTER (CENTRAL) 9/59; NEASDEN 6/60; WOODFORD HALSE 6/62; OXLEY 1/65; PATRICROFT 4/65; WITHDRAWN 6/68.

73011 NEW 8/51; LEEDS (HOLBECK) 8/51; MILLHOUSES 10/53; HOLYHEAD 2/60; LLANDUDNO JUNCTION 2/63; WOODFORD HALSE 11/63; OXLEY 1/65; PATRICROFT 4/65; WITHDRAWN 11/67.

73012 NEW 8/51; LEEDS (HOLBECK) 8/51; SHREWSBURY 9/53; SWINDON 11/56; LLANELLY 1/64; BRISTOL (BARROW ROAD) 6/64; WITHDRAWN 11/64.

73013 NEW 8/51; MILLHOUSES 8/51; SHREWSBURY 9/53; CHESTER (WEST) 7/55; CHESTER (MIDLAND) 9/59; WILLESDEN 5/60; BLETCHLEY 3/64; OXLEY 1/65; BANBURY 6/65; BOLTON 4/66; WITHDRAWN 5/66.

73014 NEW 9/51; MILLHOUSES 9/51; SHREWSBURY 9/53; CARDIFF (CANTON) 8/55; CHESTER (WEST) 8/58; CHESTER (MIDLAND) 4/60; WILLESDEN 5/60; BLETCHLEY 3/64; OXLEY 2/65; BANBURY 6/65; BOLTON 4/66; WITHDRAWN 7/67.

73015 NEW 9/51; MILLHOUSES 9/51; SHREWSBURY 9/53; DERBY 3/56; BRISTOL (BARROW ROAD) 5/57; BATH (GREEN PARK) 6/65; WITHDRAWN 8/65.

73016 NEW 9/51; GRIMESTHORPE 9/51; MILLHOUSES 3/52; DERBY 1/53; MILLHOUSES 2/53; CANKLOW 1/62; EASTLEIGH 11/62; FELTHAM 12/63; NINE ELMS 11/64; FELTHAM 10/65; WEYMOUTH 11/65; WITHDRAWN 12/66.

73017 NEW 9/51; NOTTINGHAM 9/51; SHREWSBURY 9/53; CARDIFF (CANTON) 6/56; SHREWSBURY 7/56; SWINDON 11/56; WEYMOUTH 9/58; WITHDRAWN 10/64.

73018 NEW 10/51; NOTTINGHAM 10/51; SHREWSBURY 9/53; SWINDON 11/56; WEYMOUTH 9/58; GUILDFORD 4/67; WITHDRAWN 7/67.

73019 NEW 10/51; NOTTINGHAM 10/51; BRISTOL (ST PHILLIP'S MARSH) 9/53; BATH (GREEN PARK) 6/58; BRISTOL (BARROW ROAD) 7/60; BATH (GREEN PARK) 10/60; GLOUCESTER (BARNWOOD) 4/62; GLOUCESTER (HORTON ROAD) 4/64; OXLEY 11/64; BOLTON 4/66; WITHDRAWN 1/67.

73020 NEW 10/51; CHESTER (MIDLAND) 10/51; WILLESDEN 9/52; CHESTER (MIDLAND) 10/52; CHESTER (WEST) 9/53; SHREWSBURY 9/54; SWINDON 11/56; WEYMOUTH 9/58; GUILDFORD 4/67; WITHDRAWN 7/67.

73021 NEW 10/51; CHESTER (MIDLAND) 10/51; CHESTER (WEST) 9/53; CARDIFF (CANTON) 4/59; SHREWSBURY 4/60; LLANELLY 5/60; BRISTOL (BARROW ROAD) 7/62; GLOUCESTER (BARNWOOD) 9/62; GLOUCESTER (HORTON ROAD) 4/64; OXFORD 6/65; WITHDRAWN 8/65.

73022 NEW 10/51; CHESTER (MIDLAND) 10/51; BRISTOL (ST PHILLIP'S MARSH) 9/53; LANDORE 12/53; BRISTOL (ST PHILLIP'S MARSH) 1/54; SWINDON 7/54; WEYMOUTH 9/58; EASTLEIGH 9/64; GUILDFORD 5/65; NINE ELMS 6/66; WITHDRAWN 4/67.

73023 NEW 11/51; PATRICROFT 11/51; CHESTER (WEST) 9/53; CARDIFF (CANTON) 4/59; LLANELLY 5/60; BATH (GREEN PARK) 6/64; OXFORD 9/64; WITHDRAWN 8/65.

73024 NEW 11/51; PATRICROFT 11/51; CHESTER (WEST) 9/53; SHREWSBURY 9/54; CARDIFF (CANTON) 7/56; CHESTER (WEST) 8/58; CARDIFF (CANTON) 4/59; SHREWSBURY 4/60; BRISTOL (BARROW ROAD) 7/62; GLOUCESTER (BARNWOOD) 10/62; SHREWSBURY 3/63; LLANELLY 9/63; BRISTOL (BARROW ROAD) 6/64; OXFORD 9/64; WITHDRAWN 11/64.

73025 NEW 11/51; BLACKPOOL 11/51; SHREWSBURY 9/53; CARDIFF (CANTON) 7/54; CHESTER (WEST) 8/58; SHREWSBURY 4/59; OXLEY 1/65; SHREWSBURY 3/65; AGECROFT 4/66; PATRICROFT 10/66; WITHDRAWN 10/67.

73026 NEW 11/51; BLACKPOOL 11/51; SHREWSBURY 9/53; CARDIFF (CANTON) 7/54; CHESTER (WEST) 8/58; SHREWSBURY 4/59; LEAMINGTON SPA 10/64; TYSELEY 6/65; BOLTON 4/66; WITHDRAWN 4/67.

73027 NEW 12/51; BLACKPOOL 12/51; BRISTOL (ST PHILLIP'S MARSH) 9/53; SWINDON 7/54; WITHDRAWN 2/64.

73028 NEW 12/51; BLACKPOOL 12/51; BRISTOL (ST PHILLIP'S MARSH) 9/53; BATH (GREEN PARK) 6/58; BRISTOL (BARROW ROAD) 7/60; BATH (GREEN PARK) 10/60; BRISTOL (BARROW ROAD) 5/61; SWINDON 11/63; GLOUCESTER (BARNWOOD) 1/64; GLOUCESTER (HORTON ROAD) 4/64; OXLEY 11/64; BOLTON 4/66; WITHDRAWN 12/66.

73029 NEW 1/52; BLACKPOOL 1/52; BRISTOL (ST PHILLIP'S

MARSH) 9/53; CARMARTHEN 12/53; BRISTOL (ST PHILLIP'S MARSH) 1/54; SWINDON 9/57; WEYMOUTH 9/58; EASTLEIGH 8/64; GUILDFORD 5/65; NINE ELMS 6/66; WITHDRAWN 7/67.

73030 NEW 6/53; DERBY 6/53; RUGBY TESTING STATION 6/53; DERBY 11/53; LEICESTER (MIDLAND) 1/58; PATRICROFT 5/58; EXMOUTH JUNCTION 10/63; BRISTOL (BARROW ROAD) 9/64; BATH (GREEN PARK) 1/65; BRISTOL (BARROW ROAD) 2/65; OXFORD 6/65; WITHDRAWN 8/65.

73031 NEW 7/53; DERBY 7/53; BRISTOL (BARROW ROAD) 6/57; RUGBY TESTING STATION 11/58; BATH (GREEN PARK) 11/61; GLOUCESTER (BARNWOOD) 4/62; GLOUCESTER (HORTON ROAD) 4/64; OXFORD 6/65; WITHDRAWN 9/65.

73032 NEW 7/53; KINGMOOR 7/53; BRISTOL (ST PHILLIP'S MARSH) 8/53; BIRKENHEAD 6/58; WILLESDEN 5/60; NEASDEN 10/60; WOODFORD HALSE 6/62; NUNEATON 8/64; CROES NEWYDD 5/65; WITHDRAWN 8/65.

73033 NEW 8/53; POLMADIE 8/53; SHREWSBURY 9/53; OXLEY 10/56; CHESTER (WEST) 6/58; CHESTER (MIDLAND) 9/59; WILLESDEN 5/60; CHESTER (MIDLAND) 7/62; WILLESDEN 8/62; BLETCHLEY 3/64; OXLEY 1/65; NUNEATON 3/65; PATRICROFT 7/65; WITHDRAWN 1/68.

73034 NEW 8/53; KINGMOOR 8/53 SHREWSBURY 9/53; OXLEY 10/56; SHREWSBURY 6/58; AGECROFT 4/66; PATRICROFT 10/66; WITHDRAWN 3/68.

73035 NEW 8/53; POLMADIE 8/53; SHREWSBURY 9/53; OXLEY 10/56; SHREWSBURY 6/58; PATRICROFT 7/65; WITHDRAWN 1/68.

73036 NEW 9/53; KINGMOOR 9/53; SHREWSBURY 9/53; TYSELEY 10/56; SHREWSBURY 1/58; WITHDRAWN 9/65.

73037 NEW 9/53; SHREWSBURY 9/53; TYSELEY 10/56; SHREWSBURY 1/58; LLANELLY 4/62; BRISTOL (BARROW ROAD) 6/64; OXFORD 9/64; EASTLEIGH 4/65; GUILDFORD 5/65; NINE ELMS 6/66; WITHDRAWN 7/67.

73038 NEW 9/53; CHESTER (WEST) 9/53; CHESTER (MIDLAND) 4/60; LLANDUDNO JUNCTION 11/62; WILLESDEN 11/63; BLETCHLEY 3/64; OXLEY 1/65; NUNEATON 3/65; SHREWSBURY 7/65; WITHDRAWN 9/65.

73039 NEW 9/53; BRISTOL (ST PHILLIP'S MARSH) 9/53; BIRKENHEAD 6/58; WILLESDEN 5/60; BLETCHLEY 3/64; NUNEATON 1/65; PATRICROFT 7/65; WITHDRAWN 9/67.

73040 NEW 10/53; CHESTER (MIDLAND) 10/53; WILLESDEN 11/63; BLETCHLEY 3/64; NUNEATON 1/65; CROES NEWYDD 7/65; BOLTON 4/66; PATRICROFT 4/68; WITHDRAWN 5/68.

73041 NEW 10/53; CHESTER (MIDLAND) 10/53; HOLYHEAD 7/57; GRIMESTHORPE 5/58; NINE ELMS 5/59; WEYMOUTH 11/59; EASTLEIGH 2/61; WEYMOUTH 4/61; EASTLEIGH 8/64; GUILDFORD 5/65; WITHDRAWN 6/65.

73042 NEW 10/53; CHESTER (MIDLAND) 10/53; HOLYHEAD 7/57; NINE ELMS 5/59; WEYMOUTH 11/59; EASTLEIGH 2/61; WEYMOUTH 4/61; WITHDRAWN 8/65.

73043 NEW 10/53; PATRICROFT 10/53; GRIMESTHORPE 5/58; CANKLOW 4/61; EASTLEIGH 11/62; FELTHAM 12/63; EASTLEIGH 8/64; GUILDFORD 5/65; NINE ELMS 6/66; WITHDRAWN 7/67.

73044 NEW 11/53; PATRICROFT 11/53; EXMOUTH JUNCTION 10/63; OXFORD 1/65; WITHDRAWN 3/65.

73045 NEW 11/53; LEEDS (HOLBECK) 11/53; LEICESTER (CENTRAL) 9/59; NEASDEN 6/60; WOODFORD HALSE 6/62; SHREWSBURY 9/64; NUNEATON 9/64; CROES NEWYDD 5/65; PATRICROFT 7/65; WITHDRAWN 8/67.

73046 NEW 11/53; LEICESTER (MIDLAND) 11/53; MILLHOUSES 5/58; CANKLOW 4/61; NINE ELMS 11/62; WITHDRAWN 9/64.

73047 NEW 12/53; MILLHOUSES 12/53; BATH (GREEN PARK) 8/55; SHREWSBURY 7/64; WITHDRAWN 12/64.

73048 NEW 12/53; MILLHOUSES 12/53; CHESTER (MIDLAND) 2/60; WILLESDEN 11/63; BLETCHLEY 3/64; NUNEATON 1/65; BANBURY 6/65; BOLTON 4/66; WITHDRAWN 10/67.

73049 NEW 12/53; LEICESTER (MIDLAND) 12/53; BATH (GREEN PARK) 8/55; SHREWSBURY 4/60; BRISTOL (BARROW ROAD) 6/62; BATH (GREEN PARK) 7/62; OXFORD 9/64; WITHDRAWN 3/65.

73050 NEW 6/54; BATH (GREEN PARK) 6/54; GLOUCESTER (BARNWOOD) 8/62; BATH (GREEN PARK) 11/62; LLANELLY 3/64; SHREWSBURY 4/64; AGECROFT 4/66; PATRICROFT 10/66; WITHDRAWN 6/68. ENGINE PRESERVED.

73051 NEW 6/54; BATH (GREEN PARK) 6/54; WITHDRAWN 8/65.

73052 NEW 6/54; BATH (GREEN PARK) 6/54; WITHDRAWN 12/64.

73053 NEW 6/54; LEEDS (HOLBECK) 6/54; LEICESTER (CENTRAL) 9/59; NEASDEN 6/60; WOODFORD HALSE 6/62; CRICKLEWOOD 5/63; BEDFORD 7/63; WOODFORD HALSE 8/63; SHREWSBURY 7/64; PATRICROFT 7/65; WITHDRAWN 3/68.

73054 NEW 6/54; LEEDS (HOLBECK) 6/54; DERBY 8/55; BRISTOL (BARROW ROAD) 5/57; BATH (GREEN PARK) 4/61; WITHDRAWN 8/65.

73055 NEW 6/54; POLMADIE 6/54; WITHDRAWN 5/66.

73056 NEW 7/54; POLMADIE 7/54; ABERDEEN (FERRY HILL) 7/64; WITHDRAWN 6/65.

73057 NEW 7/54; POLMADIE 7/54; CORKERHILL 6/64; WITHDRAWN 3/66.

73058 NEW 7/54; POLMADIE 7/54; ABERDEEN (FERRY HILL) 7/64; WITHDRAWN 11/64.

73059 NEW 8/54; POLMADIE 8/54; WITHDRAWN 5/67.

73060 NEW 8/54; POLMADIE 8/54; MOTHERWELL 10/55; POLMADIE 9/57; WITHDRAWN 5/67.

73061 NEW 9/54; POLMADIE 9/54; MOTHERWELL 10/55; POLMADIE 6/57; WITHDRAWN 12/64.

73062 NEW 9/54; POLMADIE 9/54; MOTHERWELL 10/55; POLMADIE 6/57; WITHDRAWN 6/65.

73063 NEW 9/54; POLMADIE 9/54; WITHDRAWN 6/66.

73064 NEW 10/54; POLMADIE 10/54; WITHDRAWN 5/67.

73065 NEW 10/54; MILLHOUSES 10/54; CANKLOW 1/62; EASTLEIGH 11/62; FELTHAM 12/63; NINE ELMS 11/64; GUILDFORD 5/65; NINE ELMS 6/66; WITHDRAWN 7/67.

73066 NEW 10/54; LEEDS (HOLBECK) 10/54; LEICESTER (CENTRAL) 10/59; NEASDEN 6/60; LEICESTER (CENTRAL) 6/62; WOODFORD HALSE 1/63; CRICKLEWOOD 5/63; LEAMINGTON SPA 10/64; TYSELEY 6/65; BOLTON 4/66; WITHDRAWN 4/67.

73067 NEW 10/54; NOTTINGHAM 10.54; LEICESTER (MIDLAND) 2/58; MILLHOUSES 5/58; HOLYHEAD 1/60; CHESTER (MIDLAND) 2/63; WILLESDEN 3/64; OXLEY 1/65; SHREWSBURY 4/65; AGECROFT 4/66; PATRICROFT 10/66; WITHDRAWN 3/68.

73068 NEW 10/54; DERBY 10/54; BRISTOL (BARROW ROAD) 5/57; GLOUCESTER (BARNWOOD) 9/62; BATH (GREEN PARK) 4/64; GLOUCESTER (HORTON ROAD) 1/65; BATH (GREEN PARK) 4/65; WITHDRAWN 12/65.

73069 NEW 11/54; DERBY 11/54; LEEDS (HOLBECK) 8/55; LEICESTER (CENTRAL) 10/59; NEASDEN 6/60; LEICESTER (CENTRAL) 6/62; WOODFORD HALSE 2/63; CRICKLEWOOD 5/63; LEAMINGTON SPA 10/64; TYSELEY 6/65; BOLTON 4/66; PATRICROFT 4/68; CARNFORTH 7/68; WITHDRAWN 8/68.

73070 NEW 11/54; CHESTER (MIDLAND) 11/54; WILLESDEN 11/63; BLETCHLEY 3/64; SHREWSBURY 6/64; BOLTON 4/66; WITHDRAWN 4/67.

73071 NEW 11/54; CHESTER (MIDLAND) 11/54; KINGS CROSS 2/56; CHESTER (MIDLAND) 3/57; CRICKLEWOOD 5/63; BEDFORD 7/63; WOODFORD HALSE 8/63; OXLEY 1/65; SHREWSBURY 4/65; PATRICROFT 7/65; WITHDRAWN 9/67.

73072 NEW 12/54; CHESTER (MIDLAND) 12/54; POLMADIE 11/58; WITHDRAWN 10/66.

73073 NEW 12/54; PATRICROFT 12/54; BATH (GREEN PARK) 3/55; LEICESTER (MIDLAND) 8/55; MILLHOUSES 5/58; HOLYHEAD 2/60; LLANDUDNO JUNCTION 2/63; WOODFORD HALSE 11/63; NUNEATON 7/64; PATRICROFT 7/65; WITHDRAWN 11/67.

73074 NEW 12/54; PATRICROFT 12/54; BATH (GREEN PARK) 3/55; MILLHOUSES 8/55; LEEDS (HOLBECK) 5/56; MILLHOUSES 3/56; GRIMESTHORPE 1/59; CANKLOW 4/61; NINE ELMS 11/62; WITHDRAWN 9/64.

73075 NEW 4/55; POLMADIE 4/55; WITHDRAWN 12/65.

73076 NEW 4/55; POLMADIE 4/55; WITHDRAWN 7/64.

73077 NEW 5/55; EASTFIELD 5/55; CORKERHILL 1/63; WITHDRAWN 1/65.

73078 NEW 5/55; EASTFIELD 5/55; CARSTAIRS 1/66; WITHDRAWN 7/66.

73079 NEW 5/55; EASTFIELD 5/55; CORKERHILL 7/55; POLMADIE 4/67; WITHDRAWN 5/67.

73080 NEW 6/55; STEWARTS LANE 6/55; NINE ELMS 5/59; WEYMOUTH 11/59; EASTLEIGH 2/61; WEYMOUTH 4/61; WITHDRAWN 12/66.

73081 NEW 6/55; STEWARTS LANE 6/55; NINE ELMS 5/59; GUILDFORD 5/65; WITHDRAWN 7/66.

73082 NEW 6/55; STEWARTS LANE 6/55; NINE ELMS 5/59; GUILDFORD 5/65; WITHDRAWN 6/66. ENGINE PRESERVED.

73083 NEW 7/55; STEWARTS LANE 7/55; NINE ELMS 5/59; FELTHAM 8/64; WEYMOUTH 11/64; WITHDRAWN 9/66.

73084 NEW 7/55; STEWARTS LANE 7/55; NINE ELMS 5/59; FELTHAM 10/65; EASTLEIGH 11/65; WITHDRAWN 12/65.

73085 NEW 8/55; STEWARTS LANE 8/55; NINE ELMS 5/59; FELTHAM 10/65; EASTLEIGH 11/65; NINE ELMS 6/66; WITHDRAWN 7/67.

73086 NEW 8/55; STEWARTS LANE 8/55; NINE ELMS 5/59; WITHDRAWN 10/66.

73087 NEW 8/55; STEWARTS LANE 8/55; BATH (GREEN PARK) 8/56; EASTLEIGH 10/56; BATH (GREEN PARK) 7/57; STEWARTS LANE 10/57; BATH (GREEN PARK) 5/58; NINE ELMS 9/58; BATH (GREEN PARK) 5/59; NINE ELMS 4/60; BATH (GREEN PARK) 6/60; NINE ELMS 6/61; FELTHAM 8/64; EASTLEIGH 9/64; GUILDFORD 5/65; WITHDRAWN 10/66.

73088 NEW 9/55; STEWARTS LANE 9/55; BATH (GREEN PARK) 5/58; NINE ELMS 9/58; GUILDFORD 10/65; WITHDRAWN 10/66.

73089 NEW 9/55; STEWARTS LANE 9/55; NINE ELMS 5/58; EASTLEIGH 9/64; GUILDFORD 10/65; WITHDRAWN 9/66.

73090 NEW 10/55; PATRICROFT 10/55; SHREWSBURY 8/58; OXLEY 1/65; SHREWSBURY 3/65; WITHDRAWN 10/65.

73091 NEW 10/55; PATRICROFT 10/55; SHREWSBURY 8/58; GLOUCESTER (BARNWOOD) 9/61; GLOUCESTER (HORTON ROAD) 4/64; WITHDRAWN 5/65.

73092 NEW 10/55; PATRICROFT 10/55; SHREWSBURY 8/58; GLOUCESTER (BARNWOOD) 9/61; GLOUCESTER (HORTON ROAD) 4/64; BATH (GREEN PARK) 7/64; EASTLEIGH 4/65; GUILDFORD 10/65; WITHDRAWN 7/67.

73093 NEW 11/55; PATRICROFT 11/55; SHREWSBURY 8/58; GLOUCESTER (BARNWOOD) 9/61; GLOUCESTER (HORTON ROAD) 4/64; BATH (GREEN PARK) 2/65; EASTLEIGH 4/65; GUILDFORD 10/65; WITHDRAWN 7/67.

73094 NEW 11/55; PATRICROFT 11/55; SHREWSBURY 8/58; BRISTOL (BARROW ROAD) 9/61; GLOUCESTER (BARNWOOD) 11/61; GLOUCESTER (HORTON ROAD) 4/64; SHREWSBURY 5/64; PATRICROFT 7/65; WITHDRAWN 5/67.

73095 NEW 11/55; PATRICROFT 11/55; SHREWSBURY 8/58; CROES NEWYDD 8/65; AGECROFT 4/66; WITHDRAWN 8/66.

73096 NEW 11/55; PATRICROFT 11/55; SHREWSBURY 8/58; GLOUCESTER (BARNWOOD) 7/62; GLOUCESTER (HORTON ROAD) 4/64; OXLEY 11/64; NUNEATON 3/65; CROES NEWYDD 6/65; PATRICROFT 7/65; WITHDRAWN 11/67. ENGINE PRESERVED.

73097 NEW 12/55; PATRICROFT 12/55; SHREWSBURY 8/58; PATRICROFT 7/65; WITHDRAWN 5/67.

73098 NEW 12/55; PATRICROFT 12/55; CHESTER (WEST) 9/58; POLMADIE 11/58; WITHDRAWN 3/66.

73099 NEW 12/55; PATRICROFT 12/55; CHESTER (WEST) 9/58; POLMADIE 11/58; HAMILTON 7/60; POLMADIE 9/61; WITHDRAWN 10/66.

73100 NEW 8/55; CORKERHILL 8/55; WITHDRAWN 1/67.

73101 NEW 8/55; CORKERHILL 8/55; WITHDRAWN 8/66.

73102 NEW 9/55; CORKERHILL 9/55; WITHDRAWN 12/66.

73103 NEW 9/55; CORKERHILL 9/55; WITHDRAWN 10/65.

73104 NEW 9/55; CORKERHILL 9/55; WITHDRAWN 10/65.

73105 NEW 12/55; EASTFIELD 12/55; GRANGEMOUTH 12/64; STIRLING 10/65; CORKERHILL 6/66; WITHDRAWN 9/66.

73106 NEW 12/55; EASTFIELD 12/55; INVERNESS 6/57; PERTH 10/57; CORKERHILL 6/64; WITHDRAWN 6/65.

73107 NEW 12/55; EASTFIELD 12/55; INVERNESS 6/57; PERTH 10/57; MOTHERWELL 6/64; WITHDRAWN 9/66.

73108 NEW 12/55; EASTFIELD 12/55; CARSTAIRS 1/66; WITHDRAWN 12/66.

73109 NEW 1/56; EASTFIELD 1/56; WITHDRAWN 10/64.

73110 NEW 10/55; NINE ELMS 10/55; EASTLEIGH 8/64; GUILDFORD 10/65; WITHDRAWN 1/67.

73111 NEW 10/55; NINE ELMS 10/55; EASTLEIGH 8/64; WITHDRAWN 10/65.

73112 NEW 10/55; NINE ELMS 10/55; EASTLEIGH 8/64; NINE ELMS 9/64; WITHDRAWN 6/65.

73113 NEW 10/55; NINE ELMS 10/55; EASTLEIGH 8/64; WEYMOUTH 10/65; WITHDRAWN 1/67.

73114 NEW 11/55; NINE ELMS 11/55; EASTLEIGH 8/64; WEYMOUTH 10/65; WITHDRAWN 6/66.

73115 NEW 11/55; NINE ELMS 11/55; EASTLEIGH 8/64; NINE ELMS 6/66; GUILDFORD 10/66; WITHDRAWN 3/67.

73116 NEW 11/55; NINE ELMS 11/55; BATH (GREEN PARK) 8/56; EASTLEIGH 10/56; BATH (GREEN PARK) 7/57; NINE ELMS 9/57; BATH (GREEN PARK) 5/58; NINE ELMS 9/58; BATH (GREEN PARK) 5/59; NINE ELMS 4/60; EASTLEIGH 8/64; WITHDRAWN 11/64.

73117 NEW 11/55; NINE ELMS 11/55; EASTLEIGH 8/64; NINE ELMS 6/66; GUILDFORD 10/66; WITHDRAWN 3/67.

73118 NEW 12/55; NINE ELMS 12/55; EASTLEIGH 8/64; NINE ELMS 6/66; GUILDFORD 10/66; WITHDRAWN 7/67.

73119 NEW 12/55; NINE ELMS 12/55; EASTLEIGH 8/64; WITHDRAWN 3/67.

73120 NEW 1/56; PERTH 1/56; CORKERHILL 1/63; WITHDRAWN 12/66.

73121 NEW 1/56; CORKERHILL 1/56; WITHDRAWN 1/66.

73122 NEW 1/56; CORKERHILL 1/56; WITHDRAWN 9/65.

73123 NEW 2/56; CORKERHILL 2/56; WITHDRAWN 5/65.

73124 NEW 2/56; CORKERHILL 2/56; WITHDRAWN 12/65.

73125 NEW 7/56; SHREWSBURY 7/56; PATRICROFT 8/58; WITHDRAWN 6/68.

73126 NEW 7/56; SHREWSBURY 7/56; PATRICROFT 8/58; WITHDRAWN 4/68.

73127 NEW 8/56; SHREWSBURY 8/56; PATRICROFT 8/58; WITHDRAWN 11/67.

73128 NEW 8/56; SHREWSBURY 8/56; PATRICROFT 8/58; ROWSLEY 2/64; PATRICROFT 4/64; WITHDRAWN 5/68.

73129 NEW 8/56; SHREWSBURY 8/56; PATRICROFT 8/58; WITHDRAWN 11/67. ENGINE PRESERVED.

73130 NEW 9/56; SHREWSBURY 9/56; PATRICROFT 8/58; WITHDRAWN 1/67.

73131 NEW 9/56; SHREWSBURY 9/56; PATRICROFT 8/58; WITHDRAWN 1/68.

73132 NEW 10/56; SHREWSBURY 10/56; PATRICROFT 8/58; WITHDRAWN 3/68.

73133 NEW 10/56; SHREWSBURY 10/56; PATRICROFT 8/58; WITHDRAWN 6/68.

73134 NEW 10/56; SHREWSBURY 10/56; PATRICROFT 8/58; WITHDRAWN 6/68.

73135 NEW 10/56; HOLYHEAD 10/56; LEICESTER (MIDLAND) 5/58; DERBY 1/59; ROWSLEY 11/59; DERBY 4/64; PATRICROFT 9/64; WITHDRAWN 3/68.

73136 NEW 11/56; HOLYHEAD 11/56; LEICESTER (MIDLAND) 5/58; DERBY 1/59; ROWLSEY 11/59; PATRICROFT 5/64; WITHDRAWN 3/68.

73137 NEW 11/56; HOLYHEAD 11/56; LEICESTER (MIDLAND) 5/58; DERBY 1/59; ROWSLEY 11/59; LEICESTER (MIDLAND) 5/62; ROWSLEY 6/62; PATRICROFT 6/64; WITHDRAWN 6/67.

73138 NEW 11/56; HOLYHEAD 11/56; LEICESTER (MIDLAND) 1/57; DERBY 1/59; ROWSLEY 11/59; PATRICROFT 5/64; WITHDRAWN 4/68.

73139 NEW 11/56; HOLYHEAD 11/56; LEICESTER (MIDLAND) 5/58; DERBY 1/59; ROWSLEY 11/59; PATRICROFT 6/64; WITHDRAWN 5/67.

73140 NEW 12/56; LEICESTER (MIDLAND) 12/56; HOLYHEAD 1/57; LEICESTER (MIDLAND) 5/58; TRAFFORD PARK 9/58; LEICESTER (MIDLAND) 10/58; DERBY 1/59; ROWSLEY 11/59; DERBY 9/61; ROWSLEY 2/62; PATRICROFT 5/64; WITHDRAWN 10/67.

73141 NEW 12/56; LEICESTER (MIDLAND) 12/56; DERBY 1/59; ROWSLEY 11/59; PATRICROFT 5/64; WITHDRAWN 7/67.

73142 NEW 12/56; LEICESTER (MIDLAND) 12/56; DERBY 1/59; ROWSLEY 11/59; DERBY 4/64; PATRICROFT 5/64; WITHDRAWN 4/68.

73143 NEW 12/56; LEICESTER (MIDLAND) 12/56; NOTTINGHAM 4/58; DERBY 1/59; ROWSLEY 11/59; PATRICROFT 2/64; WITHDRAWN 6/68.

73144 NEW 12/56; LEICESTER (MIDLAND) 12/56; NOTTINGHAM 4/58; DERBY 1/59; ROWSLEY 11/59; DERBY 9/61; ROWSLEY 2/62; DERBY 4/64; PATRICROFT 5/64; WITHDRAWN 8/67.

73145 NEW 1/57; ST ROLLOX 1/57; EASTFIELD 1/66; AYR 9/66; WITHDRAWN 9/66.

73146 NEW 2/57; ST ROLLOX 2/57; EASTFIELD 1/66; MOTHERWELL 11/66; WITHDRAWN 5/67.

73147 NEW 2/57; ST ROLLOX 2/57; WITHDRAWN 8/65.

73148 NEW 3/57; ST ROLLOX 3/57; WITHDRAWN 9/65.

73149 NEW 3/57; ST ROLLOX 3/57; STIRLING 11/66; WITHDRAWN 12/66.

73150 NEW 4/57; ST ROLLOX 4/57; STIRLING 11/66; WITHDRAWN 12/66.

73151 NEW 4/57; ST ROLLOX 4/57; WITHDRAWN 8/66.

73152 NEW 5/57; ST ROLLOX 5/57; WITHDRAWN 12/65.

73153 NEW 5/57; ST ROLLOX 5/57; STIRLING 11/66; WITHDRAWN 12/66.

73154 NEW 6/57; ST ROLLOX 6/57; STIRLING 12/65; MOTHERWELL 6/66; WITHDRAWN 12/66.

73155 NEW 12/56; NEASDEN 12/56; MILLHOUSES 5/58; CANKLOW 1/62; EASTLEIGH 11/62; FELTHAM 12/63; EASTLEIGH 11/64; GUILDFORD 4/67; WITHDRAWN 7/67.

73156 NEW 12/56; NEASDEN 12/56; MILLHOUSES 5/58; GRIMESTHORPE 1/59; DERBY 8/60; NEASDEN 9/60; LEICESTER (CENTRAL) 6/62; WOODFORD HALSE 3/63; CRICKLEWOOD 5/63; LEAMINGTON SPA 10/64; TYSELEY 6/65; BOLTON 4/66; WITHDRAWN 11/67. ENGINE PRESERVED.

73157 NEW 12/56; NEASDEN 12/56; KINGS CROSS 9/57; DARNALL 10/58; NEASDEN 12/58; DERBY 2/59; NEASDEN 6/60; CRICKLEWOOD 6/62; CHESTER (MIDLAND) 5/63; WOODFORD HALSE 11/63; OXLEY 1/65; PATRICROFT 4/65; WITHDRAWN 5/68.

73158 NEW 12/56; NEASDEN 12/56; KINGS CROSS 9/57; DARNALL 10/58; NEASDEN 12/58; DERBY 2/59; NEASDEN 6/60; CRICKLEWOOD 6/62; BEDFORD 7/63; CRICKLEWOOD 8/63; PATRICROFT 4/64; WITHDRAWN 10/67.

73159 NEW 1/57; NEASDEN 1/57; KINGS CROSS 9/57; DARNALL 10/58; NEASDEN 12/58; DERBY 2/59; NEASDEN 6/60; LEICESTER (CENTRAL) 6/62; WOODFORD HALSE 1/63; NUNEATON 9/64; PATRICROFT 7/65; WITHDRAWN 10/67.

73160 NEW 1/57; BLAYDON 1/57; NORMANTON 9/57; BLETCHLEY 4/64; OXLEY 1/65; PATRICROFT 4/65; WITHDRAWN 11/67.

73161 NEW 2/57; BLAYDON 2/57; NORMANTON 9/57; NEVILLE HILL 6/62; WAKEFIELD 6/63; EXMOUTH JUNCTION 9/63; WITHDRAWN 12/64.

73162 NEW 2/57; YORK 2/57; HUDDERSFIELD 10/58; NEVILLE HILL 6/61; WAKEFIELD 6/63; EXMOUTH JUNCTION 9/63; OXFORD 1/65; WITHDRAWN 5/65.

73163 NEW 2/57; YORK 2/57; HUDDERSFIELD 10/58; WAKEFIELD 8/64; OXLEY 11/64; PATRICROFT 4/65; WITHDRAWN 11/65.

73164 NEW 3/57; YORK 3/57; HUDDERSFIELD 10/58; BATH (GREEN PARK) 9/63; BRISTOL (BARROW ROAD) 11/63; OXFORD 9/64; WITHDRAWN 12/64.

73165 NEW 3/57; YORK 3/57; HUDDERSFIELD 10/58; WAKEFIELD 8/64; OXLEY 11/64; PATRICROFT 4/65; WITHDRAWN 9/65.

73166 NEW 3/57; YORK 3/57; HUDDERSFIELD 10/58; LEEDS (HOLBECK) 4/59; HUDDERSFIELD 9/60; LEEDS (HOLBECK) 4/62; ROYSTON 9/62; PATRICROFT 6/63; EXMOUTH JUNCTION 10/63; YEOVIL TOWN 9/64; OXFORD 6/65; WITHDRAWN 12/65.

73167 NEW 4/57; YORK 4/57; LEEDS (HOLBECK) 4/57; NORMANTON 9/57; SCARBOROUGH 2/59; NORMANTON 6/59; LEEDS (HOLBECK) 6/63; FELTHAM 9/63; SHREWSBURY 8/64; WITHDRAWN 8/65.

73168 NEW 4/57; YORK 4/57; LEEDS (HOLBECK) 4/57; SCARBOROUGH 2/59; LEEDS (HOLBECK) 6/59; NEVILLE HILL 10/61; WAKEFIELD 6/63; FELTHAM 9/63; EASTLEIGH 11/64; WITHDRAWN 12/65.

73169 NEW 4/57; YORK 4/57; LEEDS (HOLBECK) 5/57; SCARBOROUGH 2/59; LEEDS (HOLBECK) 6/59; NEVILLE HILL 6/61; WAKEFIELD 6/63; FELTHAM 9/63; EASTLEIGH 11/64; WITHDRAWN 10/66.

73170 NEW 5/57; YORK 5/57; LEEDS (HOLBECK) 5/57; SCARBOROUGH 2/59; LEEDS (HOLBECK) 6/59; ROYSTON 9/62; FELTHAM 9/63; EASTLEIGH 11/64; WITHDRAWN 6/66.

73171 NEW 5/57; YORK 5/57; LEEDS (HOLBECK) 9/57; ROYSTON 9/62; FELTHAM 9/63; EASTLEIGH 11/64; WITHDRAWN 10/66.

75000 NEW 5/51; SWINDON 5/51; SHREWSBURY 9/51; TYSELEY 8/59; OXFORD 2/61; BRISTOL (BARROW ROAD) 7/62; LEAMINGTON SPA 9/62; YEOVIL TOWN 9/63; WORCESTER 6/65; WITHDRAWN 12/65.

75001 NEW 8/51; SHREWSBURY 8/51; SWINDON 7/53; OXFORD 9/54; BRISTOL (BARROW ROAD) 3/63; YEOVIL TOWN 9/63; WITHDRAWN 12/64.

75002 NEW 8/51; SHREWSBURY 8/51; SWINDON 9/53; OSWESTRY 9/56; SWINDON 1/57; GLOUCESTER (BARNWOOD) 1/60; TEMPLECOMBE 9/61; BRISTOL (BARROW ROAD) 6/62; MACHYNLLETH 9/62; CROES NEWYDD 12/66; STOKE 6/67; WITHDRAWN 8/67.

75003 NEW 8/51; SHREWSBURY 8/51; SWINDON 12/53; WORCESTER 2/58; TYSELEY 7/60; YEOVIL TOWN 10/63; WORCESTER 6/65; WITHDRAWN 10/65.

75004 NEW 8/51; BRISTOL (BATH ROAD) 8/51; SHREWSBURY 10/51; SWINDON 9/53; OXFORD 9/54; CARDIFF (CANTON) 7/55; BRISTOL (BARROW ROAD) 9/58; TEMPLECOMBE 11/61; BATH (GREEN PARK) 5/62; MACHYNLLETH 10/62; SHREWSBURY 1/66; WITHDRAWN 3/67.

75005 NEW 9/51; SHREWSBURY 9/51; CARDIFF (CANTON) 9/53; OSWESTRY 2/54; CHESTER (WEST) 8/58; TYSELEY 4/59; WORCESTER 7/60; GLOUCESTER (HORTON ROAD) 1/64; EXMOUTH JUNCTION 3/64; YEOVIL TOWN 4/65; WORCESTER 6/65; WITHDRAWN 11/65.

75006 NEW 9/51; SWINDON 9/51; SHREWSBURY 4/52; CARDIFF (CANTON) 9/53; OSWESTRY 12/53; CHESTER (WEST) 8/58; TYSELEY 4/59; MACHYNLLETH 9/62; CROES NEWYDD 3/63; STOKE 11/64; TYSELEY 7/65; SHREWSBURY 11/65; CROES NEWYDD 3/67; STOKE 6/67; WITHDRAWN 8/67.

75007 NEW 9/51; SHREWSBURY 9/51; CARDIFF (CANTON) 9/53; OXFORD 9/58; TEMPLECOMBE 3/63; YEOVIL TOWN 9/64; WITHDRAWN 3/65.

75008 NEW 10/51; SHREWSBURY 10/51; CARDIFF (CANTON) 10/53; OXFORD 10/58; TEMPLECOMBE 7/64; EXMOUTH JUNCTION 9/64; WORCESTER 6/65; WITHDRAWN 12/65.

75009 NEW 10/51; SHREWSBURY 10/51; CARDIFF (CANTON) 9/53; WORCESTER 5/58; GLOUCESTER (BARNWOOD) 8/58; TEMPLECOMBE 9/61; MACHYNLLETH 11/62; CROES NEWYDD 3/63; LLANDUDNO JUNCTION 2/66; MACHYNLLETH 6/66; SHREWSBURY 12/66; CROES NEWYDD 3/67; LOSTOCK HALL 5/67; CARNFORTH 6/67; WITHDRAWN 8/68.

75010 NEW 11/51; PATRICROFT 11/51; LLANDUDNO JUNCTION 10/53; BANGOR 5/57; LLANDUDNO JUNCTION 7/57; NUNEATON 10/62; CHESTER (MIDLAND) 3/63; CROES NEWYDD 3/66; LOSTOCK HALL 5/67; CARNFORTH 6/67; WITHDRAWN 10/67.

75011 NEW 11/51; PATRICROFT 11/51; LLANDUDNO JUNCTION 10/53; NUNEATON 10/62; DERBY 5/63; WIGAN (SPRINGS BRANCH) 11/63; SKIPTON 3/65; WITHDRAWN 11/66.

75012 NEW 11/51; PATRICROFT 11/51; LLANDUDNO JUNCTION 10/53; BANGOR 5/57; LLANDUDNO JUNCTION 7/57; NUNEATON 10/62; CHESTER (MIDLAND) 3/63; MACHYNLLETH 1/66; CROES NEWYDD 3/66; SHREWSBURY 3/66; WITHDRAWN 1/67.

75013 NEW 11/51; PATRICROFT 11/51; LLANDUDNO JUNCTION 10/53; CHESTER (MIDLAND) 9/59; MOLD JUNCTION 4/60; BLETCHLEY 4/62; MACHYNLLETH 6/65; SHREWSBURY 12/66; CROES NEWYDD 3/67; STOKE 5/67; WITHDRAWN 8/67.

75014 NEW 11/51; PATRICROFT 11/51; LLANDUDNO JUNCTION 10/53; CHESTER (MIDLAND) 9/57; LLANDUDNO JUNCTION 6/59; CHESTER (MIDLAND) 9/59; MOLD JUNCTION 4/60; BLETCHLEY 4/62; STOKE 5/63; TYSELEY 6/64; SHREWSBURY 9/64; WITHDRAWN 12/66. ENGINE PRESERVED.

75015 NEW 12/51; SOUTHPORT 12/51; AINTREE 12/63; WIGAN (SPRINGS BRANCH) 4/64; SKIPTON 3/65; CARNFORTH 2/67; WITHDRAWN 12/67.

75016 NEW 1/52; SOUTHPORT 1/52; NUNEATON 5/63; SHREWSBURY 6/65; CROES NEWYDD 3/67; COLWICK 6/67; WITHDRAWN 7/67.

75017 NEW 1/52; SOUTHPORT 1/52; WIGAN (SPRINGS BRANCH) 12/63; SKIPTON 3/65; WITHDRAWN 1/67.

75018 NEW 3/52; SOUTHPORT 3/52; NUNEATON 5/63; BANGOR 6/63; STOKE 9/63; NUNEATON 4/66; STOKE 6/66; WITHDRAWN 6/67.

75019 NEW 3/52; SOUTHPORT 3/52; WIGAN (SPRINGS BRANCH) 12/63; SKIPTON 3/65; CARNFORTH 1/67; TEBAY 4/67; CARNFORTH 1/68; WITHDRAWN 8/68.

75020 NEW 11/53; OSWESTRY 11/53; CHESTER (WEST) 8/58; TYSELEY 4/59; MACHYNLLETH 6/59; CROES NEWYDD 3/63; STOKE 1/65; SHREWSBURY 1/66; AINTREE 3/67; CARNFORTH 6/67; WITHDRAWN 8/68.

75021 NEW 11/53; CARDIFF (CANTON) 11/53; BRISTOL (BARROW ROAD) 9/58; OXFORD 10/60; MACHYNLLETH 5/62; CROES NEWYDD 3/63; SHREWSBURY 3/66; CROES NEWYDD 7/66; CARNFORTH 4/67; WITHDRAWN 2/68.

75022 NEW 12/53; CARDIFF (CANTON) 12/53; SWANSEA (VICTORIA) 6/57; CARDIFF (CANTON) 7/57; BRISTOL (BARROW ROAD) 9/58; OXFORD 9/61; EXMOUTH JUNCTION 4/64; BRISTOL (BARROW ROAD) 1/65; EXMOUTH JUNCTION 2/65; WORCESTER 6/65; WITHDRAWN 12/65.

75023 NEW 12/53; OSWESTRY 12/53; SWINDON 9/56; WORCESTER 11/57; GLOUCESTER (BARNWOOD) 8/58; TEMPLECOMBE 9/61; MACHYNLLETH 9/62; CROES NEWYDD 3/63; STOKE 1/65; WITHDRAWN 1/66.

75024 NEW 12/53; OSWESTRY 12/53; SHREWSBURY 2/55; OXFORD 12/58; SWINDON 3/59; TYSELEY 8/59; MACHYNLLETH 11/62; CROES NEWYDD 3/63; HOLYHEAD 6/65; MACHYNLLETH 7/66; STOKE 12/66; TEBAY 5/67; WITHDRAWN 11/67.

75025 NEW 4/54; LAIRA 4/54; SWINDON 6/56; WORCESTER 11/57; MACHYNLLETH 8/60; WORCESTER 11/60; GLOUCESTER (HORTON ROAD) 1/64; EXMOUTH JUNCTION 3/64; WORCESTER 6/65; WITHDRAWN 12/65.

75026 NEW 5/54; LAIRA 5/54; SWINDON 6/56; OSWESTRY 1/57; CHESTER (WEST) 8/58; TYSELEY 4/59; MACHYNLLETH 6/59; CROES NEWYDD 3/63; BANK HALL 2/65; AINTREE 10/66; SKIPTON 11/66; CARNFORTH 4/67; TEBAY 4/67; WITHDRAWN 12/67.

75027 NEW 5/54; LAIRA 5/54; OXFORD 9/54; SWINDON 2/59; TEMPLECOMBE 2/60; MACHYNLLETH 11/62; CROES NEWYDD 3/63; BANK HALL 2/65; AINTREE 10/66; SKIPTON 11/66; CARNFORTH 1/67; TEBAY 4/67; CARNFORTH 1/68; WITHDRAWN 8/68. ENGINE PRESERVED.

75028 NEW 5/54; LAIRA 5/54; OSWESTRY 6/56; CHESTER (WEST) 8/58; RHYL 6/59; CHESTER (WEST) 9/59; WORKINGTON 4/60; MOLD JUNCTION 6/60; RHYL 6/61; MOLD JUNCTION 9/61; BLETCHLEY 4/62; MACHYNLLETH 6/65; WITHDRAWN 12/65.

75029 NEW 5/54; LAIRA 5/54; OXFORD 9/54; GLOUCESTER (HORTON ROAD) 12/54; OXFORD 1/55; SOUTHPORT 10/58; OXFORD 1/59; SWINDON 2/59; OXFORD 11/60; TYSELEY 1/61; MACHYNLLETH 11/62; CROES NEWYDD 3/63; LLANDUDNO JUNCTION 6/65; SHREWSBURY 9/66; CROES NEWYDD 3/67; STOKE 6/67; WITHDRAWN 8/67. ENGINE PRESERVED.

75030 NEW 6/53; BLETCHLEY 6/54; LLANDUDNO JUNCTION 6/54; BLETCHLEY 2/55; LLANDUDNO JUNCTION 2/55; BLETCHLEY 12/56; CHESTER (NORTHGATE) 11/59; WILLESDEN 1/60; NUNEATON 1/63; STOKE 9/63; TEBAY 5/67; WITHDRAWN 12/67.

75031 NEW 6/53; BLETCHLEY 6/53; LLANDUDNO JUNCTION 2/55; CHESTER (MIDLAND) 12/55; BANGOR 5/57; LLANDUDNO JUNCTION 7/57; CHESTER (MIDLAND) 9/57; LLANDUDNO JUNCTION 6/59; CHESTER (MIDLAND) 9/59; MOLD JUNCTION 4/60; RHYL 6/61; WILLESDEN 9/61; ASTON 12/62; STOKE 9/63; WITHDRAWN 2/66.

75032 NEW 6/53; BLETCHLEY 6/53; LLANDUDNO JUNCTION 2/55; CHESTER (MIDLAND) 12/55; LLANDUDNO JUNCTION 6/56; CHESTER (MIDLAND) 10/56; BANGOR 7/57; LLANDUDNO JUNCTION 11/57; CHESTER (MIDLAND) 9/59; LLANDUDNO JUNCTION 6/62; NUNEATON 10/62; SOUTHPORT 5/63; BANK HALL 7/63; STOKE 2/66; TEBAY 5/67; CARNFORTH 1/68; WITHDRAWN 2/68.

75033 NEW 7/53; BLETCHLEY 7/53; CHESTER (MIDLAND) 2/55; LLANDUDNO JUNCTION 6/56; CHESTER (MIDLAND) 10/56; RHYL 7/57; CHESTER (MIDLAND) 8/57; RHYL 6/59; CHESTER (WEST) 9/59; WORKINGTON 4/60; MOLD JUNCTION 6/60; RHYL 4/62; LLANDUDNO JUNCTION 9/62; NUNEATON 10/62; SOUTHPORT 5/63; BANK HALL 7/63; HEATON MERSEY 4/66; CHESTER (MIDLAND) 4/66; CROES NEWYDD 5/

66; SHREWSBURY 1/67; CROES NEWYDD 3/67; CARNFORTH 4/67; WITHDRAWN 12/67.

75034 NEW 7/53; BLETCHLEY 7/53; CHESTER (MIDLAND) 2/55; ACCRINGTON 5/56; CHESTER (MIDLAND) 8/56; RHYL 7/57; BANGOR 9/57; LLANDUDNO JUNCTION 11/57; CHESTER (MIDLAND) 9/58; RHYL 6/61; MOLD JUNCTION 9/61; RHYL 4/62; LLANDUDNO JUNCTION 9/62; NUNEATON 10/62; ASTON 12/62; STOKE 9/63; CARNFORTH 6/67; WITHDRAWN 2/68.

75035 NEW 8/53; BLETCHLEY 8/53; CHESTER (MIDLAND) 2/55; BANGOR 7/57; LLANDUDNO JUNCTION 11/57; CHESTER (MIDLAND) 9/58; LLANDUDNO JUNCTION 9/62; NUNEATON 10/62; BANGOR 6/63; NUNEATON 12/64; STOKE 6/66; TEBAY 5/67; WITHDRAWN 7/67.

75036 NEW 8/53; BLETCHLEY 8/53; LLANDUDNO JUNCTION 6/61; NUNEATON 10/62; BANGOR 6/63; NUNEATON 7/63; STOKE 9/63; WITHDRAWN 6/66.

75037 NEW 8/53; BLETCHLEY 8/53; ASTON 12/62; STOKE 9/63; TEBAY 5/67; WITHDRAWN 12/67.

75038 NEW 8/53; BLETCHLEY 8/53; SHREWSBURY 10/64; WITHDRAWN 12/65.

75039 NEW 8/53; BLETCHLEY 8/53; CHESTER (MIDLAND) 2/55; BLETCHLEY 3/62; DERBY 5/63; WIGAN (SPRINGS BRANCH) 11/63; SKIPTON 3/65; CARNFORTH 1/67; TEBAY 4/67; WITHDRAWN 9/67.

75040 NEW 8/53; BEDFORD 8/53; ACCRINGTON 10/53; BEDFORD 1/55; DERBY 1/60; LEICESTER (MIDLAND) 2/60; DERBY 9/62; STOKE 10/63; CARNFORTH 6/67; WITHDRAWN 10/67.

75041 NEW 9/53; BEDFORD 9/53; ACCRINGTON 10/53; BEDFORD 1/55; LEICESTER (MIDLAND) 1/60; DERBY 9/62; WIGAN (SPRINGS BRANCH) 11/63; SKIPTON 3/65; CARNFORTH 4/67; WITHDRAWN 1/68.

75042 NEW 9/53; BEDFORD 9/53; ACCRINGTON 10/53; BEDFORD 1/55; LEICESTER (MIDLAND) 4/59; DERBY 9/62; WIGAN (SPRINGS BRANCH) 11/63; SKIPTON 3/65; CARNFORTH 4/67; WITHDRAWN 11/67.

75043 NEW 9/53; BEDFORD 9/53; ACCRINGTON 10/53; BEDFORD 1/55; LEICESTER (MIDLAND) 1/60; DERBY 9/62; WALTON-ON-THE-HILL 11/63; AINTREE 12/63; CARNFORTH 6/67; WITHDRAWN 12/67.

75044 NEW 9/53; BEDFORD 9/53; ACCRINGTON 10/53; BEDFORD 1/55; NOTTINGHAM 1/60; LEICESTER (MIDLAND) 2/60; DERBY 9/62; WIGAN (SPRINGS BRANCH) 11/63; SKIPTON 3/65; WITHDRAWN 3/66.

75045 NEW 9/53; ACCRINGTON 9/53; BANK HALL 10/55; NUNEATON 5/63; WITHDRAWN 4/66.

75046 NEW 10/53; ACCRINGTON 10/53; BANK HALL 11/55; HEATON MERSEY 4/66; CHESTER (MIDLAND) 4/66; CROES NEWYDD 5/66; STOKE 5/67; WITHDRAWN 8/67.

75047 NEW 10/53; ACCRINGTON 10/53; BANK HALL 11/55; STOKE 2/66; CROES NEWYDD 3/66; MACHYNLLETH 7/66; CROES NEWYDD 12/66; SHREWSBURY 1/67; CROES NEWYDD 3/67; STOKE 6/67; WITHDRAWN 8/67.

75048 NEW 10/53; ACCRINGTON 10/53; BANK HALL 11/55; CHESTER (MIDLAND) 4/66; CROES NEWYDD 5/66; LOSTOCK HALL 5/67; CARNFORTH 6/67; WITHDRAWN 8/68.

75049 NEW 10/53; ACCRINGTON 10/53; BANK HALL 11/55; CHESTER (MIDLAND) 5/56; BANK HALL 8/56; WITHDRAWN 10/66.

75050 NEW 11/56; LLANDUDNO JUNCTION 11/56; CHESTER (MIDLAND) 9/57; BANGOR 6/62; LLANDUDNO JUNCTION 9/62; NUNEATON 10/62; BANK HALL 5/63; STOKE 2/66; NUNEATON 3/66; STOKE 6/66; WITHDRAWN 11/66.

75051 NEW 11/56; CHESTER (MIDLAND) 11/56; RHYL 6/58; CHESTER (MIDLAND) 9/58; BLETCHLEY 6/62; DERBY 5/63; WIGAN (SPRINGS BRANCH) 11/63; SKIPTON 3/65; WITHDRAWN 10/66.

75052 NEW 12/56; BLETCHLEY 12/56; CHESTER (NORTHGATE) 12/59; WILLESDEN 1/60; NUNEATON 1/63; HOLYHEAD 6/65; MACHYNLLETH 7/66; CROES NEWYDD 12/66; STOKE 6/67; WITHDRAWN 8/67.

75053 NEW 1/57; CHESTER (MIDLAND) 1/57; RHYL 6/58; CHESTER (MIDLAND) 9/58; RHYL 6/60; MOLD JUNCTION 9/60; BLETCHLEY 4/62; ASTON 12/62; STOKE 9/63; SHREWSBURY 9/64; WITHDRAWN 9/66.

75054 NEW 1/57; CHESTER (MIDLAND) 1/57; RHYL 6/58; CHESTER (MIDLAND) 9/58; RHYL 6/60; MOLD JUNCTION 9/60; BLETCHLEY 4/62; STOKE 1/65; WITHDRAWN 8/66.

75055 NEW 1/57; BEDFORD 1/57; NOTTINGHAM 1/60; LEICESTER (MIDLAND) 2/60; NOTTINGHAM 1/61; LEICESTER (MIDLAND) 2/62; DERBY 5/62; BLETCHLEY 5/63; SHREWSBURY 9/64; BLETCHLEY 10/64; MACHYNLLETH 6/65; SHREWSBURY 12/66; CROES NEWYDD 3/67; STOKE 5/67; WITHDRAWN 5/67.

75056 NEW 3/57; NOTTINGHAM 3/57; DERBY 9/62; BLETCHLEY 5/63; STOKE 9/63; WITHDRAWN 6/66.

75057 NEW 3/57; LEICESTER (MIDLAND) 3/57; DERBY 9/62; WIGAN (SPRINGS BRANCH) 11/63; SKIPTON 3/65; WITHDRAWN 2/66.

75058 NEW 4/57; LEICESTER (MIDLAND) 4/57; DERBY 9/62; WIGAN (SPRINGS BRANCH) 1/64; SKIPTON 3/65; CARNFORTH 4/67; WITHDRAWN 12/67.

75059 NEW 4/57; LEICESTER (MIDLAND) 4/57; DERBY 9/62; WIGAN (SPRINGS BRANCH) 11/63; SKIPTON 3/65; CARNFORTH 4/67; WITHDRAWN 7/67.

75060 NEW 5/57; LEICESTER (MIDLAND) 5/57; DERBY 9/62; WALTON-ON-THE-HILL 11/63; AINTREE 12/63; EDGE HILL 6/65; HEATON MERSEY 4/66; CHESTER (MIDLAND) 4/66; CROES NEWYDD 5/66; WITHDRAWN 4/67.

75061 NEW 5/57; LEICESTER (MIDLAND) 5/57; DERBY 9/62; WALTON-ON-THE-HILL 11/63; AINTREE 12/63; WITHDRAWN 2/67.

75062 NEW 5/57; NOTTINGHAM 5/57; DERBY 9/62; STOKE 10/63; LOSTOCK HALL 5/67; CARNFORTH 6/67; WITHDRAWN 2/68.

75063 NEW 6/57; NOTTINGHAM 6/57; DERBY 9/62; NUNEATON 5/63; SHREWSBURY 9/64; WITHDRAWN 5/66.

75064 NEW 6/57; NOTTINGHAM 6/57; DERBY 9/62; WALTON-ON-THE-HILL 11/63; AINTREE 12/63; WITHDRAWN 5/67.

75065 NEW 8/55; DOVER 8/55; BOURNEMOUTH 5/59; EASTLEIGH 8/61; BASINGSTOKE 11/62; EASTLEIGH 3/63; WITHDRAWN 9/66.

75066 NEW 9/55; DOVER 9/55; BOURNEMOUTH 5/59; EASTLEIGH 7/61; BASINGSTOKE 11/62; EASTLEIGH 3/63; WITHDRAWN 2/66.

75067 NEW 9/55; DOVER 9/55; BOURNEMOUTH 5/59; EASTLEIGH 8/61; BRIGHTON 11/62; STEWARTS LANE 4/63; NORWOOD JUNCTION 9/63; EASTLEIGH 12/63; WITHDRAWN 10/64.

75068 NEW 9/55; DOVER 9/55; BOURNEMOUTH 5/59; EASTLEIGH 5/61; BRIGHTON 11/62; STEWARTS LANE 4/63; NORWOOD JUNCTION 9/63; EASTLEIGH 12/63; WITHDRAWN 7/67.

75069 NEW 9/55; DOVER 9/55; BOURNEMOUTH 5/59; STEWARTS LANE 11/59; NINE ELMS 8/63; EASTLEIGH 5/65; WITHDRAWN 9/66. ENGINE PRESERVED.

75070 NEW 10/55; EXMOUTH JUNCTION 10/55; BATH (GREEN PARK) 6/56; EASTLEIGH 3/57; STEWARTS LANE 1/59; BRIGHTON 2/59; THREE BRIDGES 1/60; STEWARTS LANE 10/62; NINE ELMS 8/63; EASTLEIGH 5/65; WITHDRAWN 9/66.

75071 NEW 10/55; EXMOUTH JUNCTION 10/55; BATH (GREEN PARK) 6/56; TEMPLECOMBE 11/62; CROES NEWYDD 7/64; STOKE 6/67; WITHDRAWN 8/67.

75072 NEW 11/55; EXMOUTH JUNCTION 11/55; BATH (GREEN PARK) 6/56; TEMPLECOMBE 10/62; WITHDRAWN 8/67.

75073 NEW 11/55; EXMOUTH JUNCTION 11/55; EASTLEIGH 6/56; BATH (GREEN PARK) 3/57; TEMPLECOMBE 11/62; WITHDRAWN 12/65.

75074 NEW 11/55; EXMOUTH JUNCTION 11/55; EASTLEIGH 6/56; BASINGSTOKE 8/57; STEWARTS LANE 1/59; NORWOOD JUNCTION 7/63; EASTLEIGH 12/63; NINE ELMS 8/64; EASTLEIGH 5/65; WITHDRAWN 7/67.

75075 NEW 11/55; EXMOUTH JUNCTION 11/55; BASINGSTOKE 6/56; THREE BRIDGES 1/59; STEWARTS LANE 10/62; NORWOOD JUNCTION 7/63; EASTLEIGH 12/63; WITHDRAWN 7/67.

75076 NEW 12/55; EXMOUTH JUNCTION 12/55; BASINGSTOKE 6/56; NINE ELMS 3/63; EASTLEIGH 5/65; WITHDRAWN 7/67.

75077 NEW 12/55; EXMOUTH JUNCTION 12/55; BASINGSTOKE 6/56; NINE ELMS 3/63; EASTLEIGH 5/65; WITHDRAWN 7/67.

75078 NEW 1/56; EXMOUTH JUNCTION 1/56; BASINGSTOKE 6/56; NINE ELMS 3/63; EASTLEIGH 5/65; WITHDRAWN 7/66. ENGINE PRESERVED.

75079 NEW 1/56; EXMOUTH JUNCTION 1/56; BASINGSTOKE 6/56; EASTLEIGH 3/63; WITHDRAWN 11/66. ENGINE PRESERVED.

76000 NEW 12/52; MOTHERWELL 12/52; WITHDRAWN 5/67.

76001 NEW 12/52; MOTHERWELL 12/52; PERTH 4/55; MOTHERWELL 5/57; FORT WILLIAM 6/60; CORKERHILL 8/62; ARDROSSAN 4/64; AYR 2/65; WITHDRAWN 8/66.

76002 NEW 12/52; MOTHERWELL 12/52; WITHDRAWN 12/66.

76003 NEW 12/52; MOTHERWELL 12/52; WITHDRAWN 3/66.

76004 NEW 12/52; MOTHERWELL 12/52; GREENOCK (LADYBURN) 1/63; POLMADIE 12/64; WITHDRAWN 10/66.

76005 NEW 12/52; EASTLEIGH 12/52; BOURNEMOUTH 7/53; EASTLEIGH 9/53; DORCHESTER 5/54; EASTLEIGH 2/55; SALISBURY 6/55; BOURNEMOUTH 10/65; WITHDRAWN 7/67.

76006 NEW 1/53; EASTLEIGH 1/53; BOURNEMOUTH 7/53; EASTLEIGH 9/53; DORCHESTER 5/54; EASTLEIGH 2/55; SALISBURY 6/55; EASTLEIGH 3/60; BOURNEMOUTH 10/65; WITHDRAWN 7/67.

76007 NEW 1/53; EASTLEIGH 1/53; SALISBURY 5/58; BOURNEMOUTH 4/67; WITHDRAWN 7/67.

76008 NEW 2/53; EASTLEIGH 2/53; SALISBURY 6/55; BOURNEMOUTH 4/67; WITHDRAWN 5/67.

76009 NEW 2/53; EASTLEIGH 2/53; REDHILL 8/56; EASTLEIGH 1/57; YEOVIL TOWN 9/58; SALISBURY 1/59; EASTLEIGH 3/60; BOURNEMOUTH 10/65; WITHDRAWN 7/67.

76010 NEW 3/53; EASTLEIGH 3/53; YEOVIL TOWN 9/58; EASTLEIGH 1/59; BOURNEMOUTH 10/65; WITHDRAWN 9/66.

76011 NEW 3/53; EASTLEIGH 3/53; YEOVIL TOWN 9/58; EASTLEIGH 1/59; BOURNEMOUTH 10/65; WITHDRAWN 7/67.

76012 NEW 4/53; EASTLEIGH 4/53; GUILDFORD 6/66; WITHDRAWN 9/66.

76013 NEW 4/53; EASTLEIGH 4/53; BOURNEMOUTH 9/64; WITHDRAWN 9/66.

76014 NEW 5/53; EASTLEIGH 5/53; REDHILL 8/56; EASTLEIGH 1/57; BOURNEMOUTH 9/64; WITHDRAWN 9/66.

76015 NEW 5/53; EASTLEIGH 5/53; BOURNEMOUTH 6/61; WITHDRAWN 10/65.

76016 NEW 5/53; EASTLEIGH 5/53; GUILDFORD 6/66; WITHDRAWN 10/66.

76017 NEW 6/53; EASTLEIGH 6/53; SALISBURY 3/60; WITHDRAWN 7/65. ENGINE PRESERVED.

76018 NEW 6/53; EASTLEIGH 6/53; SALISBURY 3/60; EASTLEIGH 8/64; GUILDFORD 7/66; WITHDRAWN 10/66.

76019 NEW 7/53; EASTLEIGH 7/53; BOURNEMOUTH 8/61; EASTLEIGH 8/64; WITHDRAWN 2/66.

76020 NEW 12/52; DARLINGTON 12/52; KIRKBY STEPHEN 7/56; NUNEATON 5/59; SUTTON OAK 6/59; ASTON 7/62; STOKE 12/62; UTTOXETER 10/63; STOKE 12/64; CHESTER 7/65; WITHDRAWN 4/66.

76021 NEW 12/52; YORK 12/52; NEVILLE HILL 2/53; SELBY 5/53; MALTON 5/53; SELBY 1/54; WEST AUCKLAND 5/56; HURLFORD 10/63; WITHDRAWN 10/66.

76022 NEW 12/52; HULL, (DAIRYCOATES) 12/52; KIRKBY STEPHEN 5/56; LANCASTER (GREEN AYRE) 4/60; WIGAN (SPRINGS BRANCH) 2/62; ASTON 7/62; STOKE 12/62; UTTOXETER 10/63; STOURBRIDGE 8/64; OXLEY 11/64; WITHDRAWN 8/66.

76023 NEW 12/52; SUNDERLAND 12/52; WEST HARTLEPOOL 6/55; KIRKBY STEPHEN 7/56; LANCASTER (GREEN AYRE) 4/60; SUTTON OAK 8/60; ASTON 7/62; STOKE 12/62; UTTOXETER 10/63; CREWE SOUTH 6/64; STOKE 1/65; WITHDRAWN 10/65.

76024 NEW 1/53; GATESHEAD 1/53; BLAYDON 3/53; PERCY MAIN 3/53; TWEEDMOUTH 4/53; BLAYDON 4/54; WEST AUCKLAND 6/56; GATESHEAD 6/59; HEATON 11/59; SUNDERLAND 7/60; YORK 9/61; THORNABY 6/62; HURLFORD 10/63; WITHDRAWN 12/66.

76025 NEW 10/53; EASTLEIGH 10/53; BOURNEMOUTH 5/61; WITHDRAWN 10/65.

76026 NEW 10/53; EASTLEIGH 10/53; BOURNEMOUTH 8/61; WITHDRAWN 7/67.

76027 NEW 10/53; EASTLEIGH 10/53; BOURNEMOUTH 3/62; WITHDRAWN 10/65.

76028 NEW 10/53; EASTLEIGH 10/53; WITHDRAWN 5/64.

76029 NEW 11/53; EASTLEIGH 11/53; WITHDRAWN 10/64.

76030 NEW 11/53; STRATFORD 11/53; CAMBRIDGE 6/60; MARCH 9/60; BRIGHTON 11/62; GUILDFORD 9/63; EASTLEIGH 1/65; WITHDRAWN 4/65.

76031 NEW 11/53; STRATFORD 11/53; MARCH 11/60; BRIGHTON 11/62; GUILDFORD 9/63; EASTLEIGH 1/65; GUILDFORD 6/66; WITHDRAWN 7/67.

76032 NEW 12/53; STRATFORD 12/53; CAMBRIDGE 6/60; MARCH 9/60; BRIGHTON 11/62; GUILDFORD 9/63; WITHDRAWN 8/64.

76033 NEW 12/53; STRATFORD 12/53; CAMBRIDGE 6/60; MARCH 9/60; BRIGHTON 11/62; GUILDFORD 9/63; EASTLEIGH 1/65; GUILDFORD 6/66; WITHDRAWN 1/67.

76034 NEW 12/53; STRATFORD 12/53; NORWICH (THORPE) 11/60; MARCH 9/61; BRIGHTON 11/62; GUILDFORD 9/63; WITHDRAWN 9/64.

76035 NEW 5/54; NEASDEN 6/54; CRICKLEWOOD 6/62; WILLESDEN 12/64; CHESTER 7/65; WITHDRAWN 5/66.

76036 NEW 6/54; NEASDEN 6/54; CRICKLEWOOD 6/62; SALTLEY 7/64; BESCOT 3/65; STOURBRIDGE 11/65; CHESTER (MIDLAND) 4/66; WITHDRAWN 1/67.

76037 NEW 6/54; NEASDEN 6/54; CRICKLEWOOD 6/62; WILLESDEN 12/64; OXLEY 9/65; CHESTER (MIDLAND) 2/67; CROES NEWYDD 4/67; WITHDRAWN 7/67.

76038 NEW 7/54; NEASDEN 7/54; CRICKLEWOOD 6/62; SALTLEY 7/64; MACHYNLLETH 6/66; WITHDRAWN 9/66.

76039 NEW 7/54; NEASDEN 7/54; CRICKLEWOOD 6/62; WILLESDEN 12/64; OXLEY 9/65; CHESTER (MIDLAND) 3/67; CROES NEWYDD 4/67; WITHDRAWN 6/67.

76040 NEW 7/54; NEASDEN 7/54; CRICKLEWOOD 6/62; SALTLEY 7/64; ASTON 1/65; SALTLEY 10/65; CROES NEWYDD 9/66; WITHDRAWN 4/67.

76041 NEW 7/54; NEASDEN 7/54; CRICKLEWOOD 6/62; WILLESDEN 12/64; OXLEY 9/65; CHESTER (MIDLAND) 3/67; WITHDRAWN 4/67.

76042 NEW 8/54; NEASDEN 8/54; CRICKLEWOOD 7/62; SALTLEY 7/64; BESCOT 3/65; STOURBRIDGE 11/65; OXLEY 5/66; WITHDRAWN 6/66.

76043 NEW 8/54; NEASDEN 8/54; CRICKLEWOOD 7/62; SALTLEY 7/64; MACHYNLLETH 6/66; WITHDRAWN 9/66.

76044 NEW 8/54; NEASDEN 8/54; WOODFORD HALSE 6/62; STOKE 6/64; CHESTER (MIDLAND) 3/66; WITHDRAWN 10/66.

76045 NEW 3/55; GATESHEAD 3/55; BLAYDON 10/55; GATESHEAD 1/56; WEST AUCKLAND 6/56; GRANGEMOUTH 10/63; CARSTAIRS 10/65; WITHDRAWN 1/66.

76046 NEW 3/55; GATESHEAD 3/55; BLAYDON 7/55; WEST AUCKLAND 6/56; DAWSHOLM 10/63; GRANGEMOUTH 10/64; CORKERHILL 10/65; WITHDRAWN 5/67.

76047 NEW 3/55; GATESHEAD 3/55; BLAYDON 10/55; KIRKBY STEPHEN 5/56; TRAFFORD PARK 8/60; CRICKLEWOOD 9/62; STOKE 9/63; SALTLEY 10/63; BESCOT 3/65; CHESTER (MIDLAND) 3/66; WITHDRAWN 12/66.

76048 NEW 3/55; GATESHEAD 3/55; BLAYDON 10/55; KIRKBY STEPHEN 6/56; SKIPTON 11/58; HEATON MERSEY 5/59; CRICKLEWOOD 9/62; SALTLEY 7/64; CROES NEWYDD 9/66; WITHDRAWN 2/67..

76049 NEW 4/55; GATESHEAD 4/55; BLAYDON 6/55; GATESHEAD 1/56; WEST AUCKLAND 6/56; HAWICK 10/63; ST MARGARETS 10/65; BATHGATE 1/66; WITHDRAWN 1/66.

76050 NEW 8/56; DARLINGTON 8/56; WEST AUCKLAND 10/56; HAWICK 10/63; WITHDRAWN 9/66.

76051 NEW 8/56; YORK 8/56; KIRKBY STEPHEN 10/56; LANCASTER (GREEN AYRE) 4/60; WIGAN (SPRINGS BRANCH) 2/62; ASTON 7/62; STOKE 12/62; COLWICK 2/66; SUTTON OAK 11/66; WITHDRAWN 4/67.

76052 NEW 9/56; YORK 9/56; KIRKBY STEPHEN 10/56; NEASDEN 5/60; WOODFORD HALSE 7/62; SALTLEY 10/63; OXLEY 5/65; SALTLEY 7/65; CHESTER (MIDLAND) 8/65; WITHDRAWN 12/66.

76053 NEW 4/55; REDHILL 4/55; SALISBURY 4/60 GUILDFORD 6/64; FELTHAM 1/65; EASTLEIGH 7/65; GUILDFORD 6/66; WITHDRAWN 1/67.

76054 NEW 4/55; REDHILL 4/55; SALISBURY 4/60; GUILDFORD 6/64; WITHDRAWN 10/64.

76055 NEW 4/55; REDHILL 4/55; SALISBURY 4/60; GUILDFORD 6/64; FELTHAM 1/65; SALISBURY 7/65; WITHDRAWN 10/65.

76056 NEW 5/55; REDHILL 5/55; EASTLEIGH 11/59; BOURNEMOUTH 12/59; WITHDRAWN 10/65.

76057 NEW 5/55; REDHILL 5/55; EASTLEIGH 11/59; BOURNEMOUTH 12/59; WITHDRAWN 10/66.

76058 NEW 6/55; REDHILL 6/55; EASTLEIGH 11/59; BOURNEMOUTH 12/59; EASTLEIGH 2/62; GUILDFORD 6/66; WITHDRAWN 3/67.

76059 NEW 6/55; REDHILL 6/55; SALISBURY 5/59; EASTLEIGH 3/60; GUILDFORD 6/66; WITHDRAWN 9/66.

76060 NEW 7/55; REDHILL 7/55; SALISBURY 5/59; EASTLEIGH 3/60; WITHDRAWN 12/65.

76061 NEW 7/55; REDHILL 7/55; EASTLEIGH 5/59; WITHDRAWN 1/67.

76062 NEW 7/55; REDHILL 7/55; EASTLEIGH 5/59; WITHDRAWN 10/65.

76063 NEW 7/56; EASTLEIGH 7/56; WITHDRAWN 4/67.

76064 NEW 7/56; EASTLEIGH 7/56; WITHDRAWN 7/67.

76065 NEW 7/56; EASTLEIGH 7/56; WITHDRAWN 10/65.

76066 NEW 7/56; EASTLEIGH 7/56; SALISBURY 3/60; GUILDFORD 8/64; FELTHAM 1/65; EASTLEIGH 7/65; WITHDRAWN 7/67.

76067 NEW 8/56; EASTLEIGH 8/56; SALISBURY 3/60; BOURNEMOUTH 4/67; WITHDRAWN 7/67.

76068 NEW 8/56; EASTLEIGH 8/56; WITHDRAWN 10/65.

76069 NEW 8/56; EASTLEIGH 8/56; GUILDFORD 10/66; WITHDRAWN 6/67.

76070 NEW 9/56; MOTHERWELL 9/56; GREENOCK (LADYBURN) 1/63; BEATTOCK 4/64; POLMADIE 12/64; WITHDRAWN 8/66.

76071 NEW 10/56; MOTHERWELL 10/56; GREENOCK (LADYBURN) 1/63; POLMADIE 12/64; WITHDRAWN 1/66.

76072 NEW 10/56; DUMFRIES 10/56; WITHDRAWN 10/64.

76073 NEW 10/56; DUMFRIES 10/56; AYR 4/66; WITHDRAWN 6/66.

76074 NEW 11/56; EASTFIELD 11/56; PARKHEAD 8/61; GRANGEMOUTH 10/61; DAWSHOLM 11/63; DUMFRIES 10/64; AYR 3/66; WITHDRAWN 8/66.

76075 NEW 12/56; SUTTON OAK 12/56; BESCOT 10/62; STOKE 1/63; COLWICK 2/66; SUTTON OAK 11/66; WIGAN (SPRINGS BRANCH) 6/67; WITHDRAWN 10/67.

76076 NEW 12/56; SUTTON OAK 12/56; WITHDRAWN 11/66.

76077 NEW 12/56; SUTTON OAK 12/56; WIGAN (SPRINGS BRANCH) 6/67; WITHDRAWN 12/67. ENGINE PRESERVED.

76078 NEW 12/56; SUTTON OAK 12/56; WITHDRAWN 12/66.

76079 NEW 2/57; SUTTON OAK 2/57; WIGAN (SPRINGS BRANCH) 6/67; WITHDRAWN 12/67. ENGINE PRESERVED.

76080 NEW 2/57; LOWER DARWEN 2/57; SUTTON OAK 3/65; WIGAN (SPRINGS BRANCH) 6/67; WITHDRAWN 12/67.

76081 NEW 2/57; LOWER DARWEN 2/57; SUTTON OAK 3/65; WIGAN (SPRINGS BRANCH) 6/67; WITHDRAWN 7/67.

76082 NEW 3/57; LOWER DARWEN 3/57; SUTTON OAK 3/65; WITHDRAWN 10/66.

76083 NEW 3/57; LOWER DARWEN 3/57; SUTTON OAK 3/65; WITHDRAWN 10/66.

76084 NEW 4/57; LOWER DARWEN 4/57; LANCASTER (GREEN AYRE) 3/59; LANCASTER (GREEN AYRE) 2/59; LOWER DARWEN 3/59; SUTTON OAK 3/65; WIGAN (SPRINGS BRANCH) 6/67; WITHDRAWN 12/67. ENGINE PRESERVED.

76085 NEW 4/57; LEICESTER (MIDLAND) 4/57; SALTLEY 7/57; HEATON MERSEY 1/59; CRICKLEWOOD 9/62; STOKE 9/63; SALTLEY 10/63; STOKE 1/65; COLWICK 3/66; WITHDRAWN 6/66.

76086 NEW 5/57; LEICESTER (MIDLAND) 5/57; SALTLEY 7/57; TRAFFORD PARK 1/59; CRICKLEWOOD 10/62; STOKE 9/63; SALTLEY 10/63; BESCOT 3/65; SALTLEY 3/66; MACHYNLLETH 6/66; CROES NEWYDD 9/66; WITHDRAWN 9/66.

76087 NEW 5/57; TRAFFORD PARK 5/57; SALTLEY 7/57; HEATON MERSEY 1/59; WOODFORD HALSE 9/62; SALTLEY 10/63; BESCOT 3/65; STOURBRIDGE 3/66; OXLEY 5/66; WITHDRAWN 1/67.

76088 NEW 5/57; TRAFFORD PARK 5/57; NEASDEN 9/60; TRAFFORD PARK 12/60; CRICKLEWOOD 9/62; STOKE 9/63; SALTLEY 10/63; BESCOT 3/65; OXLEY 3/66; CHESTER (MIDLAND) 2/67; WITHDRAWN 6/67.

76089 NEW 6/57; TRAFFORD PARK 6/57; CRICKLEWOOD 9/62; WILLESDEN 12/64; STOKE 1/65; COLWICK 2/66; WITHDRAWN 9/66.

76090 NEW 6/57; CORKERHILL 6/57; PARKHEAD 1/61; MOTHERWELL 10/61; BEATTOCK 7/62; WITHDRAWN 12/66.

76091 NEW 6/57; CORKERHILL 6/57; PARKHEAD 1/61; CORKERHILL 10/61; HURLFORD 4/64; WITHDRAWN 12/66.

76092 NEW 6/57; CORKERHILL 6/57; HURLFORD 4/64; WITHDRAWN 8/66.

76093 NEW 7/57; CORKERHILL 7/57; PARKHEAD 1/61; CORKERHILL 10/61; WITHDRAWN 2/67.

76094 NEW 8/57; CORKERHILL 8/57; PARKHEAD 1/61; CORKERHILL 10/61; HURLFORD 6/64; BEATTOCK 11/66; WITHDRAWN 5/67.

76095 NEW 8/57; CORKERHILL 8/57; PARKHEAD 1/61; CORKERHILL 12/61; WITHDRAWN 7/64; (Reinstated) SALTLEY 9/64; ASTON 1/65; CHESTER (MIDLAND) 8/65; WITHDRAWN 3/67.

76096 NEW 9/57; CORKERHILL 9/57; AYR 5/62; WITHDRAWN 12/66.

76097 NEW 9/57; CORKERHILL 9/57; AYR 5/62; WITHDRAWN 7/64.

76098 NEW 10/57; CORKERHILL 10/57; ARDROSSAN 4/64; AYR 2/65; BEATTOCK 12/65; WITHDRAWN 5/67.

76099 NEW 11/57; CORKERHILL 11/57; AYR 5/62; CORKERHILL 1/63; ARDROSSAN 4/64; WITHDRAWN 7/64. (Reinstated) SALTLEY 9/64; STOKE 1/65; COLWICK 3/66; WITHDRAWN 8/66.

76100 NEW 5/57; DAWSHOLM 5/57; PARKHEAD 7/60; DAWSHOLM 1/61; GRANGEMOUTH 10/64; AYR 10/65; BEATTOCK 12/65; AYR 6/66; WITHDRAWN 8/66.

76101 NEW 6/57; DAWSHOLM 6/57; GRANGEMOUTH 10/64; AYR 10/65; STRANRAER 11/65; AYR 3/66; WITHDRAWN 12/66.

76102 NEW 6/57; PARKHEAD 6/57; ST ROLLOX 2/59; PARKHEAD 7/60; DAWSHOLM 12/60; GRANGEMOUTH 10/64; DUMFRIES 10/65; HURLFORD 6/66; WITHDRAWN 12/66.

76103 NEW 6/57; PARKHEAD 6/57; ST ROLLOX 3/59; PARKHEAD 7/60; ST ROLLOX 1/61; GRANGEMOUTH 10/61; DAWSHOLM 3/63; GRANGEMOUTH 10/64; DUMFRIES 10/65; POLMADIE 11/65; BEATTOCK 4/66; AYR 6/66; WITHDRAWN 7/66.

76104 NEW 7/57; KITTYBREWSTER 7/57; ABERDEEN (FERRYHILL) 6/61; BATHGATE 11/64; POLMADIE 1/66; WITHDRAWN 6/66.

76105 NEW 7/57; KITTYBREWSTER 7/57; ABERDEEN (FERRYHILL) 6/61; DALRY ROAD 12/61; BATHGATE 3/64; POLMADIE 1/66; WITHDRAWN 1/66.

76106 NEW 7/57; KITTYBREWSTER 7/57; KEITH 5/60; ABERDEEN (FERRYHILL) 6/61; DALRY ROAD 12/61; BATHGATE 3/64; WILLESDEN 8/65; WITHDRAWN 9/65.

76107 NEW 8/57; KITTYBREWSTER 8/57; KEITH 5/60; ABERDEEN (FERRYHILL) 6/61; BATHGATE 11/64; WITHDRAWN 10/65.

76108 NEW 8/57; KITTYBREWSTER 8/57; ABERDEEN (FERRYHILL) 6/61; HURLFORD 1/63; WITHDRAWN 7/66.

76109 NEW 8/57; THORNTON 8/57; DUNFERMLINE 1/60; WTHDRAWN 9/66.

76110 NEW 8/57; THORNTON 8/57; DUNFERMLINE 4/60; WITHDRAWN 12/66.

76111 NEW 8/57; THORNTON 8/57; DUNFERMLINE 4/60; THORNTON 2/62; BATHGATE 11/64; WITHDRAWN 1/66.

76112 NEW 9/57; DUMFRIES 9/57; STRANRAER 12/57; WITHDRAWN 10/65.

76113 NEW 10/57; ST ROLLOX 10/57; PARKHEAD 1/61; ST ROLLOX 11/61; GRANGEMOUTH 5/62; CARSTAIRS 10/65; WITHDRAWN 12/66.

76114 NEW 10/57; ST ROLLOX 10/57; PARKHEAD 7/60; ST ROLLOX 10/61; CORKERHILL 5/62; BEATTOCK 11/66; WITHDRAWN 12/66.

77000 NEW 2/54; DARLINGTON 2/54; WEST AUCKLAND 7/54; BRIDLINGTON 6/55; HULL (SPRINGWOOD) 1/58; HULL (DAIRYCOATES) 12/58; DARLINGTON 1/63; STOURTON 5/64; WITHDRAWN 12/66.

77001 NEW 2/54; DARLINGTON 2/54; WEST AUCKLAND 7/54; HULL (BOTANIC GARDENS) 6/55; HULL (DAIRYCOATES) 6/59; THORNABY 4/62; STOURTON 9/63; FARNLEY 12/63; MANNINGHAM 12/64; HULL (DAIRYCOATES) 11/65; GOOLE 12/65; WITHDRAWN 1/66.

77002 NEW 2/54; DARLINGTON 2/54; WEST AUCKLAND 7/54; DARLINGTON 12/62; HULL (DAIRYCOATES) 1/63; STOURTON 9/63; TWEEDMOUTH 11/64; STOURTON 7/66; YORK 10/66; WITHDRAWN 6/67.

77003 NEW 2/54; DARLINGTON 2/54; WEST AUCKLAND 7/54; STOURTON 2/64; WITHDRAWN 12/66.

77004 NEW 3/54; DARLINGTON 3/54; WEST AUCKLAND 8/54; DARLINGTON 12/54; WHITBY 10/55; DARLINGTON 11/55; YORK 8/58; WHITBY 9/58; NEVILLE HILL 4/59; SELBY 5/59; YORK 9/59; SCARBOROUGH 11/59; YORK 4/63; TWEEDMOUTH 11/64; STOURTON 7/66; WITHDRAWN 10/66.

77005 NEW 3/54; HAMILTON 3/54; POLMADIE 9/59; CARSTAIRS 5/60; MOTHERWELL 6/63; WITHDRAWN 11/66.

77006 NEW 3/54; HAMILTON 3/54; CARSTAIRS 11/62; GRANGEMOUTH 12/63; MOTHERWELL 10/65; WITHDRAWN 3/66.

77007 NEW 3/54; HAMILTON 3/54; POLMADIE 9/59; HURLFORD 8/63; WITHDRAWN 11/66.

77008 NEW 4/54; PERTH 4/54; POLMADIE 11/54; MOTHERWELL 8/63; WITHDRAWN 6/66.

77009 NEW 6/54; PERTH 6/54; POLMADIE 12/54; CARSTAIRS 8/63; GRANGEMOUTH 10/63; MOTHERWELL 10/65; WITHDRAWN 5/66.

77010 NEW 6/54; DARLINGTON 6/54; WEST AUCKLAND 8/54; DARLINGTON 6/55; BRIDLINGTON 7/55; HULL (SPRINGHEAD) 9/58; HULL (DAIRYCOATES) 12/58; THORNABY 4/62; WEST AUCKLAND 4/63; STOURTON 2/64; WITHDRAWN 11/65.

77011 NEW 6/54; DARLINGTON 6/54; WEST AUCKLAND 8/54; BLAYDON 6/55; GATESHEAD 9/59; TYNE DOCK 9/60; SOUTH BLYTH 4/61; THORNABY 10/62; STOURTON 9/63; NORTHWICH 11/64; WITHDRAWN 2/66.

77012 NEW 6/54; DARLINGTON 6/54; WEST AUCKLAND 12/54; WHITBY 11/55; YORK 12/58; STOURTON 9/63; FARNLEY 12/63; MANNINGHAM 12/64; HULL (DAIRYCOATES) 11/65; GOOLE 12/65; SOUTH BLYTH 3/66; YORK 4/66; WITHDRAWN 6/67.

77013 NEW 7/54; DARLINGTON 8/54; WHITBY 10/55; NEVILLE HILL 4/59; SELBY 5/59; YORK 9/59; SCARBOROUGH 10/60; YORK 4/63; STOURTON 9/63; WITHDRAWN 3/66.

77014 NEW 7/54; DARLINGTON 7/54; WHITBY 10/55; BLAYDON 6/56; GATESHEAD 9/59; TYNE DOCK 9/60; SOUTH BLYTH 4/61; THORNABY 10/62; STOURTON 9/63; NORTHWICH 11/64; GUILDFORD 3/66; WITHDRAWN 7/67.

77015 NEW 7/54; HURLFORD 7/54; WITHDRAWN 7/66.

77016 NEW 8/54; HURLFORD 8/54; WITHDRAWN 3/66.

77017 NEW 8/54; HURLFORD 8/54; WITHDRAWN 11/66.

77018 NEW 8/54; HURLFORD 8/54; WITHDRAWN 11/66.

77019 NEW 9/54; HURLFORD 9/54; POLMADIE 2/63; HURLFORD 10/63; WITHDRAWN 11/66.

78000 NEW 12/52; OSWESTRY 12/52; MACHYNLLETH 4/53; NOTTINGHAM 5/63; DERBY 1/64; WITHDRAWN 6/65.

78001 NEW 12/52; OSWESTRY 12/52; MACHYNLLETH 4/53; WORCESTER 5/54; GLOUCESTER (BARNWOOD) 1/64; GLOUCESTER (HORTON ROAD) 4/64; WITHDRAWN 12/65.

78002 NEW 12/52; OSWESTRY 12/52; MACHYNLLETH 5/53; WIGAN (CENTRAL) 8/63; BANK HALL 10/63; LOSTOCK HALL 6/64; WITHDRAWN 6/66.

78003 NEW 12/52; OSWESTRY 12/52; MACHYNLLETH 4/53; WORCESTER 3/58; MACHYNLLETH 5/58; BANGOR 5/63; WILLESDEN 6/65; NUNEATON 9/65; SHREWSBURY 1/66; WITHDRAWN 12/66.

78004 NEW 1/53; OSWESTRY 1/53; MACHYNLLETH 5/53; SWINDON 1/54; HEREFORD 6/57; LLANELLY 1/64; GLOUCESTER (HORTON ROAD) 7/64; WITHDRAWN 11/65.

78005 NEW 2/53; OSWESTRY 2/53; MACHYNLLETH 5/53; GLOUCESTER (BARNWOOD) 10/62; GLOUCESTER (HORTON ROAD) 4/64; WITHDRAWN 9/64.

78006 NEW 3/53; OSWESTRY 3/53; MACHYNLLETH 9/53; GLOUCESTER (BARNWOOD) 9/62; GLOUCESTER (HORTON ROAD) 4/64; WITHDRAWN 12/65.

78007 NEW 3/53; OSWESTRY 3/53; MACHYNLLETH 9/53; CREWE NORTH 6/63; CREWE SOUTH 6/64; GORTON 3/65; TRAFFORD PARK 6/65; BOLTON 8/66; WITHDRAWN 5/67.

78008 NEW 3/53; OSWESTRY 3/53; WORCESTER 7/53; WOLVERHAMPTON (STAFFORD ROAD) 3/62; OXLEY 11/62; WITHDRAWN 10/66.

78009 NEW 4/53; OSWESTRY 4/53; WORCESTER 7/53; GLOUCESTER (BARNWOOD) 3/63; WITHDRAWN 2/64.

78010 NEW 12/53; WEST AUCKLAND 12/53; NORTHALLERTON 3/55; POLMADIE 3/63; MOTHERWELL 5/63; DARLINGTON 6/63; FARNLEY 11/63; CREWE SOUTH 4/64; WITHDRAWN 9/66.

78011 NEW 12/53; WEST AUCKLAND 12/53; NORTHALLERTON 3/55; DARLINGTON 3/63; FARNLEY 11/63; MANNINGHAM 4/64; GORTON 12/64; TRAFFORD PARK 6/65; WITHDRAWN 9/65.

78012 NEW 1/54; WEST AUCKLAND 1/54; NORTHALLERTON 3/55; DARLINGTON 3/63; TWEEDMOUTH 11/63; GORTON 12/64; TRAFFORD PARK 6/65; BOLTON 8/66; WITHDRAWN 5/67.

78013 NEW 1/54; WEST AUCKLAND 1/54; NORTHALLERTON 3/55; KIRKBY STEPHEN 1/58; KIRKBY-IN-ASHFIELD 6/60; NOTTINGHAM 3/63; COALVILLE 12/63; LEICESTER (MIDLAND) 9/64; TOTON 7/66; BOLTON 11/66; WITHDRAWN 5/67.

78014 NEW 2/54; WEST AUCKLAND 2/54; NORTHALLERTON 3/55; DARLINGTON 3/63; FARNLEY 11/63; MANNINGHAM 4/64; GORTON 12/64; TRAFFORD PARK 6/65; WITHDRAWN 9/65.

78015 NEW 2/54; WEST AUCKLAND 2/54; NORTHALLERTON 12/56; DARLINGTON 3/63. WITHDRAWN 11/63.

78016 NEW 3/54; WEST AUCKLAND 3/54; KIRKBY STEPHEN 4/54; WEST AUCKLAND 3/58; MOTHERWELL 8/63; DUMFRIES 10/63; STRANRAER 2/64; WITHDRAWN 8/66.

78017 NEW 3/54; WEST AUCKLAND 3/54; KIRKBY STEPHEN 4/54; WIGAN (SPRINGS BRANCH) 4/60; RHYL 6/61; WIDNES 10/61; RHYL 3/62; STOKE 4/62; SHREWSBURY 10/66; WITHDRAWN 12/66.

78018 NEW 3/54; WEST AUCKLAND 3/54; KIRKBY STEPHEN 4/54; CHESTER (MIDLAND) 4/60; WORKINGTON 6/62; CHESTER (MIDLAND) 9/62; WILLESDEN 5/63; NUNEATON 9/65; SHREWSBURY 4/66; WITHDRAWN 11/66. ENGINE PRESERVED.

78019 NEW 3/54; KIRKBY STEPHEN 3/54; WIGAN (SPRINGS BRANCH) 4/60; NORTHWICH 6/61; WILLESDEN 5/63; NUNEATON 9/65; CREWE SOUTH 1/66; WITHDRAWN 11/66. ENGINE PRESERVED.

78020 NEW 4/54; KETTERING 4/54; NOTTINGHAM 11/59; WIGAN (CENTRAL) 12/63; WIGAN (SPRINGS BRANCH) 4/64; DERBY 5/64; TOTON 10/66; LOSTOCK HALL 11/66; WITHDRAWN 5/67.

78021 NEW 5/54; KETTERING 5/54; NOTTINGHAM 11/59; DERBY 1/64; LEICESTER (MIDLAND) 2/65; TOTON 7/66; LOSTOCK HALL 11/66; WITHDRAWN 5/67.

78022 NEW 5/54; MILLHOUSES 5/54; DONCASTER 1/62; MARCH 9/62; BARROW 12/62; AINTREE 5/63; LOSTOCK HALL 12/63; WITHDRAWN 9/66.
ENGINE PRESERVED.

78023 NEW 5/54; MILLHOUSES 5/54; DONCASTER 1/62; MARCH 9/62; BARROW 12/62; AINTREE 5/63; NOTTINGHAM 5/64; GORTON 3/65; TRAFFORD PARK 6/65; BOLTON 8/66; WITHDRAWN 5/67.

78024 NEW 5/54; MILLHOUSES 5/54; DONCASTER 1/62; MARCH 9/62; DARLINGTON 12/62; TWEEDMOUTH 10/63; GORTON 12/64; WITHDRAWN 2/65.

78025 NEW 6/54; MILLHOUSES 6/54; DONCASTER 1/62; MARCH 9/62; DARLINGTON 12/62; WEST AUCKLAND 1/63; TWEEDMOUTH 10/63; GORTON 12/64; WITHDRAWN 2/65.

78026 NEW 6/54; CANKLOW 6/54; AYR 1/62; DUMFRIES 1/63 STRANRAER 2/64; CORKERHILL 11/64; WITHDRAWN 8/66.

78027 NEW 6/54; CANKLOW 6/54; MARCH 9/62; BARROW 12/62; WIGAN (CENTRAL) 6/63; WIGAN (SPRINGS BRANCH) 4/64; DERBY 5/64; LEICESTER (MIDLAND) 9/64; WITHDRAWN 9/65.

78028 NEW 7/54; LEICESTER (MIDLAND) 7/54; KETTERING 1/59; NOTTINGHAM 11/59; COALVILLE 1/64; LEICESTER (MIDLAND) 9/64; TOTON 7/66; BOLTON 11/66; WITHDRAWN 2/67.

78029 NEW 7/54; LEICESTER (MIDLAND) 7/54; NOTTINGHAM 11/59; OSWESTRY 5/63; WATFORD 6/63; WILLESDEN 4/65; WITHDRAWN 10/65.

78030 NEW 9/54; PRESTON 9/54; CREWE NORTH 4/56; CREWE SOUTH 10/64; WITHDRAWN 10/65.

78031 NEW 9/54; TEBAY 9/54; CHESTER (NORTHGATE) 10/56; RHYL 6/59; CHESTER (MIDLAND) 4/62; WITHDRAWN 10/66.

78032 NEW 9/54; RHYL 9/54; WIDNES 5/56; CHESTER (MIDLAND) 2/60; KIRKBY STEPHEN 4/60; CHESTER (MIDLAND) 5/60; BANGOR 9/63; WILLESDEN 6/65; WITHDRAWN 10/65.

78033 NEW 9/54; RHYL 9/54; CREWE NORTH 2/55; RHYL 3/55; WIDNES 5/56; CHESTER (MIDLAND) 2/60; WILLESDEN 5/63; WITHDRAWN 10/65.

78034 NEW 10/54; RHYL 10/54; WIDNES 5/56; BANGOR 9/61; WATFORD 5/63; WILLESDEN 4/65; CREWE SOUTH 9/65; WITHDRAWN 1/66.

78035 NEW 10/54; RHYL 10/54; WIDNES 5/56; PRESTON 4/58; WIDNES 5/58; WATFORD 5/63; WILLESDEN 4/65; SHREWSBURY 9/65; WITHDRAWN 12/65.

78036 NEW 11/54; PRESTON 11/54; LOSTOCK HALL 9/61; SKIPTON 9/62; CREWE SOUTH 5/63; SHREWSBURY 11/66; WITHDRAWN 12/66.

78037 NEW 11/54; PRESTON 11/54; LOSTOCK HALL 9/61; SKIPTON 9/62; WIGAN (SPRINGS BRANCH) 3/64; DERBY 5/64; LOSTOCK HALL 3/65; WITHDRAWN 5/67.

78038 NEW 11/54; BESCOT 11/54; CHESTER (NORTHGATE) 10/56; RHYL 3/58; NORTHWICH 11/59; WILLESDEN 5/63; SHREWSBURY 9/65; WITHDRAWN 8/66.

78039 NEW 11/54; RHYL 11/54; WIDNES 5/56; WILLESDEN 5/63; NUNEATON 9/65; SHREWSBURY 4/66; WITHDRAWN 10/66.

78040 NEW 12/54; BANK HALL 12/54; WIGAN 2/57; AINTREE 1/61; LOSTOCK HALL 4/64; WITHDRAWN 1/66.

78041 NEW 12/54; BANK HALL 12/54; LOSTOCK HALL 6/64; WITHDRAWN 5/67.

78042 NEW 12/54; BANK HALL 12/54; NOTTINGHAM 5/64; TOTON 4/65; WITHDRAWN 9/65.

78043 NEW 12/54; BANK HALL 12/54; AINTREE 11/56; BANK HALL 3/57; AINTREE 9/62; WILLESDEN 5/63; WITHDRAWN 10/65.

78044 NEW 12/54; BANK HALL 12/54; AINTREE 9/62; LOSTOCK HALL 12/63; AINTREE 4/64; NOTTINGHAM 5/64; TOTON 4/65; BOLTON 11/66; WITHDRAWN 5/67.

78045 NEW 10/55; KITTYBREWSTER 10/55; KEITH 6/60; ABERDEEN (FERRYHILL) 6/61; BATHGATE 6/64; WITHDRAWN 1/66.

78046 NEW 10/55; HAWICK 10/55; BATHGATE 1/64; ST MARGARETS 9/66; WITHDRAWN 11/66.

78047 NEW 10/55; HAWICK 10/55; ST MARGARETS 10/65; BATHGATE 1/66; ST MARGARETS 9/66; WITHDRAWN 9/66.

78048 NEW 10/55; ST MARGARETS 10/55; HAWICK 7/60; WITHDRAWN 7/64.

78049 NEW 11/55; ST MARGARETS 11/55; HAWICK 6/59; ST MARGARETS 1/66; WITHDRAWN 8/66.

78050 NEW 11/55; MOTHERWELL 11/55; DAWSHOLM 10/63; BATHGATE 7/64; WITHDRAWN 1/66.

78051 NEW 11/55; MOTHERWELL 11/55; DAWSHOLM 10/63; DUMFRIES 7/64; AYR 6/66; WITHDRAWN 11/66.

78052 NEW 11/55; MOTHERWELL 11/55; INVERNESS 12/56; ST MARGARETS 9/58; AVIEMORE 11/58; PERTH 7/62; BATHGATE 11/63; WITHDRAWN 1/66.

78053 NEW 11/55; MOTHERWELL 11/55; ABERDEEN (FERRYHILL) 10/56; KEITH 12/56; ABERDEEN (FERRYHILL) 6/61; STIRLING 1/63; WITHDRAWN 7/64.

78054 NEW 12/55; MOTHERWELL 12/55; ABERDEEN (FERRYHILL) 10/56; KEITH 12/56; ABERDEEN (FERRYHILL) 6/61; BATHGATE 6/64; WITHDRAWN 12/65.

78055 NEW 8/56; CHESTER 8/56; BESCOT 7/57; CHESTER (NORTHGATE) 8/57; LLANDUDNO JUNCTION 6/59; RHYL 11/59; NORTHWICH 9/60; CREWE SOUTH 11/62; SKIPTON 5/63; AINTREE 3/64; SPEKE JUNCTION 4/64; NOTTINGHAM 5/64; TOTON 4/65; BOLTON 11/66; WITHDRAWN 2/67.

78056 NEW 8/56; CHESTER (NORTHGATE) 8/56; RHYL 4/59; STOKE 4/62; WITHDRAWN 7/66.

78057 NEW 9/56; CHESTER 9/56; RHYL 1/57; CHESTER (MIDLAND) 7/57; BANGOR 11/57; NORTHWICH 11/59; WIGAN (CENTRAL) 5/63; WIGAN (SPRINGS BRANCH) 4/64; DERBY 5/64; LOSTOCK HALL 3/65; WITHDRAWN 5/66.

78058 NEW 9/56; CHESTER (NORTHGATE) 9/56; LLANDUDNO JUNCTION 6/59; BANGOR 11/59; WILLESDEN 6/65; SHREWSBURY 9/65; WITHDRAWN 12/66.

78059 NEW 9/56; CHESTER (NORTHGATE) 9/56; LLANDUDNO JUNCTION 6/59; BANGOR 11/59; HOLYHEAD 4/64; BANGOR 10/64; WILLESDEN 6/65; NUNEATON 9/65; STOKE 6/66; CREWE SOUTH 10/66; WITHDRAWN 11/66. ENGINE PRESERVED.

78060 NEW 10/56; WIGAN (CENTRAL) 10/56; AINTREE 9/62; WILLESDEN 5/63; SHREWSBURY 9/65; WITHDRAWN 10/66.

78061 NEW 10/56; WIGAN (CENTRAL) 10/56; WIGAN (SPRINGS BRANCH) 4/64; DERBY 5/64; LEICESTER (MIDLAND) 6/64; TOTON 7/66; WITHDRAWN 11/66.

78062 NEW 10/56; WIGAN (CENTRAL) 10/56; WIGAN (SPRINGS BRANCH) 4/64; NOTTINGHAM 5/64; TOTON 4/65; GORTON 4/65; TRAFFORD PARK 6/65; BOLTON 11/66; WITHDRAWN 5/67.

78063 NEW 11/56; WIGAN (CENTRAL) 11/56; WILLESDEN 5/63; NUNEATON 9/65; SHREWSBURY 4/66; WITHDRAWN 12/66.

78064 NEW 11/56; WIGAN (CENTRAL) 11/56; DERBY 2/64; TOTON 10/66; WITHDRAWN 12/66.

80000 NEW 9/52; AYR 9/52 CORKERHILL 11/52; HURLFORD 9/61; CORKERHILL 1/62; ARDROSSAN 9/62; CORKERHILL 6/64; WITHDRAWN 12/66.

80001 NEW 10/52; POLMADIE 10/52; BEATTOCK 5/62; POLMADIE 5/64; WITHDRAWN 7/66.

80002 NEW 10/52; MOTHERWELL 10/52; POLMADIE 11/52; BEATTOCK 5/62; POLMADIE 5/64; WITHDRAWN 3/67. ENGINE PRESERVED.

80003 NEW 10/52; MOTHERWELL 10/52; POLMADIE 11/52; ST MARGARETS 6/62; WITHDRAWN 2/65.

80004 NEW 11/52; KITTYBREWSTER 11/52; BEATTOCK 6/61; EASTFIELD 1/63; DAWSHOLM 8/64; CORKERHILL 10/64; WITHDRAWN 5/67.

80005 NEW 11/52; KITTYBREWSTER 11/52; CORKERHILL 7/59; AYR 10/64; BEATTOCK 3/65; POLMADIE 11/65; WITHDRAWN 8/66.

80006 NEW 11/52; POLMADIE 11/52; BEATTOCK 6/61; POLMADIE 8/61; ST MARGARETS 5/62; WITHDRAWN 9/66.

80007 NEW 12/52; POLMADIE 12/52; ST MARGARETS 5/62; POLMADIE 11/65; WITHDRAWN 7/66.

80008 NEW 12/52; CORKERHILL 12/52; WITHDRAWN 7/64.

80009 NEW 12/52; CORKERHILL 12/52; WITHDRAWN 9/64.

80010 NEW 7/51; TUNBRIDGE WELLS WEST 7/51; BRIGHTON 11/56; THREE BRIDGES 2/59; TUNBRIDGE WELLS WEST 1/63; BRIGHTON 9/63; WITHDRAWN 6/64.

80011 NEW 7/51; TUNBRIDGE WELLS WEST 7/51; BRIGHTON 11/56; THREE BRIDGES 2/59; TUNBRIDGE WELLS WEST 1/63; BRIGHTON 9/63; REDHILL 6/64; EASTLEIGH 5/65; BOURNEMOUTH 10/65; GUILDFORD 1/66; BOURNEMOUTH 2/66; WITHDRAWN 7/67.

80012 NEW 8/51; TUNBRIDGE WELLS WEST 8/51; BRIGHTON 3/58; THREE BRIDGES 2/59; STEWARTS LANE 1/63; FELTHAM 6/63; EASTLEIGH 11/64; NINE ELMS 10/65; WITHDRAWN 3/67.

80013 NEW 8/51; TUNBRIDGE WELLS WEST 8/51; BRIGHTON 1/59; BOURNEMOUTH 6/64; WITHDRAWN 6/66.

80014 NEW 9/51; TUNBRIDGE WELLS WEST 9/51; BRIGHTON 9/63; EASTLEIGH 6/64; WITHDRAWN 5/65.

80015 NEW 9/51; TUNBRIDGE WELLS WEST 9/51; BRIGHTON 6/56; TUNBRIDGE WELLS WEST 11/56; EASTLEIGH 8/63; NINE ELMS 10/65; WITHDRAWN 7/67.

80016 NEW 9/51; TUNBRIDGE WELLS WEST 9/51; BRIGHTON 3/52; TUNBRIDGE WELLS WEST 11/56; BRIGHTON 9/63; EASTLEIGH 6/64; WITHDRAWN 7/67.

80017 NEW 10/51; TUNBRIDGE WELLS WEST 10/51; BRIGHTON 1/52; EASTBOURNE 3/52; TUNBRIDGE WELLS WEST 10/52; BRIGHTON 6/56; TUNBRIDGE WELLS WEST 11/56; BRIGHTON 9/63; EASTLEIGH 6/64; WITHDRAWN 9/64.

80018 NEW 10/51; TUNBRIDGE WELLS WEST 10/51; BRIGHTON 1/52; EASTBOURNE 3/52; REDHILL 10/52 TUNBRIDGE WELLS WEST 2/53; BRIGHTON 6/56; TUNBRIDGE WELLS WEST 11/56; BRIGHTON 9/63; FELTHAM 6/64; EASTLEIGH 11/64; WITHDRAWN 4/65.

80019 NEW 10/51; TUNBRIDGE WELLS WEST 10/51; BRIGHTON 1/52; EASTBOURNE 6/52; REDHILL 10/52; BRIGHTON 2/53; TUNBRIDGE WELLS WEST 11/56; BRIGHTON 9/63; REDHILL 6/64; BOURNEMOUTH 5/65; WITHDRAWN 3/67.

80020 NEW 10/51; KITTYBREWSTER 10/51; ARDROSSAN 6/61; CORKERHILL 7/61; WITHDRAWN 6/65.

80021 NEW 11/51; KITTYBREWSTER 11/51; ARDROSSAN 6/61; CORKERHILL 7/61; WITHDRAWN 7/64.

80022 NEW 11/51; POLMADIE 11/51; ST MARGARETS 5/62; WITHDRAWN 6/65.

80023 NEW 11/51; POLMADIE 11/51; STRANRAER 6/62; HURLFORD 9/62; DUMFRIES 3/65; WITHDRAWN 10/65.

80024 NEW 12/51; CORKERHILL 12/51; WITHDRAWN 8/66.

80025 NEW 12/51; CORKERHILL 12/51; WITHDRAWN 8/66.

80026 NEW 12/51; POLMADIE 12/51; ST MARGARETS 7/62; WITHDRAWN 9/66.

80027 NEW 1/52; POLMADIE 1/52; EASTFIELD 1/63; POLMADIE 12/64; WITHDRAWN 11/66.

80028 NEW 1/52; KITTYBREWSTER 1/52; ARDROSSAN 6/61; HURLFORD 6/62; STRANRAER 6/63; PERTH 11/63; WITHDRAWN 9/66.

80029 NEW 1/52; KITTYBREWSTER 1/52; ARDROSSAN 6/61; HURLFORD 6/62; WITHDRAWN 12/65.

80030 NEW 2/52; CORKERHILL 2/52; ARDROSSAN 10/58 CORKERHILL 12/58; WITHDRAWN 6/64.

80031 NEW 2/52; BRIGHTON 2/52; REDHILL 12/63; WITHDRAWN 9/64.

80032 NEW 3/52; BRIGHTON 3/52; REDHILL 12/63; BOURNEMOUTH 5/65; WITHDRAWN 1/67.

80033 NEW 3/52; BRIGHTON 3/52; REDHILL 12/63; FELTHAM 5/65; WITHDRAWN 10/66.

80034 NEW 4/52; CREWE NORTH 4/52; WATFORD 6/52; ASHFORD 12/59; STEWARTS LANE 5/62; BRIGHTON 8/63; REDHILL 12/63; FELTHAM 5/65; WITHDRAWN 1/66.

80035 NEW 4/52; WATFORD 4/52; ASHFORD 12/59; EXMOUTH JUNCTION 5/62; YEOVIL TOWN 9/64; EXMOUTH JUNCTION 1/65; YEOVIL TOWN 2/65; WITHDRAWN 3/65.

80036 NEW 5/52; WATFORD 5/52; ASHFORD 12/59; EXMOUTH JUNCTION 5/62; WITHDRAWN 11/64.

80037 NEW 5/52; WATFORD 5/52; ASHFORD 12/59; TONBRIDGE 5/61; EXMOUTH JUNCTION 6/62; BATH (GREEN PARK) 1/65; EXMOUTH JUNCTION 2/65; TEMPLECOMBE 6/65; WITHDRAWN 3/66.

80038 NEW 5/52; WATFORD 6/52; ASHFORD 12/59; TONBRIDGE 5/61; EXMOUTH JUNCTION 6/62; YEOVIL TOWN 7/63; EXMOUTH JUNCTION 10/63; WITHDRAWN 9/64.

80039 NEW 6/52; BLETCHLEY 6/52; LONGSIGHT 12/53; BLETCHLEY 2/55; ASHFORD 12/59; TONBRIDGE 5/61; EXMOUTH JUNCTION 6/62; BATH (GREEN PARK) 1/65; EXMOUTH JUNCTION 2/65; YEOVIL TOWN 4/65; TEMPLECOMBE 6/65; WITHDRAWN 2/66.

80040 NEW 6/52; BLETCHLEY 6/52; CHESTER (MIDLAND) 7/57; ASHFORD 12/59; TONBRIDGE 5/61; EXMOUTH JUNCTION 6/62; WITHDRAWN 5/64.

80041 NEW 7/52; BLETCHLEY 7/52; ASHFORD 12/59; TONBRIDGE 5/61; EXMOUTH JUNCTION 6/62; TEMPLECOMBE 6/65; WITHDRAWN 3/66.

80042 NEW 7/52; BLETCHLEY 7/52; ASHFORD 12/59; TONBRIDGE 5/61; EXMOUTH JUNCTION 6/62; WITHDRAWN 1/65.

80043 NEW 7/52; BLETCHLEY 7/52; DOVER 12/59; ASHFORD 1/60; TONBRIDGE 5/61; EXMOUTH JUNCTION 6/62; TEMPLECOMBE 9/64; WITHDRAWN 3/66.

80044 NEW 8/52; DERBY 8/52; BEDFORD 1/53; BURY 1/55; NEWTON HEATH 2/56; CORKERHILL 2/60; BANGOR 7/64; WITHDRAWN 11/64.

80045 NEW 9/52; BEDFORD 9/52; KENTISH TOWN 1/55; CHESTER (MIDLAND) 10/56; CORKERHILL 4/60; BEATTOCK 3/65; POLMADIE 11/65; WITHDRAWN 5/67.

80046 NEW 9/52; BEDFORD 9/52; BURY 1/55; NEWTON HEATH 2/56; BLACKPOOL 11/57; CORKERHILL 4/60; WITHDRAWN 5/67.

80047 NEW 10/52; BEDFORD 10/52; KENTISH TOWN 1/53; CHESTER (MIDLAND) 10/56; CORKERHILL 2/60; WITHDRAWN 8/66.

80048 NEW 10/52; KENTISH TOWN 10/52; CHESTER (MIDLAND) 10/56; CORKERHILL 5/60; BANGOR 7/64; SHREWSBURY 9/64; WITHDRAWN 7/65.

80049 NEW 10/52; NEWTON HEATH 12/52; CHESTER (MIDLAND) 10/56; CORKERHILL 4/60; WITHDRAWN 6/64.

80050 NEW 11/52; NEWTON HEATH 11/52; CHESTER (MIDLAND) 10/56; CORKERHILL 4/60; BANGOR 7/64; WITHDRAWN 11/64.

80051 NEW 11/52; NEWTON HEATH 11/52; CHESTER (MIDLAND) 10/56; CORKERHILL 4/60; WITHDRAWN 8/66.

80052 NEW 12/52; NEWTON HEATH 12/52; CHESTER (MIDLAND) 10/56; CORKERHILL 2/60; WITHDRAWN 7/64.

80053 NEW 12/52; NEWTON HEATH 12/52; CHESTER (MIDLAND) 10/56; CORKERHILL 4/60; WITHDRAWN 7/64.

80054 NEW 12/54; POLMADIE 12/54; ST MARGARETS 7/62; GREENOCK (LADYBURN) 11/65; WITHDRAWN 6/66.

80055 NEW 12/54; POLMADIE 12/54; ST MARGARETS 7/62; WITHDRAWN 9/66.

80056 NEW 12/54; POLMADIE 12/54; EASTFIELD 1/63; LOSTOCK HALL 9/64; WITHDRAWN 10/64.

80057 NEW 12/54; POLMADIE 12/54; EASTFIELD 1/63; POLMADIE 2/65; WITHDRAWN 12/66.

80058 NEW 1/55; POLMADIE 1/55; WITHDRAWN 7/66.

80059 NEW 3/53; KENTISH TOWN 3/53; CHESTER (MIDLAND) 10/56; BANGOR 5/58; NEASDEN 9/58; DOVER 12/59; ASHFORD 1/60; TONBRIDGE 5/61; EXMOUTH JUNCTION 6/62; TEMPLECOMBE 9/64; BRISTOL (BARROW ROAD) 6/65; BATH (GREEN PARK) 7/65; WITHDRAWN 11/65.

80060 NEW 3/53; BEDFORD 3/53; BURY 1/55; NEWTON HEATH 2/56; STIRLING 2/60; GREENOCK (LADYBURN) 7/64; POLMADIE 12/65; WITHDRAWN 2/66.

80061 NEW 4/53; BEDFORD 4/53; BURY 1/55; NEWTON HEATH 2/56; STIRLING 3/60; DUMFRIES 7/64; POLMADIE 7/65; WITHDRAWN 12/66.

80062 NEW 5/53; KENTISH TOWN 5/53; CHESTER (MIDLAND) 10/56; BIRKENHEAD 2/58; STIRLING 2/60; GREENOCK (LADYBURN) 7/64; STIRLING 8/64; WITHDRAWN 10/64.

80063 NEW 5/53; SALTLEY 5/53; KENTISH TOWN 10/54; CHESTER (MIDLAND) 10/56; BIRKENHEAD 2/57; STIRLING 2/60; CORKERHILL 7/64; WITHDRAWN 8/66.

80064 NEW 6/53; WATFORD 6/53; DOVER 12/59; ASHFORD 1/60; TONBRIDGE 5/61; EXMOUTH JUNCTION 6/62; BRISTOL (BARROW ROAD) 5/65; WITHDRAWN 9/65. ENGINE PRESERVED.

80065 NEW 6/53; WATFORD 6/53; DOVER 12/59; ASHFORD 1/60; TONBRIDGE 5/61; EASTLEIGH 6/62; WITHDRAWN 9/66.

80066 NEW 7/53; WATFORD 7/53; STEWARTS LANE 12/59; ASHFORD 1/60; TONBRIDGE 5/61; EASTLEIGH 6/62; WITHDRAWN 5/65.

80067 NEW 8/53; WATFORD 8/53; STEWARTS LANE 12/59; EXMOUTH JUNCTION 5/62; TEMPLECOMBE 9/64; BRISTOL (BARROW ROAD) 5/65; WITHDRAWN 6/65.

80068 NEW 8/53; WATFORD 8/53; STEWARTS LANE 12/59; BRIGHTON 9/63; REDHILL 12/63; FELTHAM 5/65; WITHDRAWN 10/66.

80069 NEW 9/53; PLAISTOW 9/53; TILBURY 12/56; SWANSEA EAST DOCK 8/62; NINE ELMS 7/64; WITHDRAWN 2/66.

80070 NEW 10/53; PLAISTOW 10/53; TILBURY 12/56; OLD OAK COMMON 8/62; SHREWSBURY 12/62; CROES NEWYDD 2/63; SHREWSBURY 3/63; EASTLEIGH 4/65; WITHDRAWN 6/65.

80071 NEW 10/53; PLAISTOW 10/53; TILBURY 12/56; MARCH 9/62; ARDSLEY 12/62; CARSTAIRS 10/63; WITHDRAWN 7/64.

80072 NEW 11/53; PLAISTOW 11/53; TILBURY 12/56; SWANSEA EAST DOCK 8/62; LEAMINGTON SPA 9/62; SHREWSBURY 6/65; WITHDRAWN 7/65; ENGINE PRESERVED.

80073 NEW 11/53; PLAISTOW 11/53; TILBURY 12/56; MARCH 9/62; ARDSLEY 12/62; CARSTAIRS 10/63; WITHDRAWN 7/64.

80074 NEW 11/53; PLAISTOW 11/53; TILBURY 12/56; MARCH 9/62; ARDSLEY 12/62; CARSTAIRS 10/63; WITHDRAWN 7/64.

80075 NEW 12/53; PLAISTOW 12/53; TILBURY 12/56; MARCH 9/62; ARDSLEY 12/62; CARSTAIRS 11/63; WITHDRAWN 7/64.

80076 NEW 12/53; PLAISTOW 12/53; TILBURY 12/56; MARCH 9/62; ARDSLEY 12/62; DUMFRIES 10/63; WITHDRAWN 7/64.

80077 NEW 1/54; PLAISTOW 1/54; TILBURY 12/56; MARCH 9/62; ARDSLEY 12/62; ARDROSSAN 10/63; CORKERHILL 6/64; WITHDRAWN 10/64.

80078 NEW 2/54; PLAISTOW 2/54; TILBURY 12/56; STRATFORD 6/62; SHREWSBURY 8/62; CROES NEWYDD 2/63; WITHDRAWN 7/65. ENGINE PRESERVED.

80079 NEW 3/54; PLAISTOW 3/54; TILBURY 12/56; STRATFORD 6/62; CROES NEWYDD 8/62; WITHDRAWN 7/65. ENGINE PRESERVED.

80080 NEW 3/54; PLAISTOW 3/54; TILBURY 5/54; CROES NEWYDD 8/62; WITHDRAWN 7/65. ENGINE PRESERVED,

80081 NEW 3/54; BLETCHLEY 3/54; WILLESDEN 11/59; STEWARTS LANE 12/59; WEYMOUTH 7/63; BOURNEMOUTH 8/63; WITHDRAWN 6/65.

80082 NEW 4/54; BLETCHLEY 4/54; BRICKLAYERS ARMS 12/59; EASTLEIGH 6/62; WITHDRAWN 9/66.

80083 NEW 5/54; BLETCHLEY 5/54; RUGBY 1/55; BLETCHLEY 2/55; NEASDEN 9/58; BRICKLAYERS ARMS 12/59; EASTLEIGH 6/62; WITHDRAWN 8/66.

80084 NEW 5/54; BLETCHLEY 5/54; WILLESDEN 11/59; BRICKLAYERS ARMS 12/59; STEWARTS LANE 5/62; BRIGHTON 9/63; REDHILL 12/63; WITHDRAWN 6/65.

80085 NEW 6/54; BLETCHLEY 6/54; RUGBY 1/55; BLETCHLEY 2/55; BRICKLAYERS ARMS 12/59; ASHFORD 1/61; TONBRIDGE 5/61; STEWARTS LANE 5/62; BRIGHTON 9/63; REDHILL 12/63; FELTHAM 5/65; NINE ELMS 10/66; WITHDRAWN 7/67.

80086 NEW 6/54; BURY 6/54; WAKEFIELD 8/56; CHESTER (MIDLAND) 10/56; BIRKENHEAD 2/57; CHESTER (MIDLAND) 2/58; DALRY ROAD 4/60; CARSTAIRS 10/60; POLMADIE 11/60; WITHDRAWN 5/67.

80087 NEW 7/54; BURY 7/54; BANGOR 10/56; THREE BRIDGES 12/59; ASHFORD 1/60; THREE BRIDGES 5/61; EASTLEIGH 11/62; GUILDFORD 3/63; EASTLEIGH 9/63; WITHDRAWN 6/64.

80088 NEW 7/54; BURY 7/54; BANGOR 10/56; THREE BRIDGES 12/59; TUNBRIDGE WELLS WEST 1/63; BRIGHTON 9/63; REDHILL 12/63; WITHDRAWN 6/65.

80089 NEW 8/54; BURY 8/54; BANGOR 10/56; THREE BRIDGES 12/59; STEWARTS LANE 1/63; BRIGHTON 9/63; REDHILL 12/63; FELTHAM 5/65; NINE ELMS 11/65; WITHDRAWN 10/66.

80090 NEW 8/54; BURY 8/54; BANGOR 10/56; BIRKENHEAD 12/58; DUNDEE (TAYBRIDGE) 2/60; WITHDRAWN 3/65.

80091 NEW 9/54; KENTISH TOWN 9/54; BANGOR 10/56; CHESTER (MIDLAND) 11/57; DUNDEE (TAY BRIDGE) 4/60; ST ROLLOX 9/60; HURLFORD 5/62; BEATTOCK 4/66; WITHDRAWN 11/66.

80092 NEW 10/54; KENTISH TOWN 10/54; BANGOR 10/56; WILLESDEN 12/56; BANGOR 1/57; CHESTER (MIDLAND) 11/57; PERTH 2/60; WITHDRAWN 9/66.

80093 NEW 11/54; BEDFORD 11/54; BURY 2/55; NEWTON HEATH 2/56; BLACKPOOL 11/57; PERTH 2/60; WITHDRN 9/66.

80094 NEW 11/54; KENTISH TOWN 11/54; BANGOR 10/56; THREE BRIDGES 12/59; STEWARTS LANE 1/63; BRIGHTON 9/63; REDHILL 12/63; FELTHAM 5/65; WITHDRAWN 7/66.

80095 NEW 11/54; ST ALBANS 11/54; BANGOR 10/56; TUNBRIDGE WELLS WEST 12/59; EASTLEIGH 11/62; GUILDFORD 3/63; FELTHAM 9/63; NINE ELMS 11/64; WITHDRAWN 10/66.

80096 NEW 11/54; PLAISTOW 11/54; TILBURY 11/59; SHREWSBURY 8/62; CROES NEWYDD 11/62; MACHYNLLETH 3/63; CROES NEWYDD 10/63; BOURNEMOUTH 4/65; WITHDRAWN 12/65.

80097 NEW 12/54; PLAISTOW 12/54; TILBURY 11/59; STRATFORD 6/62; SWANSEA EAST DOCK 8/62; OSWESTRY 7/63; MACHYNLLETH 6/64; WITHDRAWN 7/65. ENGINE PRESERVED.

80098 NEW 12/54; PLAISTOW 12/54; TILBURY 11/59; OLD OAK COMMON 8/62; SHREWSBURY 9/62; CROES NEWYDD 11/62; MACHYNLLETH 3/63; WITHDRAWN 7/65. ENGINE PRESERVED.

80099 NEW 1/55; PLAISTOW 1/55; TILBURY 11/59; STRATFORD 6/62; SWANSEA EAST DOCK 8/62; MACHYNLLETH 7/63; WITHDRAWN 5/65.

80100 NEW 1/55; PLAISTOW 1/55; TILBURY 11/59; STRATFORD 6/62; SHREWSBURY 8/62; WITHDRAWN 7/65. ENGINE PRESERVED.

80101 NEW 2/55; PLAISTOW 2/55; TILBURY 11/59; STRATFORD 6/62; SHREWSBURY 8/62; MACHYNLLETH 9/62; CROES NEWYDD 2/63; MACHYNLLETH 3/63; WITHDRAWN 7/65.

80102 NEW 3/55; PLAISTOW 3/55; TILBURY 11/59; OLD OAK COMMON 8/62; SHREWSBURY 12/62; BANGOR 6/64; SHREWSBURY 9/64; EASTLEIGH 4/65; WITHDRAWN 12/65.

80103 NEW 3/55; PLAISTOW 3/55; TILBURY 11/59; WITHDRAWN 9/62.

80104 NEW 3/55; PLAISTOW 3/55; TILBURY 11/59; OLD OAK COMMON 8/62; CROES NEWYDD 12/62; MACHYNLLETH 3/63; WITHDRAWN 7/65. ENGINE PRESERVED.

80105 NEW 4/55; PLAISTOW 4/55; TILBURY 11/59; MACHYNLLETH 8/62; SHREWSBURY 9/62; CROES NEWYDD 2/63; MACHYNLLETH 3/63; WITHDRAWN 7/65. ENGINE PRESERVED.

80106 NEW 10/54; KITTYBREWSTER 10/54; POLMADIE 4/57; WITHDRAWN 10/64.

80107 NEW 10/54; KITTYBREWSTER 10/54; POLMADIE 4/57; WITHDRAWN 9/64.

80108 NEW 11/54; KITTYBREWSTER 11/54; POLMADIE 4/57; WITHDRAWN 5/65.

80109 NEW 11/54; KITTYBREWSTER 11/54; POLMADIE 4/57; HAMILTON 3/59; POLMADIE 9/59; WITHDRAWN 11/65.

80110 NEW 11/54; KITTYBREWSTER 11/54; POLMADIE 6/57; CARSTAIRS 9/63; POLMADIE 5/64; WITHDRAWN 5/65.

80111 NEW 11/54; POLMADIE 11/54; KITTYBREWSTER 4/57; CORKERHILL 6/61; HURLFORD 7/61; BEATTOCK 4/66; WITHDRAWN 11/66.

80112 NEW 12/54; POLMADIE 12/54; KITTYBREWSTER 4/57; CORKERHILL 6/61; HURLFORD 7/61; CORKERHILL 6/64; WITHDRAWN 8/66.

80113 NEW 12/54; POLMADIE 12/54; KITTYBREWSTER 6/57; KEITH 6/60; HAWICK 6/61; ST MARGARETS 1/66; WITHDRAWN 9/66.

80114 NEW 12/54; POLMADIE 12/54; KITTYBREWSTER 4/57; KEITH 10/60; HAWICK 6/61; ST MARGARETS 3/62; WITHDRAWN 12/66.

80115 NEW 12/54; POLMADIE 12/54; KITTYBREWSTER 4/57; KEITH 10/60; ABERDEEN (FERRYHILL) 6/61; POLMADIE 8/61; ARDROSSAN 1/64; CORKERHILL 6/64; POLMADIE 7/64; WITHDRAWN 10/64.

80116 NEW 5/55; YORK 5/55; WHITBY 6/55; SCARBOROUGH 2/56; WHITBY 5/56; NEVILLE HILL 6/58; LEEDS (HOLBECK) 6/63; DUMFRIES 10/63; CARSTAIRS 11/63; POLMADIE 4/64; WITHDRAWN 5/67.

80117 NEW 5/55; WHITBY 5/55; NEVILLE HILL 6/58; DUMFRIES 10/63; BEATTOCK 11/65; POLMADIE 11/65; WITHDRAWN 3/66.

80118 NEW 6/55; WHITBY 6/55; NEVILLE HILL 6/58; CARSTAIRS 10/63; POLMADIE 4/64; WITHDRAWN 11/66.

80119 NEW 6/55; WHITBY 6/55; SCARBOROUGH 2/56; WHITBY 5/56; NEVILLE HILL 6/58; CARSTAIRS 10/63; DUMFRIES 11/63; WITHDRAWN 6/65.

80120 NEW 7/55; WHITBY 7/55; NEVILLE HILL 6/58; CARSTAIRS 10/63; POLMADIE 4/64; WITHDRAWN 5/67.

80121 NEW 7/55; KITTYBREWSTER 7/55; KEITH 11/55; ABERDEEN (FERRYHILL) 6/61; POLMADIE 7/61; WITHDRAWN 6/66.

80122 NEW 7/55; KITTYBREWSTER 7/55; KEITH 11/55; DALRY ROAD 6/61; ST MARGARETS 5/62; GREENOCK (LADYBURN) 11/65; WITHDRAWN 12/66.

80123 NEW 9/55; DUNDEE (TAYBRIDGE) 9/55; POLMADIE 4/65; WITHDRAWN 8/66.

80124 NEW 9/55; DUNDEE (TAYBRIDGE) 9/55; ST MARGARETS 1/66; WITHDRAWN 12/66.

80125 NEW 10/55; STIRLING 10/55; LOSTOCK HALL 8/64; WITHDRAWN 10/64.

80126 NEW 10/55; PERTH 10/55; WITHDRAWN 11/66.

80127 NEW 11/55; CORKERHILL 11/55; WITHDRAWN 7/64.

80128 NEW 11/55; CORKERHILL 11/55; HURLFORD 9/61; CORKERHILL 1/62; WITHDRAWN 4/67.

80129 NEW 12/55; POLMADIE 12/55; LOSTOCK HALL 8/64; WITHDRAWN 10/64.

80130 NEW 12/55; POLMADIE 12/55; WITHDRAWN 8/66.

80131 NEW 3/56; PLAISTOW 3/56; TILBURY 11/59; OLD OAK COMMON 8/62; SHREWSBURY 9/62; OSWESTRY 1/63; BANGOR 1/65; WITHDRAWN 5/65.

80132 NEW 3/56; PLAISTOW 3/56; TILBURY 11/59; OLD OAK COMMON 8/62; SHREWSBURY 12/62; OSWESTRY 1/63; BANGOR 1/65; EASTLEIGH 4/65; WITHDRAWN 1/66.

80133 NEW 3/56; PLAISTOW 3/56; SHOEBURYNESS 11/59; SWANSEA EAST DOCK 8/62; NEATH 3/63; LLANELLY 6/64; FELTHAM 7/64; NINE ELMS 11/64; WITHDRAWN 7/67.

80134 NEW 4/56; PLAISTOW 4/56; TILBURY 11/59; SWANSEA EAST DOCK 8/62; LLANELLY 3/64; FELTHAM 7/64; BOURNEMOUTH 8/64; WITHDRAWN 7/67.

80135 NEW 4/56; PLAISTOW 4/56; TILBURY 11/59; SHREWSBURY 8/62; OSWESTRY 1/63; SHREWSBURY 9/64; WITHDRAWN 7/65. ENGINE PRESERVED.

80136 NEW 5/56; PLAISTOW 5/56; TILBURY 11/59; SHREWSBURY 8/62; OSWESTRY 1/63; MACHYNLLETH 6/64; SHREWSBURY 9/64; WITHDRAWN 7/65. ENGINE PRESERVED.

80137 NEW 5/56; NEASDEN 5/56; TUNBRIDGE WELLS WEST 12/59; EASTLEIGH 11/62; GUILDFORD 3/63; FELTHAM 9/63; NINE ELMS 11/64; WITHDRAWN 10/65.

80138 NEW 6/56; NEASDEN 6/56; TUNBRIDGE WELLS WEST 12/59; BRIGHTON 2/61; REDHILL 12/63; BOURNEMOUTH 2/65; WITHDRAWN 10/66.

80139 NEW 6/56; NEASDEN 6/56; TUNBRIDGE WELLS WEST 12/59; BRIGHTON 9/63; REDHILL 12/63; EASTLEIGH 2/65; WITHDRAWN 7/67.

80140 NEW 7/56; NEASDEN 7/56; TUNBRIDGE WELLS WEST 12/59; BRIGHTON 9/63; REDHILL 12/63; FELTHAM 5/65; NINE ELMS 10/66; WITHDRAWN 7/67.

80141 NEW 7/56; NEASDEN 7/56; TUNBRIDGE WELLS WEST 12/59; BRIGHTON 9/63; REDHILL 12/63; FELTHAM 5/65; NINE ELMS 11/65; WITHDRAWN 2/66.

80142 NEW 8/56; NEASDEN 8/56; TUNBRIDGE WELLS WEST 12/59; BRIGHTON 9/63; REDHILL 12/63; SALISBURY 5/65; EASTLEIGH 2/66; WITHDRAWN 3/66.

80143 NEW 9/56; NEASDEN 9/56; BRIGHTON 12/59; FELTHAM 7/63; NINE ELMS 11/64; WITHDRAWN 7/67.

80144 NEW 9/56; NEASDEN 9/56; BRIGHTON 12/59; REDHILL 12/63; SALISBURY 5/65; EASTLEIGH 11/65; NINE ELMS 2/66; WITHDRAWN 5/66.

80145 NEW 10/56; BRIGHTON 10/56; REDHILL 12/63; SALISBURY 5/65; NINE ELMS 2/66; WITHDRAWN 6/67.

80146 NEW 10/56; BRIGHTON 10/56; EASTLEIGH 8/63; BOURNEMOUTH 12/63; WITHDRAWN 7/67.

80147 NEW 11/56; BRIGHTON 11/56; WEYMOUTH 7/63; BOURNEMOUTH 8/63; WITHDRAWN 6/65.

80148 NEW 11/56; BRIGHTON 11/56; FELTHAM 6/63; WITHDRAWN 6/64.

80149 NEW 12/56; BRIGHTON 12/56; REDHILL 12/63; WITHDRAWN 3/65.

80150 NEW 12/56; BRIGHTON 12/56; EASTLEIGH 8/63; WITHDRAWN 10/65. ENGINE PRESERVED.

80151 NEW 1/57; BRIGHTON 1/57; REDHILL 12/63; SALISBURY 5/65; EASTLEIGH 10/66; WITHDRAWN 5/67. ENGINE PRESERVED.

80152 NEW 2/57; BRIGHTON 2/57; REDHILL 12/63; SALISBURY 5/65; EASTLEIGH 10/66; WITHDRAWN 7/67.

80153 NEW 2/57; BRIGHTON 2/57; REDHILL 12/63; WITHDRAWN 3/65.

80154 NEW 3/57; BRIGHTON 3/57; FELTHAM 7/63; NINE ELMS 11/64; WITHDRAWN 4/67.

82000 NEW 4/52; TYSELEY 4/52; BARRY 8/53; TREHERBERT 9/53; SHREWSBURY 11/55; WREXHAM (RHOSDDU) 2/59; MACHYNLLETH 2/60; PATRICROFT 4/65; WITHDRAWN 12/66.

82001 NEW 4/52; TYSELEY 4/52; BARRY 9/53; NEWTON ABBOT 7/55; TREHERBERT 9/56; BRISTOL (BATH ROAD) 3/58; CHESTER (WEST) 7/58; CHESTER (MIDLAND) 4/60; TEMPLECOMBE 4/61; HEREFORD 9/62; EXMOUTH JUNCTION 4/63; TAUNTON 12/63; BRISTOL (BARROW ROAD) 6/64; BATH (GREEN PARK) 11/65; WITHDRAWN 12/65.

82002 NEW 4/52; TYSELEY 4/52; BARRY 9/53; NEWTON ABBOT 7/55; TREHERBERT 9/56; BRISTOL (BATH ROAD) 5/58; CHESTER (WEST) 7/58; CHESTER (MIDLAND) 4/60; TEMPLECOMBE 4/61; HEREFORD 9/62; EXMOUTH JUNCTION 4/63; WITHDRAWN 2/64.

82003 NEW 5/52; TYSELEY 5/52; BARRY 9/53; BRISTOL (BATH ROAD) 3/58; CHESTER (WEST) 7/58; CHESTER (MIDLAND) 4/60; BRISTOL (BARROW ROAD) 4/61; BRISTOL (ST PHILLIP'S MARSH) 2/62; CARMARTHEN 3/62; MACHYNLLETH 6/62; PATRICROFT 4/65; WITHDRAWN 12/66.

82004 NEW 5/52; TYSELEY 5/52; BARRY 9/53; NEWTON ABBOT 4/55; WELLINGTON 8/56; SHREWSBURY 6/59; WELLINGTON 8/59; BATH (GREEN PARK) 10/59; WITHDRAWN 10/65.

82005 NEW 5/52; TYSELEY 5/52; BARRY 9/53; NEWTON ABBOT 7/55; TREHERBERT 9/56; BRISTOL (BATH ROAD) 6/58; CHESTER (WEST) 7/58; CHESTER (MIDLAND) 4/60; SHREWSBURY 4/61; MACHYNLLETH 7/61; SHREWSBURY 10/61; MACHYNLLETH 11/61; NINE ELMS 4/65; WITHDRAWN 9/65.

82006 NEW 5/52; TYSELEY 5/52; BARRY 9/53; NEWTON ABBOT 7/55; WELLINGTON 8/56; BRISTOL (BATH ROAD) 1/60; BRISTOL (BARROW ROAD) 9/60; MACHYNLLETH 2/61; NINE ELMS 4/65; WITHDRAWN 9/66.

82007 NEW 5/52; TYSELEY 5/52; BARRY 9/53; TREHERBERT 7/55; SHREWSBURY 11/55; LEAMINGTON SPA 6/58; WELLINGTON 6/58; WREXHAM (RHOSDDU) 8/58; WORCESTER 8/58; BRISTOL (BATH ROAD) 9/58; BRISTOL (BARROW ROAD) 9/60; BRISTOL (ST PHILLIP'S MARSH) 2/61; BRISTOL (BARROW ROAD) 10/62; WITHDRAWN 6/64.

82008 NEW 6/52; TYSELEY 6/52; BARRY 9/53; KIDDERMINSTER 9/55; WORCESTER 8/57; KIDDERMINSTER 11/57; WORCESTER 1/58; MACHYNLLETH 7/61; NEYLAND 9/61; TAUNTON 10/61; WITHDRAWN 2/64.

82009 NEW 6/52; TYSELEY 6/52; BARRY 9/53; NEWTON ABBOT 4/55; WELLINGTON 9/56; SHREWSBURY 6/59; WELLINGTON 8/59; BRISTOL (BATH ROAD) 1/60; BRISTOL (BARROW ROAD) 9/60; BRISTOL (ST PHILLIP'S MARSH) 10/60; MACHYNLLETH 2/61; PATRICROFT 4/65; WITHDRAWN 11/66.

82010 NEW 6/52; EXMOUTH JUNCTION 6/52; EASTLEIGH 9/62; NINE ELMS 10/62; WITHDRAWN 4/65.

82011 NEW 7/52; EXMOUTH JUNCTION 7/52; EASTLEIGH 9/62; NINE ELMS 10/62; WITHDRAWN 8/64.

82012 NEW 7/52; EXMOUTH JUNCTION 7/52; EASTLEIGH 2/53; NINE ELMS 11/62; WITHDRAWN 5/64.

82013 NEW 7/52; EXMOUTH JUNCTION 7/52; EASTLEIGH 9/62; NINE ELMS 10/62; WITHDRAWN 6/64.

82014 NEW 8/52; EASTLEIGH 8/52; NINE ELMS 11/62; WITHDRAWN 5/64.

82015 NEW 8/52; EASTLEIGH 8/52; GUILDFORD 11/62; NINE ELMS 3/63; WITHDRAWN 12/64.

82016 NEW 8/52; EASTLEIGH 8/52; GUILDFORD 11/62; NINE ELMS 3/63; WITHDRAWN 4/65.

82017 NEW 8/52; EXMOUTH JUNCTION 8/52; EASTLEIGH 9/62; NINE ELMS 10/62; WITHDRAWN 4/65.

82018 NEW 9/52; REDHILL 9/52; EXMOUTH JUNCTION 9/52; EASTLEIGH 9/62; NINE ELMS 10/62; WITHDRAWN 6/66.

82019 NEW 9/52; REDHILL 9/52; EXMOUTH JUNCTION 9/52; EASTLEIGH 9/62; NINE ELMS 10/62; WITHDRAWN 7/67.

82020 NEW 9/54; EXMOUTH JUNCTION 9/54; NUNEATON 10/54; WREXHAM (RHOSDDU) 10/56; SHREWSBURY 1/60; MACHYNLLETH 3/60; NINE ELMS 4/65; WITHDRAWN 9/65.

82021 NEW 10/54; EXMOUTH JUNCTION 10/54; NUNEATON 10/54; WREXHAM (RHOSDDU) 10/56; SHREWSBURY 1/60; MACHYNLLETH 3/60; NINE ELMS 4/65; WITHDRAWN 10/65.

82022 NEW 10/54; EXMOUTH JUNCTION 10/54; EASTLEIGH 9/62; NINE ELMS 10/62; WITHDRAWN 10/65.

82023 NEW 10/54; EXMOUTH JUNCTION 10/54; EASTLEIGH 9/62; NINE ELMS 10/62; WITHDRAWN 11/66.

82024 NEW 10/54; EXMOUTH JUNCTION 10/54; EASTLEIGH 9/62; NINE ELMS 10/62; WITHDRAWN 2/66.

82025 NEW 11/54; EXMOUTH JUNCTION 11/54; EASTLEIGH 9/62; NINE ELMS 10/62; WITHDRAWN 8/64.

82026 NEW 11/54; KIRKBY STEPHEN 11/54; DARLINGTON 1/58; SCARBOROUGH 9/58; LOWMOOR 12/62; COPLEY HILL 4/63; GUILDFORD 9/63; BOURNEMOUTH 12/63; NINE ELMS 8/64; WITHDRAWN 6/66.

82027 NEW 11/54; KIRKBY STEPHEN 11/54; WEST HARTLEPOOL 1/58; MALTON 9/58; SCARBOROUGH 6/60; MALTON 12/62; YORK 4/63; GUILDFORD 9/63; BOURNEMOUTH 12/63; NINE ELMS 8/64; WITHDRAWN 1/66.

82028 NEW 12/54; DARLINGTON 12/54; SCARBOROUGH 9/58; MALTON 9/61; YORK 4/63; GUILDFORD 9/63; BOURNEMOUTH 12/63; NINE ELMS 8/64; WITHDRAWN 9/66.

82029 NEW 12/54; DARLINGTON 12/54; WEST HARTLEPOOL 1/58; MALTON 9/58; SCARBOROUGH 6/60; MALTON 9/61; YORK 4/63; GUILDFORD 9/63; BOURNEMOUTH 12/63; NINE ELMS 8/64; WITHDRAWN 7/67.

82030 NEW 12/54; BARRY 12/54; SHREWSBURY 5/55; WORCESTER 12/55; BRISTOL (BATH ROAD) 4/59; WORCESTER 5/59; KIDDERMINSTER 6/59; WORCESTER 7/59; WELLINGTON 10/59; BRISTOL (BATH ROAD) 1/60; BRISTOL (BARROW ROAD) 9/60; TAUNTON 10/61; EXMOUTH JUNCTION 6/64; GLOUCESTER (HORTON ROAD) 6/65; WITHDRAWN 8/65. (R) BATH (GREEN PARK) 11/65; WITHDRAWN 1/66. (R) - Reinstated.

82031 NEW 12/54; BARRY 12/54; LAIRA 1/55; NEWTON ABBOT 3/55; SHREWSBURY 5/55; WREXHAM (RHOSDDU) 2/59; MACHYNLLETH 1/60; BANGOR 6/64; PATRICROFT 4/65; WITHDRAWN 12/66.

82032 NEW 1/55; BARRY 1/55; NEWTON ABBOT 7/55; TREHERBERT 9/56; RADYR 3/58; BRISTOL (BATH ROAD) 5/58; CHESTER (WEST) 7/58; CHESTER (MIDLAND) 4/60; SHREWSBURY 4/61; MACHYNLLETH 8/61; SHREWSBURY 11/61; MACHYNLLETH 7/62; BANGOR 6/64; WITHDRAWN 5/65.

82033 NEW 1/55; NEWTON ABBOT 1/55; TREHERBERT 9/56; RADYR 3/58; BRISTOL (BATH ROAD) 5/58; BRISTOL (BARROW ROAD) 9/60; MACHYNLLETH 12/60; BANGOR 6/64; NINE ELMS 4/65; WITHDRAWN 9/65.

82034 NEW 1/55; NEWTON ABBOT 1/55; WELLINGTON 8/56; TREHERBERT 9/56; RADYR 3/58; BRISTOL (BATH ROAD) 5/58; CHESTER (WEST) 7/58; CHESTER (MIDLAND) 4/60; MACHYNLLETH 4/61; PATRICROFT 4/65; WITHDRAWN 12/66.

82035 NEW 3/55; BARRY 3/55; BRISTOL (BATH ROAD) 5/58; BRISTOL (BARROW ROAD) 9/60; BRISTOL (ST PHILLIP'S MARSH) 2/62; BRISTOL (BARROW ROAD) 10/62; EXMOUTH JUNCTION 3/64; YEOVIL TOWN 9/64; WITHDRAWN 7/65.

82036 NEW 3/55; BARRY 3/55; RADYR 3/58; BRISTOL (BATH ROAD) 5/58; CHESTER (WEST) 6/58; CHESTER (MIDLAND) 4/60; MACHYNLLETH 4/61; SHREWSBURY 11/61; BRISTOL (ST PHILLIP'S MARSH) 7/62; BRISTOL (BARROW ROAD) 10/62; WITHDRAWN 7/65.

82037 NEW 4/55; SWANSEA VICTORIA 4/55; BARRY 7/55; ABERCYNON 6/56; BARRY 7/56; RADYR 4/58; BRISTOL (BATH ROAD) 5/58; BATH (GREEN PARK); 5/58; WREXHAM (RHOSSDU) 2/59; BRISTOL (BATH ROAD) 1/60; BRISTOL (BARROW ROAD) 9/60; BRISTOL (ST PHILLIP'S MARSH) 2/62; BRISTOL (BARROW ROAD) 10/62; WITHDRAWN 9/65.

82038 NEW 5/55; NEWTON ABBOT 5/55; SHREWSBURY 10/55; WORCESTER 12/55; WELLINGTON 9/59; BRISTOL (BATH ROAD) 1/60; BRISTOL (ST PHILLIP'S MARSH) 9/60; BRISTOL (BARROW ROAD) 10/62; WITHDRAWN 7/65.

82039 NEW 5/55; BARRY 5/55; BRISTOL (BATH ROAD) 5/58; TEMPLECOMBE 2/59; BRISTOL (BARROW ROAD) 9/60; BRISTOL (ST PHILLIP'S MARSH) 2/62; BRISTOL (BARROW ROAD) 10/62; EXMOUTH JUNCTION 3/64; GLOUCESTER (HORTON ROAD) 6/65; WITHDRAWN 7/65.

82040 NEW 5/55; BARRY 5/55; BRISTOL (BATH ROAD) 5/58; BRISTOL (BARROW ROAD) 9/60; BRISTOL (ST PHILLIP'S MARSH) 2/62; BRISTOL (BARROW ROAD) 10/62; EXMOUTH JUNCTION 10/63; GLOUCESTER (HORTON ROAD) 6/65; WITHDRAWN 7/65.

82041 NEW 6/55; BARRY 6/55; BRISTOL (BATH ROAD) 5/58; BATH (GREEN PARK) 3/59; WITHDRAWN 12/65.

82042 NEW 6/55; BARRY 6/55; BRISTOL (BATH ROAD) 8/58; BRISTOL (BARROW ROAD) 9/60; NEYLAND 9/61; TAUNTON 10/61; EXMOUTH JUNCTION 6/64; GLOUCESTER (HORTON ROAD) 6/65; WITHDRAWN 8/65.

82043 NEW 6/55; BARRY 6/55; BRISTOL (BATH ROAD) 5/58; BRISTOL (BARROW ROAD) 9/60; TAUNTON 1/62; BRISTOL (ST PHILLIP'S MARSH) 2/62; BRISTOL (BARROW ROAD) 10/62; WITHDRAWN 2/64.

82044 NEW 8/55; BARRY 8/55; BRISTOL (BATH ROAD) 5/58; BRISTOL (BARROW ROAD) 9/60; NEYLAND 9/61; TAUNTON 10/61; EXMOUTH JUNCTION 6/64; GLOUCESTER (HORTON ROAD) 6/65; WITHDRAWN 8/65. (Reinstated) BATH (GREEN PARK) 9/65; WITHDRAWN 11/65.

84000 NEW 7/53; CREWE NORTH 7/53; PLODDER LANE 8/53 WREXHAM 3/54; BIRKENHEAD 8/56; WARRINGTON (DALLAM) 6/61; OSWESTRY 4/63; CROES NEWYDD 1/65; WITHDRAWN 10/65.

84001 NEW 7/53; CREWE NORTH 7/53; PLODDER LANE 8/53; WREXHAM 3/54; CHESTER (NORTHGATE) 10/55; BIRKENHEAD 1/60; WARRINGTON (DALLAM) 6/61; LLANDUDNO JUNCTION 12/62; WITHDRAWN 10/64.

84002 NEW 8/53; PLODDER LANE 8/53; WREXHAM (RHOSDDU) 3/54; CHESTER (NORTHGATE) 10/55; BLETCHLEY 8/56; WITHDRAWN 4/65.

84003 NEW 8/53; PLODDER LANE 8/53; WREXHAM 3/54; BIRKENHEAD 8/56; RHYL 9/61; LLANDUDNO JUNCTION 2/63; CROES NEWYDD 3/64; LLANDUDNO JUNCTION 6/64; WITHDRAWN 10/65.

84004 NEW 8/53; PLODDER LANE 8/53; WREXHAM (RHOSDDU) 9/54; BLETCHLEY 8/56; OSWESTRY 4/63; CROES NEWYDD 1/65; WITHDRAWN 10/65.

84005 NEW 8/53; BEDFORD 8/53; NEASDEN 6/61; BEDFORD 12/61; NEASDEN 3/62; KENTISH TOWN 7/62; WELLINGBOROUGH 1/63; BEDFORD 2/63; WELLINGBOROUGH 2/63; LEICESTER (MIDLAND) 2/64; WELLINGBOROUGH 5/64; LEICESTER (MIDLAND) 10/64; WITHDRAWN 10/65.

84006 NEW 8/53; BURTON 8/53; WELLINGBOROUGH 1/59; NEASDEN 12/61; BEDFORD 1/62; NEASDEN 3/62; ANNESLEY 4/62; WELLINGBOROUGH 7/64; LEICESTER (MIDLAND) 10/64; WITHDRAWN 10/65.

84007 NEW 9/53; BURTON 9/53; WELLINGBOROUGH 2/59; ANNESLEY 3/62; WELLINGBOROUGH 12/63; WITHDRAWN 1/64.

84008 NEW 9/53; BURTON 9/53; WELLINGBOROUGH 2/59; NEASDEN 6/61; KENTISH TOWN 7/62; LEICESTER (MIDLAND) 12/62; WELLINGBOROUGH 5/63; LEICESTER (MIDLAND) 2/64; WELLINGBOROUGH 5/64; LEICESTER (MIDLAND) 9/64; WITHDRAWN 10/65.

84009 NEW 9/53; ROYSTON 9/53; SKIPTON 1/55; ROYSTON 7/55; HULL (DAIRYCOATES) 6/59; LLANDUDNO JUNCTION 12/62; CROES NEWYDD 3/64; LLANDUDNO JUNCTION 6/64; WITHDRAWN 11/65.

84010 NEW 9/53; LOW MOOR 9/53; LEES (OLDHAM) 9/54; ROSE GROVE 5/56; FLEETWOOD 12/59; EASTLEIGH 11/65; LMR and WITHDRAWN 12/65.

84011 NEW 9/53; LOW MOOR 9/53; BANK HALL 1/55; ROSE GROVE 5/56; LOWER DARWEN 5/57; FLEETWOOD 3/61; WITHDRAWN 4/65.

84012 NEW 9/53; LOW MOOR 9/53; LEES (OLDHAM) 9/54; ROSE GROVE 5/55; BANK HALL 10/55; LOWER DARWEN 5/57; FLEETWOOD 3/61; SOUTHPORT 2/63; WITHDRAWN 10/63.

84013 NEW 9/53; LOW MOOR 9/53; BANK HALL 1/55; LEES (OLDHAM) 11/55; BOLTON 4/59; STOCKPORT 12/64; LEICESTER (MIDLAND) 5/65; STOCKPORT 7/65; EASTLEIGH 11/65; LMR + WITHDRAWN 12/65.

84014 NEW 9/53; LOW MOOR 9/53; BANK HALL 1/55; SOUTHPORT 4/55; LEES (OLDHAM) 11/55; BOLTON 2/59; STOCKPORT 12/64; EASTLEIGH 11/65; LMR + WITHDRAWN 12/65.

84015 NEW 10/53; LOW MOOR 10/53; LEES (OLDHAM) 9/54; ROSE GROVE 5/55; FLEETWOOD 10/55; LANCASTER (GREEN AYRE) 7/57; SKIPTON 7/58; EASTLEIGH 11/65; LMR + WITHDRAWN 12/65.

84016 NEW 10/53; BURY 10/53; FLEETWOOD 6/54; LANCASTER (GREEN AYRE) 7/57; FLEETWOOD 11/58; STOCKPORT 6/65; FLEETWOOD 7/65; EASTLEIGH 11/65; LMR + WITHDRAWN 12/65.

84017 NEW 10/53; BURY 10/53; FLEETWOOD 6/54; SOUTHPORT 10/63; BOLTON 6/64; STOCKPORT 6/65; EASTLEIGH 11/65 + WITHDRAWN 12/65.

84018 NEW 10/53; BURY 10/53; FLEETWOOD 6/54; WITHDRAWN 4/65.

84019 NEW 10/53; BURY 10/53; FLEETWOOD 6/54; LEES (OLDHAM) 11/55; BOLTON 4/58; EASTLEIGH 11/65; LMR + WITHDRAWN 12/65.

84020 NEW 3/57; ASHFORD 3/57; STEWARTS LANE 1/61; EXMOUTH JUNCTION 5/61; LLANDUDNO JUNCTION 9/61; WITHDRAWN 10/64.

84021 NEW 3/57; ASHFORD 3/57; BRICKLAYERS ARMS 1/61; EXMOUTH JUNCTION 5/61; LLANDUDNO JUNCTION 9/61; CREWE WORKS 7/62; WITHDRAWN 9/64.

84022 NEW 3/57; ASHFORD 3/57; BRICKLAYERS ARMS 1/61; EXMOUTH JUNCTION 5/61; LLANDUDNO JUNCTION 9/61; CREWE WORKS 7/62; WITHDRAWN 9/64.

84023 NEW 4/57; ASHFORD 4/57; BRICKLAYERS ARMS 1/61; EXMOUTH JUNCTION 5/61; LANCASTER (GREEN AYRE) 9/61; WIDNES 1/62; CREWE WORKS 7/62; WITHDRAWN 9/64.

84024 NEW 4/57; ASHFORD 4/57; BRICKLAYERS ARMS 1/61; BRIGHTON 5/61; WARRINGTON (DALLAM) 9/61; WIDNES 1/62; CREWE WORKS 7/62; WITHDRAWN 9/64.

84025 NEW 4/57; RAMSGATE 4/57; ASHFORD 5/59; BRIGHTON 5/61; NEWTON HEATH 9/61; BOLTON 11/61; EASTLEIGH 11/65; LMR + WITHDRAWN 12/65.

84026 NEW 4/57; RAMSGATE 4/57; ASHFORD 5/59; BRIGHTON 6/61; NEWTON HEATH 9/61; BOLTON 10/61; HORWICH WORKS 5/63; BOLTON 12/63; STOCKPORT 12/64; EASTLEIGH 11/65; LMR + WITHDRAWN 12/65.

84027 NEW 5/57; RAMSGATE 5/57; ASHFORD 5/59; BRIGHTON 5/61; NEWTON HEATH 9/61; BOLTON 10/61; WELLINGBOROUGH 1/62; ANNESLEY 3/62; WITHDRAWN 5/64.

84028 NEW 5/57; RAMSGATE 5/57; ASHFORD 5/59; EASTLEIGH 6/61; NEWTON HEATH 9/61; SKIPTON 10/61; EASTLEIGH 11/65; LMR + WITHDRAWN 12/65.

84029 NEW 6/57; RAMSGATE 6/57; ASHFORD 5/59; EASTLEIGH 6/61; BEDFORD 9/61; NEASDEN 1/62; KENTISH TOWN 7/62; WELLINGBOROUGH 1/63; LEICESTER (MIDLAND) 2/63; WITHDRAWN 6/64.

92000 NEW 1/54; NEWPORT (EBBW JUNCTION) 1/54; BATH (GREEN PARK) 6/61; BANBURY 9/61; OLD OAK COMMON 3/62; TYSELEY 3/62; BRISTOL (BARROW ROAD) 2/62; GLOUCESTER (HORTON ROAD) 2/65; WITHDRAWN 7/65.

92001 NEW 1/54; NEWPORT (EBBW JUNCTION) 1/54; BATH (GREEN PARK) 6/61; CARDIFF (CANTON) 6/61; BATH (GREEN PARK) 7/62; OXFORD 10/62; TYSELEY 11/62; WAKEFIELD 10/66; WITHDRAWN 1/67.

92002 NEW 1/54; NEWPORT (EBBW JUNCTION) 1/54; TYSELEY 4/63; BANBURY 7/64; TYSELEY 11/64; SALTLEY 11/66; BIRKENHEAD 12/66; WITHDRAWN 11/67.

92003 NEW 1/54; NEWPORT (EBBW JUNCTION) 1/54; CARDIFF (CANTON) 10/58; CARDIFF EAST DOCK 9/62; WITHDRAWN 3/65.

92004 NEW 1/54; NEWPORT (EBBW JUNCTION) 1/54; CARDIFF (CANTON) 9/59; SOUTHALL 2/60; NEWPORT (EBBW JUNCTION) 10/60; BRISTOL (BARROW ROAD) 1/61;

BANBURY 3/63; KINGMOOR 10/66; CARNFORTH 1/68; WITHDRAWN 3/68.

92005 NEW 2/54; NEWPORT (EBBW JUNCTION) 2/54; CARDIFF (CANTON) 10/58; NEWPORT (EBBW JUNCTION) 5/61; YORK 9/63; WITHDRAWN 8/65.

92006 NEW 2/54; NEWPORT (EBBW JUNCTION) 2/54; BATH (GREEN PARK) 6/61; NEWPORT (EBBW JUNCTION) 9/61; YORK 9/63; WAKEFIELD 10/66; WITHDRAWN 4/67.

92007 NEW 2/54; NEWPORT (EBBW JUNCTION) 2/54; BRISTOL (BARROW ROAD) 12/60; GLOUCESTER (HORTON ROAD) 2/65; CARDIFF EAST DOCK 6/65; SEVERN TUNNEL JUNCTION 7/65; GLOUCESTER (HORTON ROAD) 10/65; WITHDRAWN 12/65.

92008 NEW 3/54; WELLINGBOROUGH 3/54; SALTLEY 6/57; ROWSLEY 11/59; TOTON 1/62; ROWSLEY 2/62; SALTLEY 6/62; ROWSLEY 7/63; KIRKBY-IN-ASHFIELD 4/64; SPEKE JUNCTION 12/64; WARRINGTON 8/67; WITHDRAWN 10/67.

92009 NEW 3/54; WELLINGBOROUGH 3/54; SALTLEY 6/57; BURTON 9/57; SALTLEY 3/58; ANNESLEY 10/58; SALTLEY 11/58; ROWSLEY 11/59; SALTLEY 6/62; WESTHOUSES 7/62; ROWSLEY 10/63; KETTERING 4/64; KINGMOOR 6/64; CARNFORTH 1/68; WITHDRAWN 3/68.

92010 NEW 5/54; MARCH 5/54; ANNESLEY 2/57; WELLINGBOROUGH 3/63; LEICESTER (MIDLAND) 6/63 NEWTON HEATH 4/64; KINGMOOR 6/64; WITHDRAWN 4/66.

92011 NEW 5/54; MARCH 5/54; NEW ENGLAND 10/55; ANNESLEY 5/57; BIRKENHEAD 8/65; WITHDRAWN 11/67.

92012 NEW 5/54; MARCH 5/54; NEW ENGLAND 10/55; ANNESLEY 5/57; ROWSLEY 8/63; KETTERING 4/64; KINGMOOR 6/64; WITHDRAWN 10/67.

92013 NEW 5/54; MARCH 5/54; ANNESLEY 2/57; WOODFORD HALSE 9/59; ANNESLEY 10/59; BANBURY 6/65; SALTLEY 9/66; WITHDRAWN 10/66.

92014 NEW 5/54; MARCH 5/54; STRATFORD 8/54; MARCH 1/56; ANNESLEY 2/57; SALTLEY 4/60; TOTON 9/60; CRICKLEWOOD 7/61; ANNESLEY 10/61; BIRKENHEAD 8/65; WITHDRAWN 10/67.

92015 NEW 9/54; WELLINGBOROUGH 9/54; SALTLEY 12/57; NEWTON HEATH 6/58; BOLTON 9/62; NEWTON HEATH 12/62; KINGMOOR 6/64; WITHDRAWN 4/67.

92016 NEW 10/54; WELLINGBOROUGH 10/54; SALTLEY 12/57; NEWTON HEATH 6/58; BOLTON 9/62; NEWTON HEATH 12/62; CARNFORTH 6/67; WITHDRAWN 10/67.

92017 NEW 10/54; WELLINGBOROUGH 10/54; SALTLEY 12/57; NEWTON HEATH 6/58; BOLTON 9/62; NEWTON HEATH 12/62; KINGMOOR 6/64; WITHDRAWN 12/67.

92018 NEW 10/54; WELLINGBOROUGH 10/54; CRICKLEWOOD 12/57; WELLINGBOROUGH 1/58; ROWSLEY 3/62; KIRKBY-IN-ASHFIELD 4/64; NEWTON HEATH 9/64; KINGMOOR 8/66; WITHDRAWN 4/67.

92019 NEW 10/54; WELLINGBOROUGH 10/54; CRICKLEWOOD 12/57; WELLINGBOROUGH 1/58; TOTON 1/62; WELLINGBOROUGH 3/62; ROWSLEY 3/62; WELLINGBOROUGH 4/62; KETTERING 1/64; KINGMOOR 6/64; WITHDRAWN 6/67.

92020 NEW 5/55; WELLINGBOROUGH 5/55; KIRKBY-IN-ASHFIELD 11/63; SPEKE JUNCTION 9/64; BIRKENHEAD 1/65; WITHDRAWN 10/67.

92021 NEW 5/55; WELLINGBOROUGH 5/55; KETTERING 1/64; KINGMOOR 6/64; BIRKENHEAD 7/65; WITHDRAWN 11/67.

92022 NEW 5/55; WELLINGBOROUGH 5/55; ROWSLEY 7/63; KETTERING 4/64; NEWTON HEATH 6/64; SPEKE JUNCTION 2/66; BIRKENHEAD 2/67; WITHDRAWN 11/67.

92023 NEW 5/55; WELLINGBOROUGH 5/55; KINGMOOR 11/55; WELLINGBOROUGH 12/55; KETTERING 8/63; KINGMOOR 5/64; BIRKENHEAD 7/65; WITHDRAWN 11/67.

92024 NEW 6/55; WELLINGBOROUGH 6/55; KETTERING 1/64; KINGMOOR 5/64; BIRKENHEAD 7/65; WITHDRAWN 11/67.

92025 NEW 6/55; WELLINGBOROUGH 6/55; KETTERING 1/64; ANNESLEY 4/64; SPEKE JUNCTION 11/64; BIRKENHEAD 2/67; WITHDRAWN 11/67.

92026 NEW 6/55;; WELLINGBOROUGH 6/55; SALTLEY 3/61; WELLINGBOROUGH 4/61; KETTERING 8/63; KIRKBY-IN-ASHFIELD 11/63; NEWTON HEATH 9/64; BIRKENHEAD 5/65; WITHDRAWN 11/67.

92027 NEW 7/55; WELLINGBOROUGH 7/55; KETTERING 1/64; ANNESLEY 4/64; SPEKE JUNCTION 11/64; WITHDRAWN 8/67.

92028 NEW 7/55; WELLINGBOROUGH 7/55; KETTERING 12/60; SALTLEY 10/62; BIRKENHEAD 11/63; SALTLEY 4/64; BANBURY 3/65; SALTLEY 7/65; WITHDRAWN 10/66.

92029 NEW 7/55; WELLINGBOROUGH 7/55; KETTERING 12/60; SALTLEY 10/62; BIRKENHEAD 11/63; SALTLEY 4/64; CROES NEWYDD 5/66; SALTLEY 8/66; BIRKENHEAD 12/66; WITHDRAWN 11/67.

92030 NEW 11/54; NEW ENGLAND 11/54; ANNESLEY 5/57; BANBURY 6/65; SALTLEY 10/66; WAKEFIELD 11/66; WITHDRAWN 2/67.

92031 NEW 11/54; MARCH 11/54; NEW ENGLAND 3/55; ANNESLEY 5/57; WESTHOUSES 6/65; NEWTON HEATH 7/65; WITHDRAWN 1/67.

92032 NEW 11/54; MARCH 11/54; NEW ENGLAND 12/54; ANNESLEY 5/57; KIRKBY-IN-ASHFIELD 6/65; BIRKENHEAD 7/65; WITHDRAWN 4/67.

92033 NEW 11/54; MARCH 11/54; NEW ENGLAND 12/54; ANNESLEY 5/57; BANBURY 6/65; NORTHAMPTON 7/65; WITHDRAWN 9/65.

92034 NEW 12/54; NEW ENGLAND 12/54; FRODINGHAM 1/59; NEW ENGLAND 3/59; IMMINGHAM 6/63; WITHDRAWN 5/64.

92035 NEW 12/54; NEW ENGLAND 12/54; FRODINGHAM 1/59; NEW ENGLAND 3/59; IMMINGHAM 6/63; WITHDRAWN 2/66.

92036 NEW 12/54; NEW ENGLAND 12/54; DONCASTER 9/62; COLWICK 6/63; NEW ENGLAND 11/63; COLWICK 1/64; NEW ENGLAND 6/64; WITHDRAWN 12/64.

92037 NEW 12/54; NEW ENGLAND 12/54; IMMINGHAM 6/63; WITHDRAWN 2/65.

92038 NEW 12/54; NEW ENGLAND 12/54; IMMINGHAM 6/63; NEW ENGLAND 6/64; LANGWITH 1/65; WITHDRAWN 4/65.

92039 NEW 12/54; NEW ENGLAND 12/54; IMMINGHAM 2/59; NEW ENGLAND 9/61; DONCASTER 9/62; COLWICK 6/63; IMMINGHAM 11/63; DONCASTER 6/64; LANGWITH 6/65; WITHDRAWN 6/65.

92040 NEW 12/54; NEW ENGLAND 12/54; COLWICK 6/63; BARROW HILL 9/64; LANGWITH 1/65; WITHDRAWN 8/65.

92041 NEW 12/54; NEW ENGLAND 12/54; COLWICK 6/63; BARROW HILL 9/64; LANGWITH 1/65; WITHDRAWN 8/65.

92042 NEW 1/55; NEW ENGLAND 1/55; COLWICK 6/63; LANGWITH 1/65; COLWICK 11/65; WITHDRAWN 12/65.

92043 NEW 1/55; MARCH 1/55; ANNESLEY 2/57; BURTON 12/65; KINGMOOR 1/66; WITHDRAWN 7/66.

92044 NEW 1/55; MARCH 1/55; NEW ENGLAND 7/57; DONCASTER 9/62; COLWICK 6/63; BARROW HILL 9/64; LANGWITH 1/65; WITHDRAWN 4/65.

92045 NEW 2/55; WELLINGBOROUGH 2/55; TOTON 2/56; BIDSTON 5/56; BIRKENHEAD 1/63; WITHDRAWN 9/67.

92046 NEW 2/55; WELLINGBOROUGH 2/55; TOTON 2/56; BIDSTON 5/56; BIRKENHEAD 1/63; WITHDRAWN 10/67.

92047 NEW 2/55; WELLINGBOROUGH 2/55; BIDSTON 8/55; BIRKENHEAD 1/63; WITHDRAWN 11/67.

92048 NEW 2/55; WELLINGBOROUGH 2/55; TOTON 2/56; SALTLEY 6/57; ROWSLEY 11/59; TOTON 4/64; WARRINGTON 3/65; BIRKENHEAD 5/65; WITHDRAWN 9/67.

92049 NEW 3/55; WELLINGBOROUGH 3/55; TOTON 2/56; SALTLEY 6/57; ROWSLEY 11/59; TOTON 4/64; WARRINGTON 3/65; BIRKENHEAD 2/66; WITHDRAWN 11/67.

92050 NEW 9/55; TOTON 9/55; KINGMOOR 11/55; TOTON 12/55; ROWSLEY 11/59; KIRKBY-IN-ASHFIELD 4/64; NEWTON HEATH 10/64; SPEKE JUNCTION 2/66; WARRINGTON 8/67; WITHDRAWN 9/67.

92051 NEW 9/55; TOTON 9/55; WELLINGBOROUGH 11/55; TOTON 12/55; SALTLEY 6/57; ROWSLEY 11/59; KIRKBY-IN-ASHFIELD 4/64; NEWTON HEATH 10/64; KINGMOOR 11/65; WITHDRAWN 10/67.

92052 NEW 9/55; TOTON 9/55; WELLINGBOROUGH 3/58; SALTLEY 5/59; TOTON 6/61; ANNESLEY 10/61; ROWSLEY 3/62; TOTON 4/62; ROWSLEY 7/63; TOTON 7/63; WELLINGBOROUGH 8/63; KIRKBY-IN-ASHFIELD 10/63; NEWTON HEATH 10/64; KINGMOOR 6/67; WITHDRAWN 8/67.

92053 NEW 9/55; TOTON 9/55; BURTON 9/57; SALTLEY 3/58; WELLINGBOROUGH 11/59; TOTON 9/62; WARRINGTON 3/65; WITHDRAWN 2/66.

92054 NEW 9/55; TOTON 9/55; WELLINGBOROUGH 3/58; LEICESTER (MIDLAND) 9/62; WESTHOUSES 12/62; SPEKE JUNCTION 9/64; WITHDRAWN 5/68.

92055 NEW 9/55; TOTON 9/55; WELLINGBOROUGH 3/58; TOTON 9/60; BIDSTON 3/61; TOTON 4/61; ROWSLEY 3/62; TOTON 4/62; WELLINGBOROUGH 7/62; TOTON 9/62; WARRINGTON 3/65; SPEKE JUNCTION 10/67; WITHDRAWN 12/67.

92056 NEW 10/55; TOTON 10/55; WELLINGBOROUGH 3/58; TOTON 9/60; SALTLEY 3/62; WELLINGBOROUGH 5/62; ROWSLEY 9/62; KIRKBY-IN-ASHFIELD 4/64; NEWTON HEATH 10/64; KINGMOOR 8/66; WITHDRAWN 11/67.

92057 NEW 10/55; TOTON 10/55; WESTHOUSES 1/60; CRICKLEWOOD 9/60; ANNESLEY 10/61; TOTON 4/63; SALTLEY 10/63; BIRKENHEAD 4/64; WITHDRAWN 10/65.

92058 NEW 10/55; TOTON 10/55; WELLINGBOROUGH 3/58; TOTON 9/60; WESTHOUSES 7/62; LEICESTER (MIDLAND) 4/64; WARRINGTON 3/65; SPEKE JUNCTION 6/67; KINGMOOR 8/67; WITHDRAWN 11/67.

92059 NEW 10/55; TOTON 10/55; WELLINGBOROUGH 3/58; TOTON 9/60; WARRINGTON 3/65; BIRKENHEAD 5/65; WITHDRAWN 9/66.

92060 NEW 11/55; TYNE DOCK 11/55; WELLINGBOROUGH 12/55; TYNE DOCK 4/56; WITHDRAWN 10/66.

92061 NEW 11/55; TYNE DOCK 11/55; WELLINGBOROUGH 12/55; TYNE DOCK 4/56; WITHDRAWN 9/66.

92062 NEW 11/55; TYNE DOCK 11/55; WELLINGBOROUGH 12/55; WESTHOUSES 2/56; TYNE DOCK 5/56; WITHDRAWN 6/66.

92063 NEW 11/55; TYNE DOCK 11/55; WELLINGBOROUGH 12/55; WESTHOUSES 2/56; TYNE DOCK 5/56; WITHDRAWN 11/66.

92064 NEW 12/55; TYNE DOCK 12/55; WELLINGBOROUGH 12/55; TOTON 2/56; TYNE DOCK 5/56; WITHDRAWN 11/66.

92065 NEW 12/55; TYNE DOCK 12/55; WELLINGBOROUGH 12/55; TOTON 2/56; TYNE DOCK 5/56; WAKEFIELD 11/66; WITHDRAWN 4/67.

92066 NEW 12/55; TYNE DOCK 12/55; WELLINGBOROUGH 12/55; TOTON 2/56; TYNE DOCK 5/56; WITHDRAWN 5/65.

92067 NEW 12/55; DONCASTER 12/55; ANNESLEY 2/57; BANBURY 6/65; KINGMOOR 10/66; WITHDRAWN 11/66.

92068 NEW 12/55; DONCASTER 12/55; ANNESLEY 2/57; KIRKBY-IN-ASHFIELD 4/64; DERBY 12/65; WITHDRAWN 1/66.

92069 NEW 12/55; DONCASTER 12/55; ANNESLEY 2/57; BIRKENHEAD 5/65; SPEKE JUNCTION 11/67; WITHDRAWN 5/68.

92070 NEW 1/56; DONCASTER 1/56; ANNESLEY 2/57; SALTLEY 4/60; TOTON 9/60; WESTHOUSES 6/62; WELLINGBOROUGH 3/63; LEICESTER (MIDLAND) 5/63; WARRINGTON 3/65; BIRKENHEAD 5/65; WITHDRAWN 11/67.

92071 NEW 1/56; DONCASTER 1/56; ANNESLEY 2/57; NEWTON HEATH 7/65; KINGMOOR 11/65; WITHDRAWN 11/67.

92072 NEW 2/56; DONCASTER 2/56; ANNESLEY 2/57; KIRKBY-IN-ASHFIELD 7/65; WITHDRAWN 1/66.

92073 NEW 2/56; DONCASTER 2/56; ANNESLEY 2/57; BANBURY 6/65; BIRKENHEAD 9/66; WITHDRAWN 11/67.

92074 NEW 2/56; DONCASTER 2/56; ANNESLEY 2/57; BANBURY 6/65; SALTLEY 1/66; CROES NEWYDD 5/66; KINGMOOR 12/66; WITHDRAWN 4/67.

92075 NEW 3/56; DONCASTER 3/56; ANNESLEY 2/57; TOTON 4/63; ANNESLEY 10/63; KIRKBY-IN-ASHFIELD 7/65; KINGMOOR 4/66; WITHDRAWN 9/66.

92076 NEW 3/56; DONCASTER 3/56; ANNESLEY 2/57; ROWSLEY 10/63; KIRKBY-IN-ASHFIELD 4/64; NEWTON HEATH 10/64; KINGMOOR 1/65; WITHDRAWN 2/67.

92077 NEW 3/56; TOTON 3/56; WELLINGBOROUGH 8/63; KIRKBY-IN-ASHFIELD 10/63; NEWTON HEATH 6/64; CARNFORTH 4/67; WITHDRAWN 6/68.

92078 NEW 3/56; TOTON 3/56; WARRINGTON 3/65; WITHDRAWN 5/67.

92079 NEW 4/56; TOTON 4/56; BROMSGROVE 5/56; BIRKENHEAD 10/63; WITHDRAWN 11/67.

92080 NEW 4/56; TOTON 4/56; WELLINGBOROUGH 3/58; KETTERING 8/63; NEWTON HEATH 6/64; KINGMOOR 8/66; WITHDRAWN 5/67.

92081 NEW 5/56; TOTON 5/56; ANNESLEY 12/58; TOTON 4/59; WELLINGBOROUGH 11/59; KETTERING 8/63; NEWTON HEATH 6/64; WITHDRAWN 2/66.

92082 NEW 5/56; WELLINGBOROUGH 5/56; TOTON 1/62; WELLINGBOROUGH 3/62; SALTLEY 3/63; BIRKENHEAD 11/63; WITHDRAWN 11/67.

92083 NEW 5/56; WELLINGBOROUGH 5/56; ANNESLEY 11/60; WELLINGBOROUGH 2/61; ANNESLEY 2/63; WELLINGBOROUGH 3/63; KETTERING 1/64; LEICESTER (MIDLAND) 10/64; ANNESLEY 1/65; BIRKENHEAD 5/65; WITHDRAWN 5/67.

92084 NEW 5/56; WELLINGBOROUGH 5/56; KETTERING 1/64; SPEKE JUNCTION 9/64; BIRKENHEAD 1/65; WITHDRAWN 11/67.

92085 NEW 6/56; WELLINGBOROUGH 6/56; KETTERING 12/60; SALTLEY 10/62; TYSELEY 11/63; WILLESDEN 9/64; BIRKENHEAD 12/64; WITHDRAWN 12/66.

92086 NEW 6/56; WELLINGBOROUGH 6/56; KETTERING 1/64; LEICESTER (MIDLAND) 10/64; WARRINGTON 3/65; BIRKENHEAD 6/65; WITHDRAWN 11/67.

92087 NEW 8/56; DONCASTER 8/56; ANNESLEY 2/57; BANBURY 6/65; NORTHAMPTON 7/65; TYSELEY 9/65; CARNFORTH 11/66; WITHDRAWN 2/67.

92088 NEW 10/56; DONCASTER 10/56; ANNESLEY 2/57; TOTON 5/63; ANNESLEY 8/63; TOTON 6/65; BIRKENHEAD 7/65; CARNFORTH 11/67; WITHDRAWN 4/68.

92089 NEW 9/56; DONCASTER 9/56; ANNESLEY 2/57; LEICESTER (MIDLAND) 2/63; SPEKE JUNCTION 9/64; BIRKENHEAD 1/65; WITHDRAWN 4/67.

92090 NEW 11/56; DONCASTER 11/56; ANNESLEY 2/57; BIRKENHEAD 5/65; WITHDRAWN 5/67.

92091 NEW 11/56; DONCASTER 11/56; ANNESLEY 2/57; SPEKE JUNCTION 7/65; CARNFORTH 5/68; WITHDRAWN 5/68.

92092 NEW 12/56; DONCASTER 12/56; ANNESLEY 2/57; BIRKENHEAD 5/65; WITHDRAWN 10/66.

92093 NEW 1/57; DONCASTER 1/57; ANNESLEY 2/57; KIRKBY-IN-ASHFIELD 7/65; KINGMOOR 1/66; WITHDRAWN 9/67.

92094 NEW 2/57; DONCASTER 2/57; ANNESLEY 4/57; TOTON 12/58; ANNESLEY 4/59; BIRKENHEAD 5/65; SPEKE JUNCTION 11/67; WITHDRAWN 5/68.

92095 NEW 3/57; ANNESLEY 3/57; KIRKBY-IN-ASHFIELD 7/65; WARRINGTON 5/66; WITHDRAWN 10/66.

92096 NEW 4/57; ANNESLEY 4/57; DERBY 12/65; KINGMOOR 1/66; WITHDRAWN 2/67.

92097 NEW 6/56; TYNE DOCK 6/56; WITHDRAWN 10/66.

92098 NEW 7/56; TYNE DOCK 7/56; WITHDRAWN 7/66.

92099 NEW 7/56; TYNE DOCK 7/56; WITHDRAWN 9/66.

92100 NEW 8/56; TOTON 8/56; LEICESTER (MIDLAND) 3/58; TOTON 12/59; WESTHOUSES 1/60; WELLINGBOROUGH 3/63; LEICESTER (MIDLAND) 5/63; BIRKENHEAD 4/65; WITHDRAWN 5/67.

92101 NEW 8/56; TOTON 8/56; LEICESTER (MIDLAND) 3/58; WELLINGBOROUGH 1/60; LEICESTER (MIDLAND) 4/60; BIRKENHEAD 4/65; WITHDRAWN 10/67.

92102 NEW 8/56; TOTON 8/56; LEICESTER (MIDLAND) 3/58; BIRKENHEAD 4/65; WITHDRAWN 11/67.

92103 NEW 8/56; TOTON 8/56; LEICESTER (MIDLAND) 3/58; BIRKENHEAD 4/65; WITHDRAWN 5/67.

92104 NEW 8/56; TOTON 8/56; LEICESTER (MIDLAND) 3/58; WESTHOUSES 4/62; SPEKE JUNCTION 12/64; BIRKENHEAD 4/65; WITHDRAWN 2/67.

92105 NEW 9/56; WELLINGBOROUGH 9/56; KETTERING 11/56; WELLINGBOROUGH 3/63; KETTERING 1/64; LEICESTER (MIDLAND) 10/64; BIRKENHEAD 5/65; WITHDRAWN 1/67.

92106 NEW 9/56; WELLINGBOROUGH 9/56; KETTERING 11/56; LEICESTER (MIDLAND) 10/64; BIRKENHEAD 4/65; WITHDRAWN 7/67.

92107 NEW 9/56; WELLINGBOROUGH 9/56; SALTLEY 12/61; BANBURY 11/63; WILLESDEN 9/64; BIRKENHEAD 12/64; WITHDRAWN 2/67.

92108 NEW 10/56; WELLINGBOROUGH 10/56; CRICKLEWOOD 11/56; WELLINGBOROUGH 4/59; LEICESTER (MIDLAND) 3/60; WELLINGBOROUGH 2/62; LEICESTER (MIDLAND) 9/62; BIRKENHEAD 4/65; WITHDRAWN 11/67.

92109 NEW 10/56; TOTON 10/56; SALTLEY 3/57; WELLINGBOROUGH 6/57; LEICESTER (MIDLAND) 7/57; ANNESLEY 11/63; LEICESTER (MIDLAND) 4/64; BIRKENHEAD 4/65; WITHDRAWN 11/67.

92110 NEW 10/56; TOTON 10/56; CRICKLEWOOD 11/56; WELLINGBOROUGH 4/59; LEICESTER (MIDLAND) 3/60; WELLINGBOROUGH 7/62; LEICESTER (MIDLAND) 9/62; KIRKBY-IN-ASHFIELD 11/63; NEWTON HEATH 9/64; KINGMOOR 5/65; WITHDRAWN 12/67.

92111 NEW 11/56; CRICKLEWOOD 11/56; WELLINGBOROUGH 4/59; LEICESTER (MIDLAND) 3/60; KIRKBY-IN-ASHFIELD 11/63; SPEKE JUNCTION 9/64; BIRKENHEAD 1/65; WITHDRAWN 10/67.

92112 NEW 11/56; CRICKLEWOOD 11/56; WELLINGBOROUGH 4/59; LEICESTER (MIDLAND) 3/60; BIRKENHEAD 4/65; WITHDRAWN 11/67.

92113 NEW 11/56; WESTHOUSES 11/56; TOTON 6/60; BIDSTON 3/61; TOTON 4/61; ROWSLEY 4/62; WELLINGBOROUGH 2/64; TOTON 3/64; ANNESLEY 10/64; WESTHOUSES 7/65; BIRKENHEAD 8/65; WITHDRAWN 10/67.

92114 NEW 11/56; WESTHOUSES 11/56; TOTON 6/60; ROWSLEY 4/62; KIRKBY-IN-ASHFIELD 4/64; NEWTON HEATH 9/64; KINGMOOR 5/65; WITHDRAWN 4/67.

92115 NEW 12/56; WESTHOUSES 12/56; SPEKE JUNCTION 6/64; WITHDRAWN 2/66.

92116 NEW 12/56; WESTHOUSES 12/56; WELLINGBOROUGH 3/63; KETTERING 2/64; WARRINGTON 3/65; WITHDRAWN 11/66.

92117 NEW 12/56; WESTHOUSES 12/56; ANNESLEY 10/61; ROWSLEY 3/62; WELLINGBOROUGH 4/62; KETTERING 2/64; SPEKE JUNCTION 10/64; WITHDRAWN 12/67.

92118 NEW 12/56; WESTHOUSES 12/56; WELLINGBOROUGH 11/59; SALTLEY 1/62; BANBURY 7/64; TYSELEY 11/64; CARNFORTH 11/66; WITHDRAWN 5/68.

92119 NEW 1/57; WESTHOUSES 1/57; CRICKLEWOOD 1/59; LEICESTER (MIDLAND) 4/59; WARRINGTON 3/65; SPEKE JUNCTION 6/67; KINGMOOR 8/67; WITHDRAWN 9/67.

92120 NEW 2/57; WESTHOUSES 2/57; ANNESLEY 10/58; WESTHOUSES 11/58; SALTLEY 12/58; WELLINGBOROUGH 11/59; LEICESTER (MIDLAND) 3/60; ANNESLEY 11/60; LEICESTER (MIDLAND) 10/61; BIRKENHEAD 4/65; WITHDRAWN 7/67.

92121 NEW 2/57; WELLINGBOROUGH 2/57; SALTLEY 3/57; WELLINGBOROUGH 6/57; LEICESTER (MIDLAND) 7/57; BIRKENHEAD 4/65; WITHDRAWN 7/67.

92122 NEW 2/57; WELLINGBOROUGH 2/57; LEICESTER (MIDLAND) 3/60; WELLINGBOROUGH 7/62; LEICESTER (MIDLAND) 9/62; BIRKENHEAD 4/65; WITHDRAWN 11/67.

92123 NEW 3/57; WELLINGBOROUGH 3/57; LEICESTER (MIDLAND) 3/60; BIRKENHEAD 4/65; WITHDRAWN 10/67.

92124 NEW 3/57; WELLINGBOROUGH 3/57; KETTERING 2/64; WARRINGTON 3/65; WITHDRAWN 12/66.

92125 NEW 3/57; WELLINGBOROUGH 3/57; KETTERING 12/60; SALTLEY 11/63; CROES NEWYDD 5/66; KINGMOOR 12/66; WITHDRAWN 12/67.

92126 NEW 3/57; WELLINGBOROUGH 3/57; KETTERING 2/64; WARRINGTON 3/65; WITHDRAWN 8/67.

92127 NEW 4/57; WELLINGBOROUGH 4/57; ROWSLEY 7/63; KIRKBY-IN-ASHFIELD 4/64; SPEKE JUNCTION 10/64; BIRKENHEAD 1/65; WITHDRAWN 8/67.

92128 NEW 4/57; TOTON 4/57; LEICESTER (MIDLAND) 3/58; SALTLEY 6/62; BANBURY 7/64; SALTLEY 9/66; CARNFORTH 11/66; WITHDRAWN 11/67.

92129 NEW 4/57; SALTLEY 4/57; TOTON 6/57; KETTERING 8/59; TOTON 2/60; CRICKLEWOOD 5/60; ANNESLEY 10/61; SALTLEY 12/61; BANBURY 7/64; KINGMOOR 9/66; WITHDRAWN 7/67.

92130 NEW 4/57; SALTLEY 4/57; TOTON 6/57; KINGMOOR 5/64; WITHDRAWN 5/66.

92131 NEW 5/57; SALTLEY 5/57; TOTON 6/57; WESTHOUSES 1/60; SPEKE JUNCTION 12/64; BIRKENHEAD 5/65; WITHDRAWN 9/67.

92132 NEW 5/57; SALTLEY 5/57; WELLINGBOROUGH 12/57; KETTERING 2/64; ANNESLEY 3/64; BANBURY 6/65; NORTHAMPTON 8/65; BANBURY 9/65; WARRINGTON 8/66; KINGMOOR 10/67; WITHDRAWN 10/67.

92133 NEW 6/57; SALTLEY 6/57; WELLINGBOROUGH 12/57; LEICESTER (MIDLAND) 2/64; BIRKENHEAD 4/65; WITHDRAWN 7/67.

92134 NEW 6/57; SALTLEY 6/57; WELLINGBOROUGH 12/57; LEICESTER (MIDLAND) 2/64; BIRKENHEAD 4/65; WITHDRAWN 12/66. ENGINE PRESERVED.

92135 NEW 6/57; SALTLEY 6/57; CROES NEWYDD 5/66; WAKEFIELD 10/66; WITHDRAWN 6/67.

92136 NEW 7/57; SALTLEY 7/57; WITHDRAWN 10/66.

92137 NEW 7/57; SALTLEY 7/57; CROES NEWYDD 8/66; KINGMOOR 12/66; WITHDRAWN 9/67.

92138 NEW 7/57; SALTLEY 7/57; SPEKE JUNCTION 8/66; WITHDRAWN 7/67.

92139 NEW 7/57; SALTLEY 7/57; SPEKE JUNCTION 12/66; KINGMOOR 8/67; WITHDRAWN 9/67.

92140 NEW 7/57; NEW ENGLAND 7/57; LANGWITH 1/65; WITHDRAWN 4/65.

92141 NEW 7/57; NEW ENGLAND 7/57; DONCASTER 9/62; NEW ENGLAND 3/63; LANGWITH 1/65; COLWICK 11/65; WITHDRAWN 12/65.

92142 NEW 7/57; NEW ENGLAND 7/57; WITHDRAWN 2/65.

92143 NEW 8/57; NEW ENGLAND 8/57; WITHDRAWN 2/65.

92144 NEW 8/57; NEW ENGLAND 8/57; IMMINGHAM 9/62; NEW ENGLAND 3/63; LANGWITH 1/65; COLWICK 11/65; WITHDRAWN 12/65.

92145 NEW 8/57; NEW ENGLAND 8/57; LANGWITH 1/65; COLWICK 11/65; IMMINGHAM 12/65; WITHDRAWN 2/66.

92146 NEW 9/57; NEW ENGLAND 9/57; LANGWITH 1/65; COLWICK 11/65; DONCASTER 12/65 WITHDRAWN 4/66.

92147 NEW 9/57; NEW ENGLAND 9/57; IMMINGHAM 3/63; WITHDRAWN 4/65.

92148 NEW 9/57; NEW ENGLAND 9/57; IMMINGHAM 6/60; NEW ENGLAND 9/61; DONCASTER 3/63; COLWICK 6/63; BARROW HILL 9/64; LANGWITH 1/65; COLWICK 11/65; WITHDRAWN 12/65.

92149 NEW 10/57; NEW ENGLAND 10/57; LANGWITH 1/65; WITHDRAWN 6/65.

92150 NEW 10/57; WESTHOUSES 10/57; SALTLEY 1/59; TYSELEY 5/64; SALTLEY 6/64; WAKEFIELD 10/66; WITHDRAWN 4/67.

92151 NEW 10/57; SALTLEY 10/57; BIRKENHEAD 11/66; WITHDRAWN 4/67.

92152 NEW 10/57; SALTLEY 10/57; BIRKENHEAD 11/66; WITHDRAWN 11/67.

92153 NEW 10/57; TOTON 10/57; WESTHOUSES 10/63; SPEKE JUNCTION 6/65; WITHDRAWN 1/68.

92154 NEW 10/57; WELLINGBOROUGH 10/57; ANNESLEY 5/58; WELLINGBOROUGH 9/58; ANNESLEY 2/64; KIRKBY-IN-ASHFIELD 7/65; SPEKE JUNCTION 7/65; WITHDRAWN 7/67.

92155 NEW 11/57; SALTLEY 11/57; SPEKE JUNCTION 8/66; WITHDRAWN 11/66.

92156 NEW 11/57; TOTON 11/57; WARRINGTON 3/65; WITHDRAWN 7/67.

92157 NEW 11/57; TOTON 11/57; SALTLEY 1/59; BIRKENHEAD 4/64; WITHDRAWN 8/67.

92158 NEW 11/57; TOTON 11/57; WESTHOUSES 10/63; SPEKE JUNCTION 6/64; WITHDRAWN 7/66.

92159 NEW 11/57; WELLINGBOROUGH 11/57; CRICKLEWOOD 11/58; WELLINGBOROUGH 12/58; ROWSLEY 2/64; KIRKBY-IN-ASHFIELD 4/64; NEWTON HEATH 9/64; BIRKENHEAD 5/65; WITHDRAWN 7/67.

92160 NEW 11/57; WELLINGBOROUGH 11/57; KETTERING 9/58; WARRINGTON 3/65; BIRKENHEAD 2/66; SPEKE JUNCTION 11/67; CARNFORTH 5/68; WITHDRAWN 6/68.

92161 NEW 12/57; WESTHOUSES 12/57; NEWTON HEATH 6/58; KINGMOOR 5/65; WITHDRAWN 12/66.

92162 NEW 12/57; WESTHOUSES 12/57; NEWTON HEATH 6/58; BIRKENHEAD 5/65; WITHDRAWN 11/67.

92163 NEW 4/58; KETTERING 4/58; LEICESTER (MIDLAND) 6/59; KETTERING 11/59; WARRINGTON 3/65; BIRKENHEAD 6/65; WITHDRAWN 11/67.

92164 NEW 4/58; LEICESTER (MIDLAND) 4/58; SALTLEY 6/62; WITHDRAWN 7/66.

92165 NEW 4/58; SALTLEY 4/58; BIDSTON 6/62; BIRKENHEAD 2/63; SPEKE JUNCTION 11/67; WITHDRAWN 3/68.

92166 NEW 5/58; SALTLEY 5/58; RUGBY TESTING PLANT 8/58; SALTLEY 5/59; CARDIFF (CANTON) 8/59; NEWPORT (EBBW JUNCTION) 9/59; SALTLEY 2/60; BIDSTON 6/62; BIRKENHEAD 2/63; WITHDRAWN 11/67.

92167 NEW 5/58; SALTLEY 5/58; TYNE DOCK 5/62; SALTLEY 10/62; BIDSTON 12/62; BIRKENHEAD 2/63; CARNFORTH 11/67; WITHDRAWN 6/68.

92168 NEW 12/57; DONCASTER 12/57; WITHDRAWN 6/65.

92169 NEW 12/57; DONCASTER 12/57; WITHDRAWN 5/64.

92170 NEW 12/57; DONCASTER 12/57; WITHDRAWN 5/64.

92171 NEW 2/58; DONCASTER 2/58; NEW ENGLAND 11/63; WITHDRAWN 5/64.

92172 NEW 1/58; DONCASTER 1/58; WITHDRAWN 4/66.

92173 NEW 2/58; DONCASTER 2/58; LANGWITH 6/65; COLWICK 11/65; DONCASTER 12/65; WITHDRAWN 3/66.

92174 NEW 2/58; DONCASTER 2/58; WITHDRAWN 12/65.

92175 NEW 2/58; DONCASTER 2/58; WITHDRAWN 5/64.

92176 NEW 3/58; DONCASTER 3/58; NEW ENGLAND 11/63; WITHDRAWN 5/64.

92177 NEW 3/58; DONCASTER 3/58; WITHDRAWN 5/64.

92178 NEW 9/57; NEW ENGLAND 9/57; LANGWITH 1/65; WITHDRAWN 10/65.

92179 NEW 10/57; NEW ENGLAND 10/57; LANGWITH 1/65; COLWICK 10/65; WITHDRAWN 11/65.

92180 NEW 11/57; NEW ENGLAND 11/57; LANGWITH 1/65; WITHDRAWN 4/65.

92181 NEW 11/57; NEW ENGLAND 11/57; WITHDRAWN 2/65.

92182 NEW 12/57; NEW ENGLAND 12/57; LANGWITH 1/65; COLWICK 11/65; DONCASTER 12/65; WITHDRAWN 4/66.

92183 NEW 12/57; NEW ENGLAND 12/57; COLWICK 6/63; DONCASTER 1/65; WITHDRAWN 3/66.

92184 NEW 1/58; NEW ENGLAND 1/58; FRODINGHAM 1/59; NEW ENGLAND 6/59; COLWICK 6/63; NEW ENGLAND 11/63; IMMINGHAM 1/64; WITHDRAWN 3/66.

92185 NEW 1/58; NEW ENGLAND 1/58; COLWICK 6/63; NEW ENGLAND 11/63; IMMINGHAM 1/64; WITHDRAWN 2/65.

92186 NEW 1/58; NEW ENGLAND 1/58; COLWICK 6/63; DONCASTER 1/65; LANGWITH 6/65; WITHDRAWN 8/65.

92187 NEW 2/58; NEW ENGLAND 2/58; GRANTHAM 6/58; NEW ENGLAND 9/58; COLWICK 6/63; WITHDRAWN 2/65.

92188 NEW 2/58; NEW ENGLAND 2/58; GRANTHAM 6/58; NEW ENGLAND 9/58; COLWICK 6/63; WITHDRAWN 2/65.

92189 NEW 3/58; MEXBOROUGH 3/58; DARNALL 4/58; DONCASTER 6/58; FRODINGHAM 1/59; DONCASTER 4/59; COLWICK 9/63; LANGWITH 1/65; COLWICK 11/65; WITHDRAWN 12/65.

92190 NEW 3/58; MEXBOROUGH 3/58; DARNALL 5/58; DONCASTER 6/58; FRODINGHAM 1/59; DONCASTER 4/59; COLWICK 9/63; DONCASTER 6/64; WITHDRAWN 12/65.

92191 NEW 4/58; DARNALL 4/58; DONCASTER 6/58; COLWICK 9/63; LANGWITH 1/65; COLWICK 11/65; WITHDRAWN 12/65.

92192 NEW 5/58; DONCASTER 5/58; COLWICK 9/63; FRODINGHAM 11/63; WITHDRAWN 2/65.

92193 NEW 5/58; DONCASTER 5/58; IMMINGHAM 2/59; WITHDRAWN 6/65.

92194 NEW 6/58; DONCASTER 6/58; IMMINGHAM 2/59; WITHDRAWN 12/65.

92195 NEW 6/58; DONCASTER 6/58; IMMINGHAM 2/59; NEW ENGLAND 6/64; LANGWITH 1/65; WITHDRAWN 5/65.

92196 NEW 8/58; DONCASTER 8/58; IMMINGHAM 2/59; WITHDRAWN 12/64.

92197 NEW 9/58; DONCASTER 9/58; FRODINGHAM 2/59; DONCASTER 4/59; IMMINGHAM 9/60; WITHDRAWN 9/65.

92198 NEW 10/58; DONCASTER 10/58; FRODINGHAM 2/59; COLWICK 9/63; FRODINGHAM 11/63; WITHDRAWN 8/64.

92199 NEW 10/58; DONCASTER 10/58; COLWICK 9/63; FRODINGHAM 11/63; WITHDRAWN 8/64.

92200 NEW 11/58; DONCASTER 11/58; IMMINGHAM 9/63; DONCASTER 6/64; LANGWITH 6/65; WITHDRAWN 10/65.

92201 NEW 12/57; DONCASTER 12/58; IMMINGHAM 9/63; DONCASTER 6/64; WITHDRAWN 3/66.

92202 NEW 12/58; DONCASTER 12/58; IMMINGHAM 4/59; WITHDRAWN 12/65.

92203 NEW 4/59; BRISTOL (ST PHILLIP'S MARSH) 4/59; OLD OAK COMMON 8/59; BRISTOL (BARROW ROAD) 9/63; BIRKENHEAD 9/66; WITHDRAWN 11/67. ENGINE PRESERVED.

92204 NEW 4/59; BRISTOL (ST PHILLIP'S MARSH) 4/59; SOUTHALL 10/60; OLD OAK COMMON 11/60; BANBURY 3/63; TYSELEY 10/63; SPEKE JUNCTION 8/66; WITHDRAWN 12/67.

92205 NEW 5/59; BRISTOL (ST PHILLIP'S MARSH) 5/59; WESTBURY 10/60; EASTLEIGH 1/61; FELTHAM 6/63; YORK 9/63; WAKEFIELD 10/66; WITHDRAWN 6/67.

92206 NEW 5/59; BRISTOL (ST PHILLIP'S MARSH) 5/59; WESTBURY 10/60; EASTLEIGH 1/61; FELTHAM 6/63; YORK 9/63; WAKEFIELD 10/66; WITHDRAWN 5/67.

92207 NEW 6/59; BRISTOL (ST PHILLIP'S MARSH) 6/59; SOUTHALL 2/60; NEWPORT (EBBW JUNCTION) 11/64; WITHDRAWN 12/64. ENGINE PRESERVED.

92208 NEW 6/59; LAIRA 6/59; SOUTHALL 3/60; CARDIFF (CANTON) 11/61; CARDIFF EAST DOCK 9/62; NEWTON HEATH 10/63 KINGMOOR 6/64; WITHDRAWN 10/67.

92209 NEW 6/59; LAIRA 6/59; CARDIFF (CANTON) 8/59; NEWPORT (EBBW JUNCTION) 5/61; CARDIFF EAST DOCK 10/63; SOUTHALL 5/65; CARDIFF EAST DOCK 6/65; SEVERN TUNNEL JUNCTION 7/65; BRISTOL (BARROW ROAD) 10/65; WITHDRAWN 12/65.

92210 NEW 8/59; CARDIFF (CANTON) 8/59; BRISTOL (BARROW ROAD) 9/60; BATH (GREEN PARK) 7/62; CARDIFF (CANTON) 8/62; CARDIFF EAST DOCK 9/62; SOUTHALL 12/63; NEWPORT (EBBW JUNCTION) 6/64; WITHDRAWN 11/64.

92211 NEW 9/59; OLD OAK COMMON 9/59; WESTBURY 6/61; EASTLEIGH 8/61; FELTHAM 6/63; YORK 9/63; WAKEFIELD 10/66; WITHDRAWN 5/67.

92212 NEW 9/59; BANBURY 9/59; BATH (GREEN PARK) 6/61; NEWPORT (EBBW JUNCTION) 11/61; TYSELEY 7/62; CARNFORTH 11/66; WITHDRAWN 1/68. ENGINE PRESERVED.

92213 NEW 10/59; BRISTOL (ST PHILLIP'S MARSH) 10/59; BANBURY 12/59; KINGMOOR 10/66; WITHDRAWN 11/66.

92214 NEW 10/59; CARDIFF (CANTON) 10/59; BANBURY 11/59; NEWPORT (EBBW JUNCTION) 11/61; BATH (GREEN PARK) 5/64; NEWPORT (EBBW JUNCTION) 6/64; SEVERN TUNNEL JUNCTION 7/64; WITHDRAWN 9/65. ENGINE PRESERVED.

92215 NEW 11/59; BANBURY 11/59; TYSELEY 10/63; WAKEFIELD 10/66; WITHDRAWN 6/67.

92216 NEW 12/59; CARDIFF (CANTON) 12/59; CARDIFF EAST DOCK 9/62; NEATH 10/63; SOUTHALL 9/64; SEVERN TUNNEL JUNCTION 9/65; WITHDRAWN 10/65.

92217 NEW 12/59; CARDIFF (CANTON) 12/59; BRISTOL (ST PHILLIP'S MARSH) 1/60; BANBURY 3/63; TYSELEY 10/63; WITHDRAWN 7/66.

92218 NEW 1/60; BRISTOL (ST PHILLIP'S MARSH) 1/60; BANBURY 3/63; WARRINGTON 10/66; SPEKE JUNCTION 3/67; KINGMOOR 8/67; SPEKE JUNCTION 1/68; WITHDRAWN 5/68.

92219 NEW 1/60; BRISTOL (ST PHILLIP'S MARSH) 1/60; CARDIFF (CANTON) 2/60; CARDIFF EAST DOCK 9/62; WITHDRAWN 9/65. ENGINE PRESERVED.

92220 NEW 3/60; CARDIFF (CANTON) 3/60; BATH (GREEN PARK) 8/62; OLD OAK COMMON 10/62; OXFORD 11/62; BATH (GREEN PARK) 8/63; CARDIFF EAST DOCK 10/63; WITHDRAWN 3/65. ENGINE PRESERVED.

92221 NEW 5/58; BANBURY 5/58; LAIRA 6/59; BANBURY 3/60; LAIRA 6/60; WESTBURY 9/60; BANBURY 10/60; BRISTOL (BARROW ROAD) 11/60; YORK 9/63; WITHDRAWN 5/65.

92222 NEW 6/58; BANBURY 6/58; LAIRA 6/59; BANBURY 3/60; LAIRA 6/60; NEWPORT (EBBW JUNCTION) 10/60; NEATH 11/63; SOUTHALL 9/64; WITHDRAWN 3/65.

92223 NEW 6/58; BANBURY 6/58; LAIRA 6/59; BANBURY 3/60; LAIRA 6/60; WESTBURY 9/60; NEWPORT (EBBW JUNCTION) 3/61; BROMSGROVE 10/63; TYSELEY 3/64; SALTLEY 11/66; KINGMOOR 12/66; CARNFORTH 1/68; WITHDRAWN 4/68.

92224 NEW 6/58; BANBURY 6/58; LAIRA 7/59; SOUTHALL 7/60; OXFORD 10/62; BATH (GREEN PARK) 8/63; BRISTOL (BARROW ROAD) 9/63; CARDIFF EAST DOCK 10/63; BANBURY 11/64; WARRINGTON 8/66; WITHDRAWN 9/67.

92225 NEW 6/58; BANBURY 6/58; LAIRA 6/59; NEWPORT (EBBW JUNCTION) 3/60; NEATH 10/63; NEWPORT (EBBW JUNCTION) 6/64; WITHDRAWN 7/65.

92226 NEW 6/58; BANBURY 6/58; SOUTHALL 7/60; NEWPORT (EBBW JUNCTION) 10/60; OLD OAK COMMON 10/61; NEWPORT (EBBW JUNCTION) 11/62; BATH (GREEN PARK) 5/64; NEWPORT (EBBW JUNCTION) 6/64; SEVERN TUNNEL JUNCTION 7/64; NEWPORT (EBBW JUNCTION) 11/64; SEVERN TUNNEL JUNCTION 6/65; WITHDRAWN 9/65.

92227 NEW 7/58; BANBURY 7/58; CARDIFF (CANTON) 1/61; BANBURY 8/62; WARRINGTON 10/66; SPEKE JUNCTION 3/67; WITHDRAWN 11/67.

92228 NEW 7/58; BANBURY 7/58; SPEKE JUNCTION 10/66; WITHDRAWN 1/67.

92229 NEW 7/58; BANBURY 7/58; OLD OAK COMMON 10/58; NEWPORT (EBBW JUNCTION) 1/60; SOUTHALL 11/63; NEWPORT (EBBW JUNCTION) 6/64; WITHDRAWN 11/64.

92230 NEW 8/58; BANBURY 8/58; OLD OAK COMMON 10/58; NEWPORT (EBBW JUNCTION) 1/60; OLD OAK COMMON 9/62; NEWPORT (EBBW JUNCTION) 10/62; BROMSGROVE 1/64; NEWPORT (EBBW JUNCTION) 7/64; GLOUCESTER (HORTON ROAD) 10/65; WITHDRAWN 12/65.

92231 NEW 8/58; PONTYPOOL ROAD 8/58; SEVERN TUNNEL JUNCTION 1/59; CARDIFF (CANTON) 2/59; NEWPORT (EBBW JUNCTION) 10/59; CARDIFF (CANTON) 2/60; BRISTOL (BARROW ROAD) 10/60; EASTLEIGH 1/61; FELTHAM 6/63; YORK 9/63; WITHDRAWN 11/66.

92232 NEW 8/58; PONTYPOOL ROAD 8/58; SEVERN TUNNEL JUNCTION 1/59; CARDIFF (CANTON) 2/59; BANBURY 9/59; CARDIFF EAST DOCK 9/62; WITHDRAWN 12/64.

92233 NEW 8/58; PONTYPOOL ROAD 8/58; SEVERN TUNNEL JUNCTION 1/59; CARDIFF (CANTON) 2/59; BANBURY 9/59; CARDIFF (CANTON) 1/61; BATH (GREEN PARK) 7/62; NEWPORT (EBBW JUNCTION) 9/62; NEWTON HEATH 10/63; KINGMOOR 6/64; SPEKE JUNCTION 1/68; WITHDRAWN 2/68.

92234 NEW 8/58; PONTYPOOL ROAD 8/58; SEVERN TUNNEL JUNCTION 1/59; CARDIFF (CANTON) 2/59; BANBURY 9/59; BROMSGROVE 9/61; BANBURY 11/61; TYSELEY 8/62; BANBURY 9/64; SALTLEY 10/66; BIRKENHEAD 12/66; WITHDRAWN 11/67.

92235 NEW 8/58; PONTYPOOL ROAD 8/58; SEVERN TUNNEL JUNCTION 1/59; CARDIFF (CANTON) 2/59; NEWPORT (EBBW JUNCTION) 9/59; BRISTOL (BARROW ROAD) 10/65; WITHDRAWN 12/65.

92236 NEW 9/58; PONTYPOOL ROAD 9/58; NEWPORT (EBBW JUNCTION) 10/58; CARDIFF (CANTON) 11/58; CARDIFF EAST DOCK 9/62; SEVERN TUNNEL JUNCTION 11/64; WITHDRAWN 3/65.

92237 NEW 9/58; NEWPORT (EBBW JUNCTION) 9/58; CARDIFF (CANTON) 11/58; CARDIFF EAST DOCK 9/62; SEVERN TUNNEL JUNCTION 11/64; NEWPORT (EBBW JUNCTION) 2/65; WITHDRAWN 9/65.

92238 NEW 9/58; NEWPORT (EBBW JUNCTION) 9/58; OLD OAK COMMON 12/58; SOUTHALL 9/60; NEWPORT (EBBW JUNCTION) 12/61; BRISTOL (BARROW ROAD) 10/63; SEVERN TUNNEL JUNCTION 7/65; WITHDRAWN 9/65.

92239 NEW 9/58; NEWPORT (EBBW JUNCTION) 9/58; OLD OAK COMMON 12/58; SOUTHALL 9/60; WESTBURY 7/61; EASTLEIGH 8/61; FELTHAM 6/63; YORK 9/63; WITHDRAWN 11/66.

92240 NEW 10/58; NEWPORT (EBBW JUNCTION) 10/58; OLD OAK COMMON 11/58; SOUTHALL 9/60; WITHDRAWN 9/65. ENGINE PRESERVED.

92241 NEW 10/58; NEWPORT (EBBW JUNCTION) 10/58; OLD OAK COMMON 11/58; CARDIFF (CANTON) 10/60; CARDIFF EAST DOCK 9/62; SOUTHALL 11/63; WITHDRAWN 7/65.

92242 NEW 10/58; NEWPORT (EBBW JUNCTION) 10/58; SEVERN TUNNEL JUNCTION 11/64; WITHDRAWN 6/65.

92243 NEW 10/58; NEWPORT (EBBW JUNCTION) 10/58; OLD OAK COMMON 11/62; CARDIFF EAST DOCK 9/63; SEVERN TUNNEL JUNCTION 11/64; CARDIFF EAST DOCK 1/65; NEWPORT (EBBW JUNCTION) 7/65; BRISTOL (BARROW ROAD) 10/65; BATH (GREEN PARK) 11/65; WITHDRAWN 12/65.

92244 NEW 10/58; NEWPORT (EBBW JUNCTION) 10/58; OLD OAK COMMON 11/58; CARDIFF (CANTON) 10/60; CARDIFF EAST DOCK 9/62; OXFORD 10/62; CARDIFF EAST DOCK 11/62; NEWPORT (EBBW JUNCTION) 7/65; GLOUCESTER (HORTON ROAD) 10/65; WITHDRAWN 12/65.

92245 NEW 11/58; OLD OAK COMMON 11/58; CARDIFF (CANTON) 10/60; BATH (GREEN PARK) 6/62; OXFORD 9/62; SOUTHALL 10/62; WITHDRAWN 12/64. ENGINE PRESERVED.

92246 NEW 11/58; OLD OAK COMMON 11/58; CARDIFF (CANTON) 10/60; CARDIFF EAST DOCK 9/62; SOUTHALL 11/63; SEVERN TUNNEL JUNCTION 9/65; GLOUCESTER (HORTON ROAD) 10/65; WITHDRAWN 12/65.

92247 NEW 12/58; OLD OAK COMMON 12/58; CARDIFF (CANTON) 2/62; BANBURY 8/62; NEWTON HEATH 9/66; WITHDRAWN 10/66.

92248 NEW 12/58; NEWPORT (EBBW JUNCTION) 12/58; SALTLEY 9/59; BRISTOL (BARROW ROAD) 9/60; CARDIFF EAST DOCK 1/65; WITHDRAWN 6/65.

92249 NEW 12/58; NEWPORT (EBBW JUNCTION) 12/58; LAIRA 6/60; NEWPORT (EBBW JUNCTION) 10/60; NEWTON HEATH 10/63; KINGMOOR 6/64; SPEKE JUNCTION 1/68; WITHDRAWN 5/68.

92250 NEW 12/58; BANBURY 12/58; NEWPORT (EBBW JUNCTION) 11/59; SOUTHALL 11/63; NEWPORT (EBBW JUNCTION) 6/64; SEVERN TUNNEL JUNCTION 7/64; GLOUCESTER (HORTON ROAD) 10/65; WITHDRAWN 12/65.

SCRAPYARDS

ARNOTT YOUNG, CARMYLE
73072 5/67; 73095 1/67; 73103 2/66; 73104 2/66
75015 6/68; 75026 7/68; 75030 7/68; 75037 7/68; 75043 4/68; 75058 4/68
92010 6/66
ARNOTT YOUNG, OLD KILPATRICK
73056 9/65; 73107 6/67
78026 12/66; 78046 6/67
ARNOTT YOUNG, WEST OF SCOTLAND, SHIPBREAKING CO., TROON
76001 10/66-3/68; 76073 11/66; 76100 6/67-4/68; 76103 11/66; 76108 11/66
73145 4/67-9/67
78016 5/67
80030 3/65; 80049 3/65
92068 4/66
BIRDS, BRIDGEND
73084 4/66; 73168 4/66
80142 7/66; 80144 10/66
82004 5-7/66; 82032 11/65; 82038 10/65
92236 8-10/65
BIRDS, BYNEA
75007 8/65
80014 8/65; 80035 8/65
ARNOTT YOUNG, PARKGATE AND RAWMARSH
77010 2/66
84013 3/66; 84017 3/66; 84019 3/66; 84025 3/66; 84026 3/66
92017 4/68; 92030 7/67; 92054 6/68; 92065 8/67; 92069 10/68; 92094 9/68; 92110 3/68; 92125 4/68; 92194 3/66; 92206 9/67; 92218 7/68; 92249 9/68
ARNOTT YOUNG, DINSDALE
92088 10/68; 92223 9/68
BIRDS, LONG MARSTON
75002 2/68; 75006 2/68; 75013 2/68; 75024 4/68; 75036 8/66; 75045 8/66; 75046 2/68; 75047 2/68; 75052 2/68; 75056 8/66; 75063 8/66; 75071 2/68
76020 7/66
78024 10/65-1/66; 78025 11/65; 78056 11/66
82039 11/65; 82040 11/65
92000 11/65; 92120 2/68; 92138 12/67-2/68
BIRDS, MORRISTON, SWANSEA
75005 2/66
76005 11/67; 76006 11/67; 76011 11/67; 76031 12/67; 76064 11/67
78001 3/66; 78006 3/66
80048 4/66; 80066 10/65; 80081 10/65; 80084 10/65; 80088 10/65; 80101 4/66; 80147 1/66
82010 10/65; 82016 4/65; 82017 8/65
BIRDS, RISCA
73044 8/65; 73049 6/65; 73091 8/65
75068 2/68; 75076 12/67
76007 11/67
77014 12/67-2/68
80011 11/67-3/68; 80015 12/67-3/68; 80016 2/68; 80085 2/68; 80133 1-3/68; 80134 1-2/68; 80139 1/68; 80140 12/67; 80143 1/68; 80146 12/67-3/68; 80152 12/67-3/68
82005 12/65-2/66; 82019 12/67-3/68; 82020 1/66; 82029 1/68; 82033 12/65-2/66
BUTTIGIEGS, NEWPORT
73012 2/65; 73024 3/65; 73039 2/68; 73052 4/65; 73119 9/67; 73161 4/65
75018 11/67; 75065 12/66-3/67
76010 3/67; 76012 3/67; 76013 3/67; 76014 1/67; 76039 12/67; 76055 1/66; 76058 9-12/67; 76063 9-12/67; 76068 2/66; 76075 1-4/68; 76088 12/67
80012 9/67; 80019 11/67; 80059 3/66; 80154 10/67
82003 5/67-10/68; 82006 2/67; 82018 10/66; 82021 3/66; 82022 5/66; 82026 10/66; 82044 2/66
84000 4/66; 84002 9/66; 84004 6/66; 84005 5-9/66; 84006 5/66; 84008 1/66
92008 8/68; 92014 3-8/68; 92020 4-8/68; 92027 12/67; 92046 4-8/68; 92050 2/68; 92101 4-8/68; 92113 4-8/68; 92127 12/67; 92157 1/68; 92210 3/65
CAMPBELLS, AIRDRIE
70002 6/67; 70003 12/67; 70005 1/68; 70008 6/67; 70025 1/68; 70033 6/68; 70046 1/68; 70047 12/67; 70050 12/66; 70052 11/67
72007 3/66
73059 8/67; 73060 9/67; 73064 9/67; 73079 9/67; 73102 4/67; 73108 4/67; 73120 4/67; 73146 11/67; 73154 5/67
75009 11/68; 75019 11/68; 75020 11/68; 75035 1/68; 75048 11/68; 75059 12/67
76004 1/67; 76021 2/67; 76046 9/67; 76074 1/67; 76092 11/66; 76093 4/67; 76094 9/67; 76104 9/67
77015 11/66
80004 9/67;80028 1/67; 80045 9/67; 80046 9/67; 80092 1/67; 80093 1/67; 80116 9/67; 80120 9/67; 80126 2/67
92002 4/68; 92011 1/68; 92021 1/68; 92022 4/68; 92023 4/68; 92024 5/68; 92025 4/68; 92026 4/68; 92029 2/68; 92043 10/66; 92047 4/68; 92049 6/68; 92070 2/68; 92073 2/68; 92077 10/68; 92079 4/68; 92082 4/68; 92084 3/68; 92086 4/68; 92102 3/68; 92108 2/68; 92109 3/68; 92112 3/68; 92114 2/68; 92122 2/68; 92152 3/68; 92160 10/68;92162 5/68; 92163 5/68; 92166 3/68; 92167 11/68; 92234 2/68
CASHMORE'S, GREAT BRIDGE
73000 6/68; 73006 9/67; 73010 9/68; 73011 3/68; 73013 8/66; 73038 5/66; 73040 7/68; 73066 8/67; 73067 6/68; 73070 11/67; 73090 1/66; 73097 10/67; 73125 10/68; 73128 8/68; 73130 2-9/67; 73132 7/68; 73133 10/68; 73134 10/68; 73135 9/68; 73137 1/68; 73138 9/68; 73142 9/68; 73143 11/68; 73157 8/68; 73160 3/68; 73165 3/66
75054 1/67
76022 12/66; 76023 1/66; 76035 8/66; 76051 12/67; 76083 3/67; 76085 11/66; 76099 11/66; 76106 11/65
78000 1/66; 78008 1/67; 78027 2/66; 78028 6/67; 78029 1/66; 78030 12/65; 78032 1/66; 78033 11/65; 78035 4/66; 78038 12/66; 78043 1/66; 78055 6/67
82009 3/67
84003 2/66; 84009 12/65; 84029 10/64
92028 1/67; 92032 10/67; 92038 7/65; 92044 7/65; 92140 7/65; 92147 8/65; 92180 7/65
CASHMORE'S, NEWPORT
70017 1/67; 70026 5/67
73001 5/66; 73002 7/67-10/68; 73003 6/66; 73004 3/68; 73014 1/68; 73015 11/65; 73016 7/67-10/68; 73017 3/65; 73018 1/68; 73019 5/67; 73020 1/68; 73021 11/65; 73022 9/67; 73023 11/65; 73025 2/68; 73026 10/67; 73028 4/67; 73029 3/68; 73030 11/65; 73031 12/65; 73032 11/65; 73033 5/68; 73034 6/68; 73035 5/68; 73037 3/68; 73042 1/66; 73043 3-9/68; 73045 2/68; 73046 3/65; 73047 4/65; 73048 1/68; 73051 11/65; 73053 5/68; 73054 10/65; 73065 3/68; 73068 4/66; 73069 3/69; 73071 2-10/68; 73073 2/68; 73074 3/65; 73080 5/67; 73081 10/66; 73083 2/67; 73085 4/68; 73086 3/67; 73087 4/67; 73088 6/67; 73089 6/67; 73092 1/68; 73093 3/68; 73094 2/68; 73110 6/67; 73111 2/66; 73113 5/67; 73114 10/66; 73115 11/67; 73117 8/67; 73118 4-9/68; 73127 2-7/68; 73131 5/68; 73136 6/68; 73139 1/68; 73140 2/68; 73141 2/68; 73144 2/68; 73155 3/68; 73158 2/68; 73159 3/68; 73162 8/65; 73166 5/66; 73167 10/65; 73169 6/67; 73170 1/67 Cashmores, Weymouth Goods Yard; 73171 3/67
75001 4/65; 75004 8/67; 75064 9/67; 75066 4/66; 75070 3/67
76009 1/68; 76016 6/67; 76018 6/67; 76025 2/66; 76030 12/65; 76032 12/64; 76033 9-11/67; 76037 11/67; 76038 12/66; 76043 12/66; 76047 6/67-2/68; 76048 7/67; 76052 6/67-2/68; 76053 8/67; 76056 3/66; 76057 7/67; 76059 3/67; 76061 6/67; 76062 2/66; 76069 3/68; 76081 12/67; 76087 9/67
78003 9/67; 78004 2/66; 78005 3/65; 78010 12/66; 78017 10/67; 78031 3/67; 78036 8/67; 78039 3/67; 78058 9/67; 78060 3/67; 78063 9-12/67
80010 4/65; 80017 4/65; 80032 5/67; 80033 2/67; 80036 4/65; 80037 7/66; 80038 4/65; 80039 4/66; 80041 7/66; 80043 7/66; 80065 2/67; 80068 2/67; 80082 2/67; 80087 4/65; 80089 3/67; 80095 3/67; 80138 2/67; 80145 11/67
82000 5/67; 82001 4/66; 82007 12/64; 82015 4/65; 82023 3/67; 82028 2/67; 82030 4/66; 82031 6/67-10/68; 82034 6/67-10/68; 82035 11/65; 82036 11/65; 82037 11/65; 82041 7/66
84014 5/66
92003 7/65; 92004 7/68; 92007 2/66; 92009 7/68; 92153 6/68; 92165 6/68; 92209 3/66; 92216 4/66; 92222 7/65; 92225 9/65; 92226 12/65-2/66; 92230 3-7/66; 92235 4/66; 92237 11/65; 92238 12/65; 92241 9-12/65; 92242 8/65; 92243 4/66; 92244 4-7/66; 92246 4/66; 92248 8/65; 92250 7/66
CENTRAL WAGON CO., INCE, WIGAN
77011 5/66
78002 10/66
80050 7/65
84010 4/66; 84015 4/66; 84016 4/66; 84028 4/66
COHENS, CARGO FLEET, MIDDLESBROUGH
92066 9/65
KING'S, NORWICH
75074 10/67-2/68; 75075 10/67-2/68; 75077 10/67-2/68
76028 8/64
80013 12/66
HUGHES BOLCKOWS LTD., NORTH BLYTH
75060 10/67
84001 2/65; 84011 12/65; 84018 1/66; 84020 2/65
92062 10/66; 92179 3-5/66; 92221 9/65
GARNHAM, HARRIS & ELTON, CHESTERFIELD
75050 6/67; 75055 2/68
77002 10/67-2/68; 77012 10/67-2/68
CREWE WORKS
70007 7/65
80040 7/64; 80044 1/65; 80056 11/64; 80129 11/64
84012 10/63; 84021 10/64; 84022 10/64; 84023 10/64; 84024 10/64; 84027 6/64
92177 8/64
COHENS, MORRISTON, SWANSEA
75067 11/65
76015 1/66; 76019 6/66; 76026 9/67; 76027 1/66; 76029 3/65; 76036 7/67; 76040 9/67; 76044 3/67; 76060 5/66; 76065 6/66; 76066 11/67; 76067 11/67; 76086 5/67
80018 8/65; 80083 11/66-2/67; 80094 2/67; 80099 7/65; 80131 7/65
82024 5/66; 82025 12/64
COHENS, KETTERING
75040 3/68; 75041 8/68; 75042 3/68
76008 12/67; 76041 10/67-2/68; 76042 11/66; 76095 9/67-5/68
82011 11/64; 82012 11/64; 82013 11/64; 82014 11/64
92013 5/67; 92036 5/65; 92090 10-12/67; 92100 11/67-1/68; 92103 11/67-6/68; 92142 2/66; 92143 5/65; 92181 7/65
COX & DANKS, PARK ROYAL
80034 5/66; 80069 4/66; 80070 10/65; 80137 2/66; 80141 4/66; 80149 7/65; 80153 7/65
82027 4/66
92229 2/65
COX & DANKS, WADSLEY BRIDGE
92001 5/67
DRAPERS, HULL
73126 7/68
75049 3/67; 75053 2/67
76082 4/67; 76089 12/66
78007 12/67; 78012 10/67; 78013 10/67; 78023 10/67; 78044 10/67; 78062 10/67
92006 11/67; 92037 6/65; 92040 11/65; 92059 1/67; 92060 4/67; 92061 11/66; 92075 2/67; 92083 7/67; 92089 7/67; 92092 4/67; 92095 4/67; 92097 4/67; 92098 10/66; 92099 11/66; 92104 7/67; 92107 7/67; 92116 7/67; 92135 3/68; 92150 7-11/67; 92151 4/68; 92155 4/67; 92156 3/68; 92158 11/66; 92164 10/66; 92184 6/65; 92185 6/65; 92186 2/66; 92187 5/65; 92188 5/65; 92193 11/65; 92195 11/65; 92205 2/68; 92211 12/67; 92215 3/68; 92217 10/66;92231 4/67; 92239 4/67; 92247 4/67
EASTLEIGH WORKS
73041 by COHENS 12/65; 73116 2/65
80132 by COHENS 4/66
82002 4/64; 82008 6/64; 82043 5/64
W. GEORGE, STATION STEEL, WATH
92053 7-12/66
HAYES, BRIDGEND
75003, 2/66
76054 3/65
80042 5/65
82042 12/65-2/66
IBROX, GLASGOW
73121 spring 1966
MADEN & McKEE, STANLEY, LIVERPOOL
80125 4-6/65
THOMPSONS, STOCKTON-ON-TEES
92063 4/67; 92064 4/67; 92078 1/68; 92106 12/67; 92121 1/68; 92133 1/68; 92154 1/68; 92159 1/68
McLELLANS, BO'NESS
78053 4/65
McLELLANS, LANGLOAN
73055 1/67; 73057 6/66; 73106 10/65
80128 9/67
McWILLIAMS, SHETTLESTON
70006 11/67; 70009 6/67; 70010 1/68; 70011 4/68; 70015 2/68; 70016 12/67; 70020 6/67; 70028 2/68; 70029 3/68; 70031 3/68; 70032 3/68; 70034 10/67; 70037 2/68; 70038 2/68; 70039 2/68; 70040 12/67; 70041 10/67; 70042 10/67; 70048 10/67; 70049 3/68; 70051 3/68; 70053 10/67
72006 10/66; 72008 6/66
73075 3/66; 73124 3/66; 73152 2/66
76107 6/66
77006 6/66
80086 2/68; 80109 2/66
92012 2/68; 92015 11/67; 92016 4/68; 92052 1/68; 92058 2/68; 92067 2/67; 92076 6/67; 92080 11/67; 92087 6/67; 92096 6/67; 92126 1/68; 92128 5/68; 92208 2/68; 92213 2/67; 92224 6/68
MOTHERWELL MACHINERY & SCRAP CO., WISHAW
70001 1/67; 70018 6/67; 70027 11/67; 70036 2/67; 70054 6/67
72009 12/65
73005 10/66; 73007 6/66; 73008 12/65; 73009 9/66; 73058 3/65; 73061 3/65; 73063 10/66; 73076 2/65; 73098 6/66; 73099 6/67; 73100 5/67; 73101 11/66; 73105 2/67; 73109 2/65; 73122 1/66; 73123 7/65; 73147 11/65; 73148 1/66; 73151 10/66
75010 2/68; 75039 2/68
76000 9/67; 76002 5/67; 76003 6/66; 76045 6/66; 76049 5/66; 76070 1/67; 76071 6/66; 76097 1/65; 76105 4/66; 76109 1/67; 76111 4/66
77005 4/67; 77008 10/66; 77009 10/66; 77016 6/66
78020 11/67; 78021 11/67; 78037 11/67; 78041 11/67; 78045 4/66; 78048 4/65; 78049 12/66; 78050 4/66; 78051 3/67; 78052 4/66; 78057 8/66
80005 11/66; 80008 4/65; 80009 4/65; 80020 7/65; 80021 4/65; 80022 9/65; 80027 6/67; 80052 4/65; 80053 4/65; 80054 10/66; 80060 6/66; 80062 3/65; 80071 3/65; 80073 3/65; 80074 3/65; 80075 3/65; 80076 3/65; 80077 4/65; 80091 4/67; 80106 3/65; 80107 3/65; 80108 7/65; 80110 8/65; 80111 4/67; 80115 3/65; 80117 6/66; 80118 4/67; 80119 10/65; 80127 11/64
92018 8/67; 92019 1/68; 92051 2/68; 92056 2/68; 92071 2/68; 92074 10/67; 92093 2/68; 92119 2/68; 92129 11/67; 92130 11/66; 92132 2/68; 92137 2/68; 92139 2/68; 92161 5/67
SHIPBREAKING INDUSTRIES, FASLANE
73077 3/65; 73149 4/67; 73150 4/67; 73153 4/67
76024 4/67; 76050 11/66; 76072 1/65; 76090 4/67; 76091 4/67; 76096 7/67; 76101 5/67; 76102 5/67; 76110 4/67; 76112 2/66; 76113 4/67; 76114 4/67
78047 1/67; 78054 3/66
80000 4/67; 80001 11/66; 80003 7/65; 80006 12/66; 80007 11/66; 80023 1/66; 80024 11/66; 80025 11/66; 80026 12/66; 80029 3/66; 80047 11/66; 80051 11/66; 80055 12/66; 80057 5/67; 80058 11/66; 80061 5/67; 80063 11/66; 80090 5/65; 80112 11/66; 80113 12/66; 80114 4/67; 80121 8/66; 80122 4/67; 80123 11/66; 80124 4/67; 80130 11/66
SWINDON WORKS
73027 4/64
78009 12/64
STEEP SUPPLY CO., WEST DRAYTON
80031 4/65; 80148 4/65
STRATFORD WORKS
80103 9/62 First standard engine scrapped
WARDS, BEIGHTON, SHEFFIELD
70012 4/68; 70030 10/66; 70043 11/65; 70044 2/67; 70045 3/68
73036 12/65; 73112 11/65
75011 2/67; 75012 6/67; 75017 5/67; 75023 4/66; 75028 4/66; 75031 5/66; 75032 5/68; 75038 4/66; 75051 2/67; 75057 6/66
76078 4/67
77000 3/67; 77003 3/67; 77004 3/67; 77013 6/66
78040 5/66
92005 12/65; 92041 11/65; 92042 4/66; 92045 2/68; 92048 2/68; 92057 12/65; 92072 6/66; 92091 11/68; 92111 2/68; 92118 9/68; 92123 2/68; 92131 2/68; 92136 2/67; 92141 4/66; 92144 4/66; 92145 4/66; 92148 4/66; 92149 10/65; 92168 11/65; 92173 5/66; 92174 5/66; 92189 4/66; 92190 1/66; 92191 4/66; 92192 5/65; 92196 1/66; 92197 1/66; 92198 6/65; 92199 6/65; 92202 3/66; 92204 3/68; 92227 1/68; 92228 6/67; 92233 8/68
WARDS, INVERKEITHING
70004 4/68; 70014 4/68; 70021 2-5/68; 70022 4/68; 70035 4/68
75021 6/68; 75034 7/68; 75062 6/68
76098 3/68
WARDS, KILLAMARSH
70023 4/68; 70024 4/68
73163 2/66
75000 4/66; 75008 4/66; 75016 6/68; 75022 4/66; 75025 4/66; 75033 6/68; 75044 6/66; 75061 6/67
76076 4/67
77001 2/66
78011 12/65; 78014 12/65; 78034 4/66; 78042 12/65; 78061 3/67; 78064 3/67
92031 5/67; 92033 12/65; 92034 8/65; 92035 4/66; 92039 1/66; 92055 4/68; 92105 5/67; 92117 4/68; 92124 4/67; 92169 1/65; 92170 1/65; 92171 3/65; 92175 2/65; 92176 3/65; 92178 12/65; 92200 12/65
WARDS, WISHAW
77007 4/67; 77017 4/67; 77018 4/67; 77019 4/67
WARDS, RINGWOOD, HANTS
75072 4/66; 75073 4/66
80096 3/66 at Ringwood Goods Yard
80102 3/66 at Ringwood Goods Yard
WEST OF SCOTLAND SHIPBREAKING CO., TROON
70019 10/66-8/67
72005 7/65
73145 4-9/67
WOODS (SHIPBREAKING), QUEENBOROUGH, KENT
76034 10/64
BANBURY SHED
73164 by Friswells 4/65
WOODHAMS
76080 by 4/72
80067 9/65
92085 7/80; 92232 3/65
DARLINGTON WORKS
72000 10/63-3/64; 72001 10/63-2/64; 72002 10/63-4/64; 72003 10/63-3/64; 72004 10/63-3/64
78015 1/64
LOOMS, SPONDON
84007 11/64
W. GEORGE, STATION STEEL, WATH
92081 6/66; 92115 6/66; 92146 6-8/66; 92172 6-7/66; 92182 6-7/66; 92183 7/66; 92201 7/66

That naming ceremony, 18 March 1960. Probably for the first time, it was obvious an engine would be preserved before it was even built, but few in the 1960s thought more than a handful of static steam locos would ever survive. The notion that several dozen Standards alone, let alone all the rest, would be preserved would have been greeted with puzzled disbelief. Photograph Hugh Ballantyne.

Preservation

Locations of the preserved Standards are subject to change and this account is based on the best estimates as at early summer, 1997. Check first if your life depends on it...

70000 BRITANNIA
Built Crewe 1951. First shed Stratford. Withdrawn 5/66, final shed Newton Heath.
First BR standard built, a popular performer on the main line and on preserved railways such as Mid Hants, Nene Valley. Normally based at Didcot Railway Centre.

70013 OLIVER CROMWELL
Built at Crewe in 1951. First shed Norwich. Withdrawn 8/68, final shed Carnforth.
The last main line steam engine to be overhauled by BR, at its birthplace, Crewe. Now part of the National Collection and since withdrawal has been kept at the Bressingham Steam Museum, Diss, Norfolk.

71000 DUKE OF GLOUCESTER
Built at Crewe in 1954. Crewe North was its only shed. Withdrawn 11/62.
The 53rd engine to be moved from Barry scrapyard, in April 1974. Once known as 'Mission Impossible' the engine was restored over 12 years at Loughborough on the Great Central Railway and it now works on the main line. A proven performer, normally based at Steamtown, Carnforth.

73050
Built at Derby in 1954. First shed Bath (Green Park). Withdrawn 6/68, final shed Patricroft.
A former Somerset & Dorset engine purchased direct from BR service, is based on the Nene Valley Railway,

named 'City of Peterborough' and a regular performer on the line when not requiring an overhaul.

73082 CAMELOT
Built at Derby in 1955. First shed Stewarts Lane. Withdrawn 6/66, final shed Guildford.
The 107th engine to be moved from Barry scrapyard, in October 1979. The one surviving 'Standard Arthur' named after withdrawn Urie Arthurs. After restoration on the Bluebell Railway it was steamed in autumn 1995 - an especially happy event for me, for I am a life member of the owning Society. All contributions will be gratefully received...

73096
Built at Derby in 1955. First shed Patricroft. Withdrawn 11/67, final shed Patricroft.
The 164th engine to be moved from Barry scrapyard, in July 1985. When delivered to the Mid Hants Railway at Alresford some members were under the impression we had a Black 5 coming or even CAMELOT itself. The engine ran under the guise of 73080 MERLIN but is fitted with the wrong type of tender for this identity. It now carries its original number, sporting BR green livery.

73129
Built at Derby in 1956. First shed Shrewsbury. Withdrawn 11/67, final shed Patricroft.
The 32nd engine to be moved from Barry, in January 1973. The only survivor of thirty Caprotti Class 5s and is undergoing restoration at the Midland Railway Centre.

73156
Built at Doncaster in 1956. First shed Neasden. Withdrawn 11/67, final shed Bolton.

The 177th engine to be moved from Barry scrapyard, in October 1986. Now undergoing restoration on the East Lancashire Railway, it spent its last year in BR service in the north west of England.

75014
Built at Swindon in 1951. First shed Patricroft. Withdrawn 12/66, final shed Shrewsbury.
The 121st engine to be moved from Barry scrapyard, in February 1981. Based in the north west of England and North Wales for a good part of its BR service, is now on the North York Moors Railway and passed for main line running. Partnered 70000 on the main line in the spring of 1995. Has also worked in Scotland, between Fort William and Mallaig.

75027
Built Swindon in 1954. First shed Laira. Withdrawn 8/68, final shed Carnforth.
Purchased direct from BR service and has worked on the Bluebell Railway far longer than it worked for BR. Spent a while on the Somerset & Dorset Railway and a time in the north west of England.

75029
Built at Swindon in 1954. First shed Laira. Withdrawn 8/67, final shed Stoke.
Purchased from British Railways by the artist David Shepherd and after a period on the abortive Longmoor Railway and a time at Eastleigh Works it is now based on the East Somerset railway at Cranmore and named 'The Green Knight'.

75069
Built at Swindon in 1955. First shed Dover. Withdrawn 9/66, final shed Eastleigh.
The 37th engine to be moved from Barry scrapyard, in

March 1973. Always a Southern engine and since restoration on the Severn Valley Railway has worked on the main line, in both Central Wales and Southern England.

75078
Built at Swindon in 1956. First shed Exmouth Junction. Withdrawn 7/66, final shed Eastleigh.
The 21st engine to be moved from Barry scrapyard, in June 1972. Spent its BR life on the LSWR lines out of Waterloo; moved to the Worth Valley Railway in 1972 and since restoration has proved a popular engine on the Yorkshire line.

75079
Built at Swindon in 1956. First shed Exmouth Junction. Withdrawn 11/66, final shed Eastleigh. The 139th engine to be moved from Barry scrapyard, in March 1982. Also spent its BR life on the LSWR lines and was purchased with help from Plymouth City lottery funds. Stored at Marsh Mills, Plymouth awaiting restoration.

76017
Built at Horwich in 1953. First shed Eastleigh. Withdrawn 7/65, final shed Salisbury.
The 46th engine to be moved from Barry scrapyard, in January 1974. Based at Eastleigh for seven years and for ten years has worked near 'home', on the Mid-Hants Railway. Spent a short while at Quainton Road after movement from Barry and now awaits its second overhaul in preservation.

76077
Built at Horwich in 1956. First shed Sutton Oak. Withdrawn 12/67, final shed Wigan (Springs Branch).
The 186th engine to be moved from Barry scrapyard, in May 1987. Its working life on BR was spent in the north west of England and it is now undergoing restoration on the Gloucester & Warwickshire Railway at Toddington.

76079
Built at Horwich in 1957. First shed Sutton Oak. Withdrawn in 12/67, final shed Wigan (Spring Branch).
The 59th engine to be moved from Barry scrapyard, in July 1974. First moved to Steamport, Southport - is now based on the East Lancs Railway and has worked on the Llangollen Steam Railway.

76084
Built at Horwich in 1957. First shed Lower Darwen. Withdrawn 12/67, final shed Springs Branch. The 144th engine to be moved from Barry scrapyard, in April 1983. Another north west based engine in BR days, it is kept on a private site in North Leverton.

78018
Built at Darlington in 1954. First shed West Auckland. Withdrawn 11/66, final shed Shrewsbury.
The 97th engine to be moved from Barry, in November 1978. Started its working life in the north east, moved to the north west, had a while at Willesden shed and finished in the Midlands. Was first moved to Shackerstone but is now undergoing restoration on a site next to Darlington North Road Museum.

78019
Built at Darlington in 1954. First shed Kirkby Stephen. Withdrawn 11/66, final shed Crewe South.
The 35th engine to be moved from Barry scrapyard in March 1973. Moved from the north east to the north west, Willesden and the Midlands before withdrawal. Has been stored on the Severn Valley Railway for over 20 years awaiting restoration.

78022
Built at Darlington in 1954. First shed Millhouses. Withdrawn 9/66, final shed Lostock Hall.
The 67th engine to be moved from Barry scrapyard, in June 1975. Worked on the Eastern and London Midland Regions. Steamed on the Worth Valley at the end of 1992, now a regular performer on that line.

78059
Built at Darlington in 1956. First shed Chester (Northgate). Withdrawn 11/66, final shed Crewe South. The 145th engine to be moved from Barry scrapyard, in May 1983. An LMR engine all its working life on BR, it is now based on the Bluebell Railway where it is planned to rebuild it as a sister Class 2 2-6-2T, to be numbered 84030.

80002
Built at Derby in 1952. First shed Motherwell. Withdrawn 3/67, final shed Polmadie. Purchased direct from BR service by the Worth Valley Railway. Its final duty on BR was as a carriage heating boiler at Cowlairs; did not work on the KWVR for many years but is now back in working order.

80064
Built at Brighton in 1953. First shed Watford. Withdrawn 9/65, final shed Bristol (Barrow Road). The 34th engine to be moved from Barry scrapyard, in February 1973. Restored to working order at Buckfastleigh. Spent a number of years on the Bluebell Railway before returning to Buckfastleigh, now the South Devon Railway. Now back on the Bluebell.

80072
Built at Brighton in 1953. First shed Plaistow. Withdrawn 7/65, final shed Shrewsbury.
The 206th engine to be moved from Barry scrapyard, in July 1988. Undergoing restoration on the Llangollen Steam Railway.

80078
Built at Brighton in 1954. First shed Plaistow. Withdrawn 7/65, final shed Croes Newydd.
The 84th engine to be moved from Barry scrapyard, in September 1976. Has spent more time on the Swanage Railway than it was owned by BR. Restoration has started.

80079
Built at Brighton in 1954. First shed Plaistow. Withdrawn 7/65, final shed Croes Newydd.
The 13th engine and the first Standard to be moved from Barry scrapyard, in May 1971. Overhauled twice by the Severn Valley Railway where it has been a regular performer; has also worked on the main line and appeared at the Rainhill celebrations in 1980.

80080
Built at Brighton in 1954. First shed Plaistow. Withdrawn 7/65, final shed Croes Newydd.
The 115th engine to be moved from Barry scrapyard, in November 1980. Featured on the BBC programme *Blue Peter*, first moved to the Peak Railway and then a few years later to the Midland Railway Centre. After restoration to working order in 1987 has appeared as a regular on the main line. Worked on the Settle and Carlisle in 1993.

80097
Built at Brighton in 1954. First shed Plaistow. Withdrawn 7/65, final shed Machynlleth.
162nd engine to be moved from Barry scrapyard, in May 1985. On the East Lancashire Railway, undergoing restoration and though never based in the north west the engine should be right at home working north from Bury.

80098
Built at Brighton in 1954. First shed Plaistow. Withdrawn 7/65, final shed Machynlleth. The 157th engine to be moved from Barry scrapyard, in November 1984. First planned to be a source of spares, now undergoing restoration at the Midland Railway Centre.

80100
Built at Brighton in 1955. First shed Plaistow. Withdrawn 7/65, final shed Shrewsbury.
The 94th engine to be moved from Barry, in October 1978. Based on the Bluebell Railway, not so far from its birthplace, still in Barry condition - a long term restoration project.

80104
Built at Brighton in 1955. First shed Plaistow. Withdrawn 7/65, final shed Machynlleth. The 155th engine to be moved from Barry scrapyard, in September 1984, to the Swanage Railway. Restored to steam spring 1997, carrying the boiler from 80078.

80105
Built at Brighton in 1955. First shed Plaistow. Withdrawn 7/65, final shed Machynlleth.
The 44th engine to be moved from Barry scrapyard, in October 1973. Purchased by the Scottish RPS as a representative of the class that once worked in Scotland and is now being restored at Bo'ness.

80135
Built at Brighton in 1956. First shed Plaistow. Withdrawn 7/65, final shed Shrewsbury. The 39th engine to be moved from Barry scrapyard, in April 1973. Has been based on the NYMR for over twenty years and proved a popular engine once restored. Painted in green, a livery the class never carried in BR times.

80136
Built at Brighton in 1956. First shed Plaistow. Withdrawn 7/65, final shed Shrewsbury.
The 102nd engine to be moved from Barry scrapyard, in August 1979. Arrived at Barry via the LTS lines, West Midlands and Mid Wales and is now based on the North Staffordshire Railway at Cheddleton.

80150
Built at Brighton in 1956. First shed Brighton. Withdrawn 10/65, final shed Eastleigh. The 196th engine to be moved from Barry scrapyard in February 1988. Part of the Wales Railway Centre collection, based at Barry.

80151
Built at Brighton in 1957. First shed Brighton. Withdrawn 5/67, final shed Eastleigh. The 66th engine to be moved from Barry scrapyard, in March 1975. Has been at Chappel & Wakes Colne for twenty years, where restoration work is proceeding.

92134
Built at Crewe in 1957. First shed Saltley. Withdrawn 12/66, final shed Birkenhead. The 116th engine to be moved from Barry scrapyard, in December 1980. Purchased for eventual use on the North Yorks Moors Railway and is on a site in Essex undergoing restoration.

92203
Built at Swindon in 1959. First shed Bristol (St. Phillip's Marsh). Withdrawn 11/67, final shed Birkenhead. Purchased by the artist David Shepherd direct from BR service and after a while at Longmoor has been based on the East Somerset Railway at Cranmore. Named 'Black Prince'. In recent years it has worked on various preserved lines in England.

92207
Built at Swindon in 1959. First shed Bristol (St. Phillip's Marsh). Withdrawn 12/64, final shed Newport (Ebbw Junction). The 180th engine to be moved from Barry scrapyard in December 1986. The buyer named it 'Morning Star' but will it carry this name when working on the East Lancashire Railway where it is being restored?

92212
Built at Swindon in 1959. First shed Banbury. Withdrawn 1/68, final shed Carnforth. The 105th engine to be moved from Barry scrapyard, in September 1979. This engine is working on the GCR (restoration took place at Loughborough) and has recreated the famous Windcutter trains. Though the engine was never based on the GC proper it might have worked the line when at Banbury shed.

92214
Built at Swindon in 1959. First shed Cardiff (Canton). Withdrawn 8/65, final shed Severn Tunnel Junction. The 117th engine to be moved from Barry scrapyard, in December 1980. A Western Region engine all its short working life, it went to the Peak Railway from Barry but is now at the Midland Railway Centre undergoing restoration. Will it go main line as many of the engines based at the MRC have?

92219
Built at Swindon in 1960. First shed Bristol (St. Phillip's Marsh). Withdrawn 8/65, final shed Cardiff East Dock. The 163rd engine to be moved from Barry scrapyard, in May 1985. Also a Western Region engine all its short working life, and also at the Midland Railway Centre, having moved from the Peak Railway. Awaiting overhaul.

92220 EVENING STAR
Built at Swindon 1960. First shed Cardiff (Canton). Withdrawn 3/65, final shed Cardiff East Dock. What can be written about this engine? The last steam engine built for BR, has been in preservation for far longer than BR owned it. A crowd puller and normally kept at the National Railway Museum, York.

92240
Built at Crewe in 1958. First shed Newport (Ebbw Junction). Withdrawn 8/65, final shed Southall. The 93rd engine to be moved from Barry scrapyard, in October 1978. In its seven years service on BR 92240 was only based at three sheds. Was the first 9F to leave Barry and purchased as one of the Crewe built survivors. Should now work on the Bluebell Railway well into the 21st century.

92245
Built at Crewe in 1958. First shed Old Oak Common. Withdrawn 12/64, final shed Southall. The 195th engine to be moved from Barry scrapyard, in February 1988. Part of the Wales Railway Centre collection now stored at Barry. Still in scrapyard condition, so will it ever work again?